WASHINGTON STATE

The Inaugural Decade ❧ *1889-1899*

ROBERT E. FICKEN

Washington State University Press
Pullman, Washington

WASHINGTON STATE
UNIVERSITY
Washington State University Press
PO Box 645910
Pullman, Washington 99164-5910
Phone: 800-354-7360
Fax: 509-335-8568
E-mail: wsupress@wsu.edu
Web site: wsupress.wsu.edu

Library of Congress Cataloging-in-Publication Data

Ficken, Robert E.
  Washington State : the inaugural decade, 1889-1899 / Robert E. Ficken.
    p. cm.
  Includes bibliographical references and index.
  ISBN-13: 978-0-87422-288-3 (alk. paper)
  1. Washington (State)—History—19th century. I. Title.
  F891.F493 2007
  979.7'03—dc22

                                                          2006102026

Front cover: Inauguration day, November 18, 1889. *University of Washington Libraries (UW376)*

Back cover: Governor Elisha P. Ferry. *Museum of History and Industry, Seattle (1957.1284.5)*

Fine Quality Books from the Pacific Northwest

Table of Contents

For
Lorraine *and* Matthew

Acknowledgments

Research for *Washington State: The Inaugural Decade, 1889–1899*, was conducted at a number of libraries and archival repositories. I am especially indebted for the highly professional assistance provided by the staffs at the University of Washington Library, the Washington State University Library, and the Washington State Library. My work also was greatly facilitated, as the bibliography will attest, by reference to the many relevant books and articles produced by regional historians.

David Nicandri of the Washington State Historical Society provided helpful comments on the original draft of the text. Professor David Stratton of Washington State University likewise kindly offered a detailed critic. Neither historian, of course, is responsible for remaining errors of fact or interpretation.

At Washington State University Press, Editor-in-chief Glen Lindeman did his usual first rate job with the manuscript. I would also like to thank other WSU Press staff members for their vital contributions: Mary Read, Nancy Grunewald, Kerry Darnall, Jean Taylor, Caryn Lawton, and Jenni Lynn.

Introduction

$\mathcal{A}$FTER A LONG AND OCCASIONALLY DISHEARTENING era of territorial vassalage—36 years in all—Washington entered the union on November 11, 1889. The recently completed Northern Pacific transcontinental railroad, with a direct line to Commencement Bay, had stimulated the great burst of immigration responsible for the creation of America's 42nd state. Many years prior to this transcendent political development, however, Washington had attained an important role in world trade, eclipsing its standing as a mere territory. Since the mid-19th century, Puget Sound lumber had gone in large quantities to California and international ports around the Pacific Rim. Following the Civil War, vast grain growing areas east of the Cascades—in the inviting Walla Walla Valley and then among the grassy mounds of the Palouse country—began sending yearly consignments of wheat to far flung markets.

A fact little known to casual outside observers, Washington needed railroads to become a viable and progressive entity. The sea was a lifeline, of course, allowing San Francisco merchants to build steam powered sawmills on the northwest coast and to secure the inherent wealth of the region's forests. Sacked grain from the interior went out by wagon and riverboat to the lower Columbia, there to be hoisted aboard Liverpool bound steamers. Western Washington was, for all practical purposes, a colony of California's famed golden bay. The eastern half of the territory, meanwhile, developed as a tributary of Portland. Neither section experienced anything remotely akin to a meaningful connection—in terms of transportation, commerce or politics—with the other. And both were cut off from the American nation beyond the Rockies.

Commenced late in the territorial period and brought to fruition during the first statehood years, railway construction opened new opportunities in all fields of endeavor. The Northern Pacific would be joined by a rival, James J. Hill's Great Northern, in 1893. An intricate spider's web of feeders soon connected previously isolated places with one or the other of the transcontinental lines. People poured into the nation's far corner—farmers seeking land, workers in search of employment and capitalists expecting to get rich through well placed investments. Seattle, Tacoma and Spokane solidified their lately won stature as Washington's dominant urban areas. Late developing communities, among them Wenatchee on the upper Columbia, Anacortes and Everett on the northern Sound, and Aberdeen and South Bend on the foggy seaboard, emerged as railroad linked centers of regional consequence.

Though some were irked by the long delay of statehood, and others frankly professed indifference or even hostility to the concept, Washington's admission in 1889 turned out to be, under contemporary circumstances, perfectly timed.

Railroads and ocean going steamers allowed for efficient commerce and speedy, safe and comfortable travel. The telegraph and telephone introduced, with due allowance for delays from weather and mechanical malfunction, virtually instantaneous communication. Generated by the Industrial Revolution, surplus capital was available from London and European financial houses and from East Coast speculators for investment in all manner of endeavors. Decisions were made and funds dispatched by wire and agents sent to the Pacific coast by fast train.

Directly or indirectly, most residents of the new state were enmeshed in the world of capital. Urban merchants and real estate promoters sought financing for their enterprises. Grain growers east of the Cascades borrowed money to buy land and equipment and to harvest and ship the yearly crop. Persons otherwise sympathetic to the abuses inflicted upon laborers in the dawning industrial age nevertheless worried that corrective action in the workplace would retard outside investment. Leaders of state, municipal and county governments sold bonds to pay for much needed improvements in infrastructure—utilities, schools and roads—and to retire existing debt. Legislators rejected reformist measures, bills that might increase taxation or impose regulation on corporations, in fitful anticipation that even the discussion of such proposals might cause distant financiers to withhold loans.

Washington prospered or faltered according to the availability of money. In good times, property values increased, towns expanded and farm returns mounted with almost automatic ease. However, should faraway investors decide to withdraw credit—for reasons having little or nothing to do with regional issues—confidence gave way to despair and progress to retrogression. The prolonged effect of the Panic of 1893, lasting four gloomy years, was the decade's defining development, fully exposing the infant state's vast dependence upon a harsh outside world.

Washington's citizens experienced other equally dramatic events during the first years of statehood. In government, the Populist movement rose spectacularly by 1896, given strength due to the populace's desperation during the depth of the depression and by national debate over a silver monetary standard. In just two years, however, populism collapsed just as precipitously, enervated by the economic recovery finally beginning in 1897. Washington then reverted to its earlier Republicanism in accord with capital related economic improvements.

Gold was discovered in Alaska and the Yukon, eventually in sufficient quantities in 1897 to attract national and international attention that publicized—and profited—Puget Sound as a fitting out and departure point. War with Spain in 1898 had far reaching ramifications, causing an unanticipated extension of American hegemony across the Pacific to Hawaii, Guam, the Philippine archipelago and the very edge of Asia. Having emerged from national isolation in 1889, Washington found itself, a mere ten years later, occupying a key geographical location and in control of resources best suited to exploit an oceanic commercial empire.

Washington's first state governor, Elisha P. Ferry, who previously held two appointments as territorial governor in 1872–1880. *Museum of History and Industry, Seattle (1957.1284.5)*

Chapter One

More than Magical Transformations

*Events are crowding fast upon the heels of time in the northwest. The transforma-
tions going on under the influence of railroad construction are more than magi-
cal, for they are real and not visionary. They come not by the waving of a fairy
wand, nor do they vanish. Cities, towns, factories, mines, farms and a thousand
other things are appearing where but a short time ago there was nothing, and
people with money, brains and energy are coming in a steady stream to aid in the
work.—West Shore.*[1]

RIPPING CLOUDS GAVE WAY and a dull, if appropriately beneficent, late
morning sun shined upon Olympia on November 18, 1889, the day
Washington finally commenced the business of state government. Assembling
in the business district, local citizens and out-of-town guests formed a loosely
organized parade open to anyone who cared to ride in a carriage or march on
foot. Militia companies, tootling fraternal bands and assorted dignitaries, well
fortified for the occasion, led the way through the streets toward the elevated
grounds of the capitol building. Erected in earliest territorial days, the two story
frame structure sagged among misty firs and rotting stumps and was widely, and
justifiably, considered a genuine public embarrassment.[2]

Recently white-washed, the place had been cleaned up to the fullest possible
extent for the great celebration. Bunting and swags of evergreen hung from the
second floor portico. A stuffed eagle and an out-of-control floral bouquet—roses,
chrysanthemums, violets and geraniums provided by ladies of refined society—
graced the special oath taking platform. Fixed in prominent display, a banner
proclaimed in the old Chinook trade jargon an appropriate, if hardly original,
motto. "Living hitherto in the past," the words announced in rough translation,
"we now begin to live in the future."[3]

Noon approaching, the bands burst forth with "America," the favored
national anthem of the time, then faded into the strains of "Hail to the Chief"
as Elisha P. Ferry, Washington's first elected governor, stepped forward to address
the crowd and assume the duties of high and distinguished office. Thinning hair,
whitening muttonchops and a slightly discombobulated air made Ferry resemble
an aging school principal somehow attired in the finely tailored trappings of a

railroad attorney and tidewater statesman. Barely heard in the closest ranks of the audience, his turgid remarks explored the past and anticipated the future of the newly born commonwealth, the unavoidable theme of the festivities. Oldtimers, the governor himself included, had waited so long for statehood that "they almost despaired of the realization of their hopes." Untroubled by historic frustration, recent immigrants (the overwhelming majority of the population) might properly look forward to the blessings of "resources superior to those of any other equal area." Pioneers and newcomers alike should go forth "proudly" aware of their presence at the exact moment when "the wheels of government" were "put into motion for the first time."[4]

Upon completion of the oratory and the swearing-in of Ferry and other statewide officials, soldiers fired a final cannon salute. Regular folks retraced their steps to warm downtown haunts, intent upon the pleasures of strong drink and hearty meals. "Every hotel and restaurant was soon tested to its utmost capacity," one celebrant wrote. Invited corporate representatives retired with the politicians to more refined quarters, to sip quality whiskey, inhale the luxurious smoke of fine cigars and debate the vital necessity of the new state avoiding such capital-repelling horrors as high taxation, genuine regulation of business and interference with the private exploitation of public resources. "Washington, but yesterday in…vassalage," a Puget Sound editorialist commented in reflecting upon the governmental transformation just completed in Olympia, "is to-day as much a state as though she were one of the original thirteen."[5]

America's 42nd state had, as a contemporary analysis of demographic trends pointed out, "actually been built within the last decade." The 357,000 residents tallied by the 1890 federal census represented a five-fold increase over the 1880 figure, a rate of growth 16 times the national pace for the 10 year period. At its birth, Washington ranked 34th among all states and territories, four places above neighboring Oregon. West of the Rockies, only California claimed a larger population.[6]

More growth took place in the Pacific Northwest during the 1880s, according to an amazed witness, than "in all the time previous since the first white settlement was established at Astoria in 1811." Recent developments within the boundaries of the new state were also worthy of note. For much of the territorial period, eastern Washington had been more dynamic than western, accounting in large part for frequent Walla Walla-based secession campaigns. Immigration continued to mount on the far side of the mountains in the final years of the territory; as the Palouse filled in, wheat ranchers moved into the Big Bend country and irrigation agriculture developed in the Yakima and Wenatchee river valleys. Recent railroad construction, however, had encouraged a substantially greater movement of people to Puget Sound and other tide-water points. Though two-thirds of the state lay east of the Cascades, by 1890 two-thirds of the population resided in western Washington.[7]

Of equal significance, a state often, and not incorrectly, portrayed in terms of vast forests and open-to-the-sky wheat prairies was newly and heavily urbanized. In 1880, only Walla Walla, Seattle and Vancouver on the Columbia recorded populations in excess of 1,000. Discounting for local booster exaggeration, three dozen towns had since moved beyond that mark. Seattle trailed Walla Walla slightly in 1880, but was now 10 times the size of its permanently displaced rival. Claiming barely a tenth of Walla Walla's population at the beginning of the decade, Spokane Falls had passed the older eastern Washington community by a factor of four. Together, Seattle, Tacoma and Spokane had slightly over 100,000 inhabitants, nearly a third of the entire state population, and twice the combined figure for the remainder of the 20 largest cities.[8]

Through most of its history, Washington Territory maintained a large non-white population, primarily Native Americans. This, too, had changed with the influx of immigration. The 1890 census listed precisely 1,602 black, 360 Japanese and 3,160 Chinese residents. Still holding legal title to 7,000,000 acres, encompassed within 18 reservations, the 4,000 remaining Indians had, as one newspaper somewhat indelicately noted, been "thinned out" as a percentage of the overall figure. Sympathetic pioneers familiar with the old days bemoaned the decline of native culture and worried over the problematic tribal attempts to sustain subsistence fishing and hunting activities in a time of rapid industrialization and urbanization.[9]

Except in certain specialized fields, such as Puget Sound commercial fishing and hop picking, Native Americans no longer played vital roles in the regional economy. Developers and homesteaders attempted, by one means or another, to procure valuable portions of the reservations. Grays Harbor timber interests demanded federal allotment of the Quinault agency, so that forested tracts might eventually be opened to exploitation by mill companies. East of the Cascades, settlers applied similar pressure to the Yakama reservation. Otherwise, Indians drew the interest of white Washingtonians only upon the periodic and widely reported urban excursions of such personages as Chief Joseph or Chief Moses. News coverage of the latter's horse selling expedition to Spokane in 1890 described in detail the visitor's "gorgeous tobacco sack," impressive leggings and "long buckskin coat of a beautiful shade of tan, heavily beaded and fringed and trimmed with otter skins."[10] A living history exhibit, the stout old man served as a dignified reminder of a marginalized people.

Composing two-thirds of the population, men dominated the state. No county came even remotely close to having an equal number of male and female residents. As in territorial times, various marriage societies and lonely hearts bureaus attempted to recruit "self-sacrificing young women" in the East as brides for love starved Washingtonians. Alice Houghton, Spokane's "Real East Queen," and Fay Fuller, the first of her sex to climb Mount Rainier, achieved modest public notoriety. For the most part, however, the daily and weekly press ignored female accomplishments and issues. The suffrage question, occasionally revisited after brief experimentation in the previous decade, was dismissed in most quarters as theoretical and dangerous nonsense. The *Seattle Post-Intelligencer* feared that women, if politically empowered, would attempt to "enact emotions and moral abstractions rather than practical laws." Submitted to the statewide electorate in 1889, the matter went down to defeat, amongst no great outcry of protest, by a two-to-one margin. Allowed to vote in local school elections, females participated at a significantly lower rate than men, suggesting a general disinclination for involvement in public affairs.[11]

≈≈≈

Washington Territory was, according to the many commentaries regarding a series of symbolic conflagrations, "consumed by fire" in its final months. Pedestrian causes of ignition—in one instance an untended glue pot—combined with ill timed breezes, wooden structures and ineffectual suppression efforts had decimated three of the prospective state's most important communities. On June 6, 1889, flames destroyed an estimated $15 million worth of property in Seattle, including offices, stores, mills, all but two of the Elliott Bay wharves and most of the city's vital public and personal documents. A month later, an aptly described "ocean of flame" swept through Ellensburg on the far side of Snoqualmie Pass. In the first week of August, fire burned 30 square blocks in Spokane Falls. For months thereafter, dispossessed residents dined on greasy over-priced ham and egg fare in dirty canvas tent restaurants alongside the Spokane River. "The tobacco smoke and beer fumes," one refugee claimed in recalling the strange absence of flies and other nagging insects in such rough-and-ready establishments, "killed them deader than a door nail." Urban dwellers from the Spokane River falls to the shores of Puget Sound faced the mettle-proving task of rebuilding on ash heap foundations of "ruin, rubbish and the remnants of lost fortune."[12]

Somehow, statehood appeared to have encouraged an outright epidemic of urban fire. "Hardly a month passes," wrote one of the Oregonians happy to celebrate disaster in neighboring Washington, "without the news coming that the best part of a city or town has been destroyed." Only the fortuitous absence of wind prevented complete destruction of Yakima in May 1890. The pioneer Walla Walla Valley town of Dayton went up in smoke in August 1890 and again the following January. Major outbreaks in August and October 1891 consumed numerous important structures in Walla Walla City, among them the offices of the *Union-Journal*, one of the oldest newspapers of the Pacific Northwest. North of the Snake River, Pullman, a grain shipping center on the verge of becoming a college town, fell victim to flames in mid-1890. Colfax burned in 1891, 1892— the local brewery was a particularly tragic victim—and 1893. On the rainy side of the Cascades, Mount Vernon, the important Skagit River trading point, was decimated in July 1891. Later in the year, Centralia, midway between the Sound and the Columbia, suffered damages calculated at $150,000. Ocosta, a favored Grays Harbor site for speculation by investors connected with the Northern Pacific, lost its entire business district in March 1892.[13]

Major urban areas victimized by the 1889 conflagrations, in contrast, avoided further devastation. Brick and stone, the modern construction materials of a newly created state, provided substantially better protection than the wooden structures still favored by smaller communities. Considering Ellensburg's modest population, some 1,500 permanent residents at the time of Washington's admission to the Union, it made the most impressive recovery. Work began on a new and better city within days of the July fire, thanks to the rapid infusion of capital from eastern and Puget Sound sources. Within a year, 300 buildings, including 75 "fireproof" structures, lined elegantly graded streets. An electric commuter railway, a system of streetlights and an impressive high school neared completion. The only apparent obstacle to the rapid growth of the Kittitas Valley metropolis was the difficulty experienced by local brick yards in keeping up with demand.[14]

Spokane's quick-time recovery drew widespread attention. "As one looks down the various…streets," the *Spokane Falls Review* reported in late 1889, "and sees the long lines of business blocks, from four to six stories high, nearly ready for occupation, it is a source of wonder and amazement…when it is remembered that less than four months ago all was desolation and ruin." Six million dollars were eventually spent on the erection of new brick, stone and iron buildings, including a $300,000 opera house and the Spokane Hotel, the finest hostelry in the state. Property valuations doubled between 1889 and 1890, as more land transactions were recorded than in Portland, Tacoma or Seattle. "You can no more keep Spokane real estate down," local boosters proclaimed, "than you can keep a cork below water."[15]

Certain discriminating visitors were, to be sure, less than fully impressed by the hustling Spokane scene. Outside investors privately derided the parochial townsfolk as so "fully convinced that a great city is to grow up in a day" that they tended, from naive greed, to "rush into enterprises without counting the cost." Elizabeth Bacon Custer, the famous Indian campaigner's wife and America's most enduring professional widow, complained of the endless "blasting," not to mention the "rattling" and "din," experienced in the course of her thoroughly unpleasant stay. The Austrian Archduke Franz Ferdinand, passing through while on a spare-no-cost New World tour, hated everything about the place. The "monotonous" ill painted buildings "presented no refreshing sight" and the muddy streets brought to mind horrid recollections of "conditions in small localities in Asia Minor." Even the Spokane River falls, a feature of the city rarely criticized, were "in reality only mill dams."[16]

Though traduced by a condescending son of debased European nobility, those very falls were actually the basis for a local conviction that "the fates have been kind to Spokane." Although Washington possessed more potential for hydroelectricity than either Oregon or California, Spokane was one of the few contemporary locations where water power could be effectively utilized. Dropping in a furious froth over a series of dark basaltic ledges in the middle of town, the Spokane River generated enormous energy. "Owing to the distribution of its flow…and its successive leaps over rapids and cataracts," one duly impressed hydrologist pointed out, "the available horse power it furnishes is greater than that which has built up Minneapolis." At the upstream end, the Spokane Water Power Company provided the motive force for lumber and flour manufactories. Organized in 1889, the Washington Water Power Company already had a dam in place, the first step in a largescale development scheme.[17]

Real estate, rather than water power, energized Seattle. Liberated from a past of wooden buildings and pioneer tawdriness, from a downtown "hastily, and in many respects, rudely constructed," community leaders immediately set about erecting an up-to-date city. Workers tore down blackened walls, hauled away rubble and built makeshift wharves and depots. Newspapers appeared on schedule, with the *Seattle Times* operating from a tent and the *Post-Intelligencer*, famously dubbed the "*P-I*," publishing on an open air press. Every incoming train and steamer deposited laborers, contractors and commission-hungry architects in the midst of the burnt-over district. Ready for customers by the end of summer, the ostentatiously temporary Rainier Hotel accommodated the better heeled opportunity seekers.[18]

Even the onset of the fall rains failed to slow the pace of reconstruction. A thousand structures, most of them trade oriented, were completed by Thanksgiving. Over a hundred fireproof commercial blocks, three to eight stories tall, soon graced the streets of new Seattle. Merchants moved in at ground level before workers finished the upper floors. According to a locally accepted estimate, 10,000 residents were added prior to the 1890 federal census count. Given the chance to modernize their properties, waterfront interests installed coal bunkers of the latest design and built 60 wharves along the two miles of bayside.[19]

Local citizens and touring outsiders alike expressed amazement over Seattle's hurried rebirth. On the two month anniversary of the blaze, attorney and longtime resident Thomas Burke wrote of experiencing "difficulty…in locating myself" among the unfamiliar downtown streets and structures. Calling frequently to keep track of his extensive real estate holdings, lumberman Cyrus Walker, a difficult person to impress, found that "the amount of work they have done…is simply astonishing." Visiting for the first time since the conflagration, the editor of the Portland *Oregonian* also was astounded: "Go where you like in…Seattle, and everything is as distinctly stamped 'Push,' as though the words themselves were painted thereon."[20]

Although hard headed types like Thomas Burke and Cyrus Walker avoided such forms of expression, literate Seattleites tended to credit their triumph to a providential "Spirit," a pro-growth enthusiasm apparently imbibed from Elliott Bay's early times. Here was born, in response to the fire, the exceptionalist ideology—a way of thinking readily projected back into the dimmest mudhole years of local history—proclaiming Seattle as the "Queen City" of the Pacific Northwest. "Seattle is not given to introspection," noted the *Seattle Telegraph*, the editorial voice of respectable business Democrats. "Its face is toward the future." In bipartisan accord on this basic tenet of faith, the soundly Republican *P-I* insisted that "the Seattle spirit is shown by the dogged pertinacity with which it will follow a project until it has been proved to be hopeless." Each year on the date of the fire, the newspapers honored, by way of glorious remembrance, the manner in which the city had converted "what might have been a disaster into an opportunity for grand achievement."[21]

Much of the hoopla bore scant resemblance to reality. "In the work of reconstruction," the *Post-Intelligencer* falsely boasted, "there have been no animosities, no contention of parties, no hindrance of selfish interests, and there have been no drones." Greed, albeit boldly employed, trumped concern for the general welfare, the downtrodden and the longterm interests of the city. Cyrus Walker steamed over from Port Ludlow in a mill company tug to personally evict fire victims who had dared to set up shelters on his Seattle property. Henry Yesler, another reconstruction curmudgeon, successfully obstructed efforts to straighten the streets in the business district, a much needed reform likely to impinge upon his waterfront holdings. Merchants moving into new buildings demanded that the municipal authorities enforce the town ordinance restricting usage of tents, alleged eyesores still in use by less fortunate commercial rivals.[22]

In a decidedly symbolic instance of malfeasance, the secretary of the well-endowed fire relief fund absconded with several thousand charitable dollars assigned to his uncertain care. Owners of surviving structures took advantage of the happy opportunity to raise rents. Relying on credit for financing, developers overbuilt expensive business blocks, leaving Seattle with a potential glut of high end office and store space likely to drag the local economy down in the event of hard times. Contractors ignored, on the other hand, the growing demand for common residential construction, the cheaper housing required if workers were to be attracted to the community to build and maintain the new city. Prominent local residents, including Henry Yesler and members of the Denny family, opposed essential public works related to population growth, arguing that such undertakings would increase their taxes and reduce private profiting opportunities.[23]

There was nothing unique, moreover, about the Seattle Spirit. The rhetoric actually was a conscious and near exact borrowing from Chicago's much bally-hooed response to the Great Fire of 1871. Spokane and Ellensburg residents expressed themselves in the same self-glorifying fashion. On the yearly anniversary of "the fire of Hope," Spokane honored its communal effort as producing a reborn community with "more life and excitement to the square inch than in any other town in America." Rising, Phoenix-like, upon the "ruins of the old," residents of Ellensburg claimed to have been motivated by "brave hearts and an undying faith in the living destiny of their city." Smaller places, meanwhile, boasted of the "Yakima Idea" and the "Aberdeen Rustle." Once the people of Pasco "thoroughly make up their minds to obtain a point," a local observer wrote of his spirited friends at the mouth of the Snake River, "they always obtain it." Spared a major conflagration, Tacoma nonetheless manifested unbridled get-up-and-go. "A misfortune may stun us but it cannot end us," one editor noted in affirming that "the right sort of material has been used in making the people of Tacoma."[24]

Seattle's near destruction produced deliberate efforts in Tacoma to prevent a similar disaster, including a ban of Fourth of July fireworks. At the same time, Commencement Bay boosters complained that the fire had given Seattle an unfair advantage in the form of an artificial economic stimulus on the eve of the 1890 census. "This abnormal industrial movement was attended by a speculative activity," a local editor grumbled, "and…large numbers of people were attracted there, whose residence may not be permanent." Tacomans in their "City of Destiny" all but openly mourned their own avoidance of prosperity inducing flame. Unfortunately, two hotel fires, neither of significant impact, provided the closest approximation of fruitful devastation.[25]

Bitter reflection upon a commercial rival's blessed suffering reflected the enduring strength of regional animosities. Continuing a longtime debate, and providing endless amusement to citizens in other parts of the state, Seattleites daily gazed, weather permitting, upon the startling bulk of "Mount Rainier." However, outdoors enthusiasts from Commencement Bay, including Fay Fuller, climbed the same peak, calling it "Mount Tacoma," or "Tahoma." Seattle made fun of the "City of Uncertain Destiny" and was in return dubbed "Mortgageville" for its boom-and-bust reputation. Tacomans claimed that Seattle's number one rating in the 1890 census was based upon assorted fraudulent methods, among them a last minute extension of the municipal limits and by the counting of cemetery "ghosts," visiting steamship crews and passing railroad passengers. Readily dismissed by outsiders as silly bombast—"one should be called Omnipotence and the other Infinity," a bemused newspaper joked of the two cities—the nasty exchanges represented a serious struggle for economic dominance in western Washington.[26]

Distracted in a sometimes unhealthy manner by what a Puget Sound observer termed "the heavy ball and chain of Seattle…rivalry," Tacomans often forgot that their own town site possessed attractions every bit the equal of those on Elliott Bay. Visible from all points, imposing Mount Rainier/Tahoma seemed to rise practically from sea level, though in reality dozens of miles distant. "The older resident, as well as the latest arrival," a visiting Oregonian reported, "always finds something new to admire in the varying shades of light and color that play upon its sides." Climbing the tide-flats hillside, the streets assumed "the general form," said railroad journalist E.V. Smalley, "of...what railway engineers call a 'reverse curve.'" At the highest elevation, an extensive plateau, still relatively empty of human habitation, ran west toward the public wilderness of Point Defiance and the constricted Puget Sound passage, the Narrows.[27]

In an age obsessed with the material exploitation of nature, certain aspects of Tacoma's scenery were especially appealing. The blufftop onlooker could look eastward and ponder the flats at the mouth of the Puyallup River—vast expanses targeted for full development and already home to the impressive St. Paul & Tacoma milling complex. Below the vantage point, the Northern Pacific's concentration of some 60 miles of interconnecting tracks and spurs, with modern shops, warehouses and office quarters, dominated a bustling waterfront. To the west, in the direction of pioneer Old Tacoma, tall-masted lumber schooners— "some weighted down, their decks covered ten feet high, and some light, with only the first thousand feet of their cargo"—loaded fresh cut sawmill products at sagging wharves. Railroad coal bunkers and grain elevators accommodated the largest steamers in regional waters. Far out on the city limits, a long anticipated smelter, the first facility of its kind on Puget Sound, began processing ore in 1890, completing what was then sometimes called the "poetry" of local industrialization. Together, scenic attraction, manufacturing and trade made the place a genuine rival to Seattle. "Even the tramps who flock here," one editor exclaimed, "are evidence that Tacoma is flourishing."[28]

What really distinguished the two cities was the substantially greater money making capacity of Seattle. The most profitable Elliott Bay enterprises tended to be controlled by individuals—people with resources of their own and investment connections in the East and Europe. Seattle was a real estate town in a large and more positive meaning of the expression—a community where citizens could take advantage of profit opportunities in a timely fashion. Tacoma, in contrast, was dominated by the Northern Pacific and its corporate land and utility affiliates. A blessing in terms of the community's original prosperity, the relationship tended to later stifle development. Commencement Bay might have gained a second transcontinental railway in 1890 when the Union Pacific expressed genuine interest in building to Puget Sound, but the NP frustrated attempts to open the necessary right-of-way. NP holdings interfered with the extension of public streets to the waterfront and the development of independent enterprises there. Supplies of water and energy lagged behind the needs of the growing population. Railroad executives and stockholders promoted competing Washington towns, to Tacoma's detriment. Years of habit, moreover, caused residents to rely far too much upon the Northern Pacific, an uncertain patron of progressive works.[29]

Modestly influenced by the fires at the time of statehood, an enduring commercial center pattern had been established east and west of the Cascades. During the territorial period, towns prospered, faltered and declined on a regular basis. Olympia and Steilacoom, the early centers of population, had long since lost stature, the former regaining momentary significance only when the biennial legislature convened. New places of temporary importance—on the Sound, the several timber ports, and east of the mountains, Walla Walla—had developed on a basis of natural resources extraction and prevailing territorial transportation networks. At the birth of the state, however, Seattle, Tacoma and Spokane, situated at strategic points connected to railroads and profiting from regional, national and foreign markets, attained permanent ranking as the predominant urban concentrations. Observers at the time recognized that all three had expanded to virtually self-sustaining scales. "Its development will proceed from within, quite as much as by accretion from without," an editorialist noted in regard to Tacoma. "That is to say, it has become a point of so much intrinsic consequence that to a degree it compels the location here of manufactures and other business establishments, and the enlargement of facilities for transportation."[30]

Capitalists, rather than hard working government officials or stalwart settlers, would determine the course of state history. Washington joined the Union at an opportune moment, for the industrial revolution had only recently generated enormous amounts of surplus money, especially in Great Britain. Modern means of transportation and communication, moreover, facilitated farflung investment. The London banker could easily dispatch agents across the Atlantic and on to the distant West by steamer and train. The telegraph, on land and below the sea, enabled near instant decision making and rapid transfers of funds. Wealthy Americans—in New York and Boston, Chicago and the Twin Cities—acted in accordance with the same motivations and methods.[31]

Territorial Washington suffered, until very late, from a notable deficiency of development credit. The only sources were locally based moneylenders and rudimentary banks, with little to offer and at high short-term rates, and San Francisco firms and investors, where interest was limited to the exploitation of Northwest timber and coal. Though "a long way from the East," as a sage observer noted, the New Washington now was wide open for business. "Money is pouring into the state from all quarters," a financial publication reported in 1890. "It seeks every opportunity; it enters into every avenue; it creates cities, makes farms, irrigates lands and establishes industries of different kinds." Loans were sought with the same avidity east and west of the Cascades. Perceptive individuals pointed out that the incoming cash flow made Washington fiscally dependent upon easterners and Europeans, a problematical risk worth taking, however, in exchange for growth and prosperity. Distant creditors possessed such unbounded faith in the resources of the Pacific Northwest, a Tacoma newspaper enthused, that "there need be no fear that this state will be brought up with a round turn and have to go through a threatening period of balancing the books."[32]

In the quest for loans, Washington possessed important advantages over "web-foot friends" south of the Columbia, advantages credited by many analysts to the new state's 1890 census lead. Oregonians themselves admitted that "mossbackism," defined as the tendency of long entrenched Portland interests to impede new-coming rivals, diverted outside money to more energetic points. "The laws of Washington," the bi-monthly *West Shore* magazine noted in reference to a more substantive difference, "favor investment of capital, while the laws of Oregon practically forbid it." The 42nd state had lower taxes, declined to tax mortgage interest and avoided effectual restrictions upon usury, all factors sure to be noted in New York and London counting houses. The result—"by their system of financial legislation," a Willamette Valley journal complained of the authorities in Salem, "Oregon is being drained of its available capital by Washington"—was evident to all quarters, domestic and foreign.[33]

Borrowed money was the chief factor in what one Puget Sounder called "the longest kind of a boom," i.e., new railroads. The great transcontinentals were the most famous and lucrative American corporations, with gross earnings of $965 million in 1890 and $7.4 billion in outstanding stocks and bonds. Washington, as the *Spokane Falls Review* proudly and correctly maintained, was "by far the banner state of the West" in railway construction. Under the most conservative statistical tabulations of completed annual mileage, the state ranked first nationally in 1889, second in 1890 and third in 1891. For the three year period, twice as much track was laid as in Oregon and California combined.[34]

At statehood, Washington was served by a single transcontinental road. The recently completed direct Northern Pacific line ran southwest from Spokane Falls to Pasco at the mouth of the Snake River, then up the Yakima Valley to Stampede Pass and crossed the Cascade crest, by deep tunnel, to tidewater. Expecting competition, NP's management instituted an expensive improvement program, straightening curves, replacing rails and ties and upgrading bridges and trestles, the better to serve passengers and freight. Other moves were calculated to overcome years of distrust in Seattle and to preempt potential rivals. In December 1889, the Northern Pacific took legal control of the Puget Sound Shore, or "Orphan Road," the existing and previously inadequate rail connection between Elliott Bay and Tacoma. In formal control of its own line into Seattle, the company introduced the same rates and fares charged Tacomans, eliminating a traditional source of discriminatory complaint.[35]

Prospective Northern Pacific opponents were easily identified, justifying the expense of improved service. "At present," a Spokane observer noted in November 1889, "the new state of Washington is the…chess board on which the great railroad magnates are making the moves." The Union Pacific had just taken over the Oregon Railway & Navigation Company, the Portland oriented wheat

Daniel C. Corbin, builder of lucrative railway ventures in the Coeur d'Alenes and developer of the Spokane Falls & Northern. *Museum of Arts & Culture, Spokane (L93-18.128)*

shipping outlet for the Walla Walla Valley and much of the Palouse. Early in 1890, the UP began work west of the Cascades on a costly Columbia River bridge, projected as the initial phase in an extension to Puget Sound. Another potential rival, the Seattle, Lake Shore & Eastern, was, for the moment, in a weakened state as the result of financial and legal difficulties. The original plan, to connect the Sound with Spokane, had been abandoned. Construction proceeded north of Seattle, however, with track laid up the Stillaguamish River in the direction of the Cascades and another line surveyed to the Canadian border. The aim remained eventual takeover by one of the major railways, providing Elliott Bay with a connection to the East independent of the Northern Pacific.[36]

One additional alternative—international railroading—drew positive attention in both western and eastern Washington. Feeders from the Canadian Pacific to the 49th parallel might easily be connected to roads coming north from Seattle and Spokane. The resulting haul to U.S. points east of the Rockies would be roundabout, but bonded goods carried in sealed cars could be sent back and forth across the "invisible border" free of customs duties. Travel already followed the basic route, with British Columbia merchants complaining that "95 per cent of the immigrants" arriving in Vancouver via the CP continued on to Puget Sound by steamer. Besides, competition—foreign or domestic—was the key factor in preventing the Northern Pacific from charging monopoly rates. "The more roads the better for everybody," asserted the *Tacoma Daily News* in reference to the guiding principle of commercial progress.[37]

Various regional railroads were fitted into the developing transportation framework. On the east side of the Cascades, loosely organized lines constructed by promoter George W. Hunt linked the Walla Walla Valley to Wallula and the Northern Pacific. The advent of the Union Pacific also terminated the longstanding division-of-territory between the NP and the Oregon Railway & Navigation Company, the former having operated north and the latter south of the Snake River. The UP moved aggressively into the Palouse, with its affiliated lines soon connecting the wheat country with both Spokane and Portland. Spokane also became the focus of development in other directions. The NP-related Washington

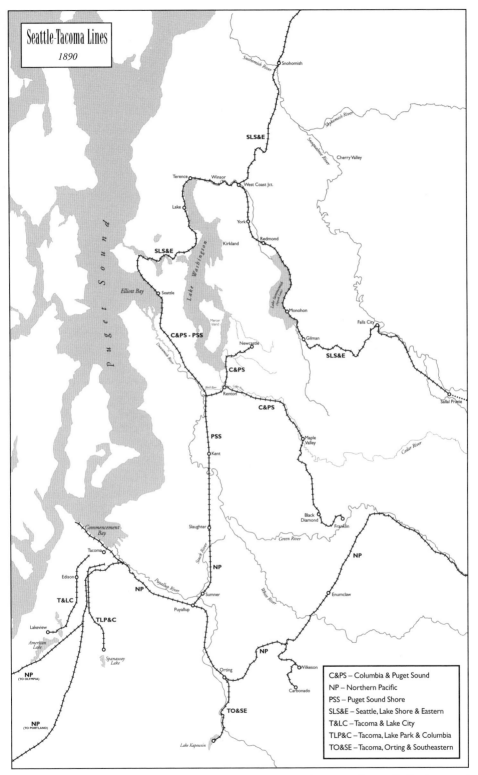

Seattle-Tacoma Lines
1890

C&PS – Columbia & Puget Sound
NP – Northern Pacific
PSS – Puget Sound Shore
SLS&E – Seattle, Lake Shore & Eastern
T&LC – Tacoma & Lake City
TLP&C – Tacoma, Lake Park & Columbia
TO&SE – Tacoma, Orting & Southeastern

From K. Armbruster, *Orphan Road* (WSU Press, 1999).

Central ran from Cheney through Davenport all the way, by mid-1890, to the brink of the Grand Coulee. Daniel C. Corbin, previously the developer of transport links to the Coeur d'Alene mines, built northward from Spokane, reaching the Columbia above Kettle Falls in the summer of 1890. Relying for the moment upon steamer transfers to the border, his Spokane Falls & Northern Railway advanced along the Kettle River at a steady pace toward the 49th parallel.[38]

West of the mountains, the Oregon Improvement Company, owner of the Columbia & Puget Sound running from the King County coal operations at Newcastle and Black Diamond to Elliott Bay, initiated ambitious transportation ventures. On the north, the Oregon Improvement Company built roads to Anacortes, a Fidalgo Island townsite promoted by the OIC, and up the Skagit River, opening service to Seattle in late 1890. The concern's heavily subsidized Port Townsend Southern affiliate began work along the western shore of Hood Canal, on a route intending to connect the Strait of Juan de Fuca with Olympia. Acquiring the territorial-era Tenino feeder linking the capital city with the Northern Pacific, the OIC looked forward to opening a direct connection with Portland. The overall goal was two fold—control of the key points on the upper Sound, with Anacortes on one side and Port Townsend on the other, and eventual consolidation at substantial profit with a transcontinental railroad.[39]

Competing with the Oregon Improvement Company, Nelson Bennett, previously a regular NP contractor and still a major developmental factor in Tacoma, operated from Fairhaven, his new town site on Bellingham Bay. On the eve of statehood, Bennett pointed the Fairhaven & Southern in the direction of the Skagit. Heading up that stream in a construction race with the OIC, he intended to wrest from Anacortes the trade at Sedro and other mining communities. Bennett also built north in early 1890, grading right-of-way and laying track toward the border in expectation of being the first American line to connect with the Canadian Pacific feeder from New Westminster. Like other regional promoters, he anticipated an eventual merger with one or another of the big cross country lines.[40]

Railroading also spread to the Washington coast, a region still dependent upon steamers from Portland. In late 1889, the Port Blakely Mill Company opened common carrier service on 24 miles of its logging road between Kamilche, a remote Puget Sound timber landing with water connections to Olympia, and Montesano at the head of navigation on the Chehalis River. The NP soon purchased this pioneer linkage between the Sound and Grays Harbor, and laid track from Tacoma through the state capital toward a junction point with its new line. In February 1891, trains began running direct through Elma to Montesano, where passengers transferred to boats for the 15 miles to Aberdeen at the mouth of the river. Previously a two day journey under the best of weather conditions, the trip from Commencement Bay to Grays Harbor now took a mere six hours.[41]

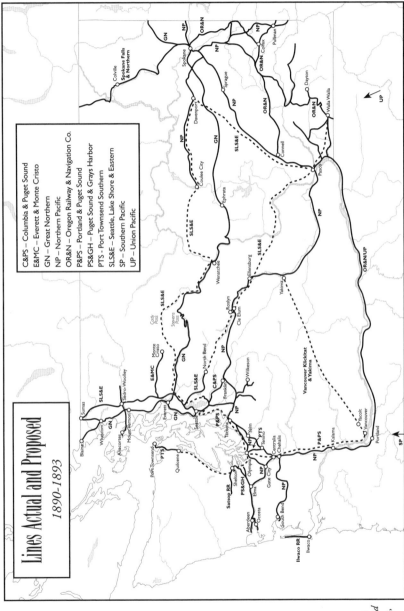

Lines Actual and Proposed
1890-1893

C&PS – Columbia & Puget Sound
E&MC – Everett & Monte Cristo
GN – Great Northern
NP – Northern Pacific
OR&N – Oregon Railway & Navigation Co.
P&PS – Portland & Puget Sound
PS&GH – Puget Sound & Grays Harbor
PTS – Port Townsend Southern
SLS&E – Seattle, Lake Shore & Eastern
SP – Southern Pacific
UP – Union Pacific

From K.
Armbruster,
Orphan Road
(WSU Press,
1999).

Other NP construction crews pushed work on a road from the mainline at Centralia, following the Chehalis River downstream to Montesano and Aberdeen. Twice daily service began on this route in 1891. Shifting his promotional energies to western Washington, George Hunt ran a parallel line along the Chehalis, in return for subsidies from land development interests on Grays Harbor. Outside analysts wondered how the chronically underfinanced Hunt could afford to compete with the NP, especially with the larger firm in possession of a transportation corridor bottleneck just east of Aberdeen. The two projects had different objectives, however, as Hunt was bound for the harbor's northern shore and the Northern Pacific for Ocosta by the Sea, a townsite favored by prominent stockholders. A damp and foggy place promptly dubbed "Ocosta in the Mud" by detractors, Ocosta was not the transcontinental's final destination in the region. Railroad management projected a further extension to South Bend, where the Willapa River emptied into Shoalwater Bay. Actual work began in 1890 upon a second NP connection to the Willapa, over 50 miles of hilly right-of-way between tidewater and the Puget Sound-Columbia River mainline. Important in its own right, the undertaking was the first phase in a proposed cross-Cascades export outlet for the Yakima Valley.[42]

<hr />

"Everybody," the OIC's Seattle based general manager exclaimed in June 1890, "seems to be building railroad." The most dramatic participant also was the most recent entrant. James J. Hill, backed by wealthy associates and heavy foreign capital, had organized the transcontinental Great Northern Railway the previous September. Although Hill's exact plans were not immediately apparent, most observers expected him to quickly acquire the Seattle, Lake Shore & Eastern as a means of securing access to Puget Sound and points north of Elliott Bay. In a neat Wall Street maneuver, however, the Northern Pacific removed this option by itself taking control of that line. A new railroading concern, the Seattle & Montana, thus became the original public face of the Great Northern on the Sound. Purchasing Nelson Bennett's Fairhaven & Southern, Hill also gained a route along the east side of the Sound country, plus the impending 49th parallel juncture with the Canadian Pacific.[43]

Hill was an entirely new type of business operator—a builder rather than a grabber, a plain talker instead of a blatant manipulator. Lumbermen had traditionally ignored law and even reason in exploiting a vast and cheaply removed natural resource. The first transcontinental railroads were undertaken for purposes of profit from construction, land sales and townsite promotion. "The people of Washington," a Seattle newspaper observed in celebrating the advent of the Great Northern, "have been accustomed to different ideas and different practices upon the part of transportation companies, whose object has been to extract every dollar possible from the products handled, without reference to the…development of the country."[44] A kind of regional admiration society soon exaggerated James J. Hill's contrasting virtues. However, the man, indeed, expressed genuine insight. Canadian born and in his early fifties, Hill was stocky, balding, gray bearded, and rather grandfatherly in appearance. His authority derived from his financial resources and from a vision focused upon a simple principle. In a much quoted remark, the GN founder described his motivation as "purely selfish"—nothing was more elevated than the making of money. To secure the most profitable return, though, he also knew he must enable GN customers to achieve the same goal.

"The prosperity of this country and the successful operation of his railroad are one," a Puget Sound observer noted of the fundamental dynamic at work. Hill stressed the point again and again in well received speeches, delivered during regular inspection tours to the coast. According to a local reporter, his much discussed September 1891 disquisition before the Spokane chamber of commerce was "better than anything [Sarah] Bernhardt can give at $5 a seat." Another Hill admirer suggested that the state print his speeches at public expense, as a means of educating the citizenry at large in the proper standards for business conduct.[45]

Aside from the top management's shrewd intelligence, certain practical concerns figured into the making of Great Northern policy. Unlike its famous transcontinental predecessors, the GN was built without land grants or townsite subsidies. Engineering calculations, enabling trains to cover the most direct practicable routes at the least gradient, were of paramount concern to an undertaking dependent upon long haul freight and passenger income. "An engine on the Great Northern," a Washington editor noted of the advantage provided by this necessary attention to technical detail, "will be able to pull more than twice as many loaded cars over the mountains as an engine of equal power will be able to pull on any other Pacific road."[46]

Vast sparsely settled territories between the Dakotas and eastern Washington had to be traversed, at considerable cost, before the Great Northern could begin generating substantial earnings. Although speedy construction through to the coast was an obvious necessity, Hill took time to send survey parties along all possible routes. "Nobody yet knows just what line will be adopted," Thomas Burke, the GN's Puget Sound attorney, informed an associate in March 1890. Politicians, journalists and everyday citizens in saloons and on street corners debated the possibilities and spread rumors. "If there is a single spot in all the wide West where the Great Northern has not been going to run," a Spokane newspaper quipped, "the public has yet to hear of it." Bemused at a distance by the hoopla, an Idaho commentator joked that "the next we hear of the line it will be skylarking around in Alaska."[47]

Within the boundaries of Washington, much of the route was determined by topography. West of Spokane, the GN had to pass between the regions already served by the main Northern Pacific to one side and the NP's Washington Central on the other. Casual map-readers grasped this point without truly understanding the difficult nature of the terrain. There was no possibility of following a straight line across the Big Bend to the Columbia, a river flowing through a deep canyon, with only occasional breaks in the looming volcanic escarpment. Two options initially appeared, or so experienced persons maintained in assessing Hill's construction problem. The Great Northern could follow Foster Creek to the Columbia, reaching the stream just above the mouth of the Okanogan River. The gradient was less than ideal, but the road would be in position to tap potentially rich mines in the Okanogan country. Alternatively, the GN might take the Moses Coulee route, striking the Columbia near Wenatchee. Although the distance to be covered would be reduced, the grade was no better and the freight-carrying potential, from initial study of the bleak surroundings, was inferior. Unimpressed by either possibility, Hill's engineers, directed by John Stevens, eventually located a better line, via Crab Creek to Rock Island Rapids, also close to Wenatchee.[48]

Detailed mountain survey work revealed that the winding Wenatchee River provided, as Stevens wrote, "the correct solution to the knotty problem" of access to the Cascades and the actual crossing to tidewater. After much hard labor among the rugged peaks, Stevens located the pass that would bear his name. Pending completion of an expensive tunnel, James J. Hill's new railroad would have to rely upon a temporary switchback system across the crest. According to an early passenger, this solution at one precipitous point went "back and forth six times on the same sidehill." Although the GN had fewer miles of track between the Idaho border and Puget Sound than the NP, its overall gradient was, for the time being, actually greater than that followed by the supposedly inferior transcontinental rival.[49]

Problems at the eastern end of the cross-Washington line, meanwhile, were not easily addressed by technical ingenuity. Served by the NP and feeder roads in all directions, Spokane's commercial leaders regarded a decision on the part of the GN to purchase a right-of-way and build through their community as both rational and inevitable. Instead of conceding the point, however, Hill requested a free and unfettered right-of-way. Otherwise, the GN would pass to the north, leaving Spokane with only a sidetrack connection. When dealing with the city's business interests, as a contemporary analyst noted, Hill "has given them much taffy, but at the end of the stick he has stated with much frankness what he wanted." Failing in a brief attempt to deal directly with property owners, the company made the right-of-way issue a stand-and-deliver public responsibility. Covert obstruction on the part of the NP delayed a resolution and the $300,000 fund necessary for purchase of the desired route was not fully subscribed until February 1892. Only then was Spokane, the self-promoted transportation hub of the interior Northwest, guaranteed through service by a second transcontinental railroad.[50]

To the west of the Cascades, Hill apparently and secretly intended from the beginning to make Elliott Bay the Puget Sound terminus. "Their views and purposes in relation to Seattle," attorney Thomas Burke privately reported after a

June 1890 conference with GN officials, "are of the most comprehensive character." For good reasons of "business policy," however, the firm declined to "show its hand too early in the day." Hill himself spoke in public of the mainline as "the head of the rake," with the various tidewater towns serving as the "prongs," a metaphor bound to stimulate region-wide aspirations. Communities large and small were, in ambitious fact, eager to be swept up by the Great Northern "rake." Fairhaven residents expressed confidence that the line would terminate at Bellingham Bay. Wealthy investors behind the development of Everett expressed a similar conviction for their Port Gardner townsite. Tacomans, too, had terminal ambitions, though Hill, as one wit observed, would have to go "zig-zagging up and down the Cascade mountains, dodging out of one pass and hiding in another" in order to reach Commencement Bay.[51]

Possible alternatives to Seattle provided Hill with considerable bargaining leverage as he pushed into the city. Existing lines controlled the southern approaches to the waterfront. Created by the municipality in 1887 and running on reclaimed harbor land, however, Railroad Avenue facilitated entrance from the north (see map, p. 98). With the politically influential Burke adroitly handling the details, the GN-affiliated Seattle & Montana secured an ample right-of-way along the thoroughfare in March 1890. "It was kept perfectly quiet," according to the confidential account of one business insider, and "submitted to a special session of the Council who passed the necessary ordinance under suspension of rules in the absence of the Mayor and two Councilmen." The Northern Pacific and the Oregon Improvement Company, the latter holding the strategically vital and preexisting "Ram's Horn" franchise at the southern end of town, countered with a series of obstructive maneuvers. Barring a satisfactory agreement with these rivals, Burke warned Hill, "we are going to have an ugly fight to get across their property."[52]

Declining to compromise, or to give up on Seattle, Hill demonstrated his commitment to Elliott Bay as the GN terminus. The struggle was prolonged, brutal and thoroughly confusing in detail. The antagonists engaged in legal battle, partisan contest and editorial debate, not to mention occasional attempts at preemptive track-laying. Fortified by the courts in its claims to the Ram's Horn, the Oregon Improvement Company held a particularly strong position. The firm's managers, however, feared a hostile public response should the GN actually be driven away from Seattle. In return for a relatively modest compensatory payment, Hill finally secured unrestricted access to the waterfront in the winter of 1895.[53]

Bullying its way to prime bayside acreage, the Great Northern was, without doubt, the most aggressive and successful combatant in the "great railroad war…to get possession of the northwest territory." Elliott Bay residents celebrated a revived market in real estate, said to be "dragging" in the aftermath of post-fire reconstruction, and welcomed the official incorporation of the Seattle and Montana by the GN as another example of the locally "indomitable"

Seattle Spirit. Except, possibly, for the aggrieved stockholders of the Oregon Improvement Company—and even the OIC made good money from land sales—Washingtonians east and west embraced the new railway. This pending arrival of a second transcontinental, plus the completion of numerous regional roads, meant greater competition and lower freight charges, as well as economic growth and increased rates of immigration and investment. Though barely a year had passed since admission to the Union, the state appeared squarely on course to a prosperous future. Washington's "storehouse has as yet been untouched," the *Tacoma News* noted in a confident forecast, "and it remains for the 'open sesame' of the iron horse to throw open the doors and pour its treasures into our lap."[54]

∽≈≈≫

Urban and rural Washingtonians alike eagerly anticipated the appearance of railway surveyors. The compass and chain professionals might be "engaged," as the *Seattle P-I* suggested, "in the performance of that ostentatious theodolitic demonstration of trigonometrical survey known in railroad technology as 'running a bluff.'" More often than not, however, survey crews were the genuine advance agents of that fundamental regional necessity, capital. Washington had to pay "a double tribute," according to a contemporary analyst of the new moneyed order. "We have our share of the American obligations to Europe, and in addition send tribute to the older sections of our own country." The ratio of benefit to cost was nonetheless positive, another observer noted, so long as "men of money look upon this state as presenting the very solidest opportunities for investment."[55] The inherent difficulty was that the same mechanisms of national and international finance responsible for prosperity could just as readily deny loans.

A sudden economic downturn in the fall of 1890 revealed this harsh truth. The causes were worldwide, ranging from fiscal crises in Argentina and Brazil to negative crop forecasts and protectionist trade policies in the United States. At this time, even the large-scale British withdrawal of gold from overseas investments failed to prevent the dramatic collapse of Baring Brothers, a venerable London money house. In New York, American stocks, especially securities issued by the railroads, dropped sharply, which spread alarm. "The decline," a Tacoma newspaper succinctly recounted, "has…weak holders anxious to sell when nobody wanted to buy." *West Shore* magazine conveyed the sense of panic on the stock exchange in a few bold lines:

> Great excitement in Wall street; bulls and bears bellowing and roaring, tossing their horns and showing their savage teeth; stocks going down like mercury before a Dakota blizzard; the whole country looking on in fear that a national financial crisis will be precipitate.[56]

Residents of the Pacific Northwest insisted that the stock market crisis was no cause for local alarm. "Imprudent investments" on the part of Wall Street "gamblers" had, at worst, temporarily interfered with the flow of capital. The panic, moreover, would actually turn out to be beneficial, as chastened and speculation averse investors turned to profit guaranteed development of land and resources in America's far northwest corner. "After the storm," one of the many Washington observers working this theme noted, "we shall have clear skies…and the wheels will go round with the same merry hum we were used to hear." All that was necessary, regionally and nationally, was a simple restoration of confidence.[57]

These sustained efforts, minimizing "the little unpleasantness on Wall Street," ignored the unhappy reality that the withholding of capital was bound to have negative consequences for the new Washington. In Spokane, one of the major banks quickly failed and hard pressed merchants demanded emergency rent reductions from overextended landlords. On account of "a diminution in the speculative demand for lots," the Washington Water Power Company was unable to secure financing for renewed development work at the falls. West of the Cascades, Elliott Bay promoters complained that "almost a complete stop" had taken place in "lending" from outside money markets. "Everybody," a Seattle attorney advised, "is hanging on by the eyelids." The city lost two of its five daily papers, the *P-I* taking over the *Journal,* and the *Press* combining with the *Times.* Townsite "booming" came to a halt on both sides of the mountains.[58]

One accurate and troubling concern emerged from the early assessment of the Wall Street affair. "The extreme depression of railroad securities," the *Tacoma Ledger* feared, "may…hamper railroad extension, and if it does we shall have cause to seriously regret it." Forced to reorganize, the Union Pacific abandoned plans to build north from Portland to Puget Sound. Badly managed and in debt to creditors large and small, the Oregon Improvement Company declared bankruptcy in November 1890. Continuing in business under a court appointed receiver, the firm set aside its ambitious regional transportation scheme, in favor of efforts to sell off existing holdings. George Hunt, another operator unable to survive without loans, sold his eastern Washington interests to a consortium headed by Charles B. Wright, the Philadelphia financier prominently involved in both the Northern Pacific and Tacoma's land development. Hunt also halted construction on the Chehalis River, leaving the NP in control of the Grays Harbor trade.[59]

James J. Hill, on the other hand, profited while regional rivals struggled to merely survive. "Before the Barings had got into difficulty," Thomas Burke wrote in explaining the fortunate circumstance of his employer, "the Great Northern loan to the extent of $10,000,000 had been placed and the money brought over to this side." The Fairhaven & Southern linked up with the Canadian Pacific at the 49th parallel in early 1891. The GN reached the Sedro terminus of the old Bennett Skagit River line, sending the first through train to the border from Seattle in late November. For the first time, Elliott Bay enjoyed transcontinental service independent of the Northern Pacific. "It affords our people," one newspaper enthused of the historic occasion, "the needed means of doing their business without reference to the great corporation which has so long been the public enemy."[60]

Work progressed as well on the GN's cross-state mainline, proceeding toward Stevens Pass from both sides of the Cascades. In a ceremony noteworthy for a complete lack of "fuss and feathers," a few pistol shots celebrated the driving of the last spike seven miles west of the pass in January 1893. The low-key nature of the proceedings contrasted with the expensive pomp and circumstance orchestrated a decade earlier by Henry Villard on behalf of the Northern Pacific. "There were no large-girthed European capitalists," a reporter emphasized, "no state or national dignitaries, and only a few of the minor officials of the road, together with contractors and laborers."[61] The business-like Great Northern, built with attention to detail and efficient expenditure, was through to the coast. Seattle now had its own direct connection to the interior Northwest and points beyond, and was able, henceforth, to ignore its temporary benefactor, the Canadian Pacific.

Next to railroading, townsite promotion attracted the most attention from investors. The relationship between transportation and urban speculation was both obvious and intimate. "This is an age of railroads," a champion of one particularly aggressive community pointed out, "and without them there is no development or progress." Original claimholders, having staked out likely places at tidewater or on navigable rivers, expected the arrival of trains to sooner or later make their fortunes. Holders of stock in the transcontinental lines anticipated the profitable sale of lots and industrial acreage. Money was to be made by all and metropolitan energy was everywhere evident. "I noticed one or more 'real estate offices' in every town," a visiting federal official reported in August 1890 of the dozen Northern Pacific stops between Tacoma and Seattle, "and…they were doing a 'thriving business!'"[62]

Land booming misbehavior, especially in western Washington, drew censorious notice even in the East. "That there are such a thing as paper cities," the *Tacoma Ledger* admitted, "no one who has had any experience in the Sound country would for a moment deny." From Bellingham Bay south, and out to the coast, unethical promoters—"keen, alert, inexhaustible in schemes for taking advantage of the unwary"—mulcted new arrivals and distant clients. "All over the state," the *P-I* noted, "little clusters of cabins are being magnified into mushroom 'cities' with…'extensions' innumerable, heralded by…prospectuses as 'terminals'…for unthought of and impossible railroad connections." Agents descended upon depots and hotel lobbies, outfitted with spurious maps depicting make believe railways and non-existent harbors. "At least two towns," a newspaper observed, "have been boomed by using the name of the Southern Pacific railroad, which so far as known, has as yet found no intention to extend its line to this part of the world." One sports savvy promoter staged professional wrestling matches to attract buyers to his development site.[63]

Puget Sound real estate, the railroad writer E.V. Smalley suggested, was "a game with loaded dice, where the money all goes into the pockets of smart speculators and the lot buyers are left with a few square feet of worthless wilderness land." The scamster and the sucker became prime targets of regional humor. Land agents, a Bellingham Bay wit claimed, "like to handle outlying suburbs, and the suburb that can outlie all the rest is the one preferred." Another resident wrote of a would-be community located on a precipitous hillside where "the birds play hide-and-seek in the clouds." Another promotion occupied terrain so swampy that "to look at the property is to wet your feet." At the pace things were going west of the Cascades, one editor joked, "the water-lapped shore…will be one continuous row of planted townsites, and the names of most of them will be synonymous with that of their southern termini at Cape Disappointment."[64]

Some voices defended boosterism, no matter how rampant, as a necessary and beneficial aspect of development. After all, a promoter explained, "capitalists don't invest their money in a town where the real estate brokers play checkers…all day long and merchants close their doors to go fishing." Serious-minded critics nonetheless condemned town booming. Speculation was an economically viable enterprise, E.V. Smalley and others pointed out, only "as long as the public is in a mood to buy lots." Bound to dissipate sooner or later, the money fever also had immediately negative consequences. Washington's image was tarnished and investors might choose, as a result, to avoid genuine exploitation of the state's abundant natural resources. Reflecting upon the 42 towns platted in Skagit County during the first three months of 1890, the *Tacoma Ledger* raised a prudent query: "Would it not be much better…if forty-two new farms had been opened…or if an equal number of productive enterprises of some other kind were started?"[65]

Assorted failed speculations provided ready examples for citation by boom detractors. Detroit, near the southern end of Hood Canal, attracted brief attention in the spring of 1890 as a likely lumber manufacturing center. Writing of "the cheerful shout of the bullwhacker in the timber" and the landing of construction supplies, an impressed visitor departed before a collapse induced by the stock market crisis occurred. Grays Harbor City, close to the ocean several miles beyond Hoquiam, expected to prosper as the terminus of George Hunt's railroad. Investors spent several hundred thousand dollars on buildings and a deep water wharf, only to lose everything when Hunt's project shut down. "This alleged city," a newspaper unkindly recounted in August 1891, "which a year ago was so thriving and popular that its lots were selling to the unsuspecting…tenderfoot at $4000 and $5000 each, is now simply a resort for bats and owls." Other promotions, too, including towns planned for the Olympic Peninsula and the mouth of the Nisqually River on the Sound, failed at the outset, having generated no investment interest.[66]

Towns served by railroads prior to the Wall Street crash achieved permanent, if troubled, status. East of the Cascades, the Washington Central promoted settlement of the Big Bend, with immigrants taking up claims all the way to the Grand Coulee and establishing what E.V. Smalley called "a thin skirmish line of civilization" above the startling precipice. Already founded by the Northern Pacific on the edge of the pine country west of Spokane, Cheney recovered from a devastating 1888 fire to secure genuine urban stature in the first year of statehood. Fifteen hundred persons resided there, served by five churches, a bank, two newspapers and recently installed water and electric light plants. Continuing rail construction produced a series of promising communities—Medical Lake, Davenport, Wilbur, Almira and, at the one point where a road could be built across the great natural chasm, Coulee City.[67]

Down on the Columbia, Wenatchee prospered as "a Great Northern town." Originally established by investors associated with the Seattle, Lake Shore & Eastern, the place made little progress prior to Washington's admission to the Union. Despite occupying a strategic site near a main river crossing and the route to Stevens Pass, Wenatchee required expensive irrigation works in order to attract settlers. To secure the necessary funding, Thomas Burke, one of the promoters, dealt James J. Hill a quarter interest in the undertaking in 1891. Buildings and residents were moved approximately a mile to a location better suited to depot and shop facilities. "Wenatchee people are becoming affected with the spirit of Western boom," a visitor reported, "and if a sale of real estate is not effected almost daily they say that it is very dull."[68]

More than justifying its namesake claim as a "good country," Wenatchee developed a reputation for prime peach, apricot and apple orchards. The town's initial importance rested, however, upon its occupancy of the place where the rails met the Columbia. The Great Northern provided access to markets east and west. Rock Island Rapids blocked downstream navigation, but the Columbia was open for steamboat traffic a substantial distance upriver, so long as the water ran high and captains exercised due caution. Tied up at Wenatchee for the past several years, the *City of Ellensburgh* was refurbished and put into regular twice-weekly service to the mouth of the Okanogan in 1892. A half dozen vessels soon joined in the lucrative business of transferring freight and passengers to and from the trains.[69]

To the west of the Cascades, many genuine towns grew up with the railroads. Sedro, previously an obscure Skagit River point controlling access to assorted varieties of mineral wealth, became the target of competing lines in the spring of 1890. In a matter of months, the site progressed from "a tangle of blackened stumps and half burned tree trunks" to a $100,000 developed center, featuring business blocks, a hotel and schoolhouse. On the NP track between Puget Sound and the lower Columbia, Centralia and Chehalis added population at a rapid pace. Both had mills, banks, mercantile emporiums and saloons, plus the usual quota of professional people, numerous real estate agents included. Smaller places, such as Bucoda and Winlock, also opened along the right-of-way, performing trade and service functions for the surrounding countryside.[70]

On a larger scale of urban significance, Bellingham Bay, in the doldrums since the Fraser River gold rush of 1858, achieved sustained prosperity. At the end of the territorial era, a local resident noted, Whatcom had consisted of "but two business houses," while Sehome, the other boom-and-busted relic, "existed only as a village, containing a few scattered buildings." Though still proclaiming from long habit the greatness of their vast saltwater bay, dispirited boosters also confessed that, thanks to severe tidal ebbs and flows, the only "safe" anchorage was "about three thousand feet from shore." Pilings, driven in rickety support of ramshackle structures and above-the-flow outhouses, cluttered the mudflats inside that line. "Awakening from its reposeful state," Bellingham Bay looked toward railroading instead of to seaborne commerce for its salvation.[71]

Nelson Bennett's road, plus the overblown conviction that the bay was likely to become the effectual western terminus of the Canadian Pacific system, set off a real estate boom reminiscent of the glorious gold excitement days. The pioneer towns of Whatcom and Sehome merged in early 1890 as New Whatcom. By spring, the revivified community claimed to have 7,000 residents, nine churches, five sawmills and more miles of planked roadway than any metropolis in the state. Around a rocky promontory to the south, Bennett's Fairhaven developed with equal rapidity. Remarking, after a mid-year visit, upon the "handsome residences," graded streets, electric transit line and expensive hotel, E.V. Smalley concluded that Fairhaven was "just now the liveliest place of its size in the whole Sound Country." Already "touching elbows," as many commentators pointed out, New Whatcom and Fairhaven appeared on the way to eventual union.[72]

To the south, Anacortes—the original claimant insisted upon the name in honor of his wife—competed with the Bellingham Bay settlements. Founded in the winter of 1890 by the Oregon Improvement Company and investors associated with the Northern Pacific, Governor Elisha Ferry included, the townsite was located on Fidalgo Island and fronted six square miles of deep water on the margin of the Skagit River delta. Featuring brick business blocks, two dozen dwellings, a schoolhouse and a telephone exchange, Anacortes frustrated its promoters once the initial burst of enthusiasm had dissipated. The NP lacked genuine interest and the OIC possessed neither expertise nor sufficient funding. Lots were poorly laid out, leading one resident manager to privately recommend "refunding the money paid and starting over on an entirely new basis." The firm declined to erect more than the minimal number of structures, leaving to newcomers the task of filling the wide-open undeveloped and inadvertently unappealing places. One would-be investor discovered that the suspiciously overactive train traffic consisted of a single locomotive, which was kept busy pulling the same two cars back and forth during the course of his visit. Discerning capitalists departed, money still firmly in hand, convinced that Anacortes was a "fake."[73]

Problems of this sort were rarely encountered at Everett, the potent nemesis of Anacortes. Located on a stubby peninsula between the Snohomish River and Port Gardner Bay, the place was the only major town founded after the 1890 panic, a testimony-in-timing to the financial standing of its promoters. Everett, sometimes known as Port Gardner, began with a plan by John D. Rockefeller and other wealthy eastern investors to manufacture whaleback barges on the Pacific coast. By happenstance a member of the group, Charles Colby, in the course of an ocean excursion to Alaska, met Henry Hewitt Jr., a partner in the St. Paul and Tacoma Lumber Company. Hewitt, who owned considerable timber acreage along the Snohomish, convinced his new friend that the stream's mouth was an ideal site for manufacturing and the most likely terminal point for the Great Northern. As a result, the so-called "City of Industry," named for Colby's son, was born in 1891.[74]

Unanticipated difficulties challenged the investors. Local convictions to the contrary, the GN ignored Everett. Although boosters insisted that the lower Snohomish was navigable by ocean shipping, the river's several outlet channels were, in uncomfortable fact, "practically dry" at low tide. Fortunately, Hewitt, Colby and their less active associates possessed the resources and the wisdom to avoid common speculation-related mistakes. "They had a good deal of money," E.V. Smalley pointed out, "and they determined to first create…solid enterprises that would support a population and then invite population to occupy their lots and streets." The first pulp operation on local waters, sawmills, nail works and the signature barge factory went up on the bayfront and along the banks of the Snohomish. Commercial and residential buildings were "constructed almost daily," according to a report, along with wharves and planked thoroughfares. "They are laying out a town," lumberman Cyrus Walker exclaimed with only slight exaggeration after a July 1892 visit, "large enough for a million people." Another railroad, maybe even the Great Northern should James J. Hill come to his senses, would surely arrive in the near future.[75]

While Everett emerged as a new place with large ambitions, Grays Harbor remained at statehood an old locale with long denied aspirations—a place, as a local editor conceded, "where even canoes patiently moved with the rise and fall of the tide." Slowly uncoiling beneath banks overgrown in tangled vegetation, the Chehalis River—reminding E.V. Smalley "a little of the bayous in Louisiana"— entered the harbor at Aberdeen. From that point to the sea, a good dozen miles, three major streams, the Wishkah, the Hoquiam and the Humptulips, ran in from the north, draining the dark green foothills of the Olympics. "One of the largest bays on the Pacific Coast" when studied on a map, Grays Harbor was "really a vast mud flat" in the considered opinion of expert engineers and surveyors.[76]

In addition to the usual complications of tidal flow, the harbor was obstructed by bars immediately west and east of Hoquiam. Although there was ample water at the harbor's mouth, the unmarked channel shifted position at disconcertingly random intervals. Army engineers had studied the situation for years, but regular entreaties from local business interests had yet to result in actual navigation improvement work. Due to the failure of the government to provide even a beacon light, sawmill magnate George Emerson complained that a "long list of vessels" lay "buried" in the sand. An active marine trade persisted in defiance of the hazards. Thirteen small steamers hauled goods and passengers between the various settlements. Weather permitting, lumber schooners were towed to sea often enough to secure profits for timber companies. Larger vessels, though, could not enter Grays Harbor, a genuine handicap so far as economic development was concerned.[77]

Unless the federal government could somehow be persuaded to fund a massive dredging project and expensive jetties, Grays Harbor was likely to remain "a local port" in the view of business executives. "A worse feature than the bar" at the mouth of the bay, a non-investing visitor reported, "is the fact that there is no harbor after you get over it that amounts to anything." Thanks to the Northern Pacific and the momentary promise of the competing Hunt road, the much maligned waterway was, however, "on the eve of great things." Now with the opening of a rail route eastward, investor attention turned to the north side of the harbor, where sawmills could most easily be supplied with logs. The population of Hoquiam—the headquarters of George Emerson's North Western Lumber Company since 1882—tripled in the first six months of statehood. Three miles to the east at the mouth of the Wishkah, Aberdeen grew up—as one enthusiast claimed, "like a fir tree in the wilderness." Blessed with extensive deep water anchorage, the community had four lumber mills and three salmon canneries. Addressing tidal conditions, Hoquiam and Aberdeen elevated their principal streets, filling in the flats with excavated earth and building upon piles.[78]

Pending completion of the Grays Harbor railroad network, delayed by quarreling between Aberdeen and Hoquiam, another long-neglected location appeared to have even better prospects. Shoalwater Bay remained the active resort of oyster harvesters, who shipped over 30,000 sacks of shellfish to San Francisco and Portland in 1891. The harbor mouth, at the far northern extremity of the North Beach Peninsula, was officially rated by the federal government as possessing sufficient depth and protection for oceangoing vessels. Taking cynical advantage of its commercially deflating place-name, "Shoalwater Bay," rival sections insisted that the finding was the corrupt product of "windy real estate boomers" and "Munchausen" Army surveyors. "Schooners, which alone can cross the bar," a Tacoma newspaper warned, "have to enter along the trough of the sea, and once in they have to lay for 10 weeks at a time...unable to get out."[79]

Conditions inside the mouth closely resembled those on Grays Harbor; the retreat of the tide uncovered vast and thoroughly dank mud flats. Tributary streams, primarily the Willapa on the north and the Nasel to the south, deposited sediment and snags, further inhibiting navigation. Unable to afford dredging, local interests turned first to public relations. "The throngs of eager, speculative men seeking in the new State of Washington for opportunities to make fortunes…were naturally repelled by the name of Shoalwater on the map," E.V. Smalley wrote, "and very few people thought it worth while to make a long journey away from the regular routes of travel to ascertain whether the water…was really shallow or not." Consequently, the relevant federal authorities provided the necessary remedy, officially changing the harbor name to Willapa Bay in June 1890.[80]

Situated three miles up the Willapa River from open water, South Bend consisted at statehood of little more than a rundown North Western Lumber Company mill, with attached store and unpainted worker housing. Railroad construction, as well as the prospect of federal navigation work, attracted eastern investors to the place as a likely transportation hub of the future. "That a large city will grow up here," the developers proclaimed in their local newspaper, "is a prevalent opinion as strong as positive knowledge." By late 1890, a planked street, teetering above the tide on piling, ran from the old mill east along the narrow corridor intervening between rain-washed hills and the river. The business district featured two banks, one strongly constructed of brick, a hotel and several mercantile establishments. Amenities included a waterworks, an electric plant and a municipal railway. An odd mixture of urbanity and salty contrariness prevailed, best exemplified on the day that a newcomer "dude" opened a lawn tennis club next door to the chambers where inebriated town council members conducted a fisticuff-punctuated public meeting.[81]

Like other boom towns, South Bend suffered in the aftermath of the 1890 financial crisis. Investors also discovered that they would have to engage in costly dredging if the town was to be made truly accessible for large sea-going vessels. "Day and night, Sundays and week days," a reporter noted of an enormous dredge hauled by sea from Tacoma, "its machinery is employed in sucking up the alluvial deposit in the bottom of the…river." If nothing else, South Bend secured a solid physical foundation—the "mixed clay and mud" excavated from the Willapa forming a "smooth, dry hard surface" when spread upon reclaimed tidal land.[82]

Despite capital dislocations, infant Washington registered substantial, even remarkable, progress in railroading and urban development—and in the process remade commercial transportation networks. The state still had 2,000 miles of stage routes in 1890. Much of the traffic, though, was on the eastside, rather than in the rapidly growing regions west of the Cascades. Stagecoaches, moreover, could not accommodate heavy freight, or passengers interested in rapid and comfortable travel. Puget Sound always had relied upon water transportation—a hard-to-avoid choice given the relative lack of decent, not to mention indecent, shore adjacent roads. Since earliest territorial times, "weather-beaten relics," as one pioneer editor cogently described the steam driven vessels in common usage, had served the Sound, "stopping at every milk ranch."[83]

At first, the arrival of new settlers stimulated traditional waterway commerce. "The regular boats…have been crowded to the guards every trip," a Tacoma newspaper reported in February 1890, "and every old tub that could be made to float at all has been…put into commission." Government inspectors guarded the principal docks, intent, if bribes were not forthcoming from pursers, on preventing overloading. Freshly constructed vessels—"swift, commodious, [and] modern"—entered the trade, the owners anticipating ample profits. "There could not be a better indication of the way in which the country is being developed," a Seattle editor enthused. Rapid completion of the main railroads, however, soon diverted passengers and compelled a sharp reduction in fares. Some steamers, among them the new and truly elegant *Bailey Gatzert*, were tied up by disconsolate investors, while the surviving transit firms struggled to form combinations for the control of rates.[84]

Seattle, the principal port-of-call for nearly all steamers, had dominated Puget Sound commerce, one observer recalled, "ever since Mr. Yesler began to saw lumber," but railroads were rising toward the forefront. Railroads also allowed Tacoma—and to a certain extent places like Fairhaven, Anacortes and Everett—to compete in an ever growing regional market. Beyond the Cascades, Spokane already had established a rail hinterland in the Palouse and across the Idaho line into the Coeur d'Alenes. The city now expected the Washington Central and D.C. Corbin's 49th-parallel-bound railroad to open new opportunities. The mines of the Okanogan and the orchards of the suddenly bustling Wenatchee Valley also could be incorporated into what Spokane Falls had, with deliberation, begun calling the "Inland Empire." Expecting to generate greater region-wide appeal, the community dropped the "Falls" from its name in the winter of 1891, emerging as a streamlined and business ready "Spokane."[85]

❧

Washington represented, to residents in general and to avid promoters in particular, the culmination of the centuries long American westering experience. "The occupation of the star of empire is gone," a Grays Harbor editor asserted. "Just a little way west of us the Pacific breaks on the beach and our west is done." Recently admitted to the Union, Washington might be "one of the baby states," the Portland *Oregonian* advised, but, thanks to an abundance of timber, grain, fish and coal, it already was "one of the great states." Always observing affairs north of the Columbia, the widely read Oregon daily proffered an appropriate, though entirely unofficial, statehood motto: "'Here,' said nature, 'is the spot where I want to lavish all my wealth. Here shall be the second garden of Eden.'"[86]

Empire's restored Eden and final star of destination, the far Northwest drew to itself wealth and labor. "All over the East, wherever there are men looking for new homes and anxious to better their condition," a Spokane paper affirmed, "the name of one state is everywhere heard—and that state is Washington." Unlike other places—for example, speculation-wracked California and supposedly moss-backed Oregon—the counties west and east of the Cascades offered opportunities and riches to persons willing to work hard. "What a country for young men is the new State of Washington!" exclaimed E.V. Smalley after attending a Tacoma banquet. Of the 60 or 70 guests, Smalley noticed, two at most had gray hair. "In the East," he observed, "these men would be overshadowed by older men and would have to be contented with subordinate positions." In Washington, however, there was "room on all the rounds...to climb up," provided that the aspirant possessed "the requisite force of character." Confirming regional myth, "every train or boat" arrived, judging from unending cross-state accounts, "crowded with passengers" bound with ambition firmly in hand for instant cities and newly turned fields.[87]

Notes

1. *West Shore*, 16 (March 15, 1890), 323.
2. The building formally was known as the legislative hall. The governor and other officials worked in rented quarters located in various parts of town. "The state officers are scattered all over Olympia," a visitor complained, "and...persons having business with them [are] put to great annoyance and inconvenience in finding the proper places." In an "Omnibus Bill," Congress granted statehood to North and South Dakota, Montana, and Washington in 1889. Olympia *Washington Standard*, Nov. 22, 1889; Norman J. Johnston, *Washington's Audacious State Capitol and Its Builders* (Seattle: University of Washington Press, 1988), 13–14; *Tacoma Daily Ledger*, Jan. 27, 1891.
3. Olympia *Washington Standard*, Nov. 22, 1889.
4. Ibid.; *Walla Walla Union*, Nov. 23, 1889.
5. Olympia *Washington Standard*, Nov. 22, 1889; Cyrus Walker to Charles Talbot, Nov. 20, 1889, Cyrus Walker Letterbooks, Ames Coll., University of Washington Library; *Seattle Morning Journal*, Nov. 12, 1889.
6. Washington advanced eight places, and Oregon dropped one, from the 1880 rankings. *Spokane Falls Review*, Jan. 16, 1890; Aug. 22, 1890; *Seattle Post-Intelligencer*, July 16, 1890; Jan. 1, 1891; *Ellensburgh Capital*, Jan. 12, 1893; *West Shore*, 17 (Sept. 13, 1890), 74.
7. The five largest counties in area—Okanogan, Stevens, Yakima, Douglas and Kittitas—and eight of the top ten were in eastern Washington. *Spokane Review*, April 14, 1892; *Seattle Post-Intelligencer*, July 26, 1890; Feb. 5, 1891; *Tacoma Daily Ledger*, Aug. 6, 1890; *Seattle Press-Times*, Sept. 9, 1891.
8. *Seattle Post-Intelligencer*, Jan. 1, 1891; *Tacoma Morning Globe*, Sept. 14, 1891; *Spokane Falls Review*, Aug. 22, 1890; *Seattle Press-Times*, Sept. 9, 1891.
9. Although Washington had passed Oregon in the total figure, its minority population was only two-thirds of that for the neighboring state. Washington, however, tallied three times as many Indians as Oregon in the 1890 census. Arizona, California, New Mexico and South Dakota were the only states or territories with a larger Native American population. Quintard Taylor, *In Search of the Racial Frontier: African Americans in the American West*,

1528–1990 (New York: W.W. Norton, 1998), 135; *Seattle Post-Intelligencer*, Jan. 1, 1891; Nov. 19, 1892; Olympia *Washington Standard*, Oct. 14, 1892; S. Frank Miyamoto, "The Japanese Minority in the Pacific Northwest," *Pacific Northwest Quarterly* [hereafter cited as *PNQ*], 54 (Oct. 1963), 143; *Tacoma Daily News*, July 11, 1891; *Seattle Press-Times*, Feb. 10, 1891.

10. *Tacoma Daily News*, Sept. 11, 1893; Kenneth Tollefson, "The Snoqualmie Indians as Hop Pickers," *Columbia: The Magazine of Northwest History* [hereafter cited as *Columbia*], 8 (Winter 1994–1995), 39–44; *Spokane Falls Review*, Jan. 1; Sept. 24, 1890; *Tacoma Daily Ledger*, July 18, 1890; George H. Emerson to C.F. White, June 9, 1903, George H. Emerson Letterbooks, University of Washington Library; *Aberdeen Herald*, Jan. 28, 1892; Spokane *Spokesman-Review*, April 16, 1899; Portland *Oregonian*, Oct. 3, 1891; *Seattle Post-Intelligencer*, Nov. 3, 1890.

11. Whitman County came closest to parity, with 10,528 men and 8,310 women. Mining-oriented Okanogan County was the most masculine, by a five-to-one ratio. Oregon maintained a better balance between the sexes, reporting 182,000 male and 132,000 female residents. *Spokane Review*, Jan. 14, 1893; *Tacoma Daily News*, Feb. 7, 1893; *Seattle Telegraph*, Aug. 21, 1893; *Seattle Press-Times*, Sept. 30, 1891; March 8, 1894; Olympia *Washington Standard*, Nov. 6, 1891; *Seattle Post-Intelligencer*, Sept. 11, 1890; Dec. 27, 1891; Jan. 22, 1892; Oct. 29, 1893; Oct. 31, 1898; *Tacoma Daily Ledger*, June 4, 1891; Spokane *Spokesman-Review*, Feb. 14, 1895; Oct. 23, 1897; Seattle *Argus*, Feb. 13, 1897; Sept. 10, 1898; T.A. Larson, "The Woman Suffrage Movement in Washington," *PNQ*, 67 (April 1976), 55.

12. *Seattle Times*, June 10; Aug. 5, 6, 1889; *West Shore*, 15 (Sept. 21, 1889), 37; 16 (March 1, 1890), 261; Spokane *Spokesman-Review*, June 6, 1899; Robert E. Ficken and Charles P. LeWarne, *Washington: A Centennial History* (Seattle: University of Washington Press, 1988), xix–xx; Murray Morgan, *Skid Road: An Informal Portrait of Seattle* (Seattle: University of Washington Press, 1951, 1982 ed.), 107–13; Kent R. Davies, "Sea of Fire," *Columbia*, 15 (Summer 2001), 32–37; H.W. McNeill to Elijah Smith, Nov. 14, 1889, Oregon Improvement Co. Records, University of Washington Library; *Seattle Press*, Feb. 9, 1891; Thomas Burke to Mrs. S. Louise Ackerson, Feb. 19, 1890, Thomas Burke Papers, University of Washington Library; *Ellensburgh Capital*, July 8, 1889; Katherine G. Morrissey, *Mental Territories: Mapping the Inland Empire* (Ithaca: Cornell University Press, 1997), 43–57; *Spokane Falls Review*, Dec. 29, 1889; Nov. 26, 1890.

13. Other admission-era fire victims included Ritzville on the Northern Pacific mainline to Spokane, Pataha City in the Walla Walla country, and Tekoa, a farming community on the Idaho border. *Spokane Review*, Sept. 6, 1892, rep. from Portland *Telegram*, April 23, 1893; Spokane Falls *Spokesman*, July 4, 1890; *Spokane Falls Review*, May 27; July 6, 1890; Olympia *Washington Standard*, Sept. 19, 1890; Feb. 27; July 17; Oct. 9, 1891; Jan. 22; Sept. 16, 1892; April 21, 1893; *Tacoma Daily Ledger*, April 21, 1891; *Seattle Post-Intelligencer*, Aug. 19, 1890; March 19, 1892; *West Shore*, 17 (Jan. 10, 1891), 27; *The Dalles Times-Mountaineer*, Sept. 17, 1892; Portland *Oregonian*, Sept. 16, 1891; *Yakima Herald*, Dec. 3, 1891.

14. The closest thing to a major post-statehood fire disaster in one of the large cities was the June 1892 destruction of Seattle's Schwabacker Brothers mercantile emporium. *West Shore*, 15 (Oct. 5, 1889), 121; 16 (March 1, 1890), 261–62; (July 5, 1890), 838; *Ellensburgh Capital*, Nov. 23, 1893; Samuel R. Mohler, "Boom Days in Ellensburg, 1888–1891," *PNQ*, 36 (Oct. 1945), 302–3; Jeffrey Karl Ochsner, "Willis A. Ritchie: Public Architecture in Washington, 1889–1905," *PNQ*, 87 (Fall 1996), 199–200; *Seattle Press-Times*, June 28, 1892.

15. *Seattle Post-Intelligencer*, Jan. 27, 1890; *Spokane Falls Review*, Nov. 28, 1889; Jan. 1; June 12; Aug. 5, 1890; *West Shore*, 15 (Dec. 21, 1889), 456; 16 (Jan. 4, 1890), 9; (March 8, 1890), 296; (April 12, 1890), 454–55; 17 (Sept. 6, 1890), 59; *Spokane Spokesman*, Oct. 23, 1890; John Fahey, "The Million-Dollar Corner: The Development of Downtown Spokane, 1890–1920," *PNQ*, 62 (April 1971), 77–80.

16. Alfred S. Moore to Herbert C. Moore, May 23, 1890, Washington Water Power Co. Records, Washington State University Library; *Spokane Review*, July 26, 1891; C.S. Kingston, "Franz Ferdinand in Spokane, 1893," *Washington Historical Quarterly* [hereafter cited as *WHQ*], 16 (Jan. 1925), 6–7; J. William T. Youngs, *The Fair and the Falls: Spokane's Expo '74; Transforming an American Environment* (Cheney: Eastern Washington University Press, 1996), 69–72.

17. *Spokane Review*, Oct. 10, 1891; C. Edward Magnusson, "Hydro-Electric Power in Washington," *WHQ*, 19 (April 1928), 97; *West Shore*, 16 (Feb. 8, 1890), 171–73; Bailey Avery, "Spokane Falls," *Northwest*, 8 (April 1890), 22, 24; Portland *Oregonian*, July 30, 1888; William Willard Howard, "Spokane Falls and Its Exposition," *Harper's Weekly*, 34 (Aug. 30, 1890), 692.

18. Seattle, one editor noted, had been "baptized by fire and born again." Writing to an absent colleague, attorney Thomas Burke claimed that the 1889 blaze "cleared the way for...newcomers by breaking up all the old lives, and, to some extent, the old associations." *Seattle Times*, June 10, 12, 13, 1889; *West Shore*, 15 (June 1889), supp.; (Sept. 21, 1889), 35; *Seattle Morning Journal*, Oct. 14, 17, 19, 1889; Burke to W. Benson, July 7, 1891; to Hanson Rasin, Oct. 25, 1889, Burke Papers; Jeffrey Karl Ochsner, "A.B. Chamberlain: The Illustration of Seattle Architecture, 1890–1896," *PNQ*, 81 (Oct. 1990), 134–37; and "Public Architecture in Washington," 196–99; *Seattle Telegraph*, June 6, 1891.

19. Pressed by mounting labor and supply costs, Thomas Burke, an active participant in the boom, was forced to borrow an additional $100,000 from German lenders to complete his namesake office building. *Seattle Morning Journal*, Oct. 22; Nov. 2, 11, 21, 22, 1889; *West Shore*, 17 (Jan. 10, 1891), 20; *Northwest*, 8 (Feb. 1890), 12–13; McNeill to Smith, Sept. 17; Nov. 4, 1889, Oregon Improvement Co. Records; Burke to D.H. Gilman, April 3, 1891; to B. Goldsmith, Jan. 5, 7, 14, 1891, Burke Papers.

20. Widely reprinted in Puget Sound newspapers, a contemporary joke captured the city's apparently unquenchable energy. "A Seattle woman," the unknown humorist advised, "has been married twice, divorced once and is now suing for a divorce from her second husband, all within 14 months, and yet some people say Seattle is a slow place." Burke to Caroline Burke, Aug. 11, 1889, Burke Papers; Walker to C. Talbot, March 31, 1890, Walker Letterbooks; to Puget Mill Co., April 5, 1890, Puget Mill Co. Records, Ames Coll., University of Washington Library; Portland *Oregonian*, April 26, 1890; *Walla Walla Statesman*, Dec. 3, 1891; *Seattle Press-Times*, Aug. 24, 1891, rep. from Port Townsend *Leader*.

21. The acerbic weekly *Argus*, beginning publication in 1894, provided a rare local counterpoint, dismissing "Seattle Spirit" as a "blowhard idea" conceived to justify the city in taking "every opportunity to sound its own horn." Meaning the comparison to be complimentary, visitors captured the more pedestrian nature of local affairs by likening Seattle to Kansas City and Galveston. John R. Finger, "The Seattle Spirit, 1851–1893," *Journal of the West*, 13 (July 1974), 28–45; *Seattle Telegraph*, June 22, 1891; June 6, 1892; June 6, 1893; *Seattle Post-Intelligencer*, June 6; Sept. 16, 1890; June 22, 1891; June 27, 1897; E.V. Smalley, "The Rebuilding and Remarkable New Growth of the Chief City of Washington," *Northwest*, 9 (Feb. 1891), 13; Erastus Brainerd, "Seattle," *Harper's Weekly*, 41 (Nov. 13, 1897), 1127; Seattle *Argus*, Aug. 24, 1895.

22. *Seattle Post-Intelligencer*, April 22, 27; June 6, 1890; Walker to W.H. Talbot, June 11, 17, 1889, Walker Letterbooks; *Seattle Times*, June 15, 26, 28, 1889; *Seattle Morning Journal*, Nov. 21, 1889. On the strange configuration of the city's downtown streets, a product of pioneer land claim arrangements, see Roger Sale, *Seattle: Past to Present* (Seattle: University of Washington Press, 1976), 20–21.

23. The shortage of affordable worker housing was also a problem in Spokane. Olympia *Washington Standard*, May 2, 1890; *Tacoma Daily Ledger*, May 29, 1890; *Seattle Post-Intelligencer*, Aug. 19; Oct. 25, 1890; Burke to C. Burke, Aug. 11, 1889, Burke Papers; Seattle *Argus*, May 19; Sept. 15, 1894; *Seattle Morning Journal*, Oct. 23, 1889; *Seattle Telegraph*, Sept. 8, 1890; Spokane Falls *Spokesman*, March 11, 1890; *Spokane Falls Review*, April 3, 1890. For the Spokane relief fund scandal, see *West Shore*, 15 (Sept. 21, 1889), 34.

24. William Cronon, *Nature's Metropolis: Chicago and the Great West* (New York: W.W. Norton, 1991), 345–46; *Spokane Falls Review*, Nov. 28, 1891; Jan. 1; Aug. 5; Sept. 21, 1890; *West Shore*, 16 (May 17, 1890), 616; (July 5, 1890), 838; (July 19, 1890), 916; *Yakima Herald*, Aug. 3, 1899; *Seattle Post-Intelligencer*, Nov. 3, 1899, rep. from Cosmopolis *Enterprise*; Pasco *News-Recorder*, June 24, 1899; *Tacoma Daily News*, July 26, 1893; *Tacoma Morning Globe*, Feb. 18, 1891; *Tacoma Daily Ledger*, Nov. 4, 1890.

25. *Tacoma Morning Globe*, July 5, 1890; *Tacoma Daily Ledger*, Nov. 15; Dec. 21, 1889; June 7; Aug. 27, 1890; *Tacoma Daily News*, July 2, 3, 1890.

26. Neither city was willing to accept a proposed compromise renaming the mountain after President Benjamin Harrison. Seattle contended that it was substantially undercounted in 1890, due to illicit political pressure from Tacoma. Prestige-related complaints about the census were common. Oregonians argued that pro-Washington bias enabled the new state to incorrectly take the lead in population. Yakima contended that census takers missed half its residents. *Tacoma Daily Ledger*, July 2, 3, 31, 1890; June 4; Oct. 6, 1891; *Tacoma Daily News*, Jan. 31; July 7, 1890; July 13, 1897; *Seattle Post-Intelligencer*, July 2, 31, rep. from Whatcom *Bulletin*; Oct. 9, 1890; Dec. 13, 1891; *Spokane Falls Review*, Sept. 26, 1890; Murray Morgan, *Puget Sound: A Narrative of Early Tacoma and the Southern Sound* (Seattle: University of Washington Press, 1979), 293–96; Portland *Oregonian*, Aug. 26; Sept. 10, 1891; *Seattle Press-Times*, March 30, 1892; *Seattle Telegraph*, Dec. 2, 1890; Olympia *Washington Standard*, Sept. 23, 1892; *Tacoma Morning Globe*, July 3, 1891; *Yakima Herald*, July 10, 1890.

27. *Seattle Post-Intelligencer*, July 31, 1892, rep. from Snohomish *Sun*; William Willard Howard, "The City of Tacoma," *Harper's Weekly*, 35 (June 20, 1891), 469; Portland *Oregonian*, Jan. 1, 1890; E.V. Smalley, "Tacoma: Remarkable Progress of the New Commercial City on Puget Sound," *Northwest*, 9 (July 1891), 20; and "Westward in Winter: A February Journey from St. Paul to Puget Sound," *Northwest*, 10 (April 1892), 4.

28. *Tacoma Daily News*, April 26, 1890; Sept. 10, 1892; *Northwest*, 10 (June 1892), 45; Emerson to A.M. Simpson, Aug. 5, 1892, Emerson Letterbooks; Murray Morgan, *The Mill on the Boot: The Story of the St. Paul and Tacoma Lumber Company* (Seattle: University of Washington Press, 1982), 3–64; *West Shore*, 16 (Feb. 1, 1890), 138; Smalley, "Tacoma," 20; Portland *Oregonian*, Jan. 1, 1890; *Tacoma Daily Ledger*, Jan. 3; Sept. 19, 1890; *Tacoma Morning Globe*, Sept. 19, 1890.

29. Poor customer service on NP trains supposedly caused Tacoma-bound immigrants to change their minds and settle elsewhere. *Seattle Press*, Feb. 17, 1891; *Tacoma Morning Globe*, Jan. 5; Aug. 8, 1890; Nov. 13, 1891; *Tacoma Daily News*, Feb. 26; March 10; May 8; June 26; July 23; Aug. 7; Nov. 4, 1890; Dec. 10, 1891. On the prevailing state of Seattle business enterprise, see Norbert MacDonald, *Distant Neighbors: A Comparative History of Seattle and Vancouver* (Lincoln: University of Nebraska Press, 1987), 32–42.

30. *Spokane Falls Review*, Jan. 1, 1891; *Tacoma Daily Ledger*, April 17, 1890. For territorial developments, see Robert E. Ficken, *Washington Territory* (Pullman: Washington State University Press, 2002).

31. During 1888 and 1889, English capitalists invested an average of $1 million a week in the United States. By 1914, Britain had nearly £4 billion invested overseas, half this sum in America. *Tacoma Daily Ledger*, Feb. 17, 1890; Niall Ferguson, *Empire* (New York: Basic Books, 2003), 242.

32. Reflecting the rabid local demand for capital, a gentlemanly English confidence artist was able to steal a considerable sum of money from gullible Puget Sounders by posing as the representative of a London investment firm. *Seattle Press-Times*, Oct. 8, 1891; *West Shore*, 16 (Nov. 19, 1890), 251; *Seattle Post-Intelligencer*, March 14, 1890; *Spokane Review*, April 1, 1892; *Tacoma Morning Globe*, Aug. 14, 1890; *Tacoma Daily Ledger*, Jan. 7, 1892. The essential work on the network of capital is William G. Robbins, *Colony and Empire: The Capitalist Transformation of the American West* (Lawrence: University Press of Kansas, 1994). On territorial financial methods, see Ficken, *Washington Territory*; and William L. Lang, *Confederacy of Ambition: William Winlock Miller and the Making of Washington Territory* (Seattle: University of Washington Press, 1996).

33. *Tacoma Daily Ledger*, Nov. 24, 1889; Aug. 31; Oct. 25; Dec. 26, 1890; *The Dalles Times-Mountaineer*, Nov. 1, 1890; *Seattle Post-Intelligencer*, Sept. 14, 1890; *Tacoma Daily News*, Sept. 6, 1890; *Spokane Falls Review*, July 27, 1890; *West Shore*, 16 (Nov. 29, 1890), 251; (Dec. 20, 1890), rep. from Corvallis *Gazette*; *Tacoma Morning Globe*, Sept. 1, 1890.

34. *Tacoma Daily News*, April 14; Sept. 13; Dec. 20, 1890; *Spokane Falls Review*, Jan. 8, 1890; *Seattle Post-Intelligencer*, Jan. 1, 1891; Jan. 28, 1892; *Tacoma Daily Ledger*, July 28, 1890; *West Shore*, 17 (Aug. 16, 1890), 12; (April 11, 1891), 237; *Seattle Press-Times*, Aug. 15, 1891.

35. The modernization effort included removal of the Stampede Pass Switchback, the dramatic original means of getting trains across the Cascades. Portland *Oregonian*, April 16; Sept. 30, 1891; Olympia *Washington Standard*, May 29, 1891; *Seattle Telegraph*, Dec. 21, 1892; *Seattle Times*, May 17, 1889; Burke to Gilman, Nov. 20, 1888, Burke Papers; *West Shore*, 15 (Nov. 16, 1889), 317; (Dec. 7, 1889), 388; *Seattle Morning Journal*, Nov. 4; Dec. 10, 11, 1889; Jan. 15, 1890; McNeill to Smith, Jan. 21, 1890, Oregon Improvement Co. Records; Kurt E. Armbruster, *Orphan Road: The Railroad Comes to Seattle, 1853–1911* (Pullman: Washington State University Press, 1999), 143; *Seattle Post-Intelligencer*, Dec. 9, 1889; *Tacoma Daily Ledger*, Dec. 11, 1889. On the origin of anti-NP sentiment in Seattle, see Ficken, *Washington Territory*, 152–54.

36. The UP takeover of the OR&N completed a process begun under an 1887 lease arrangement. *Spokane Falls Review*, Nov. 2, 1889; *Tacoma Daily Ledger*, Dec. 5, 1889; Jan. 22; March 20, 26; Aug. 21, 1890; *The Dalles Times-Mountaineer*, Jan. 18, 1890; D.W. Meinig, *The Great Columbia Plain: A Historical Geography, 1805–1910* (Seattle: University of Washington Press, 1968), 270; Peter J. Lewty, *Across the Columbia Plain: Railroad Expansion in the Interior Northwest, 1885–1893* (Pullman: Washington State University Press), 4–5, 17–18; *West Shore*, 15 (Dec. 14, 1889), 430; 16 (Oct. 25, 1890), 170; (Nov. 15, 1890), 218; *Tacoma Daily News*, Feb. 20; March 26; April 7–9; May 23, 1890; *Seattle Post-Intelligencer*, March 27; April 2; May 22; June 8, 1890; *Olympia Tribune*, Aug. 18, 1890; Burke to W.P. Clough, March 26, 1890; to C. Burke, Jan. 25, 1890; to F.M. Jones, March 11, 1890; to G.W. Griffith, March 17, 1890, Burke Papers; McNeill to Smith, Sept. 23, 1889; Jan. 21; Feb. 13, 1890, Oregon Improvement Co. Records; *Seattle Times*, June 5, 1889; *Seattle Morning Journal*, Nov. 25, 1889.

37. *West Shore*, 15 (June 1889), 342; 16 (Feb. 1, 1890), 132; (Feb. 8, 1890), 178; (April 21, 1890), 472; 17 (March 14, 1891), 168; *Tacoma Daily Ledger*, April 14, 1890; *Tacoma Daily News*, May 17, 1890; *Seattle Post-Intelligencer*, May 28, 1890.

38. The Oregon and Washington Territory Railway, popularly known as the Hunt system, was backed by individuals affiliated with the NP and by local subsidies. As of 1890, Hunt planned to build down the north bank of the Columbia to Portland. *West Shore*, 15 (June 1889), 342; (July 1889), 376, 378–79; 16 (March 15, 1890), 344; (Oct. 11, 1890), 133; (Nov. 15, 1890), 219; *The Dalles Times-Mountaineer*, Feb. 8, 1890; Meinig, *Great Columbia Plain*, 260, 273–75; Lewty, *Across the Columbia Plain*, 79–90, 133–38; John Fahey, *The Inland Empire: Unfolding Years, 1879–1929* (Seattle: University of Washington Press, 1986), 34; and *Inland Empire: D.C. Corbin and Spokane* (Seattle: University of Washington Press, 1965), 109–13, 117–18; *Tacoma Daily Ledger*, March 23; Nov. 7, 1891; *Walla Walla Statesman*, Aug. 5, 1891; Michael P. Malone, *James J. Hill: Empire Builder of the Northwest* (Norman: University of Oklahoma Press, 1996), 138–39; *Tacoma Daily News*, July 25, 1891; May 12, 1892; *Tacoma Morning Globe*, July 25, 1891; Portland *Oregonian*, Dec. 30, 1889; *Spokane Falls Review*, Jan. 28; April 1; May 29; Aug. 16, 1890; E.V. Smalley, "In the Big Bend Country," *Northwest*, 8 (May 1890), 14.

39. Founded, but no longer controlled, by Henry Villard, the far flung OIC properties included mines, steamers, town developments and even a timber carrying flume network in eastern Washington. E.H. Morrison to W.H. Starbuck, Jan. 31, 1891; C.J. Smith to Smith, Sept. 26, 1890; McNeill to Smith, Feb. 13, 21; March 25; April 14, 24, 26, 27; May 11; June 12 (two letters of this date), 1890, all Oregon Improvement Co. Records; *West Shore*, 16 (May 10, 1890), 597; (Nov. 29, 1890), 250; *Northwest*, 8 (Oct. 1890), 40–41; Ficken, *Washington Territory*, 136, 147.

40. Many Tacomans considered Bennett a traitor for attempting to build up a rival trade center. *Seattle Times*, May 16, 1889; *West Shore*, 16 (Feb. 1, 1890), 134; (Feb. 8, 1890), 163; (Feb. 15, 1890), 197–98; (April 26, 1890), 534; (Oct. 25, 1890), 171; McNeill to Smith, Feb. 13; March 25; April 27; May 11; June 12, 1890, Oregon Improvement Co. Records; *Tacoma Daily News*, May 5, 1890.

41. The NP purchase thwarted Oregon Improvement Company designs upon the Port Blakely road. *Seattle Telegraph*, Sept. 30, 1891; Portland *Oregonian*, April 2, 10, 1891; *West Shore*, 15 (Nov. 9, 1889), 261; 16 (April 19, 1890), 482; (May 17, 1890), 628; *Northwest*, 8 (May 1890), 32; E.V. Smalley, "The Gray's Harbor Basin," *Northwest*, 8 (March 1890), 12, 14; Renton, Holmes & Co. to Port Blakely Mill Co., Oct. 23, 1889, Port Blakely Mill Co. Records, University of Washington Library; McNeill to Smith, April 14, 26; May 11, 13, 1890, Oregon Improvement Co. Records; Richard C. Berner, "The Port Blakely Mill Company, 1876–89," *PNQ*, 57 (Oct. 1966), 161–63; *Tacoma Morning Globe*, May 9, 1890; *Tacoma Daily Ledger*, June 9, 1890; *Hoquiam Washingtonian*, Jan. 15; Feb. 12, 1891.

42. *West Shore*, 16 (March 1, 1890), 265; (April 19, 1890), 482; (May 17, 1890), 628; *Northwest*, 8 (Aug. 1890), 39; Olympia *Washington Standard*, Feb. 13, 1891; McNeill to Smith, May 11; June 12, 1890, Oregon Improvement Co. Records; *Hoquiam Washingtonian*, April 30; Aug. 6, 1891; *Aberdeen Herald*, Nov. 5, 26, 1891; Emerson to Simpson, June 22, 1891; to E.J. Holt, March 4, 16, 21, 1891, Emerson Letterbooks; *South Bend Enterprise*, April 5; June 6, 13; July 11, 1890; *Yakima Herald*, Dec. 4, 1890; *Tacoma Daily News*, May 1, 1890.

43. Thomas Burke, a founder of the Seattle, Lake Shore & Eastern, gave up his affiliation with the line upon the NP takeover. McNeill to Smith, March 10, 25; June 12, 1890, Oregon Improvement Co. Records; Albro Martin, *James J. Hill and the Opening of the Northwest*

(New York: Oxford University Press, 1976), 376–78; Malone, *Empire Builder,* 128–29, 145; *Seattle Morning Journal,* Nov. 15, 1889; *West Shore,* 16 (Feb. 22, 1890), 248–49; (March 1, 1890), 323; (June 28, 1890), 822; (July 5, 1890), 854; (Aug. 2, 1890), 973; *Northwest,* 8 (March 1890), 8; (Aug. 1890), 39; Burke to Gilman, June 17, 1890; to C. Burke, March 11, 1890; to D.P. Jenkins, June 4, 1891, Burke Papers; *Seattle Press-Times,* Feb. 27, 1891; Carlos A. Schwantes, *Railroad Signatures across the Pacific Northwest* (Seattle: University of Washington Press, 1993), 76–77.

44. *Seattle Press-Times,* Sept. 2, 1891.
45. Martin, *Hill and the Opening of the Northwest,* 301; *Seattle Press-Times,* Sept. 14, 18, 1891; Feb. 17; July 23, 1892; *Tacoma Daily Ledger,* Jan. 14; Feb. 20, 1892; *Seattle Telegraph,* Jan. 7, 1893; Portland *Oregonian,* Sept. 22, 1891; Burke to Gilman, June 17, 1890, Burke Papers; *Spokane Review,* Sept. 15, 1891; *Tacoma Morning Globe,* Sept. 17, 1891.
46. Hill's original railroad success, the Manitoba line, possessed granted acreage in Minnesota and Dakota. Some observers thought that the Great Northern would be unable to actually build to the Pacific coast. *Ellensburgh Capital,* Oct. 29, 1891; *Seattle Press-Times,* Aug. 20, 1891; June 8, 1893; *Spokane Review,* Sept. 15, 1891; Sept. 16, 1892; *Tacoma Daily News,* April 21, 1890. For elaboration on the theme of GN distinction, see Malone, *Empire Builder,* 149–50; and, in general, Claire Strom, *Profiting from the Plains: The Great Northern Railway and Corporate Development of the American West* (Seattle: University of Washington Press, 2003).
47. *Seattle Morning Journal,* Jan. 12, 1890; Burke to John R. Reavis, March 16, 1890, Burke Papers; *Spokane Falls Review,* Sept. 19, 28; Oct. 16, 1890; Feb. 11, 19, 1891; *Yakima Herald,* Oct. 9, 1890; *Northwest,* 9 (Aug. 1891), 36.
48. Expecting the Great Northern to follow Foster Creek, Connecticut investors founded Bridgeport at the mouth of the stream. Figuring that Hill would then build down the right bank of the Columbia, Spokane interests located a town site at the outlet of the Entiat River. Smalley, "Westward in Winter," 4; Meinig, *Great Columbia Plain,* 372; *Northwest,* 8 (Sept. 1890), 30–31; 9 (Aug. 1891), 36–37; *Spokane Review,* Aug. 12, 1891; Jan. 16, 1892; John F. Stevens–"Great Northern Railway," *WHQ,* 20 (April 1929), 111; Lewty, *Across the Columbia Plain,* 159–60; *Wenatchee Advance,* May 26, 1894; *Tacoma Morning Globe,* Nov. 23, 1891.
49. Selection of the Wenatchee Valley route compromised the efficiency of the Foster Creek line to the Columbia. *West Shore,* 16 (Oct. 11, 1890), 140; Stevens, "Great Northern Railway," 111–13; *Wenatchee Advance,* May 26, 1894; *Ellensburgh Capital,* May 7; July 16, 1891; Lewty, *Across the Columbia Plain,* 158–59, 163–66; Olympia *Washington Standard,* Sept. 30, 1892; *Northwest,* 9 (Aug. 1891), 37.
50. In addition to the lucrative Great Northern payroll, the sweeteners offered Spokane included competitive, possibly even preferential, rates. Should he choose to bypass Spokane on the north, Hill anticipated using D.C. Corbin's Spokane Falls & Northern for indirect service to the city. *Spokane Falls Review,* April 1, 4; Sept. 19; Nov. 22, 1890; *West Shore,* 16 (March 8, 1890), 291; *Spokane Spokesman,* Oct. 12, 15, 1890; *Tacoma Daily Ledger,* Feb. 19, 1892; *Spokane Review,* Aug. 9; Sept. 18, 1891; Jan. 6, 29; Feb. 13, 14; Oct. 12, 16, 18, 20, 21, 23, 25, 1892; Malone, *Empire Builder,* 136–37; Lewty, *Across the Columbia Plain,* 160–61.
51. Burke to Clough, March 20, 1890; to Griffith, March 17, 1890; to Elisha P. Ferry, March 21, 1890; to Gilman, June 17, 1890, Burke Papers; Martin, *Hill and the Opening of the Northwest,* 392; Malone, *Empire Builder,* 141; *Tacoma Daily News,* May 21, 1890; *Spokane Review,* May 21; Oct. 31, 1891; C. Smith to Smith, Oct. 4, 6, 1890, Oregon Improvement

Co. Records; *Everett Herald*, Feb. 11, 1892; *Everett News*, Feb. 19, 26, 1892; *Tacoma Daily Ledger*, May 19, 1891; Feb. 20, 1892; *Seattle Press-Times*, Feb. 26; July 23, 1892; Norman H. Clark, *Mill Town* (Seattle: University of Washington Press, 1970), 6; *Tacoma Morning Globe*, July 26, 1890; Sept. 8, 1891; Feb. 19, 1892; *South Bend Journal*, Aug. 8, 1890.

52. The Union Pacific briefly sought access to the Seattle waterfront via Railroad Avenue. The name Rams Horn referred to both a specific piece of land and, more generally, the original territorial right-of-way grant to the Orphan Road. Burke & Haller to F.W. James, Feb. 1, 1887; Burke to Clough, April 4, 19, 25, 1890, all Burke Papers; Robert C. Nesbit, *"He Built Seattle": A Biography of Judge Thomas Burke* (Seattle: University of Washington Press, 1961), 116–17; 215–17; Armbruster, *Orphan Road*, 126–27; *Seattle Times*, June 19; July 15, 1889; *Seattle Morning Journal*, Oct. 11, 1889; C.H. Hanford, "The Orphan Road and the Rams Horn Right of Way," *WHQ*, 14 (April 1923), 89–90; McNeill to Smith, April 5, 1890, Oregon Improvement Co. Records; Frank Leonard, "'Wise, Swift and Sure'? The Great Northern Entry into Seattle, 1889–1894," *PNQ*, 92 (Spring 2001), 83–84; *Tacoma Daily News*, March 24, 1890; *West Shore*, 16 (March 29, 1890), 387; *Seattle Press-Times*, June 18, 1891; Feb. 15, 1892.

53. *Seattle Press-Times*, Feb. 15, 25; Oct. 11, 1892; Gilman to Burke, March 2, 1892, Burke Papers; McNeill to Smith, April 5, 27; May 20, 1890; C. Smith to C.B. Tedcastle, Sept. 17, 1891; to Starbuck, June 9; July 30, 1892; May 31, 1893, all Oregon Improvement Co. Records. The struggle is fully covered in Leonard, "Great Northern Entry into Seattle," 81–90. Also see Nesbit, *"He Built Seattle,"* 218–36.

54. All sorts of visionary railroad projects were put forward in the first months of statehood. Various interests promoted a line between the Strait of Juan de Fuca and Grays Harbor, to be built along the shoreline west of the Olympic Range. A Portland-Shoalwater Bay road also drew considerable notice. The overly enthusiastic, meanwhile, postulated railways from Washington north to Alaska and south to Mexico. *Spokane Falls Review*, Feb. 15, 1890; McNeill to Smith, March 29; April 5, 27, 1890, Oregon Improvement Co. Records; *Seattle Telegraph*, Feb. 27, 1891; Feb. 2, 1892; *Seattle Press-Times*, Feb. 27, 1891; *Tacoma Daily Ledger*, March 7, 1890; Nov. 4, 1891; *Tacoma Daily News*, April 12; May 17, 1890; *Olympia Tribune*, Dec. 23, 1890; *South Bend Enterprise*, April 5, 1890; Portland *Oregonian*, Sept. 27, 1891; *West Shore*, 16 (April 19, 1890), 502; (June 7, 1890), 717; (Nov. 1, 1890), 186; *Seattle Post-Intelligencer*, Oct. 21, 1890.

55. *Seattle Post-Intelligencer*, April 17, 1890; *Spokane Review*, April 1, 1892; *Tacoma Morning Globe*, Aug. 14, 1890.

56. *Tacoma Daily Ledger*, Sept. 23; Oct. 26; Nov. 11, 12, 14, 1890; *Tacoma Daily News*, Sept. 15, 17, 1890; *Spokane Falls Review*, Sept. 14; Nov. 18, 1890; *Spokane Spokesman*, Sept. 16; Dec. 11, 1890; *Seattle Telegraph*, Nov. 16, 1890; *West Shore*, 16 (Nov. 15, 1890), 211.

57. "The industries and business of this state, being of a more stable and substantial character," the *Seattle P-I* insisted, "are but little affected by Eastern financial flurries." *Spokane Spokesman*, Sept. 16; Dec. 11, 1890; *Tacoma Daily News*, Nov. 13, 14, 18; Dec. 9, 15, 1890; *Spokane Falls Review*, Nov. 15, 1890; *Tacoma Daily Ledger*, Nov. 18, 1890; *Seattle Post-Intelligencer*, Dec. 18, 1890.

58. *Tacoma Daily News*, Nov. 13, 1890; *Seattle Post-Intelligencer*, Dec. 18, 1890; *Tacoma Daily Ledger*, Dec. 18, 1890; *Seattle Telegraph*, Jan. 8, 1891; Theodore S. Woolsey to W.S. Norman, May 8, 1891, Washington Water Power Co. Records; Burke to J.J. McGilvra, Nov. 30, 1890; to A.B. Wyckoff, Dec. 13, 1890; to Gilman, Feb. 10, 1891; to Don C. Corbett, April 1, 1891, Burke Papers; L.C. Gilman to Gilman, Feb. ?, 1891, Daniel H. Gilman Papers, University of Washington Library; *Spokane Falls Review*, Feb. 12, 1891.

59. *Tacoma Daily Ledger*, Nov. 14; Dec. 17, 1890; *Tacoma Daily News*, Dec. 16, 1890; June 10, 1891; Olympia *Washington Standard*, March 6; May 1, 1891; McNeill to C. Smith, Nov. 18, 1890; to Smith, Nov. 28, 1890; C. Smith to P.W. Smith, Dec. 6, 1890; to Starbuck, April 6, 1891; Jos. Simon to Jordan T. Davies, Dec. 27, 1890, all Oregon Improvement Co. Records; *Northwest*, 9 (Feb. 1891), 6; *West Shore*, 16 (Nov. 29, 1890), 247; 17 (March 7, 1891), 152; *Seattle Post-Intelligencer*, Nov. 27, 1890; Burke to McGilvra, Nov. 30, 1890, Burke Papers; *Seattle Telegraph*, Jan. 16, 1891; *Spokane Falls Review*, March 4, 6, 1891; *Walla Walla Statesman*, Aug. 5, 1891; Lewty, *Across the Columbia Plain*, 90–91.

60. Burke to McGilvra, Nov. 30, 1890, Burke Papers; Martin, *Hill and the Opening of the Northwest*, 385; *West Shore*, 17 (Jan. 17, 1891), 40; *Northwest*, 9 (Feb. 1891), 8; Olympia *Washington Standard*, June 26, 1891; *Seattle Press-Times*, Nov. 27, 1891; March 16, 1892; *Seattle Telegraph*, Oct. 13; Nov. 27, 1891.

61. *Yakima Herald*, Jan. 12, 1893; Lewty, *Across the Columbia Plain*, 166.

62. Port Angeles *Times*, April 11, 1891; *Tacoma Daily News*, Sept. 3, 1890.

63. *Tacoma Daily Ledger*, May 20; Nov. 29, 1891; *Seattle Post-Intelligencer*, April 8; Sept. 15, 1890; *Northwest*, 8 (Feb. 1890), 12; (May 1890), 13; (June 1890), 3; *West Shore*, 16 (March 22, 1890), 357.

64. "To say that real estate is active [on Puget Sound]," humorist Bill Nye maintained, "is just simply about as powerful as the remark made by the frontiersman who came home…one afternoon and found that the Indians had burned up his buildings, massacred his wife… and killed his children. He looked over the bloody scene and then said to himself with great feeling: 'This, it seems to me, is perfectly ridiculous.'" *Northwest*, 8 (May 1890), 13; (July 1890), 5; *Spokane Falls Review*, Nov. 30, 1890, rep. from Fairhaven *Herald*; *Seattle Post-Intelligencer*, Sept. 29, 1890, rep. from Whatcom *Reveille*; *Yakima Herald*, May 15, 1890.

65. *Everett News*, April 16, 1892; *Northwest*, 8 (Feb. 1890), 12; *Hoquiam Washingtonian*, Aug. 27, 1891; *Seattle Post-Intelligencer*, April 8, 1890; *Tacoma Daily Ledger*, Jan. 26; March 24; Oct. 20, 1890; Aug. 19, 1891; *Tacoma Morning Globe*, Oct. 18, 1891.

66. *West Shore*, 16 (April 19, 1890), 503; (May 10, 1890), 599; (May 31, 1890), 695; Portland *Oregonian*, May 3, 1890; *Northwest*, 8 (March 1890), 26–27; (May 1890), 31; 9 (Feb. 1891), 49; (Sept. 1891), 40; *Tacoma Daily Ledger*, Aug. 22, 1891.

67. Coulee City, a San Francisco newspaper reported, was "one of those brand-new little towns which have of late years been starting up by the dozen in the state of Washington." Smalley, "In the Big Bend Country," 14–20; *West Shore*, 15 (Sept. 14, 1889), 23; 16 (June 21, 1890), 778; Olympia *Washington Standard*, May 22, 1891; Meinig, *Great Columbia Plain*, 274–75, 334–37; *Spokane Review*, June 27, 1891, rep. from San Francisco *Chronicle*.

68. Burke disposed of settlers opposed to the relocation of Wenatchee by calling in loans and securing, through political connections, transfer of the post office from the old to the new site. Burke to Corbett, Feb. 10, 1890; April 1; June 27, 1891; April 14, 29, 1892; to James J. Hill, June 8, 1891; May 5, 1892; to Morgan J. Carkeek, Nov. 17, 1891; to John B. Allen, June 1, 1892, Burke Papers; *Spokane Review*, July 25, 1891. On the early history of Wenatchee, see Strom, *Profiting from the Plains*, 50–54; and Robert E. Ficken, *Rufus Woods, the Columbia River, and the Building of Modern Washington* (Pullman: Washington State University Press, 1995), 10–11.

69. *Seattle Post-Intelligencer*, Aug. 25, 1892; *Spokane Review*, July 25, 1891; Olympia *Washington Standard*, April 15; May 20, 1892; March 24, 1893; Meinig, *Great Columbia Plain*, 373–74; Randall V. Mills, *Stern-Wheelers Up Columbia: A Century of Steamboating in the Oregon Country* (Palo Alto: Pacific Books, 1947), 91–92.

70. *Northwest,* 8 (May 1890), 26–30; (Dec. 1890), 39; 9 (Feb. 1891), 8; (March 1891), 40; *West Shore,* 16 (April 12, 1890), 454; (April 19, 1890), 495; (April 26, 1890), 516–18; (May 17, 1890), 627–28; (Nov. 1, 1890), 183; McNeill to Smith, April 27, 1890, Oregon Improvement Co. Records.

71. *Fairhaven Herald,* March 20, 1891; *West Shore,* 15 (June 1889), 329; 16 (Feb. 1, 1890), 133. On the earlier rise and fall of Bellingham Bay, see Robert E. Ficken, *Unsettled Boundaries: Fraser Gold and the British-American Northwest* (Pullman: Washington State University Press, 2003), 57–59, 84–87.

72. In an additional selling point for settlers, New Whatcom had no taxes, the municipal revenue coming entirely from saloon licenses. The combined New Whatcom-Fairhaven population may have been as high as 15,000 by the end of 1890. An interurban electrified railway was constructed that winter. Portland *Oregonian,* April 25, 1890; *West Shore,* 16 (Feb. 1, 1890), 133–34; (April 26, 1890), 532; (May 31, 1890), 678; (June 21, 1890), 787–88; (Oct. 4, 1890), 123; *Northwest,* 8 (May 1890), 31; (June 1890), 4; (Nov. 1890), 40; 9 (Feb. 1891), 8; *Fairhaven Herald,* March 14, 20; April 7, 1891; Olympia *Washington Standard,* Jan. 23; April 3, 1891; *Tacoma Morning Globe,* Feb. 7, 1890; *Spokane Review,* Oct. 2, 1891; *Seattle Post-Intelligencer,* July 6, 1890, rep. from Bellingham Bay *Express;* McNeill to Smith, Nov. 3, 1889, Oregon Improvement Co. Records. For the spatial relationship between the bay towns, see Beth Kraig, "The Bellingham Bay Improvement Company: Boomers or Boosters?" *PNQ,* 80 (Oct. 1989), 125.

73. Ferry considered his Anacortes investment to be worth $50,000. McNeill to Smith, Nov. 3; Dec. 20, 1889; Jan. 1, 5, 21, 25; Feb. 13; March 6; April 13; Nov. 24, 1890; C. Smith to Tedcastle, Sept. 17, 1891, all Oregon Improvement Co. Records; E.V. Smalley, "Anacortes: New Seaport at the Lower End of Puget Sound," *Northwest,* 9 (April 1891), 16, 19; Eugene Semple to Sister, Feb. 13, 1890, Eugene Semple Papers, University of Washington Library; Olympia *Washington Standard,* May 1; Sept. 18, 1891; *Seattle Post-Intelligencer,* Oct. 31, 1890, rep. from Anacortes *Progress;* S.L. Moore to H. Moore, April 9, 1890, Washington Water Power Co. Records; *Yakima Herald,* May 8, 1890; Ferry to James McNaught, March 22, 1892, Elisha P. Ferry Papers, University of Washington Library.

74. Rockefeller's involvement in the remote Pacific Northwest astounded many observers. "We thought it absurd," one newspaper reflected, "that a man of Mr. Rockefeller's great wealth…should have even heard of Everett, much less given such a scheme his countenance and encouragement." C. Smith to Starbuck, May 7, 1891, Oregon Improvement Co. Records; Walker to W. Talbot, Dec. 14, 1891, Walker Letterbooks; E.V. Smalley, "Everett, Washington: The New Manufacturing and Commercial Town on Puget Sound," *Northwest,* 10 (April 1892), 24; Clark, *Mill Town,* 19–28; T.W. Symons to Thomas L. Casey, Oct. 12, 1892, in *Annual Report of the Chief of Engineers, 1893,* 3465–66; *Tacoma Daily Ledger,* Oct. 21, 1891. For usage of the Port Gardner alternate name, see *Spokane Review,* Oct. 22, 1891. The progression of events at Everett suggested the scope of the profits to be anticipated in urban speculation. Local pioneer E.C. Ferguson acquired the town site from the Indian widow of the original claimant in 1890, then sold the tract to Hewitt for $10 an acre. Six months later, Hewitt transferred title to the Everett Land Company for $180 an acre. Olympia *Washington Standard,* Feb. 23, 1894.

75. *Everett Herald,* Jan. 21; Feb. 1, 1892; *Everett News,* Feb. 19, 26, 1892; Walker to W. Talbot, July 11, 19, 1892, Puget Mill Co. Records; Symons to Casey, Oct. 12, 14, 1892, in *Annual Report of the Chief of Engineers, 1893,* 3463, 3465–66; Smalley, "Everett," 24–26; Clark, *Mill Town,* 28–42; Olympia *Washington Standard,* July 24, 1891; May 20; Aug. 5, 1892.

76. The south side tributaries of Grays Harbor, including the Charlie, the Johns and the Elk, were shorter in length and substantially smaller in drainage, factors accounting in large part

for the concentration of logging activity on the north. *Northwest*, 8 (Aug. 1890), 39, rep. from Montesano *Vidette*, T.S. Morris, "Aberdeen, Washington," *Northwest*, 8 (Jan. 1890), 14; Smalley, "Gray's Harbor Basin," 16; H.M. Chittenden, "Ports of the Pacific," American Society of Civil Engineers, *Transactions*, 76:177; *Aberdeen Herald*, Dec. 25, 1890.

77. Morris, "Aberdeen," 14; Smalley, "Gray's Harbor Basin," 12; Charles F. Powell to Chief of Engineers, Jan. 25, 1882, Portland District Records, U.S. Army Corps of Engineers, RG 77, Federal Records Center, Seattle; *West Shore*, 16 (Jan. 11, 1890), 44–45; Emerson to John L. Wilson, Feb. 9, 1892, Emerson Letterbooks; *Northwest*, 9 (May 1891), 38; *Seattle Post-Intelligencer*, Jan. 3, 1893.

78. McNeill to Smith, April 26, 1890; C. Smith to Tedcastle, April 1, 1892, both Oregon Improvement Co. Records; *West Shore*, 16 (April 19, 1890), 482; *Aberdeen Herald*, March 26; June 4, 1891; Chester A. Congdon to Harry C. Heermans, Jan. 16, 1895, Harry C. Heermans Papers, University of Washington Library; Smalley, "Gray's Harbor Basin," 17, 20; *Hoquiam Washingtonian*, Jan. 1, 1891; *Northwest*, 8 (May 1890), 31; Morris, "Aberdeen," 16–17; Louise Schafer, "Report from Aberdeen," *PNQ*, 47 (Jan. 1956), 9.

79. Colloquially, the North Beach Peninsula often is referred to as the "Long Beach" Peninsula. *Tacoma Daily Ledger*, July 30, 1891; Robert A. Habersham to Symons, Oct. 10, 1890, in *Annual Report of the Chief of Engineers, 1891*, 3267; *West Shore*, 16 (June 7, 1890), 724; *Aberdeen Herald*, May 26, 1892; *Tacoma Daily News*, May 13, 1890.

80. Powell to Chief of Engineers, Jan. 30, 1882, Portland District Records; E.V. Smalley, "South Bend: A New Commercial City on the Pacific Coast of Washington," *Northwest*, 9 (May 1891), 21; *West Shore*, 16 (March 8, 1890), 310; (June 28, 1890), 821; *South Bend Enterprise*, Feb. 7; March 7, 1890.

81. The rapid development of South Bend forced the eastern King County town of the same name to become *North* Bend. A detailed 1891 Army engineer study resulted in the opening of a channel through the shoals at the mouth of the Willapa River. Smalley, "South Bend," 22–23; *South Bend Enterprise*, April 5, 1890; Emerson to Holt, March 16, 1891, Emerson Letterbooks; *South Bend Journal*, Nov. 7, 1890; *West Shore*, 16 (May 24, 1890), 658; *Northwest*, 10 (July 1892), 31; Olympia *Washington Standard*, Oct. 24, 1890; Sept. 4, 1891; Portland *Oregonian*, April 22, 1891; *Tacoma Daily Ledger*, July 29, 1891; Symons to Casey, May 2, 1891, in *Annual Report of the Chief of Engineers, 1891*, 3268–70.

82. According to a presumably apocryphal account, an inbound steamer went off course in the Willapa and "in a vain effort to hook out a new channel through the flats…got into a neighboring pasture, and was finally lassoed and brought on to South Bend by the [tug] Edgar." Emerson to Holt, July 23, 1891, Emerson Letterbooks; *Tacoma Daily News*, July 28, 1890; Portland *Oregonian*, Sept. 2, 1891; *Northwest*, 10 (July 1892), 31; *Tacoma Daily Ledger*, Nov. 30, 1891, rep. from Olympia *Tribune*.

83. Olympia *Washington Standard*, Dec. 26, 1890; *Fairhaven Herald*, March 20, 1891. On the persistence of post-admission stage travel, see Carlos A. Schwantes, *Long Day's Journey: The Steamboat and Stagecoach Era in the Northern West* (Seattle: University of Washington Press, 1999), 351–52.

84. *Tacoma Morning Globe*, Feb. 17, 1890; McNeill to Smith, Feb. 10, 1890; C. Smith to Starbuck, Sept. 1, 1891, both Oregon Improvement Co. Records; *Seattle Press-Times*, April 1; Sept. 23; Oct. 9, 1891; *Seattle Morning Journal*, Jan. 15, 1890; *West Shore*, 16 (April 12, 1890), 459; Olympia *Washington Standard*, Feb. 6, 1891.

85. Spokane, said an outside editor, "has won the right to be called the empress of this Inland Empire." A Seattle writer thought the shortened name Spokane "more in keeping with…enterprising people." The change prompted a number of simplification proposals,

including suggestions that the "New" be dropped from New Whatcom, the "North" from North Yakima and one of the "Wallas" from Walla Walla. *Seattle Press-Times*, March 30, 1891; March 26, 1892; *Tacoma Daily Ledger*, Aug. 15, 1890; *Spokane Review*, March 5, 24, rep. from Yakima *Herald*, 1892; May 4, 1893; *West Shore*, 16 (Nov. 18, 1890), 195; *Seattle Post-Intelligencer*, May 28, 1893; *Tacoma Daily News*, May 13, 1891. The concept and term "Inland Empire" had been in use throughout the 1880s, as much in Portland as in Spokane and applied to both Washington and Oregon east of the Cascades. For the recent closer identification with Spokane, see Meinig, *Great Columbia Plain*, 323; and, in general, Morrissey, *Mental Territories*.

86. *Aberdeen Herald*, June 11, 1891; Portland *Oregonian*, Jan. 1, 1890.
87. Spokane Falls *Spokesman*, March 24, 1890; *Northwest*, 8 (May 1890), 13; *Seattle Morning Journal*, Oct. 19, 1889.

Judge Thomas Burke, an entrepreneur accredited by others with thoroughly imbuing Seattle "Spirit." *Museum of History and Industry, Seattle (SHS 12455)*

Chapter Two

Another Way of Saying God's Country

The state of Washington...is the most inviting place on this coast. It is a more open country, open, we mean, to new comers, than California and Oregon. In both those states it has been the regular policy for years to create a system of business which would make it difficult for the next comers to get in as competitors. There has been a peculiar jealousy of new men and new enterprises in those states.... This state, on the other hand, is friendly to new men and new enterprises, and any man coming here with money or industry has been welcome....It is every man's country, which is but another way of saying that it is 'God's country,' for no country can truly be said to be His, which does not set before every man 'an open door.' The struggle for existence must be made here, it is true....But there is no part of the United States where the disadvantages arising from human selfishness are less than here....There is no state which has so large a variety of opportunities. Almost every industry in the United States may be successfully undertaken here.—Tacoma Daily Ledger.[1]

*W*ASHINGTON RESIDENTS NEVER FULLY ACCEPTED the name of their territory and new state. The earliest pioneers criticized Congress for setting aside their local favorite, Columbia, in the 1853 legislation establishing a separate territorial administration for the northern regions of Oregon. During the 1880s, with admission on the horizon, the inhabitants suggested a number of alternatives, to better represent the region and its distinct identity. The sentiment persisted after 1889, with critics complaining that a distant federal government knew little and cared less about the Pacific Northwest. "It is exceedingly unpleasant," a Tacoma newspaper pointed out in reflecting upon a distasteful subject, "to be forced to constantly explain that you do not live in the national capital." One wit demanded that a change be made, at the least, to a full "George Washington," so as to avoid "much confusion," as well as the necessity of using the thoroughly undignified official postal abbreviation of "Wash" on personal and business correspondence.[2]

Poorly designated by act of congress, Washington might still be provided with a proper nickname by its own citizens. An early suggestion, "The Corner State," was geographically to the point, but hardly scintillating in popular appeal. The "Evergreen State," however, passed into widespread use within two years of

admission. Appropriately, given contemporary preoccupations with land speculation, the slogan was devised by a Seattle real estate brokerage, Crawford and
Conover, to headline a promotional brochure published in 1890.[3] The snappy
name invented to peddle tidewater housing lots failed, though, to convey genuine
meaning for an entire, often other-than-green, commonwealth.

⧼≈≈≈⧽

Washington's borders encompassed nearly 70,000 square miles, with two-thirds
east of the Cascades. Some truly magnificent portions were far from settled areas
and visited only by Indians, cowboys, prospectors or foolhardy explorers. Grand
Coulee, the product of prehistoric flooding so catastrophic as to befuddle end-
of-the-century analysis, was, said an awed California visitor, a "temple of desolation." High basaltic walls, a broad sage and grass covered floor and the spectacular
coulee mouth, suspended high above the Columbia River, provided scale enough
to frustrate human comprehension. The "enormous rent in the face of mother
earth," another traveler estimated while passing through in a wagon, varied "from
three to eight miles in width, and only God knows how many in depth." A
few herders tended cattle "Bedouin fashion," E.V. Smalley reported after a tour,
"roaming about and having no other homes than little dirt-roofed shacks."[4]

Lake Chelan, another romantic geological wonder, ran for 60 miles from
deep in the northern Cascades, before dropping 300 feet in a final three miles of
"perfect torrent" in descending to the Columbia. Miners traveled to backcountry
diggings aboard steamers based in the new village of Chelan, a tumbled-together
supply station described by one writer as "a badly-scattered lumber yard." Towing
scows loaded with pack animals, the boats huffed around the many bends in the
two-mile wide lake, straining against the wind when passing beneath towering
snowy crags. "The mountains increase in height and become more precipitous
and wild," a touring merchant noted, "and the scenery correspondingly more
magnificent." Passengers also remarked upon the sierra-clear waters, supposedly
the "deepest" in North America. "We easily countered the boulders near shore at
a depth of thirty or forty feet," one prospector recalled, "but generally the great
depth of the water gives the lake's surface an appearance of inky blackness...so
pure...that photographers in surrounding towns keep a supply on hand for use
in preparing negatives."[5]

On tidewater, the Olympics soared above Puget Sound, seeming near and at
the same time far away, in jagged heaps of snow, ice and rock. "A confused mass of
mountains" interspersed with bits of prairie, the range appeared to possess "every
requisite for a national park." Minds of promotional bent thought that the tall
timber, the many bands of elk and the mineral deposits sure to be found in the
interior fastnesses ought to be exploited at the earliest possible date. As "sparsely
settled...as Kentucky was in the days of Daniel Boone," the lower elevations
appeared ideally suited to agriculture. The problem was access, an obstacle more

than adequately documented by the wretched experiences of the first exploring expeditions to venture into the pathless wilderness. "In all likelihood," the monthly *Northwest* magazine reflected in late 1890, the central part of the Olympic Peninsula "will be permitted to remain…what it has been for ages past, the undisputed home of the elk and bear."[6]

Such places were wisely ignored by persons eager to make the most money with the least expenditure of time and effort. For the majority of the population, Washington's prime geologic feature was therefore the great dividing range of the Cascades, bisecting the state from the 49th parallel to the Oregon border. Blocking the marine air coming in from the humid Pacific, the high peaks produced two vast climatic provinces, one abundantly wet and the other uncommonly dry. So much rain fell on the west side that "a bright old lady" visiting Seattle supposedly "remarked that the noble mountain…must have been called Rainier because it was rainier there than in any other section of the globe." According to another story, no doubt apocryphal, two men strolling on a Fairhaven pier in the midst of a typical vision-obscuring downpour innocently stepped off the final plank into the chilly waters of Bellingham Bay. Government weather reports, meanwhile, tallied an annual precipitation rate of barely 16 inches for eastern Washington, with hardly any rain falling between May and October.[7] Climate related economic differences established in earliest territorial times persisted into statehood, distinguishing the regions and hardening cross-Cascades rivalries.

~~~~~~~

Trees were not lacking east of the mountains—only two of the state's counties, Adams and Franklin, were officially considered without forest cover—but commercial timber exploitation was predominantly a tidewater activity. Riding the newly laid train routes, the ubiquitous E.V. Smalley wrote of giant firs and cedars growing "so close together that when felled…their trunks are heaped up like grass before the scythe." At a comfortable distance, prospective investors studied government documents calculating that western Washington timber resources were worth at least a quarter billion dollars. The 1890 federal census ranked the new state as America's fifth largest lumber producer. Five hundred mills turned out $14 million of finished product that year, more than the combined output of Oregon and California competitors.[8]

Most visitors to Puget Sound expressed amazement at the many instant and at least superficially cultured cities to be found on the shores of the great estuary. Informed persons knew, in contrast, that regional prosperity—past, present and future—depended far more upon the remote forest resources of the Sound and Grays Harbor, with waterways offering access to timber of "such a quantity…that no child born into the world today can expect to see it used up." The new railroads allowed Washington manufacturers to introduce themselves to eastern customers and investors. The Chicago World's Fair, in particular, provided numerous promotional opportunities. The Port Blakely mill sent a giant display log, measuring well over a hundred feet in length, to the fair, delicately conveyed aboard five spring-attached flat cars. Another "leviathan monster" cut near Snoqualmie Pass became the famous polished bar of the Pabst Brewing Company concession. Two hundred carloads of rail-shipped lumber went into Washington state's own large exhibit building.[9]

Great Lakes lumbermen, close to cutting out the last prime stands in the nation's traditional timber producing region, certainly knew of the Pacific Northwest. The Merrill & Ring interests of Michigan, among others, organized syndicates "to look up desirable lands in Washington." Frederick Weyerhaeuser, America's best known forest industrialist, visited in 1891, touring, as he informed a relative, "by rail, skiff, steam boat and wagons" in search of worthwhile investments. Arriving on a regular basis, wealthy purchasers expressed "open-eyed wonderment at the immense supply of big timber in the Sound Country."[10]

San Francisco investment had dominated the region's mainstay industry since the founding of the territory, growing "fat," a critic of California control asserted, "on the meat taken from our bones." At statehood, seven of the eight largest sawmills were in Bay Area ownership, shipping by sea into the coastwise and export trade. One hundred and fifty cargoes of Puget Sound lumber were shipped to foreign ports in 1889, a third in vessels sailing to Australia and much of the remainder to South America and Hawaii. Although the combined Pope & Talbot operations at Gamble, Ludlow and Utsalady led in overall production, the Port Blakely mill, on Bainbridge Island opposite Seattle, claimed to be the largest single operation on local waters, if not in the world. A well calibrated maelstrom of cables, tramways and high pitched saws, the Blakely plant was a perfect example of expensive efficiency. "The celerity of the work," a visitor recounted, "the exact mechanism which moves…immense logs and places them to a nicety just where the saw does the work, is a revelation."[11]

Unfortunately, nearly all of the aptly named "cargo mills" were on the western shore of Puget Sound, the wrong location once railroads and eager new investors arrived upon the scene. The eastern U.S. trade, an industry veteran pointed out, "bids fair to revolutionize the lumber business on the Coast." Transcontinental lines charged by weight rather than by footage, as aboard ship, forcing older plants to acquire costly kilns and other equipment to dry lumber coming off the saws. The east Sound mills, moreover, could serve multiple land and sea markets, shifting from one to the other as circumstances dictated. Isolated on the other side of the Sound, the pioneer era producers could not compete for the vital new rail business. Connected to all points in up-to-date manner, Commencement Bay, home of the modern St. Paul & Tacoma Lumber Company and the older Tacoma Mill Company, quickly emerged as the state's leading lumber producing point.[12]

Railroading also opened up other new opportunities in forest resources. Growing in profuse supply across the rain country, cedar was easily split and resistant to weather. Excursionists happened in 1891 upon a long abandoned pile of cedar logs—"still sound, though overgrown with moss"—cut by the McClellan railroad survey of 1853. Dismantling an ancient settler cabin, promoters sent the shingles to the World's Fair "to illustrate their wonderful lasting qualities." Though light, roofing materials took up much space, even when bundled, and were seldom shipped as ocean cargo. Cedar not used for lumber usually went to timber company scrap piles and burners. Providing access to eastern markets, the transcontinental lines put an end to this tradition of waste. "They are...putting up Shingle Mills all over this country," Cyrus Walker reported in letters to his partners in San Francisco.[13]

Stimulated by favorable railway freights, shingle production doubled in the first three years of statehood. By 1892, Washington turned out fully a third of the nation's shingles. "A year ago the wholesale dealers were inclined to elevate their noses when Coast shingles were mentioned," a Chicago trade journal noted in May. "Now they are complaining that they cannot get them forward fast enough to meet the demand." Straining to fill orders, Puget Sound mills shipped 500 carloads a month. The 22 Skagit County plants on the northern Sound assigned a joint sales agent to Kansas City. A thousand laborers found work in the 42 Bellingham Bay mills, producing two million shingles daily. Activity also was brisk on Grays Harbor, where a single Montesano facility loaded 200,000 shingles per day.[14]

Dramatic in its sudden growth, shingle manufacturing reduced waste in the woods and in the mills, utilizing cedar trunks and other previously left-behind debris. The new industry struggled, though, with a number of endemic problems. Extremely thin, per-unit, profit margins exposed operators to serious negative consequences should costs increase or prices decline, and shortages of rolling stock interfered with the prompt shipment of orders. Unscrupulous firms sent inferior product east to unhappy customers. "The demand has been so urgent," Chicago buyers complained in 1892, "that some mill men may have concluded that most anything in the shape of shingles will go in this market." Better financed companies cut prices to make sales, while fiscally weak competitors sold regardless of return to cover debt obligations, undermining organized efforts to limit production.[15]

In these respects, at least, the shingle business resembled traditional lumbering. Until completion of the Great Northern in 1893, the Northern Pacific resisted industry demands for reduced freight rates in the interest of making Pacific Northwest forest products more competitive east of the Rockies. Even a modest cut, a Grays Harbor newspaper declared, would be "a matter...next in importance to the discovery of America." National tariff policies, especially after the election of Democrat Grover Cleveland to a second presidential term in 1892, encouraged the sale of British Columbia lumber in the United States. "We cannot afford," Washington interests fumed with respect to the supposed cost advantages enjoyed by cross border rivals, "to throw the little market we have open to competition from mills which employ only Chinese and Indians at starvation wages."[16]

Washington's rise to lumber production prominence, meanwhile, amounted to an ironical curse. Sawmill construction was vastly "overdone," the veteran Cyrus Walker admitted, to the extent of forestalling industry wide profit for "the next ten years." Combinations for the regulation of output were frequently and blatantly attempted, leading one editor to quip that "the mills...are about to combine and raise the price of sawdust." Mutual suspicion among the wary participants sooner or later frustrated pooling efforts. At bottom, too many companies produced too much timber for the markets to handle at a sustained profitable return. No great surprise, therefore, ensued when two of the oldest Washington cargo operations, Port Madison on the northern end of Bainbridge Island and Port Discovery on the Strait of Juan de Fuca, closed forever after declaring bankruptcy.[17]

Chronic overproduction raised as well a new concern among perceptive individuals. Washington's magnificent forests, James Bryce observed in a widely reprinted bit of succinct eloquence, were "being sadly squandered." No one knew this fundamental truth better than the larger private owners, many of whom railed at the utter folly of cutting trees in order to sell lumber at a loss. "We are now destroying our timber land for nothing," Cyrus Walker fulminated in unhappy missives to his Pope & Talbot associates, "which if kept would some day be valuable!" Another insider critic, George Emerson, expressed the same angry concern. He wrote of prevailing cut-and-run practices as "a record of crazy men, fools and idiots." For "a parallel case," said the Hoquiam lumberman, one need only consider "the extinction of the Buffalo." Absent an unlikely "reformation," however, no one familiar with contemporary business methods anticipated abandonment of the forget-about-tomorrow and log-for-today approach to timber management.[18]

A growing, if thus far ineffectual, industry desire for preserving long term investment values coincided with an increasing public conviction that trees had intrinsic worth. "Forests," a Spokane newspaper declared in making a popular argument for conservation, "increase the rainfall of a country...are a preventative of floods and...keep up the supply of water late into the season." Proceeding from different perspectives, one private and the other oriented toward the general welfare, the demand for timber protection focused upon forest fires. Late summer was the season of conflagration in the Pacific Northwest when temperatures were high, winds brisk and vegetation at its driest. Farmers recklessly burned debris from cleared land, and careless prospectors and campers failed to tend or extinguish fires. "Cutting and slashing in every direction," loggers left behind enormous masses of refuse. "A lighted match dropped upon...the ground" in such places, one writer pointed out, "causes a flame which if not at once extinguished is likely to spread over many miles." Within minutes, an entire forest might easily become "a sea of roaring flames."[19]

On hot summer days and nights, towering clouds of noxious smoke filtered through the mountain passes to plague eastern as much as western Washington.

Tourists complained of being unable to view Mount Rainier or the Olympics. "When the East wind prevails," George Emerson reported of the seasonal visitations, "the smoke…is so intense that it lays like a fog bank," precluding navigation on Grays Harbor and the lower Chehalis River. The overcast skies were so awful in 1891 that a Tacoma religious cult proclaimed that the end of the world was at hand. A delegation of eastern foresters became "enveloped in the smoke of forest fires" and, as a result, failed to complete their government funded mission to the Pacific Northwest. Lecturing on the Sound, Mark Twain worked caustic complaints about personal discomfort and ruined scenery-viewing opportunities into his regular humor routine.[20]

More than just tourism, prospective investors might be appalled by the devastation, many commentators warned, to the extent even of withholding capital. "People who visit Western Washington," a journalist noted regarding this significant consideration, "are astonished at the reckless, almost criminal waste of timber that they note on every side." Wanton destruction of a resource sure to increase substantially in value over the years would eventually cost the state and its residents "millions" in revenue and profit. Existing legislation regulated field burning and penalized those responsible for destruction of property. Such laws, though, were widely ignored and seldom enforced. Farm representatives complained of "onerous burdens" imposed upon settlers wishing to clear claims. Many lumber industry leaders opposed abandonment of traditional practices, some from economic necessity, some because they had no plans for sustained operations and some out of congenital irresponsibility. So long as politically influential interests persisted in spoliation, real achievements in this regard would be more an objective than a reality of contemporary life.[21]

Unrestrained timber exploitation impinged upon waterways as well. Mills dumped sawdust and other refuse into rivers and bays. The impact upon salmon, the closest thing to a signature regional animal, was obvious to all, and alarming to some. The state legislature prohibited gross forms of pollution—a statute subsequently described by industry as an "insolent and defiant" violation of traditional business practices. Mill company owners and attorneys claimed, to minimal hoots of derision, that "the accumulation of sawdust" actually benefited fish, providing the fortunate creatures with "a safe harbor in which to deposit their spawn." Should manufacturers be forced to burn debris, they also pointed out, the result would be "a cloud of smoke over the cities…compelling the inhabitants to breathe foul air" in order that salmon "might have more comfortable habit."[22]

❧

Early contention over stream pollution demonstrated, in addition to the despoilers' clever capacity for ingenious argument, that progress by one industry could be detrimental to other means of doing business. Despite vast acreage and an enormous resource base, Washington was unable to accommodate all comers. Nature had limits—a new and difficult concept first revealed to intelligent observers by the changing fortunes of an environmentally distressed enterprise. Many sporting enthusiasts fished with dynamite—occasionally blowing themselves up by accident—in wielding an ultimate weapon of efficient harvest. Columbia River commercial interests also favored methods of nearly equal destructive power—barriers of nets near the river's mouth and monster mechanical wheels further upstream. Although the scientific research was not exacting—one supposed expert insisted that salmon returned to the ocean after spawning—the great fishery appeared grossly and heedlessly exploited. Two dozen canneries, serviced by over 1,000 boats, recorded distressingly low catches in 1889 and 1890. "The business," *West Shore* magazine reflected, "seems to have been pushed…beyond the limits of supply and demand." Far upriver, where Indian subsistence and white recreational opportunities were together impacted, public opinion condemned the packers for having "practically exterminated the salmon."[23]

Attention shifted from the troubled Columbia to Grays Harbor, where cannery production commenced in true earnest on the eve of statehood, and to Puget Sound as well. In the latter body of water, fish supposedly congregated in schools so thick and active "that they jump into boats…and save lazy men the trouble of catching them." Between 1891, when only a few hundred persons were employed in the Sound fishery, and the end of the decade, 19 new packing plants went into business. Many were close to Canada, tapping the enormous Fraser River runs along the 49th parallel. In some years, the catch on the Sound actually exceeded the more famous Columbia River fishery.[24]

"The quantity of fish consumed each year is growing larger," protection advocates observed, "and if the fish are allowed to be caught the year round, the time will come when we will find a scarcity." Unfortunately, the first state legislation on the subject catered primarily to church going by banning Sunday fishing. Also, statutes restricting the catch at times when salmon were least likely to be present produced confusion and derision. Oregon and Washington also failed to agree on common regulations for the lower Columbia, leading to an 1893 comedic episode. Authorities of the neighboring commonwealth crossed the river and arrested Evergreen State residents, hauling the hijacked prisoners back to the south side for trial and guaranteed conviction under Oregon law. Both states installed rudimentary hatcheries, as artificial propagation was perceived as a painless answer to all the fishery related problems.[25] As in the case of logging, the Pacific Northwest failed to address a definitive dilemma—the balancing of short-term profit with long-range economic vitality.

❧❦❧

Western Washington residents never gave up on the unlikely prospect that their rain drenched region was "an exceptionally good field" for agricultural endeavor. Tidewater boosters complained that immigrants—formerly accustomed to the broad treeless prairies east of the Rockies—were too "easily discouraged" by the task of clearing timber. Already well placed along the Puyallup River, hop ranching supposedly demonstrated the commercial potential of Puget Sound farming. Developed tracts sold at up to $500 an acre. Much celebrated, the hop trade was, however, in dire straits, threatened by overproduction, indifferent attention to quality, picker shortages and pest infestation. Interurban railroading suggested an alternative in the form of truck gardening, at least in places like the White River Valley, where an alluvial plain was seasonally replenished by glacial stream flooding from Mount Rainier. The ongoing campaign to establish a public market in nearby Seattle offered the prospect of a viable outlet for fresh produce.[26]

No amount of back-to-the-soil propagandizing could detract from the fact that true commercial farming primarily would be an east-of-the-Cascades venture. Modern transportation now incorporated the once remote back areas into national and international trade networks. "The whistle of the engine has taken the place of the mountain lion's scream," a Spokane newspaper proclaimed, "and the rattle of the header, self-binder and thresher" had replaced "the oppressive silence of the uninhabited plain." Built nearly straight from Spokane Falls to the mouth of the Snake River, the Northern Pacific had once been considered an unintentional impediment to settlement and investment. "For dust, glare, heat and dreary monotony of scenery," a disgusted passenger complained of the foul travel experience, "a midsummer ride through that section…is unsurpassed on any other portion of the Great American Desert." The subsequent construction of regional feeders and the arrival of the Great Northern opened up new territory, places away from the old NP mainline with enough water and deep soil to astound newcomers from the nation's premier farming centers.[27]

Something of a dime novel aspect still prevailed east of the Cascades, with thieves running off horses and cattle from the open range in true Wild West fashion. "A system of stealing seems to extend over the entire eastern portion of the state," a Big Bend editor noted in 1892, "and so well has it been organized and manned that the efforts…to break it up seem to have been pretty nearly barren of any great results." Rustlers in the Okanogan, where grassy vistas ran all the way to Canada, drove stolen stock across the border. The remote hills of the Palouse became known as a "rendezvous of outlaws." Giving up on the law, rancher protection associations offered private rewards, maintained and circulated brand books and often resorted to violent reprisal. A vigilante posse hanged at least one thief, an unlucky desperado known only as "Texas Jack."[28]

According to the 1890 federal census, Washington citizens owned a half-million cattle and more than a hundred-thousand horses. Domesticated cows were still found "roaming the streets at their own sweet leisure" in sleepy towns in the Walla Walla Valley, but otherwise the era of unfenced range, with stock left out to fend for themselves, was giving way before the tide of settlement and agricultural expansion. Grazers soon confined their operations, for lack of better options, to fringe areas of limited water and inferior grass along the semi-arid mid-Columbia, the lower Snake and Yakima rivers and in the Okanogan. "Only in the more remote and thinly settled sections," a newspaper recounted, did "the old ways still prevail."[29]

Harsh and prolonged winter weather in 1890 exposed the dangers of a business based on free roaming, unsupervised animals. "Stock running at large was almost completely wiped out," an account from the Big Bend reported. In the Yakima Valley, losses were conservatively estimated at 50 percent, with two-thirds of that figure suffered by a half dozen ranchers. Limited to smaller bits of open country, the free roaming cattle trade never fully recovered from the disaster. Sheep, in contrast, were better equipped for a roaming subsistence and could be closely tended by herders. "Where a few thousand sheep ranged," a Spokane newspaper noted of an ongoing rangeland transformation in 1892, "hundreds of thousands now thrive."[30]

Farming advanced as stock grazing retreated. Government land offices east of the Cascades sold 700,000 acres in the fiscal year ending June 30, 1890, all but exhausting the readily available tillable soil from the public domain. "They are coming by families, colonies and train loads," a Spokane County editor wrote of the newcomers, "and those who have arrived report that thousands are preparing to come at the earliest day possible." Laggard immigrants, E.V. Smalley reported of the claim taking frenzy, "must not expect to find any free Government lands for homesteading or any cheap railroad lands or, indeed, any lands at all that will seem to them cheap." Some federal registers and receivers supposedly resigned in disgust because the inevitable drop off in sales reduced the opportunity for theft of public receipts. The only worthwhile tracts left were far from rail lines and markets, forcing years of isolation and financial hardship upon unwary pioneers.[31]

Walla Walla and its tributary valleys had long since been settled and incorporated into Portland's economic orbit, first by river steamers and then railroads. Begun in the early 1870s, the settlement of the Palouse north of the Snake and along the Idaho border was completed in the initial two years of statehood. Well watered, lacking in timber, and overgrown prior to the original plowing in vast expanses of billowing grass, the region was a homesteader's revelation—"the scene," a local editor enthused, "that brings new life to the emigrant." Writing of the most distinctive feature, the rolling topography, E.V. Smalley thought the Palouse a "queer" place featuring "bulges…of every imaginable shape," and best described as "a hilly prairie."[32]

Settlers, as opposed to scenery-minded travelers, focused upon the incredible fecundity of the soil. "Stories of the productiveness of the Palouse, of undoubted truthfulness," one observer stated, "tax the credulity of the farmer from the most prosperous parts of the east." In 1891, a farmer outside Pullman reported harvesting 40 bushels of wheat to the acre. Another rancher, from nearby Palouse City, claimed a 62 bushel return. A third operator earned back the cost of his investment, plus a tidy profit, from the initial harvest. Circulating wholesale, similar stories encouraged a doubling of land values between the spring plantings of 1890 and 1891. A 900 acre spread on the outskirts of Colfax garnered a sales price of $57,200 for its original owner.[33]

Opening up at the time of Washington's admission to the Union, the Big Bend was the second choice of late arriving immigrants, for all practical purposes a substitute Palouse. The land was not as good, with the basaltic outcroppings and sand impregnated soil drawing negative assessments from persons in search of ideal farming conditions. Cultivated acreage nonetheless tripled during the first decade of statehood. "Instead of a garden patch here and there," the Coulee City newspaper reported by mid-1891, "it is almost one continual field of green from the Grand Coulee to the eastern limits of the State." Along railway lines in place and projected—including the Washington Central, Great Northern and Northern Pacific—close to 20,000 settlers occupied the newest boom region east of the Cascades.[34]

In the Palouse, the Big Bend and the Walla Walla Valley, wheat was the prime crop, as vital to eastern Washington as timber was to the west side. "If two men stopped to shake hands and talk of the harvest," a resident observed of every day street corner behavior in small country towns, "in a moment a dozen would have gathered around and a quiet conversation would be turned into a common council." Three-fourths of the half million acres planted in grain at the time of statehood were devoted to wheat. Walla Walla and Whitman counties, the latter in the heart of the Palouse, together accounted for two-thirds of the total production. After increasing by a factor of four during the last decade of the territorial era, regional output continued to mount at a dizzying pace in the post admission years—the crop doubled between 1889 and 1891 from 7 million to 15 million bushels. Transportation firms struggled to keep up, with the Oregon Railway & Navigation Company alone erecting two dozen elevators along its interior Northwest lines in 1889.[35]

Grain cultivation was an unusually sensitive endeavor with all sorts of variables figuring into the yearly calculation of profit and loss. Fierce winter storms, though inconvenient, provided a welcome foretaste of good crops to be expected in the following season. Heavy snowfall in the Cascades supposedly translated into "from 25 to 50 bushels of wheat per acre." Three days of heavy rain, in another estimate, eventually meant an extra $2 million in earnings for Whitman County ranchers. Conversely, an ill timed harvest downpour could result in "thousands of dollars" of damage to un-threshed or poorly stored wheat.[36]

Shipping in "bulk" supposedly exposed grain to spoilage from excessive heat during the two crossings of the equator required on a five month voyage from Northwest ports to Liverpool. Farmers therefore preferred to "sack" their wheat, which allowed for greater air circulation during shipment. Unfortunately, sacks invariably were in short supply, with production failing to keep pace with the enormous annual increases in harvest output. Sacks were, in the aggregate, expensive as well, with a single bag adding 2¢ to the cost of a bushel of grain. In 1890, wheat ranchers spent a million dollars altogether for an item that could be used only once. A partial solution emerged indirectly from the general public indignation over allegations of luxury spending at the state penitentiary—the inmates even had turkey at Thanksgiving, one theatrically outraged politician spluttered. Mandating that prisoners engage in self support as opposed to tax-payer financed indolence, the legislature established a jute factory at the Walla Walla institution in 1891, providing farmers with a more dependable, if still costly, source of sacks.[37]

Exporting in the international marketplace, eastern Washington producers also necessarily paid attention to global conditions. Flooding in the Mississippi Valley, drought in Russia or blight in Australia, among other developments, might increase demand for the state's wheat in any one year. "These catastrophes of nature," a Walla Walla editor reflected, "are almost as good as a war for raising the price of grain." With virtually all the wheat produced in the interior North-west destined for shipment to England, the expense of rail haulage to tidewater became an additional factor in determining the return per bushel. Costing $2 million in the 1890 harvest season, freight charges accounted for the ongoing anti-corporate enmity expressed in farm country.[38]

Ranchers were at the mercy of historical trade patterns and traffic arrange-ments. As a general rule, producers along the Union Pacific lines, formerly the Oregon Railway & Navigation Company, shipped to Portland, while those served by the Northern Pacific sent wheat to Puget Sound. Due to a long standing divi-sion of territory between the railroads, the NP declined to build into Colfax, forc-ing a large part of the Palouse to have market connections with Oregon. Portland enjoyed a further advantage in that longer, and therefore more efficient, trains could be used on the gravity route down the Columbia, "designed," or so Orego-nians claimed, "by nature as an outlet" for the produce of eastern Washington. By contrast, "in getting to the seaboard," *West Shore* magazine pointed out regarding the direct-to-the-Sound situation, "the Northern Pacific must cross the Cascade mountains and a locomotive can draw but few cars on those heavy grades."[39]

Dependence on railroads and overseas markets by no means represented all the linkage between remote farms and distant capital. Mortgages and other forms of credit were essential for the purchase of additional land and new machinery, entailing close, confusing and often contentious involvements in the world of international finance. English mercantile houses maintained agencies on the Sound, dispatching representatives east of the mountains to buy crops. "Liverpool money" in excess of $7 million reportedly financed the 1890 state harvest. When other economic activities were depressed, regional business leaders expected the yearly infusion of wheat related cash to rescue Washington from true disaster.[40]

However, proof that "sagacity" was needed to successfully grow, harvest and sell wheat became vividly apparent in the fall of 1890. Over the preceding year, deep winter snow banks inspired enormous confidence in the coming harvest. "More snow has fallen than during the whole of last winter," a first-of-the-year report from farm country advised, "and there is very little frost in the ground, not enough to interfere with its absorbing the water when the thaw comes." Ranchers looked forward to "the first great wheat year of the Palouse country." Experienced forecasters anticipated an average of 35 bushels to the acre, "fully double what it was two years ago." Writing from the Walla Walla Valley, a journalist insisted that "no such yield" had "ever been seen…before." Across the eastern expanses of the state, farmers and small town merchants were universally "jubilant" over the approaching harvest.[41]

Indeed, it proved to be an abundant harvest, but then things went wrong, causing a truly horrific constriction of trade arteries—the "blockade" of 1890. As "the biggest crop ever raised on a similar acreage in the world" was put on the market, initial harvest time prices dropped to a disappointing low level. Farmers withheld wheat to compel an upswing, then, when this gambit failed, attempted to force grain upon a marketplace choking with surplus. The shipping pressure was more than the existing transportation network could bear. Railroad managers insisted that they could hardly "keep on hand idle for four years out of five twenty or thirty locomotives and a thousand box cars in order to be fully prepared for a possible phenomenal crop the fifth year." Grain interests countered that the railroads should have anticipated that the 1890 production was no phenomenon, but the new norm for eastern Washington agriculture.[42]

"Hundreds of thousands of bushels," east side reports proclaimed, "now lie piled up about the stations, waiting shipment, and but slightly protected from the weather." Barely half the crop had been hauled in from the fields, as buyers declined to make new purchases, citing the lack of storage and transportation. At Pasco, where the NP crossed the Columbia, 600 loaded box cars sat for weeks on a sidetrack, without locomotives to take them on to Puget Sound. "Hotheaded" ranchers threatened to blow up warehouses and bridges. The railroads canceled passenger service, making additional engines available to relieve the blockade. A perfect commercial storm of unintended consequences, the crisis lasted until mid-December, when the first positive reports in months declared that the embargo was "diminishing."[43]

Once past the immediate tribulation, the blockade became almost a "blessing" for many in the grain trade. The dramatic events generated national publicity, advertising "eastern Washington as nothing else could have," stated the *Spokane Review*. "It was universally agreed," the Inland Empire daily reasoned, "that a region which could stall two transcontinental lines with its products must be a wonderful one." The railroads were encouraged to substantially increase rolling stock and motive power—UP shops turned out new engines "at the rate of one a day" by the end of 1890—in order to avoid similar embarrassment in future years. The expansion of flour milling east of the Cascades also provided a growing local outlet for grain that otherwise would have been exported on the main railways.[44]

As a result of the distressing 1890 experience and to reduce dependence on "blood-sucking railroad corporations," eager wheat ranchers drove the recently founded Farmers' Alliance into prominence. The organization more than doubled by the next spring, with 50 chapters in Whitman County alone, a quarter of the state total. Viewed by alarmists as a "vicious" exponent of class warfare, the alliance was at this early stage more of a self help than a political movement. In 1891, the organization opened cooperative implement stores and warehouses across the grain country. Regardless of its supposed radicalism, the alliance worked with moneyed interests whenever it was mutually beneficial, going into partnership with the NP-affiliated Tacoma Land Company to build a wheat storage facility on Commencement Bay.[45]

Portland continued for a time to dominate the eastern Washington wheat trade. The Oregon metropolis suffered, however, from a singular difficulty, the infamous hazards at the Columbia's mouth. The federal government had built an expensive jetty in the previous decade, leading the city's shameless champions to insist that "there no longer exists a bar to obstruct free navigation by the largest vessels afloat." When not laughing themselves senseless over this dubious assertion, Washingtonians publicized the still potent nature of the obstructions. "No device which the ingenuity of man has invented, or is likely to invent," a Puget Sound editor noted of the Columbia, "can control the storms, which…year after year cover its deadly bar with its wrecks." A newspaper also claimed the army engineers, in expending a huge amount of taxpayer money on an ill conceived objective, had achieved a navigation improvement "of use only in fair weather."[46]

Washington's far superior tidal estuary, Puget Sound, supposedly in contrast was "free from bars, sandspits, shoals, rocks and shallow water." Without hazard, except during the occasional worst winter storm, the Sound was open to all large vessels. Steamship masters also avoided extortionate charges for pilotage and towing and lighter service, regular facets of Columbia navigation. The sea captain bound for Seattle or Tacoma with "correct charts," an Elliott Bay resident pointed out, "has no more need of a pilot than he has of two rudders." Indeed, cargo was handled more efficiently and port costs were kept to a comparative minimum. A 2,000 ton ship, for instance, paid $9,000 in total when sailing to and from Commencement Bay, substantially less than the $15,000 required on a Portland voyage.[47]

Thanks to the NP, Tacoma was first to benefit from the maritime advantages of Puget Sound. A vessel bringing in rails for NP construction in 1881 had departed with the initial consignment of grain. Additional cargoes followed, as circumstances allowed, until completion of the transcontinental line through the Stampede Pass tunnel in 1887. Exports mounted thereafter at an impressive pace, with over five million bushels shipped in 1891, a four-fold increase in two years. Two hundred carloads of wheat arrived daily during harvest season, filling elevators and warehouses. Ten steamers at a time tied up at the Tacoma docks, and the city installed three new deepwater anchor buoys to serve waiting ships. Although Portlanders insisted that the reported lower Puget Sound costs were "wholly untrue," eastern Washington farmers believed they could "realize from one to two cents per bushel more" by sending grain direct to portside on the NP.[48]

Elliott Bay lagged behind in this regional competition. At statehood, Seattle's grain handling capacity was succinctly and correctly described as "incomplete if not inadequate." With the NP abandoning its longtime pro-Tacoma rate policy, however, local interests and outside investors combined to build a waterfront elevator in West Seattle, connecting the facility with the main railroad depots by trestle across the Duwamish flats. Tacomans joked that the structure was promptly "given up to rats and bats," but 20 cargoes of wheat were handled in 1891, enough business to encourage serious expansion. Work began, too, on a West Seattle flour mill of sufficient size to produce 1,000 barrels per day. Still a distant third to Portland and Tacoma, the community expected to surge ahead upon completion of the Great Northern.[49]

Direct access to railroads was a defining development in late territorial and early statehood history. Crossed by one transcontinental line and with another on the way, "the Cascade mountains," an interior editor proclaimed, "no longer form a barrier between Eastern and Western Washington." Agriculture and commerce complemented one another, the former profiting from cheaper export costs and the latter from a general stimulus of economic progress. "As the country beyond the Cascades grows, produces and accumulates wealth," a Puget Sounder reflected, "the outlets here prosper." By establishing a mutually dependent relationship, another observer claimed, wheat had brought to an end the unhappy era in which Washington "was held in leading strings by Oregon."[50] Moreover, the larger significance of these advances—even if the development was by no means complete—was in bringing closer together Washington's historically contentious eastern and western regions.

❧❧❧

More fields could, in theory, be placed under the plow in eastern Washington. Just east of the Cascades, the problem was that most precipitation fell at the wrong time of year for nurturing crops. "To assert that this land can raise anything," a self styled dry lands expert noted, "is to challenge incredulity." Outfitted in an aptly named "duster" coat, the unfortunate summer traveler endured mile after mile of depressing landscape in the mid-Columbia area, with the "pale line of…dried sage" providing the only color or approximate sign of life. On a more positive note, the soil was undeniably decent, light and porous. Nearby mountain ranges clearly featured ample supplies of water. "The most important and urgent question" facing the interior Northwest, a Yakima Valley editor proclaimed in 1890, was finding a means to add water to the soil in the interest of new homesteads.[51]

Irrigation was of as much importance to urban as to rural areas. Washington's rivers, said one advocate, were "the heritage of all the people forever" and must, by right and by necessity, be devoted to the general welfare. In this reasoning, large landholdings would be broken up because of the cost and nature of irrigated farming, spreading property ownership among the citizenry and encouraging a more democratic utilization of resources. The final settlement of the West in 1890 ended what a legion of famous and obscure writers termed as "the great safety valve" that previously provided relief for social discontent. "The fact," a Seattle newspaper stated in one of many regional commentaries on the subject, "that as a last resource there was always a portion of public lands open to entry...has brought many an emigrant from the crowded sections of the east." By putting water upon dried out acreage, the argument went, an "outlet for the unemployed" would be reopened "for years to come."[52]

At statehood, Washington had 1,000 irrigated farms, averaging 47 acres in size and all located east of the Cascades. The greater Yakima Valley, claiming two-thirds of the irrigated farmsteads and four-fifths of the total acreage, was the focal point. "But a few years ago," a report from the newly watered desert advised, "the waste prairies of those sections were regarded as being utterly worthless." The land was "lifeless and disheartening," and most homestead tracts were "thought to be not worth the taxes charged upon them." Naysayers, though, had ignored the potential value of the many mountain streams that might, with relative ease, be diverted to thirsty acreage. "There is no other portion of Washington," a federal reclamation bulletin study pronounced in 1890, "which enjoys such facilities for the bringing out of water upon large bodies of fertile land."[53]

There were two methods for bringing more water to parched ground. Artesian wells were effective in some places, including the Yakima Valley's Moxee district, and at the Whitman County crossroads town of Pullman, but this entailed an inordinate expense and a distressingly high rate of failure. The better alternative relied upon the rivers of the Columbia system. Although enough water currently was "running to waste...to irrigate every acre of arid land in the state," unfortunately those streams had eroded down into deep canyons below the reach of simple diversion. The example of "ancient ruins throughout the deserts of Asia" suggested the obvious solution, the building of distant storage dams and canals to bring water to farms. The enormous cost of such projects, though, exceeded the fiscal capacity of most settlers. As in so many aspects of Washington life, outside capital provided the essential component for funding irrigation.[54]

Public construction of irrigation works was widely, if not universally, rejected as exceeding the constitutional powers of government. Legislation in support of private undertakings was another matter. Borrowing from California law, the first session of the state legislature authorized formation of local irrigation districts. The concept, an eastern Washington newspaper pointed out, was "somewhat after the fashion that prevails in cities as to grading streets." Actual landholders organized the districts, assessed themselves for the cost of construction and marketed bonds to secure financing. The never quite realized expectation was that individual ownership, rather than corporate monopoly, would be encouraged.[55]

Under private or district direction, an irrigation boom developed east of the Cascades. The Wenatchee Development Company instituted a number of canal projects, eventually serving 9,000 acres. Work began outside Ellensburg in 1892 on the "Big Ditch," an undertaking financed by borrowing and meant to reclaim 30,000 acres in the Kittitas Valley. Near the remote hamlet of Hooper, adjacent to the western part of the Palouse Hills, excavation commenced on a 30-mile canal from the Palouse River to a 7,000 acre tract. Two other schemes, one backed by the NP and the other a local development, also proposed to use Palouse water for extensive reclamation in the Pasco vicinity. Bold visionaries even suggested conversion of the Grand Coulee into a reservoir, storing the waters of the Columbia for distribution across the Big Bend.[56]

Canal digging was most notable, however, in the "the Yakima country," as John Wesley Powell affirmed on the basis of a personal inspection. He claimed it was "the richest, most beautiful and most prosperous section of the northwest." North Yakima, the principal settlement, boasted a mid-1890 population exceeding 3,000. "Five years ago," one daily newspaper noted in celebrating the Northern Pacific's town site speculation, the place had been "a desert of sagebrush and rocks." Arriving passengers now rode from the depot to their hotels, a tourist reported, with "the ripple of running water in the air," courtesy of the railroad-provided ditches. Shade trees lined the streets, and the better quality dwellings featured "yards green with grass or gay with a riotous growth of roses." Vacant houses were nowhere to be found in this new paradise, forcing promotion minded citizens to erect a "large and commodious" tenement for temporary accommodation of immigrants.[57]

The Yakima River, above and below its constriction at Union Gap, wound through broad open plains, with the high snowy Cascades to the west and bare forbidding ridgelines on the east. Wagons churned down powdery country roads, throwing up clouds of dust sufficient enough, remarked one traveler, to "have proved an ample guide by day for the children of Israel." Recognizing the underlying capacity of the soil and the success to date of rudimentary reclamation projects, investors began buying acreage under terms of the federal Desert Land Act. Intending to "make a complete artificial water shed" in the Yakima Valley, these interests initiated a number of ambitious projects in the first years of statehood. A 40 percent increase in irrigated acreage in 1890 provided evidence that reclamation was no "experiment." The Selah ditch, for example, ran for 20 miles, bringing 16,000 acres under cultivation. [58]

By far the most dramatic manifestation was undertaken by a corporate affiliate of the Northern Pacific. Organized in 1890, the Yakima & Kittitas Irrigation Company, directed by longtime NP executive Paul Schulze, proposed sending water through 60 miles of canal from north of Union Gap to Prosser, reclaiming tens of thousands of acres. Construction was delayed by a dispute with the federal government over the impact upon the Yakama Indian Reservation along the right bank, but work finally began on the dam and diversion works in late 1891. The first 25 miles of the Sunnyside canal were excavated the following spring and summer.[59]

Reflecting upon the Sunnyside project in particular, newspapers on both sides of the Cascades celebrated the transformation of "desert into a blossoming, fruitful garden." Washington residents, those on Puget Sound in particular, had complained for years of their dependence upon California for fresh fruit, a luxury item that was both expensive and less than wholesome in appearance and taste. Now that they had water, the newly reclaimed areas east of the Cascades could at last take advantage of orchard-ideal soil and climatic conditions. "Experiments have shown," said one booster, "that almost all kinds of fruit flourish on this land." The relatively small size of irrigated farms, a practical result of the costs involved, encouraged a focus on intensive agriculture, and the railroads opened new urban markets. "Each year," a Spokane newspaper reported, "sees thousands of additional trees set out."[60]

Quite literally, in the view of one orchard customer, the state deserved to be called "Fruitful Washington." During the 1891 season, the Yakima Valley shipped 1,000 pounds of strawberries per day to Puget Sound. The first eastern consignment, a carload of Walla Walla pears, went to St. Paul over the NP in 1892. Wenatchee fruit, meanwhile, secured a region-wide reputation for quality, the apples being praised for "solidity, enormous size and incomparable flavor." This Great Northern-connected town produced 16,000 pounds of apples in 1893, as well as large quantities of peaches and grapes, even though orchardists confronted lice and other pests that attacked growing fruit prior to harvest. Though railroad freight rates varied from year to year, impacting sales on the Sound and in the East, a prosperous agricultural enterprise was firmly implanted, linking previously remote regions in mutual commercial benefit.[61]

❧❦❧

Mining likewise was accorded importance on both sides of the Cascades. Famous gold strikes—in the California Sierra, along the Fraser River, on the Nez Perce reservation, and in eastern Oregon, western Montana and the Coeur d'Alenes of northern Idaho—were major events in territorial history. All were in border areas, however, with Washington itself never quite becoming a center of production.

In 1889, the new state produced less than a quarter million dollars in mineral wealth, one-fourth the figure for Oregon and mere pocket change when tallied against the $17 million recorded by Idaho and $13 million by California. This dismal comparative record supposedly reflected a failure of initiative, rather than any lack of hidden riches. "It is the misfortune of the mining business," a Tacoma editor claimed, "that conservative men who have means for the most part look upon it as gambling, and that inexperienced men, who have little means, look to it with confidence as a road to fortune." Supposedly being feckless, often ill prepared and easily disheartened, the latter gave up after minimal effort, their failure discouraging persons possessing common sense and the capacity for work. Pioneers nonetheless maintained faith. The state geologist explained in 1891 that Washington's mines would "at no very distant day" achieve the same regional status as "fields of grain and forests of fir and pine."[62]

Mineral pipedreams were pursued in diverse locations. "It is well known," a local paper broadcast in 1892, "that the Wenatchee is gold-bearing its entire length." Precious metal also was found, according to enthusiasts, in the hills above Kalama, the oft-waterlogged port on the lower Columbia. The "excitement" there "reached such a state of intoxication that most anything in the shape of rock is carefully carried to the assayer to learn…what it contains." The sandy beaches around Westport at the southern entrance to Grays Harbor concealed golden wealth in abundance, asserted reports from the scene. Other prospectors claimed to have discovered silver near Port Angeles on the Strait of Juan de Fuca.[63]

Of more substantial note, wealth actually was uncovered in several areas. Extending from Canada to the Columbia along the eastern Cascades, Okanogan County encompassed a truly remote backcountry, including a quarter of the state's unsurveyed lands. Trails choked in dust—"it would actually work its way into an hermetically sealed can," a traveler noted—provided the only means of communication. The region experienced one of its periodic gold and silver rushes in 1891. Miners filed 4,000 claims and demanded the opening of the Colville Indian Reservation so that they might conveniently pass to and from Spokane, the principal supply point. "If half the tales told in the past few weeks are true," one editor wrote of accounts from the diggings, "numerous hiding places of the golden metal have been brought to light." One fortunate prospector sold his claim for $200,000. Developers planned not one, but two, railways into the Okanogan, thereby hoping to emulate the exploitation methods previously used in the Coeur d'Alenes. Pending the arrival of trains, concentrated ore from primitive stamp mills was hauled by wagon to the Columbia for shipment to Wenatchee aboard steamers.[64]

Gold also was discovered in 1891 among the tangled pine ridges above the Kittitas Valley. "Hardly a day passes," an Ellensburg paper observed in midsummer, "that pack horses are not seen in our streets loaded with supplies for the sanguine prospectors." The rush to Swauk Creek and other focal points of the excitement provided a much needed economic stimulus for the town, in the doldrums since the Wall Street crisis of the previous fall. Reports that deposits from some of the canyons were worth $1,000 to the ton attracted outside investors with the funds to build flumes and concentrators. A Wild West atmosphere prevailed in the troubled foothills, with claim jumping activity and white miners running off Chinese competitors at gun point.[65]

Prospectors and capitalists alike expected to get rich in the northernmost Cascades. A thousand miners worked the Stehekin country at the head of Lake Chelan in the summers of 1891 and 1892. On both side of the Cascades, the rugged "aspect" of the topography was in itself enough to convince self-appointed experts of the existence of "rich mineral lodes." In the first year of statehood, individuals wielding shovel and pan found sufficient dust in the lower rivers and creeks to support a conviction that the peaks above guarded deposits to "last till the trump of doom." All the way from "Mount Rainier to the British boundary," an excited Seattle editor announced, "the…mountains are ribbed with ores containing lead, iron, copper, silver and gold."[66]

Prospectors spent the summers of 1890 and 1891 working up the brush-lined creeks of the Snohomish, Stillaguamish and Skagit basins. "Little by little," E.V. Smalley recounted in *Northwest* magazine, "the evidence of the existence of wide veins of paying ores accumulated." One operation traced a single outcropping over several ridgelines. At an elevation of 7,000 feet, another stumbled upon the Boston deposit, where a glacier had stripped away an entire mountainside, exposing gold, silver and lead. Original claim takers took advantage of immediate opportunities for profit. The Boston mine, for instance, sold to an outside investment syndicate in late 1890 for $150,000. Other discoveries, most notably at Silver Creek and Monte Cristo, became regionally famous wilderness camps.[67]

Remotely located in the Sauk Creek section of eastern Snohomish County, Monte Cristo drew special attention from wealthy Everett promoters. The various mineral deposits already unearthed, plus discoveries yet to be made, would provide raw material for industries to be situated on Port Gardner Bay. In January 1892, John D. Rockefeller—whose personal investment reportedly was $3 million—and his associates bought out the first claimants and began building a railroad up the Stillaguamish River in the direction of the mines.[68]

Backed by America's most famous tycoon, the Monte Cristo project was celebrated around the Sound as "the first and greatest step in the development of the contiguous iron deposits." All analysts agreed that a mineral processing industry was needed if the region was to advance beyond just extracting and exporting raw ore. Established near Port Townsend in 1880, the Irondale facility operated the largest furnace on the coast. Assorted problems, including poor design, bad management and distance from markets, forced a shutdown in 1889, leaving Washington without an iron manufactory. The state nonetheless had ample supplies of ore, coal and labor. Industrialization, once implemented, would provide local enterprise with a cheaper alternative to eastern iron. Railroad rails produced at foundries on Puget Sound, meanwhile, could be exported to China and Japan, the much touted new foreign customers of the Pacific coastal states.[69]

Seattle investors, like the Rockefeller interests, grasped at the newly available industrial opportunities. After lengthy negotiations, Peter Kirk, a developer from Scotland, joined Leigh S.J. Hunt, the owner of the *P-I*, Arthur Denny and other associates in forming the Great Western Iron & Steel Company. Although Tacomans dismissed the Kirkland project as "simply a townsite speculation," work began in impressive earnest on the eastern shore of Lake Washington in 1891. Planning for the expensive complex focused upon the construction of four blast furnaces, each with a weekly capacity in excess of 1,000 tons, plus ancillary mills, warehouses and bunkers. Residences and stores for managers and laborers also were included.[70] Once completed, the owners expected their industrialized lakefront property to rival, if not excel, the heavily publicized efforts at Everett.

For the time being, with development at Monte Cristo and Kirkland proceeding, the focus was on smelting. Located by its original backers just outside the city limits, the Tacoma smelter was taken over by W.R. Rust, a Colorado investor, prior to opening for business in September 1890. Supplied by the Northern Pacific, the plant produced close to a million dollars worth of gold, silver and lead in the first 11 months of 1891. Activation of a second belching smokestack soon doubled capacity. Benefiting from its own rail network, Spokane opened the state's second smelter in 1891. The local press, at least, credited the facility with making the Inland Empire metropolis "the greatest ore center west of Denver."[71]

The installation of smelters reflected the desire of Washington's largest cities to promote regional hinterlands. "Forgetting all about town lots," Spokane sought the trade of the Coeur d'Alenes and of newer mining localities, the Okanogan and the Kootenay district of southeast British Columbia. "One hope lies near the heart of every man and woman in Spokane," the editor of the *Review* proclaimed. "It is the desire to see her reach out for empire." Tacoma citizens expressed the same aim with regard to every point, mines included, reached by the Northern Pacific. The city, a Commencement Bay journalist claimed, "must have…marts of trade in all parts of Washington, closely connected to her by indissoluble ties of mutually advantageous commerce." Seattle, too, developed imperial aspirations respecting places served by the Great Northern. "Every acre reduced to cultivation, every new mine, or mill or factory," the *P-I* insisted, "must directly or indirectly and to a greater or less extent, contribute to the prosperity of this city."[72] Building railroads and developing mineral opportunities, capital fueled an aggressive profit making climate across the Pacific Northwest.

Another new force to be reckoned with in Northwest industrial and commercial development was organized labor. Emerging in the late territorial period, the Knights of Labor fought nobly in the coal mines—and ignobly against the Chinese—before foundering amidst internal division and employer disdain. The simple old days of management domination, however, were beyond restoration. "There is a strong inclination among the employees," the tough lumberman Cyrus Walker lamented, "to become high toned as to how they shall live, the time they shall work, the amount of work they do & the pay they receive." Many employers, too, appeared to have gone soft. "The idea of being called a *good fellow* is far too prevalent among some of the heads of the departments here," Walker wrote from his Port Ludlow headquarters.[73]

Certain aspects of the post-admission economic boom sustained the union movement. The need for construction workers and skilled mechanics overstrained the available supply of men, allowing workers to make demands on management as they provided their much needed laboring services. Prosperous conditions in the cities also attracted ambitious and talented individuals into the commercial trades and professions—men who otherwise would be workers in industry. "If you get a man that is good for anything," Cyrus Walker unhappily observed, "he will naturally want to do something better than to work all his life for a salary." Consequently, pressure developed for a reduction in the standard working day from 10 hours to 8. An eastern Washington editor quipped that married men ought to be careful lest they encourage a similar domestic demand on the part of their wives, but a favorable outcome for the campaign appeared certain. Fretful employers expressed relief only when the 1890 Wall Street crisis transformed a laboring shortage into a surplus, even allowing for cuts in pay.[74]

In the best of times, general working conditions encouraged militancy. Many laborers of the new industrialized age lived outside conventional society, moving from place to place according to the dictates of distant markets and the decisions of faraway investors. "The iron heel of monopolistic despotism," said a sympathetic Tacoma newspaper, was "keenly felt" in the form of take-it-or-leave-it wage offers and high priced company stores. Instituting production cutbacks or slashing pay, management often gave little thought to the impact upon employees and their families. As a graphic example of the inherent dangers of the working man's existence, an explosion at the Roslyn coal mine, just east of Snoqualmie Pass, killed 45 men in May 1892. Investigators concluded that the tunnels had been poorly ventilated and the operator, a subsidiary of the NP, long had been aware of the gross hazard to safety. The railroad nonetheless blamed the disaster on the carelessness of the deceased miners. The town's company paid preacher added the helpful thought that God had properly punished the victims for aboveground drinking and gambling.[75]

Ministerial lackeys and company excusers excepted, public opinion tended to be critical of corporate policies regarding labor. Urban residents, with independent merchants in the lead, condemned the company store system as "a species of robbery." The Washington state constitution prohibited, in theory, the employment of armed security forces. Thus, most citizens expressed misgivings over corporation-hired "Pinkertonism," represented in the Pacific Northwest by the lawless actions of operatives supplied by Portland's Sullivan agency in hounding labor organizations. "It raises the blood of an American," a Bellingham Bay editor exclaimed, "to have prowling around watching him a band of men who are little better than cut-throats." The North had won the Civil War, asserted the *Seattle Telegraph*, only to have "the crack of the slave driver's whip" replaced by "the crack of the Pinkerton Winchesters." Every decent person, an eastern Washington paper agreed, wanted "a stop…put to the work of these hired assassins."[76]

Generally sympathizing with workers, middle class Washingtonians expressed minimal fears regarding the many localized disputes associated with the 1890 Wall Street troubles. Unionized carpenters shut down construction of a Spokane exhibition hall that fall. The city's teachers also walked out, demanding that salaries be increased to $50 a month. Seattle newsboys went on strike against the daily papers, and all but four of the city's firefighters quit in response to a pay reduction. Grays Harbor boat operators ceased fishing in an argument with the Aberdeen canneries over the price of salmon. Tacoma bakery union members lost their jobs when shop owners imported lower paid replacements. Colfax, the Whitman County seat, experienced a general strike when the town's laborers protested the engagement of an Italian crew by street contractors. Walla Walla penitentiary inmates also refused to work, on account of the bread-and-water diet imposed by cost paring prison administrators.[77]

Early in the decade, Washington's most dramatic conflict arose from difficult times in the coaling trade. The state's 11 mines produced nearly a million tons in 1889, with Seattle alone shipping close to half that amount to San Francisco. Cheaper and arguably better British Columbia and Australian coal, unfortunately, soon captured a large share of the vital California market. Years of struggle with the Knights of Labor compromised morale and increased costs in the industry. So also did the "broken" and "unreliable" nature of the veins found in most coal mining operations. Attempts to make up for declining earnings by assessing higher prices on captive local customers generated widespread consumer discontent on Puget Sound.[78]

Long the dominant force in the industry, the Oregon Improvement Company was especially troubled by these developments. A persistent fire forced closure of the Franklin mine for a lengthy period. Newcastle, the firm's other King County property, needed expensive modernization. Continued worker militancy compelled management to grant a 15 percent wage increase in 1890. The response eventually decided upon, importation of black miners to the Franklin operation, emulated a cynical NP strategy adopted several years previously at Roslyn. In early 1891, the plan entailed a full reopening of the Franklin mine, displacement of the white employees and restoration of the old pay scale. The ultimate goal, according to an OIC executive, was two-fold—substantial cost reduction and providing "an element of certainty in the operation." The initial expenditure for recruitment, transportation and security would be large, but the company in a deft economizing touch expected to deduct the sum required from the reduced paychecks of black workers.[79]

Under a heavy escort of hired guards, 600 blacks, family members included, arrived at Franklin on May 18, 1891. "At every point in and about the town," a report from the scene noted in describing the deliberate intimidation, "stand armed guards with Winchester rifles ready to fall in line at a moment's notice and deal out death to the white miners of the town." Barbed wire surrounded the main buildings and tunnel entrances. Initially, reaction from the normally pro-business press was both forthrightly critical and subtly racist. "Nobody cares to see the population increased in this unwholesome way," the *Tacoma Ledger* sniffed. The *Seattle P-I* disdainfully described the black miners as "distinctly inferior to the men whose places they have come to fill." Ignoring the fact that the newcomers, by all accounts, produced more coal than their predecessors, the Elliott Bay daily also worried that capitalists would be discouraged from investing in Washington.[80]

Angry white workers closed the Black Diamond, Gilman and Newcastle mines, but Franklin, literally an armed camp, ran at capacity. Emboldened by this triumph, the company attempted to send black strikebreakers to Newcastle in late June. The ill conceived provocation resulted in an exchange of gunfire, the killing of two protesting miners and, in what was widely considered the most heinous act of the day, the wounding of two employees' wives. "Armed men have made human life so insecure," a Seattle paper reported, "that women and children have fled to the woods for shelter." OIC detectives carried the female casualties to a bullet riddled hut, then left them without medical attention. Gun carrying toughs, strongly fortified with alcohol, patrolled muddy streets, evicting persons suspected of disloyalty to the firm from homes and threatening to kill strikers.[81]

Governor Elisha Ferry, citing the need to restore law and order, sent five National Guard companies to Franklin. Tracing its historical roots to the volunteering tradition of early pioneer days, the guard was a fairly new entity as a formal organization. In 1888, the territorial legislature established the permanent militia, funded by a special annual tax levy. In effect, it had little other conceivable purpose than for one-sided use in labor disputes. Many hardliners approved the assignment of soldiers to the mine as a necessary response to bloodshed and the destruction of property, but public opinion in general was condemnatory. Critics could not help noting that the commander at the scene, Colonel J.C. Haines, just happened to be the lead attorney for the Oregon Improvement Company. Under this less-than-dispassionate leadership, Washington's publicly financed national guard was placed "on exactly the same footing as Pinkerton's gangs," the

Seattle Telegraph pointed out. All things considered, cynical observers suggested, the cause of patriotism was well served by the unavailability of the compromised militia units to march, as planned, in Puget Sound's July Fourth parades.[82]

Making no real attempt to carry out its ostensible official mission of disarming both pro- and anti-management forces, the guard put a point-of-the-bayonet end to the dispute. By fall, the Oregon Improvement Company produced more coal at less cost than at the beginning of the year. To obtain employment, workers had to accept a 25 percent wage cut and sign a no-strike pledge. Beyond the firm's short term victory, the entire episode was widely perceived as a full blown and thoroughly disturbing exercise in corporate exploitation. A growing public feeling that something had gone awry in late 19th century Washington was not assuaged when Governor Ferry demanded that King County taxpayers reimburse the state for costs incurred in the intervention.[83]

Thoughtful people, partially aware of an ongoing shift in America away from traditional rural values and individual self reliance, viewed such episodes in an ambivalent, even contradictory, manner. "Organized labor is a comparatively new social force," a Tacoma editor pointed out in the aftermath of Franklin, "and the boundaries and limitations of its rights are as yet but little understood." With the mutual dependence of employer and employee remaining a self evident truth—one could hardly prosper without the other—most Washingtonians endorsed the basic concept of unionization. "No sensible man," a newspaper in the state capital declared, "will deny the right of workmen to combine to get as high wages or as short hours as possible." A single person could not stand against modern corporate power, nor should industrialists be allowed to form combinations without extending the same privilege to workers.[84]

Confusion prevailed when the discussion shifted to the means by which labor organizations might actually achieve their objectives. "We believe the principle of trade unionism to be correct," the *Seattle Telegraph* maintained, "but we also believe…unreasonable and reckless use of the power acquired by unions to be very injurious." The strike, the most effective anti-management weapon, was in particular a "terribly pernicious" and virtually un-American device, a Spokane daily suggested. Discontented employees certainly had a right to quit, but they could not prevent others from taking the jobs thus vacated. "If this is to continue a free country, one principle has to be established," a Walla Walla Valley editorialist declared, "and that is that a man has a right to employ whom he pleases to do his work, and has also the right to work for whom he pleases, if the terms of employment suit him." Otherwise, alien concepts of class warfare would surely prevail in Washington and throughout the United States, thwarting the ambitious and the hard working in the name of "equality."[85]

Violence in the Coeur d'Alene mines of Idaho hardly encouraged the reconciliation of contradictory thoughts and emotions. A prolonged and nasty dispute over wages, during which both management and labor outfitted themselves with large supplies of munitions, came to a dramatic climax in July 1892 when union workers blew up the Frisco mine. Six persons, three on each side, died in the explosion and related exchanges of gunfire. Miners drove strikebreakers from the region, but were in turn put down by the intervention of federal troops and the declaration of martial law. The horrors and implications of the Coeur d'Alene troubles were as vivid on one side of the state line as on the other. "By outrage and murder," a Seattle paper asserted of those setting the dynamite charges, "they have made of themselves common criminals." The strike was "no longer a labor dispute," the *P-I* insisted. "It is treason." Idaho's miners, an Ellensburg journal affirmed, were "savage beasts," who had "forfeited any sympathy which they might have obtained" for a cause tainted in blood.[86]

Even the *Tacoma News*, a publication normally convinced that labor organizers were "as honest and right as Cromwell," denounced the apparent revolution in the Coeur d'Alene mines. Similar violence, as suggested by the Franklin crisis of the previous year, might just as easily take place in Washington. "Anarchy and communistic principles," a Walla Walla weekly decried, "are things the American people will not tolerate for an instant." A Grays Harbor editor, meanwhile, called for a national "war of extermination" against anarchists, socialists and wielders of dynamite.[87] Most residents of the state, presumably, would not go that far, but the events of 1891 and 1892 cost the union movement dearly in terms of good will and tolerance.

◈◈◈

At the end of its westering to the Pacific, the United States in 1889 faced the necessity of devising a new imperial dynamic for the approaching 20th century. With its internal lands settled, the nation required, according to a Puget Sound observer, "a more aggressive foreign policy" focused upon the development of overseas markets and protecting ocean trade routes. The coastal states, in particular, ought to cultivate relations with China and Japan. "Washington," an Aberdeen publisher advised, "must look seriously to her West, that is to the East, for aid to her commercial greatness."[88]

Trade between Asia and America already was being conducted at an impressive rate. Forty percent of Japan's exports went across the Pacific to U.S. buyers in 1890, and trade also was developed with China. Well established in terms of ocean commerce, Puget Sound was ideally situated to take advantage of the newly opening markets. Steamers sailing from Tacoma were 600 miles closer to Yokohama than rivals leaving California. A voyage from the Sound to this premier Japanese port took 12 days, under normal weather conditions, versus 52 days for ships departing England. The distance from Commencement Bay to China was roughly 4,000 miles, less than a third of the distance for British competitors.[89]

Due to these factors, favorable cost differentials led to the early establishment of formal trade connections between Washington and Asia. As one newspaper pointed out, the transcontinental railroads had been constructed "with an eye to the expanding commerce from the Orient." The Northern Pacific's steamship line commenced regular service—the initial voyage of the thousand ton *Phra Nang* was celebrated with appropriate pomp and circumstance—between Tacoma and Japanese and Chinese ports in 1892. The Great Northern's *Crown of England* began a similar business from Seattle in 1893. Inland Empire grain, ground into flour at Puget Sound mills, provided the basic export, with the vessels returning with tea and silk for distribution by rail throughout the United States.[90] Indeed, from the earliest days of settlement, Puget Sound had been part of a Pacific Rim trade network, with irregular trips conducted by timber company vessels. Now, at the outset of a new era, the entire state was a major component of a substantially larger and more efficient commercial network, the product of capital, modern transportation and new economic development.

Notes

1. *Tacoma Daily Ledger*, March 1, 1890.
2. "If the state is ever divided," another tidewater journal asserted, "we trust the eastern part will take…Washington and give us a chance to get an appropriate and character-istic name." Robert E. Ficken, "Columbia, Washington or Tacoma? The Naming and Attempted Renaming of Washington Territory," *Columbia: The Magazine of Northwest History* [hereafter cited as *Columbia*], 17 (Spring 2003), 25–27; *Tacoma Daily News*, Feb. 22; Oct. 10, 1892; *Seattle Post-Intelligencer*, Jan. 5, 1891, rep. from Aberdeen *Herald*.
3. A Puget Sound newspaper invited easterners in January 1891 to visit "the Evergreen state of Washington." The 1895 *Seattle P-I* New Year special supplement appeared under the title "Evergreen State." Portland *Oregonian*, Nov. 12, 1893; Olympia *Washington Stan-dard*, April 18, 1890; *The Dalles Times-Mountaineer*, Sept. 10, 1892; *Northwest*, 10 (Oct. 1892), 31; *Tacoma Daily News*, Jan. 9, 1891, rep. from Orting *Oracle*; *Seattle Post-Intel-ligencer*, Jan. 1, 1895.
4. *West Shore*, 15 (June 1889), 342; (Dec. 14, 1889), 421; *Spokane Review*, June 27, 1891, rep. from San Francisco *Chronicle*; *Spokane Falls Review*, June 20, 1890; E.V. Smalley, "In the Big Bend Country," *Northwest*, 8 (May 1890), 20.
5. *West Shore*, 15 (Sept. 28, 1889), 74–76; Portland *Oregonian*, Aug. 27, 1897; *Seattle Post-Intelligencer*, July 25, 1890, rep. from Waterville *Immigrant*; *Spokane Review*, May 29; July 4, 1891; *Seattle Press-Times*, Aug. 3, 1892; *Northwest*, 9 (July 1891), 45.
6. Visiting the northern Olympic Peninsula, forester Gifford Pinchot encountered "timber so thick" that his party needed "6 hours to make 2 to 2½ miles." *Seattle Post-Intelligencer*, Jan. 10, rep. from Union City *Tribune*; Feb. 8, 1891, rep. from Port Angeles *Tribune*; *Northwest*, 8 (Sept. 1890), 30; J.P. O'Neil, "The Last Home of the Elk," *Northwest*, 10 (July 1892), 5; *Tacoma Daily Ledger*, Nov. 26, 1890; *Seattle Press-Times*, Aug. 10, 1891; Portland *Oregonian*, Sept. 28, 1893; *Spokane Review*, Nov. 9, 1892; Robert L. Wood, "The O'Neil Expeditions," *Columbia*, 4 (Summer 1990), 40–45; Diary entry, Aug. 21, 1897, Gifford Pinchot Papers, Library of Congress.
7. *Yakima Herald*, Dec. 10, 1891; Olympia *Washington Standard*, Jan. 2, 1891; *Spokane Review*, June 14, 1893.

8. Colorado, a Spokane newspaper suggested, "would go into ecstacies" if possessed with the timber resources of eastern Washington. Oregon had more sawmills than Washington, but those in the newer state were larger and more efficient. *Spokane Review,* Jan. 26, 1893; Jan. 22, 1894; *Northwest,* 9 (Feb. 1891), 8; *Seattle Times,* July 16, 1895; Robert E. Ficken, *The Forested Land: A History of Lumbering in Western Washington* (Seattle: University of Washington Press, 1987), 75; Cyrus Walker to W.H. Talbot, May 14, 1892, Cyrus Walker Letterbooks, Ames Coll., University of Washington Library; Olympia *Washington Standard,* Jan. 15, 1892; *Seattle Press-Times,* March 27, 1893; *West Shore,* 15 (Dec. 21, 1889), 461.

9. Local timber also gained an international reputation, with the British government purchasing a large consignment of "fine quality" Washington lumber in 1891 for use in constructing railroads in the Himalayan foothills. Kirk Munroe, "The Cities of the Sound," *Harper's Weekly,* 38 (Jan. 13, 1894), 35; *Tacoma Daily Ledger,* June 26, 1890; *Aberdeen Herald,* June 18, 1891; *West Shore,* 16 (Aug. 9, 1890), 998; (Oct. 25, 1890), 171; Olympia *Washington Standard,* July 17, 1891; *Ellensburgh Capital,* Dec. 15, 1892; *Seattle Post-Intelligencer,* May 31, 1891, rep. from Snohomish *Eye.*

10. Agreement of April 21, 1888 at Saginaw, Michigan, Merrill & Ring Lumber Co. Records, University of Washington Library; Frederick Weyerhaeuser to J.P. Weyerhaeuser, April 6, 1891, Weyerhaeuser Family Papers, Minnesota Historical Society; *Seattle Press-Times,* Aug. 3, 4, 1891; *Seattle Post-Intelligencer,* Feb. 14, 1892; George H. Emerson to Wm. S. Brackett, March 1, 1892, George H. Emerson Letterbooks, University of Washington Library.

11. Close to half of the vessels in Puget Sound ports in November 1891 were tied up at mill company docks. Reflecting the close Washington-California connection, 14 million board feet of the 26 million feet of lumber imported by San Francisco Bay in April 1891 came from either the Sound or Grays Harbor. *Tacoma Daily News,* Feb. 21, 1890; *Tacoma Daily Ledger,* Jan. 1, 1890; March 28, 1891; *Seattle Post-Intelligencer,* Jan. 1, 1891; *Northwest,* 9 (March 1891), 40; *Everett News,* Jan. 1, 1892; Emerson to A.M. Simpson, May 15, 1894, Emerson Letterbooks; Walker to Talbot, July 30, 1895, Walker Letterbooks; *Olympia Tribune,* Nov. 2, 1891; *Aberdeen Herald,* May 28, 1891.

12. In May 1893, Hoquiam lumberman George Emerson exported 60,000 board feet a day by vessel and sent 20,000 feet a day east on rail cars. Emerson to E.J. Holt, Sept. 7, 1895; to Samuel Perkins, May 3, 1893, Emerson Letterbooks; *Seattle Telegraph,* Dec. 12, 1892; *Tacoma Morning Globe,* Jan. 1, 1892; Renton, Holmes & Co. to Port Blakely Mill Co., Dec. 12, 1889, Port Blakely Mill Co. Records, University of Washington Library; Chauncey Griggs to L.B. Royce, Aug. 7, 1896, St. Paul & Tacoma Lumber Co. Records, University of Washington Library.

13. Olympia *Washington Standard,* April 24, 1891; *Seattle Press-Times,* Sept. 7, 1892; Walker to Talbot, May 20; July 11, 1892, Puget Mill Co. Records, Ames Coll., University of Washington Library; Emerson to Simpson, July 14, 1892, Emerson Letterbooks.

14. *Seattle Press-Times,* June 29; Dec. 28, 1892; Walker to Talbot, Sept. 21, 1892, Puget Mill Co. Records; Ficken, *Forested Land,* 60; *Seattle Post-Intelligencer,* June 3, 1892, rep. from *Northwestern Lumberman;* Olympia *Washington Standard,* March 25, 1892; Jan. 27, 1893; *West Shore,* 16 (Nov. 29, 1890), 251.

15. Richard White, *Land Use, Environment, and Social Change: The Shaping of Island County, Washington* (Seattle: University of Washington Press, 1980), 95; Walker to Talbot, May 14, 1892, Walker Letterbooks; May 20; July 11; Sept. 21, 1892, Puget Mill Co. Records; Emerson to Simpson, July 14, 1892, Emerson Letterbooks; Fred S. Stimson to T.D.

Stimson, May 2, 1893, Stimson Mill Co. Records, University of Washington Library; Olympia *Washington Standard*, Aug. 26, 1892; *Seattle Telegraph*, Dec. 26, 1892, rep. from *Northwestern Lumberman*, *Tacoma Daily Ledger*, Nov. 10, 1891; *Seattle Post-Intelligencer*, April 24; May 24, 1893.

16. *Aberdeen Herald*, Feb. 16, 1893; *Seattle Telegraph*, Nov. 19, 1891; *Tacoma Daily Ledger*, Jan. 17, 1892; Aug. 18, 1893; Oct. 3, 5, 1894; *Seattle Post-Intelligencer*, Feb. 13; July 26, 1892; *Walla Walla Statesman*, Dec. 8, 1893; Emerson to Frank B. Cole, Feb. 8, 1892; to John L. Wilson, Feb. 9, 1892, Emerson Letterbooks; Gordon Hak, *Turning Trees into Dollars: The British Columbia Coastal Lumber Industry, 1858–1913* (Toronto: University of Toronto Press, 2000), 17–18.

17. The owners of the Port Discovery mill attempted to sell the property to Frederick Weyerhaeuser. Walker to Talbot, July 22, 1890; Jan. 9, 16; Feb. 5; May 14, 1892; to A.W. Jackson, Nov. 21, 1889, Walker Letterbooks, to Puget Mill Co., April 5; Aug. 20, 1890, Puget Mill Co. Records; *Spokane Falls Review*, Nov. 12, 1890, rep. from Grays Harbor *Times*; Ficken, *Forested Land*, 64–68; Olympia *Washington Standard*, Aug. 12, 1892; A.D. Moore to Weyerhaeuser, July 3, 1893, Weyerhaeuser Family Papers.

18. James Bryce, *The American Commonwealth* (New York: Macmillan, 2 vols., 3d ed., 1895), 1:585; *Northwest*, 8 (April 1890), 36; Walker to Jackson, Nov. 21, 1889; to Talbot, July 22, 1890, Walker Letterbooks; Emerson to Simpson, Feb. 10, 1896; to John L. Harris, April 18, 1896, Emerson Letterbooks.

19. *Spokane Review*, Feb. 8; Aug. 23, 1893; *Seattle Post-Intelligencer*, May 13; June 10, 1891; Aug. 13, 1892; *Tacoma Daily Ledger*, Sept. 23, 1890; *Tacoma Morning Globe*, Aug. 24, 1890; July 27; Sept. 27, 1891.

20. Forest fires also were common in eastern Washington. In 1892, for instance, regional news accounts told of blazes "burning" on both sides of the Columbia River. *Spokane Review*, July 30, 1891; *Tacoma Morning Globe*, July 2, 11, 24, 1891; Olympia *Washington Standard*, Aug. 7, 1891; Emerson to Simpson, Aug. 31, 1894; Aug. 15, 1895, Emerson Letterbooks; Herbert Hunt and Floyd C. Kaylor, *Washington, West of the Cascades* (Chicago: S.J. Clarke, 3 vols., 1917), 1:363; Steven J. Pyne, *Fire in America: A Cultural History of Wildland and Rural Fire* (Princeton: Princeton University Press, 1982), 192; Ruth A. Burnet, "Mark Twain in the Northwest, 1895," *Pacific Northwest Quarterly* [hereafter cited as *PNQ*],42 (July 1951), 193–94; *Seattle Post-Intelligencer*, Sept. 24, 1892, rep. from Wilbur *Register*.

21. *Tacoma Morning Globe*, July 2, 11, 24, 1891; *Seattle Post-Intelligencer*, Oct. 4, 1890, rep. from Cowlitz *Advocate*, Jan. 23, 1892; *Spokane Review*, Feb. 8, 1893; *Seattle Press-Times*, Sept. 9, 1893.

22. *Seattle Post-Intelligencer*, Jan. 23, 1890; Olympia *Washington Standard*, Dec. 19, 1890; Robert Bunting, *The Pacific Raincoast: Environment and Culture in an American Eden, 1778–1900* (Lawrence: University Press of Kansas, 1997), 145–46; *West Shore*, 17 (Aug. 23, 1890), 27; *Spokane Daily Chronicle*, June 9, 1898; Portland *Oregonian*, May 19, 1891; *Spokane Falls Review*, May 2; July 19, 1890; *Tacoma Daily News*, Aug. 11, 1890.

23. *Seattle Press-Times*, June 27, 1892; Olympia *Washington Standard*, Sept. 16, 1892; *Walla Walla Statesman*, April 18, 1893; *Tacoma Daily News*, Sept. 8, 1893; *Seattle Post-Intelligencer*, Sept. 15, 1890; *West Shore*, 15 (Sept. 21, 1889), 44; 16 (June 21, 1890), 778; (Aug. 2, 1890), 959; Joseph E. Taylor III, *Making Salmon: An Environmental History of the Northwest Fisheries Crisis* (Seattle: University of Washington Press, 1999), 138; *Spokane Review*, Dec. 11, 1892.

24. Railroad connections also stimulated Puget Sound output. Tacoma shipped a quarter million pounds of fish east on the Northern Pacific between August 1889 and February 1890. Olympia *Washington Standard,* July 24; Nov. 13, 1891; April 7, 1893; T.S. Morris, "Aberdeen, Washington," *Northwest,* 8 (Jan. 1890), 16; *Seattle Press,* Jan. 14, 1891; David R. Montgomery, *King of Fish: The Thousand-Year Run of Salmon* (Boulder: Westview Press, 2003), 136–37; Daniel L. Boxberger, *To Fish in Common: The Ethnohistory of Lummi Indian Salmon Fishing* (Seattle: University of Washington Press ed., 1999, 1989), 36; South Bend *Willapa Harbor Pilot,* April 22, 1898; *Tacoma Daily Ledger,* Feb. 25, 1890.

25. The legislature also created a fish commission to study the industry's problems. *Tacoma Daily News,* May 4, 1891, rep. from Fairhaven *Herald; Tacoma Daily Ledger,* Feb. 15; June 4, 1890; *Spokane Review,* Dec. 11, 22, 1892; April 12, 1893; Olympia *Washington Standard,* July 24, 1891; Feb. 3, 1893; *Tacoma Morning Globe,* July 16, 1890; *Seattle Telegraph,* Oct. 26, 1892; *Seattle Press,* Jan. 31, 1891; *Seattle Press-Times,* June 12, 1893; *Seattle Post-Intelligencer,* April 10, 1896; *West Shore,* 17 (Feb. 7, 1891), 94; Taylor, *Making Salmon,* 93.

26. Inventors kept busy devising machinery for the removal of stumps. *Seattle Post-Intelligencer,* Nov. 30, 1890; May 26, 1891; *Tacoma Daily Ledger,* Jan. 5; Aug. 17; Sept. 13, 1890; *Seattle Telegraph,* Jan. 26, 1892; *Seattle Times,* July 15, 16, 1895; *West Shore,* 16 (Nov. 1, 1890), 186; Olympia *Washington Standard,* Sept. 26, 1890; Feb. 27, 1891; *Tacoma Daily News,* Jan. 2, 1893; *Olympia Tribune,* July 17, 1892; Seattle *Argus,* Nov. 7, 21, 1896.

27. The eastern Washington traveler formerly having "to thread his way on a sweating broncho through the hills and canyons," the Colfax *Gazette* reported, now "boards a palace car," lolling "in cushioned chairs, eating peanuts and reading morning papers" en route to an urban destination. *Spokane Review,* Aug. 12, 1891; Kirk Munroe, "Eastern Washington and the Water Miracle of Yakima," *Harper's Weekly,* 38 (May 19, 1894), 466; *Seattle Press-Times,* Sept. 23, 1891; *Seattle Post-Intelligencer,* Aug. 26, 1890, rep. from Colfax *Gazette.*

28. *Spokane Review,* April 3, 1892, rep. from Davenport *Lincoln County Times;* Olympia *Washington Standard,* Sept. 26, 1890; Aug. 21, 1891; June 24, 1892; *Seattle Post-Intelligencer,* March 13, rep. from Colfax *Gazette,* 15, 19, rep. from Colfax *Gazette,* 1893; J. Orin Oliphant, *On the Cattle Ranges of the Oregon Country* (Seattle: University of Washington Press, 1968), 218–19; Portland *Oregonian,* Aug. 25, 1891.

29. *Spokane Review,* Aug. 28; Sept. 5; Dec. 23, 1891; May 1, 1892; *Seattle Post-Intelligencer,* Sept. 16, 1890, rep. from Dayton *Columbia Chronicle; Seattle Press-Times,* April 1, 1891; *Walla Walla Statesman,* May 5, 1893; Alexander Campbell McGregor, *Counting Sheep: From Open Range to Agribusiness on the Columbia Plateau* (Seattle: University of Washington Press, 1982), 26–28; John Fahey, *The Inland Empire: Unfolding Years, 1879–1929* (Seattle: University of Washington Press, 1986), 7.

30. Walla Walla County reported having more sheep in 1891 than cattle and horses combined. *Seattle Post-Intelligencer,* March 13, 1890, rep. from Davenport *Lincoln County Times; Yakima Herald,* March 6, 1890; D.W. Meinig, *The Great Columbia Plain: A Historical Geography, 1805–1910* (Seattle: University of Washington Press, 1968), 339–40; McGregor, *Counting Sheep,* 28–29, 37–38; *Spokane Review,* Feb. 14, 1892; *West Shore,* 16 (June 14, 1890), 740–43; Portland *Oregonian,* Aug. 28, 1891.

31. Immigrants also squatted on unsurveyed land, occupying a third of the 22 million acres in this category statewide. As of 1890, eastern Washington had three quarters of the state's improved farm acreage. *Seattle Post-Intelligencer,* Jan. 1, 1891; March 31, 1892, rep. from Colfax *Gazette;* Spokane *Spokesman-Review,* Sept. 2, 1894; *Spokane Falls Review,* Dec.

17, 1889, rep. from Spangle *Record;* *Seattle Morning Journal,* Jan. 11, 1890; E.V. Smalley, "In the Palouse Country," *Northwest,* 10 (Sept. 1892), 22; *Spokane Review,* Dec. 9, 1891; July 17, 1892, rep. from Olympia *Olympian;* March 20; July 18, 1893; Robert C. Nesbit and Charles M. Gates, "Agriculture in Eastern Washington, 1890–1910," *PNQ,* 37 (Oct. 1946), 279.

32. William G. Robbins, *Landscapes of Promise: The Oregon Story, 1800–1940* (Seattle: University of Washington Press, 1997), 146–48; Robert E. Ficken, *Washington Territory* (Pullman: Washington State University Press, 2002), 121–22; Meinig, *Great Columbia Plain,* 330; Nesbit and Gates, "Agriculture in Eastern Washington," 283; Portland *Oregonian,* May 6, 1890, rep. from Farmington *Register;* *West Shore,* 16 (July 19, 1890), 912; Smalley, "In the Palouse Country," 22–23.

33. *West Shore,* 16 (July 19, 1890), 912; *Seattle Press-Times,* Sept. 16, 23, 1891; Portland *Oregonian,* May 1; Aug. 15, 1891; *Spokane Review,* Nov. 21, 1891; Nesbit and Gates, "Agriculture in Eastern Washington," 283; Olympia *Washington Standard,* July 22, 1892.

34. Meinig, *Great Columbia Plain,* 372–73; Glen Lindeman, "Golden Harvest: Wheat Farming on the Columbia Plateau," *Columbia,* 6 (Summer 1992), 25; Smalley, "In the Big Bend Country," 14, 18; *West Shore,* 16 (June 28, 1890), 818; Nesbit and Gates, "Agriculture in Eastern Washington," 284; *Northwest,* 9 (July 1891), 55, rep. from Coulee City *News,* *Spokane Review,* April 7, 1893.

35. *Seattle Post-Intelligencer,* July 23, 1890, rep. from Walla Walla *Union;* May 20, 1892; *Seattle Telegraph,* June 10, 1892; *Spokane Review,* Aug. 28, 1891; *Tacoma Morning Globe,* Jan. 1, 1892; *West Shore,* 15 (Nov. 23, 1889), 329.

36. According to one estimate, a farmer had to average 28 bushels to the acre, selling this output at 53¢ a bushel, in order to generate a $2 per acre net return. *West Shore,* 15 (Dec. 7, 1889), 398; *Seattle Telegraph,* May 21, 1892; Pomeroy *Washington Independent,* Jan. 16, 1890; Olympia *Washington Standard,* July 10, 1891; *Tacoma Daily Ledger,* Jan. 7, 1890; *Ellensburgh Capital,* Jan. 14, 1892; *Walla Walla Statesman,* Sept. 12, 1893.

37. The first bulk cargo of Washington wheat for the English market was shipped from Puget Sound in June 1891. *Northwest,* 10 (Feb. 1892), 22; Meinig, *Great Columbia Plain,* 397–98; Fahey, *Inland Empire,* 56–57; *Spokane Falls Review,* Jan. 3, 1891; *Ellensburgh Capital,* Aug. 31, 1893; *West Shore,* 15 (Nov. 23, 1889), 328; Olympia *Washington Standard,* Dec. 12, 1890; *Tacoma Daily Ledger,* Aug. 15, 1893.

38. A small amount of wheat went east on the transcontinental railroads. Dayton *Columbia Chronicle,* June 11, 1892; Meinig, *Great Columbia Plain,* 354; *Spokane Falls Review,* July 5, 1890; *Seattle Press,* Feb. 5, 1891; *Yakima Herald,* Nov. 20, 1890.

39. Colfax *Palouse Gazette,* Nov. 28, 1890; *Walla Walla Statesman,* Aug. 5, 1891; Meinig, *Great Columbia Plain,* 353–54; *Tacoma Morning Globe,* July 12, 1819; *Tacoma Daily News,* May 12, 1892; *West Shore,* 16 (Dec. 6, 1890), 258, 262–63.

40. Colfax *Palouse Gazette,* Aug. 1, 1890; Fahey, *Inland Empire,* 49–52; *Tacoma Daily News,* Aug. 29; Sept. 19, 1890; July 23, 1891; July 10, 1893; Thomas Burke to Mary M. Miller, Sept. 25, 1891, Thomas Burke Papers, University of Washington Library.

41. *Spokane Review,* Aug. 23, 1891; *Spokane Falls Review,* Dec. 31, 1889, rep. from Palouse City *News,* June 11; Sept. 28, 30, rep. from Colfax *Gazette,* 1890; *West Shore,* 16 (Nov. 8, 1890), 202; *Tacoma Daily Ledger,* Aug. 21, 1890; *Seattle Post-Intelligencer,* July 22, 1890, rep. from Pomeroy *Washingtonian.*

42. One expert calculated that nearly 2,000 trains, each composed of 15 cars, were needed to haul the output of the Palouse to tidewater in timely fashion. Suggesting the difficulty of the task, the Northern Pacific was presently equipped to pull barely a hundred cars a

day over Stampede Pass. The Union Pacific admitted on the eve of the harvest to being 4,000 cars short of the capacity required to take care of the anticipated crop. *West Shore,* 16 (Dec. 6, 1890), 262–63; *Seattle Post-Intelligencer,* Sept. 19; Nov. 29, 1890; *Northwest,* 9 (Jan. 1891), 36; Colfax *Palouse Gazette,* Sept. 26; Nov. 28, 1890; *Seattle Telegraph,* Dec. 4, 1890; *Tacoma Daily News,* Aug. 19, 1890.

43. *Tacoma Daily Ledger,* Nov. 25; Dec. 3, 1890; *Yakima Herald,* Nov. 20, 1890; *Spokane Falls Review,* Oct. 19, 23; Nov. 5, 18, 1890; *West Shore,* 16 (Dec. 6, 1890), 262; 17 (Jan. 24, 1891), 63; *Northwest,* 9 (Jan. 1891), 36; *Seattle Telegraph,* Nov. 27, 1890.

44. *Spokane Review,* May 7; Nov. 21; Dec. 24, 1891; *Tacoma Daily Ledger,* Nov. 28, 1890; *West Shore,* 17 (Jan. 3, 1891), 11.

45. The less assertive Grange had a mere 30 chapters statewide. "Farmers," a Palouse newspaper reported, "are forming companies and building warehouses at every railroad siding and on every available piece of ground." Colfax *Palouse Gazette,* April 25, 1890; Portland *Oregonian,* Aug. 19; Sept. 17, 1891; *Spokane Falls Review,* Dec. 17, 1890; Olympia *Washington Standard,* Feb. 6; April 3, 1891; April 29, 1892; April 14, 1893; *Northwest,* 9 (April 1891), 34; *Seattle Press-Times,* May 13, 1891; *The Dalles Times-Mountaineer,* Aug. 1, 1891, rep. from Colfax *Gazette.*

46. Fifty-three vessels carried grain from the Columbia River in 1890, compared to 25 from Puget Sound. The Portland advantage was somewhat exaggerated, however, as its figure included wheat from both the Willamette Valley and interior points. When the *Oregonian* occasionally neglected its promotional mission to the extent of reporting "a massive deadlock at the mouth of the river," Washington papers eagerly reprinted the oversight. The Washington press also noted the symbolism when the Navy refused to allow the battleship *Oregon* to cross the bar and steam up the Columbia to Portland. Meinig, *Great Columbia Plain,* 354; *West Shore,* 15 (Sept. 14, 1889), 8–10; Portland *Oregonian,* Jan. 15, 1893; *Tacoma Daily Ledger,* May 19, 1890; Nov. 2, 1891; Jan. 10; Feb. 1, 3, 1892; April 28, 1897; *Tacoma Daily News,* Feb. 4, 1890; *Tacoma Morning Globe,* Aug. 1, 1890; *Seattle Press-Times,* Sept. 28; Nov. 6, 1891; *Spokane Review,* Oct. 27, 1891, rep. from *Oregonian.*

47. *Fairhaven Herald,* March 26, 1891; Munroe, "Cities of the Sound," 35; *Seattle Press-Times,* Nov. 18, 1891; *Tacoma Daily Ledger,* Nov. 2, 1891; Jan. 10, 1892; Sept. 4, 1893.

48. An Astoria newspaper reported in 1890 that wheat was "worth 4 cents per bushel more in Seattle than it is in Portland." Some Walla Walla grain shipped to Portland over the OR & N-Union Pacific system went to Tacoma via the old Columbia River-Puget Sound branch line. Flour shipments also increased, from three cargoes in 1890 to eleven in 1892. *Tacoma Daily Ledger,* Sept. 10, 1890; Oct. 29, 1891; Jan. 10; June 4, 1892; *Tacoma Morning Globe,* April 19, 1890; Sept. 30; Dec. 21, 25, 1891; Jan. 1, 1892; Spokane *Spokesman-Review,* Aug. 20, 1895; *Tacoma Daily News,* July 24, 1890; Sept. 28, 1892; Olympia *Washington Standard,* Jan. 1, 1892; Portland *Oregonian,* Sept. 8, 1891; *Seattle Post-Intelligencer,* Nov. 20, 1890, rep. from Astoria *Columbian.*

49. *Tacoma Daily Ledger,* May 6, 1891; *Seattle Morning Journal,* Oct. 28, 1889; *Seattle Post-Intelligencer,* Dec. 11, 1889; *Spokane Falls Review,* May 7, 1890; *West Shore,* 16 (March 29, 1890), 394; *Seattle Telegraph,* Aug. 14, 1890; Oct. 7, 1891; *Tacoma Daily News,* June 8, 1893; *Northwest,* 10 (March 1892), 35; Portland *Oregonian,* April 18, 1891; *Seattle Press-Times,* Feb. 27, 1891; Walker to Talbot, March 9, 1891, Walker Letterbooks.

50. "Every farmer who raises a bushel of wheat which is shipped to these [Puget Sound] points," a Spokane paper noted, "contributes his share toward enhancing their value." *Seattle Post-Intelligencer,* May 2, 1893, rep. from Sprague *Mail;* Olympia *Morning*

Olympian, Aug. 27, 1891; *Seattle Telegraph*, Oct. 21, 1890; *Spokane Falls Review*, Feb. 13, 1890.

51. *Tacoma Daily News*, March 24, 1893; *Tacoma Morning Globe*, Feb. 10, 1890, rep. from Ellensburgh *Register*, July 16, 1891; Munroe, "Eastern Washington and the Water Miracle," 466; *West Shore*, 15 (July 14, 1889), 5.

52. According to government figures, Washington irrigation ditches cost $4.03 per acre of reclaimed land to excavate, and 75¢ an acre for yearly maintenance. *Yakima Herald*, Jan. 2, 1890; *Seattle Post-Intelligencer*, March 25, 1890, rep. from Yakima *Republic*, Ellensburgh *Capital*, April 9, 1891; *Seattle Press-Times*, Aug. 3, 1893; *Tacoma Daily Ledger*, Sept. 9, 1891; *Tacoma Daily News*, July 18, 1892.

53. Federal surveyors rated a bit over a million acres of Washington land as adaptable to irrigation. However, Washington had barely a quarter of the irrigated acreage found in Oregon. *Spokane Review*, July 20, 1892; *Tacoma Daily Ledger*, July 21, 1890; *Walla Walla Statesman*, May 5, 1893; *Seattle Post-Intelligencer*, July 29; Aug. 2, 1892; Olympia *Washington Standard*, Feb. 19, 1892; Nesbit and Gates, "Agriculture in Eastern Washington," 286; Olympia *Morning Olympian*, March 26, 1892; Portland *Oregonian*, April 22, 1891.

54. Tree planting, widely and dismally implemented on the Great Plains, was generally dismissed in the Pacific Northwest as a "delusional theory" of reclamation. Professional rainmakers occasionally plied their peculiar talents east of the Cascades, to no recorded benefit. The average cost of watering an acre of land by artesian well was $18.88, more than twice the amount by irrigation ditch. Pullman claimed to be "the town of flowing wells." *Seattle Post-Intelligencer*, March 30; July 29, 1892; *Yakima Herald*, Jan. 2, 1890; Aug. 27, 1891; *Spokane Review*, Feb. 12; April 26, 1893; *West Shore*, 16 (Oct. 18, 1890), 156; *Northwest*, 8 (Jan. 1890), 26; Portland *Oregonian*, March 25; April 17; Aug. 19; Sept. 2, 1891; *Spokane Falls Review*, May 14, 1890; Feb. 28, 1891; *Ellensburgh Capital*, Feb. 12, 1891; April 5, 1894.

55. Many reclamation supporters called for the transfer of arid land from the public domain to state control, a concept adopted under the federal Carey Act of 1894. *Spokane Review*, June 27, 1893; *Tacoma Daily Ledger*, Dec. 13, 1889; *Seattle Press-Times*, Sept. 18, 1891; *Yakima Herald*, Feb. 13; March 6, 1890; *Tacoma Daily News*, June 13, 1891; *Northwest*, 9 (Feb. 1891), 6; *Spokane Falls Review*, April 11, 1890; Rose M. Boening, "History of Irrigation in the State of Washington," *Washington Historical Quarterly* [hereafter cited as *WHQ*], 10 (Jan. 1919), 40; Donald J. Pisani, *To Reclaim a Divided West: Water, Law, and Public Policy, 1848–1902* (Albuquerque: University of New Mexico Press, 1992), 252; and *From the Family Farm to Agribusiness: The Irrigation Crusade in California and the West, 1850–1931* (Berkeley: University of California Press, 1984), chapt. 9; Norris Hundley, Jr., *The Great Thirst: Californians and Water, 1770s–1990s* (Berkeley: University of California Press, 1992), 97–102.

56. Reflecting the anti-monopoly ideology, many Wenatchee settlers wanted to replace company irrigation with district reclamation. Burke to Don C. Corbett, April 1, 1891, Burke Papers; Fahey, *Inland Empire*, 96–97; Robert E. Ficken, "Rufus Woods, Wenatchee, and the Columbia Basin Reclamation Vision," *PNQ*, 87 (Spring 1996), 72–73; *Ellensburgh Capital*, Aug. 11, 1892; April 26, 1894; Olympia *Washington Standard*, April 14, 1893; *Spokane Review*, April 15, 1893; McGregor, *Counting Sheep*, 220; *Spokane Falls Review*, June 12, 1890; *Seattle Post-Intelligencer*, Feb. 24, 1893; *Seattle Press-Times*, April 10, 1893; *Northwest*, 10 (Nov. 1892), 20; *Walla Walla Statesman*, April 29, 1893; C.F.B. Haskell to D.H. Gilman, July 19, 1894, Daniel H. Gilman Papers, University of Washington Library. On another significant project, the attempted irrigation of land near Kennewick,

see Dorothy Zeisler-Vralsted, "Reclaiming the Arid West: The Role of the Northern Pacific Railway in Irrigating Kennewick, Washington," *PNQ,* 84 (Oct. 1993), 131–32.

57. Yakima County, a Puget Sound editor agreed, was "the most prolific in the state." Located on the Yakima River in the upper Kittitas County section, Ellensburg bristled at suggestions it was "in the Yakima valley." In 1892, settlers reoccupied the site of Yakima City, the valley's original urban center three miles south of North Yakima, abandoned in 1885 at the behest of the railroad. *Spokane Review,* Oct. 30; Dec. 13, 1892; Boening, "History of Irrigation," 25–26; *Yakima Herald,* June 12, 1890; Munroe, "Eastern Washington and the Water Miracle," 466; *Northwest,* 8 (May 1890), 31; *Olympia Tribune,* Oct. 7, 1891; *Ellensburgh Capital,* March 29, 1894; Ficken, *Washington Territory,* 161–63; Olympia *Washington Standard,* March 25, 1892.

58. The Desert Land Act of 1877 authorized purchase of up to 640 acres of arid land for $1.25 an acre, provided crop-sufficient water was supplied to the tract within three years. Munroe, "Eastern Washington and the Water Miracle," 466; *Northwest,* 10 (April 1892), 36; *Seattle Press-Times,* Sept. 21; Oct. 1, 1891; *Tacoma Morning Globe,* Sept. 2, 1890; Aug. 21, 1891; *Yakima Herald,* Jan. 9, 1890; *West Shore,* 16 (May 24, 1890), 661; *Spokane Falls Review,* June 28, 1890; Portland *Oregonian,* Aug. 19, 1891; Pisani, *To Reclaim a Divided West,* 88–89. For details on Yakima irrigation projects, see Boening, "History of Irrigation," 21–23; and Calvin B. Coulter, "The Victory of National Irrigation in the Yakima Valley, 1902–1906," *PNQ,* 42 (April 1951), 99–102.

59. The NP provided much of the land to be reclaimed and guaranteed the irrigation company's bonds. Schulze publicly denounced the commissioner of Indian affairs as "a crank philanthropist." *Yakima Herald,* May 15, 1890; *Tacoma Daily Ledger,* May 8, 1890; Nov. 8, 1891; March 27, 1892; *Tacoma Daily News,* March 21, 1892; *Northwest,* 10 (April 1892), 36–37; *West Shore,* 17 (Sept. 6, 1890), 58; Munroe, "Eastern Washington and the Water Miracle," 466; Olympia *Washington Standard,* Feb. 19, 1892; *Spokane Review,* March 29, 1892.

60. *Tacoma Daily News,* March 21, 1892; *Spokane Review,* July 19, 1892; April 6, 22, 1893; *Seattle Telegraph,* Sept. 7, 1890; Aug. 17, 1893; *Seattle Press-Times,* Feb. 6, 1892.

61. In one advertising ploy, the Northern Pacific shipped a four-box Yakima Valley sampler to Bismarck, the German chancellor. At this early period of orchard activity, peaches made up the lead crop, in part because apple trees required several years of growth to come into full bearing stage. Reflecting the new importance of fruit, a Snake River orchard was sold in 1892 for the highest farmland price yet recorded in Whitman County. Orondo, a fruit raising community on the Columbia upstream from Wenatchee, was statistically the fastest growing town in the state. *Tacoma Daily News,* June 5, 1891, rep. from Montesano *Vidette;* Olympia *Washington Standard,* June 19, 1891; March 25; June 17; Sept. 2, 1892; *Spokane Review,* July 25, 1891; July 19, 22, 1892; March 27, 1893; *Seattle Telegraph,* July 29; Oct. 2; Nov. 27, 1891; *Wenatchee Advance,* May 26, 1894; *Seattle Post-Intelligencer,* July 24; Aug. 18, 1890; Feb. 4, 1894; Portland *Oregonian,* April 30, 1890.

62. *West Shore,* 16 (Jan. 25, 1890), 107; 17 (Feb. 14, 1891), 113; *Tacoma Daily Ledger,* Oct. 17, 1891; *Tacoma Morning Globe,* Oct. 1, 1891; Feb. 9, 1892; *Seattle Press-Times,* Feb. 24, 1891.

63. *Seattle Press-Times,* Sept. 22, 1892, rep. from Wenatchee *Graphic;* Olympia *Washington Standard,* Aug. 7, 1891; *Seattle Telegraph,* Aug. 18, 1891; Dec. 20, 1892; July 10, rep. from Sumner *Hellas;* Aug. 24, 1893.

64. *West Shore*, 16 (May 10, 1890), 598; *Spokane Review*, Aug. 28; Oct. 23, 1891; March 2; July 22; Aug. 9, 1892; *Seattle Telegraph*, July 28, 1891; *Tacoma Morning Globe*, Oct. 1, 1891; *Spokane Falls Review*, July 11, 1890; *Wenatchee Advance*, May 26, 1894.

65. Suggesting the prospector's capacity for self-delusion, miners claimed to have come across an active volcano with "lava running down its sides." *Ellensburgh Capital*, July 30; Aug. 6, 20; Sept. 3, 1891; Olympia *Washington Standard*, Aug. 28; Oct. 2, 1891; *Seattle Post-Intelligencer*, Jan. 7, 29, 1893.

66. *Spokane Review*, May 29; July 4, 1891; Olympia *Washington Standard*, Aug. 26, 1892; William F. Phelps, "In the Cascade Mountains: A Tramp in Search of Silver Mines," *Northwest*, 10 (Dec. 1892), 5; *Tacoma Morning Globe*, Sept. 2, 1891; *Seattle Telegraph*, July 28, 1891; *Seattle Press-Times*, Aug. 22, 1891.

67. *Northwest*, 9 (Feb. 1891), 6–7; *West Shore*, 17 (Oct. 4, 1890), 123; *Seattle Telegraph*, Aug. 22, 1891; *Tacoma Morning Globe*, Oct. 1, 1891; Phelps, "In the Cascade Mountains," 5.

68. *Everett News*, Jan. 1, 8, 1892; *Everett Herald*, Jan. 28; May 12, 1892; June 7, 1894; Gilman to Burke, Jan. 22, 1892, Burke Papers; Walker to Talbot, May 7, 1892, Walker Letterbooks; June 4, 1892, Puget Mill Co. Records; Norman H. Clark, *Mill Town* (Seattle: University of Washington Press, 1970), 10, 32.

69. *Everett Herald*, April 28, 1892; *Seattle Telegraph*, Sept. 24, 1891; Port Townsend *Morning Leader*, Jan. 1, 1890; Diane F. Britton, *The Iron and Steel Industry in the Far West: Irondale, Washington* (Niwot: University Press of Colorado, 1991), chapt. 1; Joseph Daniels, "History of Pig Iron Manufacture on the Pacific Coast," *WHQ*, 17 (July 1926), 178–79; *Tacoma Daily Ledger*, March 5, 1890.

70. *Seattle Post-Intelligencer*, May 29, 1890; *West Shore*, 16 (June 21, 1890), 790; *Tacoma Morning Globe*, Aug. 23, 1890; William R. Sherrard, "The Kirkland Steel Mill: Adventure in Western Enterprise," *PNQ*, 53 (Oct. 1962), 134–35; Britton, *Iron and Steel Industry*, 33–35.

71. Seattleites hoped to complement the Kirkland development with a smelter on Lake Washington. *Tacoma Daily Ledger*, Jan. 3; Sept. 19, 1890; *Tacoma Daily News*, Sept. 16, 1890; July 6, 1891; *Tacoma Morning Globe*, Sept. 19, 1890; Jan. 1, 1892; *Spokane Falls Review*, Nov. 1, 1889; Jan. 30; May 8; July 1; Sept. 17, 1890; *West Shore*, 16 (April 5, 1890), 438; (April 26, 1890), 533; Spokane Falls *Spokesman*, May 10, 1890; *Spokane Review*, Aug. 8, 1891; *Seattle Post-Intelligencer*, Dec. 1, 1890; May 14, 1891.

72. Smaller towns also had hinterland aspirations. Ellensburg, for example, actively sought the trade of the Okanogan. *Spokane Falls Review*, Jan. 12, 1890; April 24, 1891; *Spokane Review*, Jan. 1; Oct. 23, 1892; *Tacoma Morning Globe*, Aug. 6, 1890; *Tacoma Daily Ledger*, May 17, 1890; *Seattle Post-Intelligencer*, July 24, 1890; *Seattle Telegraph*, July 2, 1893; *Ellensburgh Capital*, March 31, 1892. On the hinterland theme in regional historiography, see Carlos A. Schwantes, *The Pacific Northwest: An Interpretive History* (Lincoln: University of Nebraska Press, 1989, 1996).

73. *Spokane Falls Review*, May 28, 1890; Carlos A. Schwantes, *Radical Heritage: Labor, Socialism, and Reform in Washington and British Columbia, 1885–1917* (Seattle: University of Washington Press, 1979), 29–32; Walker to Talbot, April 27, 1890; Aug. 3, 1893; to Jackson, Aug. 1, 1893, Walker Letterbooks.

74. *Tacoma Daily Ledger*, Dec. 24, 1889; April 18; May 26; July 14; Nov. 10, 1890; *West Shore*, 17 (Sept. 20, 1890), 90; Walker to Talbot, April 17, 1890, Walker Letterbooks; *Tacoma Daily News*, April 10, 1890; *Spokane Falls Review*, May 6, 1890; *Seattle Post-Intelligencer*, Jan. 29, 1891; Portland *Oregonian*, May 10, 1890, rep. from Walla Walla *Union*;

Emerson to Holt, Sept. 3, 1891; to Simpson, May 2, 1892, Emerson Letterbooks. On the Knights of Labor and the 10 hour day, see Ficken, *Forested Land,* 70–72.

75. According to an 1892 account, residents of the coal company town of Roslyn were "actually suffering for food, and a large number are subsisting on nettles." Carlos A. Schwantes, "The Concept of the Wageworkers' Frontier: A Framework for Future Research," *Western Historical Quarterly,* 18 (Jan. 1987), 39–55; *Tacoma Daily News,* Feb. 25, 1890; May 13, 14, 1892; *Seattle Press-Times,* May 13, 1892; Olympia *Washington Standard,* May 13, 1892; *Spokane Review,* May 12, 17, 1892; *Seattle Telegraph,* May 20, 1892; *Seattle Post-Intelligencer,* April 17, 1892, rep. from Ellensburgh *Capital.*

76. Schwantes, *Radical Heritage,* 32; *Seattle Morning Journal,* Nov. 30, 1889; *Tacoma Daily News,* Jan. 28; Feb. 25; May 5; July 19, 1890; July 7, 1892; *Tacoma Daily Ledger,* Jan. 30, 1890; *Seattle Press-Times,* Sept. 18, 1891, rep. from Bellingham Bay *Express,* July 7, 1892; *Seattle Telegraph,* April 4, 9; Nov. 1, 1891; July 8, 1892; *Ellensburgh Capital,* July 14, 1892; *Tacoma Morning Globe,* July 17, 1891.

77. *Spokane Falls Review,* Sept. 18–20, 1890; *Spokane Spokesman,* Dec. 2, 1890; *Tacoma Daily Ledger,* April 6, 1891; Feb. 12, 1892; Olympia *Washington Standard,* Aug. 7, 1891; June 10; Sept. 9, 1892; Portland *Oregonian,* Sept. 3, 1891.

78. In 1889, Washington shipments to the Golden State fell to less than half the combined B.C.-Australian figure. Holding large contracts to supply the railroads, the Roslyn mine on the eastern slopes of the Cascades became the leading source of state output. *West Shore,* 16 (Jan. 18, 1890), 77; (Oct. 18, 1890), 156; *Seattle Morning Journal,* Oct. 22; Dec. 20, 23, 1889; *Northwest,* 8 (Aug. 1890), 38; Portland *Oregonian,* Oct. 1, 1891; *Spokane Falls Review,* April 1, 1891; Schwantes, *Radical Heritage,* 29–32; Alan Hynding, *The Public Life of Eugene Semple: Promoter and Politician of the Pacific Northwest* (Seattle: University of Washington Press, 1973), 97–113; John Hanscom, "Company Coal Town: Franklin and the Oregon Improvement Company," *Columbia,* 8 (Spring 1994), 15–16; H.W. McNeill to Elijah Smith, April 27, 1890, Oregon Improvement Co. Records, University of Washington Library.

79. "The persistence with which the San Francisco end finds reasons why they cannot do anything that will pay this branch of the O.I. Co. is wonderful," the Seattle resident manager complained of the firm's habitual incompetence. "It is only equalled by the ingenuity with which they explain the reason for it." Six of the miners killed in the 1892 Roslyn explosion were black. McNeill to Smith, Dec. 10, 1889; March 5; June 12 (two letters of this date), 1890; C.J. Smith to Smith, Sept. 27; Oct. 8, 17, 30, 1890; to W.H. Starbuck, Jan. 16, 28; April 11; May 7, 1891, all Oregon Improvement Co. Records; Hanscom, "Company Town," 15–16; Schwantes, *Radical Heritage,* 30; Robert A. Campbell, "Blacks and the Coal Mines of Western Washington, 1888–1896," *PNQ,* 73 (Oct. 1982), 148–50. The Roslyn experiment had interesting consequences. By 1891, at least 15 of the imported miners had filed homestead claims in the vicinity. Roslyn resident A.A. Garner became one of the first black attorneys in the state. Olympia *Washington Standard,* Nov. 20, 1891; May 13, 1892; Portland *Oregonian,* Aug. 16, 1891.

80. Some commentators saw no point in subtlety. "This state has all the coons it wants," a Port Townsend weekly exclaimed. "Matters are in a deplorable condition," another newspaper pronounced, "when a large body of white men are thrown out on the world without employment, and their places supplied by negroes." Fearing, apparently, that drunken blacks would engage in all sorts of mayhem, King County ordered the closure of all saloons on the eve of Franklin's first new pay day. C. Smith to Starbuck, May 27, 1891, Oregon Improvement Co. Records; Campbell, "Blacks and the Coal Mines," 150–52;

Hanscom, "Company Town," 16; *Tacoma Daily Ledger*, May 21, 1891; *Seattle Post-Intelligencer*, May 19, 31, rep. from San Juan *Graphic*, 1891; Portland *Oregonian*, Aug. 23, 1891, rep. from Port Townsend *Leader*, Olympia *Washington Standard*, June 26, 1891.

81. C. Smith to Starbuck, May 27, 1891, Oregon Improvement Co. Records; *Seattle Telegraph*, June 30; July 4, 1891; Campbell, "Blacks and the Coal Mines," 153; Hanscom, "Company Town," 17.

82. Washington spent a substantially larger sum of money on the National Guard than Oregon. "The 'boys in blue,'" a Tacoma paper claimed, "are...being used as hired Hessians under the command of a hired corporation lawyer." *West Shore*, 16 (July 12, 1890), 868; 17 (Sept. 6, 1890), 52; 17 (Jan. 17, 1891), 34–35; *Tacoma Daily Ledger*, April 3, 1890; July 4, 1891; *Seattle Press-Times*, Aug. 14, 1891; *Seattle Telegraph*, July 1, 10, 1891; *Tacoma Daily News*, July 1, 1891; *Yakima Herald*, July 16, 1891; *Spokane Review*, Sept. 23, 1891.

83. *Tacoma Morning Globe*, July 10, 1891; *Seattle Telegraph*, July 3, 9, 23; Sept. 21, 1891; C. Smith to C.B. Tedcastle, Sept. 17, 1891, Oregon Improvement Co. Records; Campbell, "Blacks and the Coal Mines," 153–54; Hanscom, "Company Town," 17; Olympia *Morning Olympian*, Aug. 5, 1891; *Tacoma Daily Ledger*, Sept. 21, 1891.

84. *Tacoma Daily News*, Aug. 24, 1892; *Spokane Falls Review*, April 27; Sept. 2, 1890; *Olympia Tribune*, Aug. 25, 1890; Seattle *Argus*, April 28, 1894.

85. *Seattle Telegraph*, July 2, 1891; *Spokane Review*, July 23, 1892; Dayton *Columbia Chronicle*, July 30, 1892; *Aberdeen Herald*, July 21, 1892; *Tacoma Daily Ledger*, April 27, 1891; Jan. 6, 1892.

86. Residents of the neighboring state to the west always paid close attention to events in northern Idaho. Commenting upon the unrest in the Coeur d'Alenes, one Washington editor was "glad that the panhandle was not given us when we wanted it," a reference to the annexation campaigns of bygone territorial days. Mark Wyman, *Hard Rock Epic: Western Miners and the Industrial Revolution, 1860–1910* (Berkeley: University of California Press, 1979), 169–70; J. Anthony Lukas, *Big Trouble* (New York: Simon and Schuster, 1997), 98–105; *Spokane Review*, July 12–17, 20, rep. from Tekoa *Globe*, 1892; *Seattle Press-Times*, July 15, 1892; *Seattle Post-Intelligencer*, July 15, 1892; *Ellensburgh Capital*, July 21, 1892.

87. *Tacoma Daily News*, July 13, 14, 24, 28, rep. from Westport *World*, 1892; *Spokane Review*, July 17, 1892, rep. from Walla Walla *Statesman*.

88. *Tacoma Daily News*, July 22, 1890; June 29, 1892, rep. from Aberdeen *Herald*; *Seattle Morning Journal*, Oct. 21, 1889; *Seattle Telegraph*, March 14, 1891; Nov. 27, 1892; May 4, 1894; *Spokane Review*, July 23, 1893; *Tacoma Daily Ledger*, March 15, 1890.

89. *Tacoma Daily Ledger*, March 2, 3, 5, 12, 15, 1890; *Seattle Telegraph*, Nov. 27, 1892; *Tacoma Morning Globe*, Aug. 27, 1891; *Spokane Falls Review*, Dec. 13, 1890.

90. Railroad affiliated steamer links were also introduced at Portland and Vancouver, the former under Union Pacific and the latter under Canadian Pacific auspices. *Spokane Falls Review*, Dec. 13, 1890; Feb. 22, 1891; *Tacoma Daily Ledger*, Sept. 14, 1890; May 24; June 17; Aug. 6, 1892; *Seattle Press-Times*, June 20, 1892; *Seattle Telegraph*, June 19, 26, 1892; *Seattle Post-Intelligencer*, Oct. 16, 1893; Hunt and Kaylor, *Washington West of the Cascades*, 1:364; *West Shore*, 17 (Jan. 31, 1891), 80; *Ellensburgh Capital*, Aug. 13, 1891.

Watson C. Squire, selected for the U.S. senate in 1889. He earlier had served a term as territorial governor, 1884–1887. *University of Washington Libraries (UW3792)*

Chapter Three

The Promise of Future Greatness

The possibilities which await this state when its great resources shall have been fully developed are beyond calculation. Even at this date, with the work of improvement just begun and with its varied industries just in their infancy, the promise given of future greatness is most brilliant, and the present successes are most encouraging.—Spokane Review.[1]

Residents of Washington, regardless of whether they lived east or west of the Cascades, agreed upon a fundamental point. Their recently admitted state was, in every possible way, superior to southern California. Large numbers of Americans had flocked to Los Angeles and San Diego in 1887, drawn by cheap rail fares and vivid promotion. Old Hispanic communities were transformed into Pacific outposts of midwestern culture. "The people actually went wild," a Seattle editor recalled of the excitement. "Men stood in line all night…for the mere privilege and opportunity to buy lots." Another bemused Puget Sound observer traced the boom to a misbegotten "dream of idleness, a conception of life of dolce far niente" in a "semi-tropical" paradise beyond winter and care. The enticing vision soon turned into nothing more tangible than a citrus fruit mania clogged market, which depressed the economy and, in the view from the Pacific Northwest, destroyed hope.[2]

No wonder, then, that the so-called tide of immigration had shifted yet again, this time in Washington's direction. "The climatic conditions of Southern California, while pleasing to the Latin races," the *Spokane Falls Review* suggested, "offer nothing that is of lasting satisfaction to…men of Anglo-Saxon, Celtic and Teuton ancestry." Abandoning Los Angeles homes, transplanted midwesterners turned away from the unpromised land of "the long siesta and the endless glare of the sun," joining the exodus to America's newest, and best, state. Nature, after all, had specifically designed Washington for settlers wanting to "seek work, not to shirk it."[3]

A vigorous, activity stimulating climate was hardly the sole factor accounting for the newfound popularity of the Pacific Northwest. Placing their faith in real estate and oranges, Californians had briefly followed what one critic derided as "the cart-before-the-horse principle." Southern California's misconceived boom was "purely speculative," the *Seattle Post-Intelligencer* claimed in a negative assessment. "The country had no agriculture; there were no minerals; there were no facilities for commerce; no timber; no coal; no iron." Puget Sound, in contrast, possessed untapped forests and mines. Eastern Washington properly boasted of its vast fields of grain. The railroad connections were better, the distance to Asia shorter and the opportunities for capital more substantial. The state possessed a guaranteed "solid and permanent" future, secure against all challenges, foreign and domestic.[4]

Washington, a commentator noted in celebrating the fourth anniversary of admission to the Union, was "almost a virgin state." Age aside, the commonwealth was anything but virginal in the conduct of its often seedy political life. Certain truisms determined the course of governance. Possessing two-fifths of the population, King, Pierce and Spokane counties dominated affairs. Because Seattle would, as the saying went, always "vote one way and Tacoma the other," Spokane held the balance of power, siding with one or the other of the Puget Sound cities. The otherwise enviable position of the Inland Empire metropolis was, however, complicated by a long standing personal rivalry. Spokane's John L. Wilson, an Indiana born attorney, was the state's first elected member of congress. George Turner, onetime territorial supreme court judge and thereafter Washington's most prominent Northern Pacific critic, contested Wilson's aspirations for the Republican nomination. The incumbent made good use of federal patronage and hardball tactics in prevailing for a second time in 1890. Turner received more votes at the Spokane County convention, but Wilson won three of the five wards—securing the third when his followers, controlling the proceedings, disqualified a sufficient number of opposition delegates—and received the nomination. Seattleites and Tacomans attempting to form alliances with the Inland Empire faced a daunting obstacle in deciding between the locally influential antagonists.[5]

Though two-thirds of the population resided west of the Cascades at statehood, a "tacit" or "sentimental" arrangement required that one of the U.S. senators be from eastern Washington. While westsiders "could elect both…regardless of geographical location," the *Seattle P-I* observed of a necessary concession to state unity, "it is doubtful if such a move would meet with general approval." When the 1890 census resulted in Washington gaining a second U.S. representative in congress, the legislature failed in attempts to devise districts with roughly equal numbers of residents. Because of the regional demographic imbalance, any division would have to run on an east-west, rather than north-south, line, raising the distinct possibility that both positions would fall to Puget Sounders. An at-large system was instead selected, to operate by the same informal rule applied to senatorial contests. Spokane's John Wilson, elected to a third term in 1892—the first election under the procedure—was joined in the house by William Doolittle, a Tacoma lawyer and Civil War veteran.[6]

Republicanism stood supremely triumphant in 1889, facilitating such behind-the-scenes arrangements. Governor Elisha Ferry, who had occupied the appointed territorial gubernatorial chair for two terms in the 1870s, was the "Grand Old Man" of state and party affairs. One of the few remaining politicians able to profit from the precious Lincoln connection, thanks to pre-war associations at the Illinois bar, Ferry was well past his prime, in poor health and consigned by circumstance and preference to a figurehead role. Leadership fell by default to the rather more dynamic senators, Watson Squire and John Allen, the former from Seattle and the latter residing in Walla Walla. Elected in October 1889, the first state legislature—the body that sent Squire and Allen to the nation's capital—was to say the least overwhelmingly Republican. All but one of the 35 senate seats, and 63 of 70 in the house of representatives, belonged, by popular mandate, to the party. Except for the 20 members who might by a broad definition be considered farmers or stock grazers, the members supported corporations in general and railroads in particular.[7]

Insider government was further encouraged by a general public indifference to politics. Less than half the eligible males, according to one contemporary estimate, bothered to register, much less vote. Largely composed of recent arrivals, the citizenry was preoccupied with claims, business enterprises and the search for remunerative employment. "Most of us are strangers to each other," an Everett editor wrote in assessing the all-to-obvious lack of civic spirit. "We, as individuals, are too busy trying to get a lot or two...to waste our time on any occupation less absorbing." Involvement in public affairs, no matter how limited in extent, moreover was bound to be sordid at worst and unedifying at best. "The political stream...is filled with hidden rocks, and broken by many wild cascades," a Spokane observer reflected. "And few who launch their boats upon its troubled waters escape with clean hands and gentle hearts."[8]

Under the prevailing methods, candidates for general elections were selected in closed party primaries and conventions. "Trades, manipulations, combinations, and other shrewd...tricks" were preferred, said one critic, the result being that "not one-quarter of the nominees...are the choice of the people." Introduced in 1890, the Australian secret ballot represented a genuine reform. Another innovation, annual voter registration, however, was easily manipulated by political interests to reduce the participation of independent minded citizens. Registrars in the larger cities worked in obscurely located offices during weekday business hours only, limiting the chance that busy employers and workers might make an appearance. Persons professionally engaged on behalf of party tickets, in contrast, had ample time and incentive to register. Certificates to be presented at the polls on election day were easily sold or distributed to partisan hangers-on. The documents "were offered for sale by the hundred" outside balloting places, a Seattle newspaper reported. In Tacoma, "a large gang of imported and local toughs" invariably gathered, prepared "to vote once or more on fraudulent certificates." The respectable middle class was therefore justified in denouncing politics as "demoralizing…expensive, ridiculous and tragic."[9]

Taxation, universally suspected of being cruel and unfair, was the one subject likely to generate real public interest. Washington relied heavily on the property tax, assessed and collected at the county level and distributed among statewide and local programs, schools and roads included. The system was easily manipulated by influential corporations and individuals. Protesting an "entirely arbitrary" Chehalis County increase upon the holdings of the North Western Lumber Company, timber man George Emerson utilized some unspecified form of under-the-table incentive to procure a substantially reduced assessment. Seattle industrialist Robert Moran experienced the same treatment in King County, securing a reduction in tax valuation, on no evidence beyond his personal word, from $61,000 to $11,000. "To cast any reflection upon Mr. Robert Moran's oath in this particular case," a tidewater newspaper observed of the casual methods used in such matters, "would have been an innovation in the history of the Board—for they have always taken the 'sworn statement' of reputable men as being correct." In Pierce County, neighboring 80 acre tracts of equal quality were assessed, respectively, at $750 and $150, the difference being that the latter belonged to a politically connected individual.[10]

Certain classes of property secured suspiciously low valuations. Port Townsend alone had four financial institutions, but the holdings of all Jefferson County banks supposedly totaled a mere $365 in 1891. Banking deposits held by the residents of Clark County failed to exceed $500. Garfield County farmers possessed firearms, jewelry, watches and clocks worth a combined $45. Such hard-to-believe figures, a rural editor pointed out, indicated that "the rich men are determined to make the common people pay all or the bulk of taxes." Regular folks, though, also appeared to have influence with assessors. The citizens of Kittitas County, along the course of the Yakima River and other streams, together owned boats valued at $10. A single sheep was to be found, officially, in all of Jefferson County. Federal surveyors tallied over 600,000 head of sheep in the state, more than twice the figure to be derived from the assessment books.[11]

Land speculation complicated the tax question, generating pressure for artificial inflation of property values as an inducement to investment and immigration. The increased assessment of Seattle real estate from $16 million in 1889 to $26 million in 1890 thus presented "a picture of wealth-creation almost as fairy-like as…any tale from the Arabian nights." In 1891, after Douglas County officials reduced their valuations, Big Bend landowners convened an indignation meeting, reasoning that the seemingly beneficial action would lead to a loss of outsider confidence in the prospects for their region. The initially unforeseen problem was that higher assessed rates forced residents to pay a larger percentage of state taxes, which were apportioned among the counties according to locally reported wealth. Recognizing this unfortunate tendency, Spokane and Tacoma citizens not involved in the buying and selling of lots protested attempts to keep up with Seattle's figures. Out-of-the-way counties, meantime, were encouraged to deliberately under-value property, thereby limiting local liabilities.[12]

Washington's tax system was aptly described by a bemused observer as "experimental," dependent upon the honesty and capacity of elected county assessors. "Human nature crops out very decidedly in the returns," the *P-I* commented in editorial scorn. In 1891, average per-acre values ranged from $35.77 in Pierce County, to $24.72 in Whatcom County, to a low of $1.68 in Adams County east of the Cascades. Whitman County, with nearly twice the population, reported the same total valuation as Walla Walla County. Yakima County agricultural acreage was assessed at one-eighth the figure for farming tracts west of the mountains in Chehalis County (today's Grays Harbor County). Meeting annually, the state board of equalization, a panel composed of the auditor, land commissioner, and secretary of state, was supposed to repair obvious disparities, raising some figures, lowering others and assigning specific revenue liabilities to each of the counties. "Mutterings" from locales instructed to pay more suggested that the correction based upon insufficient data and subject to political pressure was far from perfect. The process "resulted," claimed one critic, "in greater incongruities than the original evil."[13]

Happily, or so matters appeared in 1889, Washington had been granted an "almost priceless estate" by the federal government. Two-and-a-half million acres of the public domain dedicated to education and other worthy purposes passed into its ownership upon admission to the Union. Prudent analysts argued that the acreage should be managed carefully as a long term investment, with most tracts retained in anticipation of future increases in value. Persons more concerned with present-day tax burdens instead advocated immediate sale as a means of painlessly financing the commonwealth. "There is no reason why this generation should go through life hungry, cold or ignorant," the *Tacoma Ledger* maintained, "in order that some generations hence may have a property that this generation has the first claim upon." Washingtonians were clearly perplexed by the need to maintain government on the one hand and, on the other, a widespread simplistic conviction that services ought somehow to be free of charge.[14]

⬿⧓⬿

Conceived by the nation's founders as a distinguished institution where the country's most honored citizens would debate and decide great issues, the U.S. Senate had declined in stature since the days of Webster, Calhoun and Clay. The Bellingham Bay developer Nelson Bennett supposedly threatened a libel suit against a newspaper for merely suggesting his name as a senatorial candidate, a no doubt apocryphal story reflecting public attitudes toward a less-than-august body. The indirect election of senators by state legislatures, mandated in the federal constitution as a means of avoiding public passion, had over time produced "a millionaire's club," the members corrupting themselves by in effect purchasing their seats. Washington, unfortunately, possessed few if any actual and truly competent millionaires. "In a state like this," a student of local politics lamented, "the number of men whose means are such as to enable them to keep up the dignity of the office with independent fortune is limited."[15]

Senators Watson Squire and John Allen came closest to a degraded standard, hence their principal qualification for service. Wealthy by virtue of marriage, Squire had fled New York a decade earlier to avoid charges of embezzlement, regaining a semblance of respectability as the second-largest property owner in Seattle and through appointment as territorial governor. Corpulent—"he is one of the few senators big enough," a rival joked, "to stand on both sides of the silver question"—and lazy, Squire preferred to spend his time attending high society functions, avoiding public responsibility to the fullest pleasurable extent. According to a widely circulated report, he lounged in a luxurious bath during daylight hours, dictating correspondence to a male secretary. Lacking his effete colleague's money and style, Allen at least acted the part of apprentice millionaire, thanks to backing from the Northern Pacific. The Indiana native had been a U.S. attorney in eastern Washington and NP counsel east of the mountains before election in 1888 as the territory's last delegate to congress.[16]

Montana, North and South Dakota and Washington all entered the Union in 1889, forcing the new senators to draw lots in order to determine the duration of their initial terms. Squire, to his chagrin, came up shortest, meaning that he would have to run for reelection in January 1891. Allen secured a four year slot until 1893. The practical result, an outcome harmful to the public interest, was that state legislators devoted the first five biennial sessions to the controversial task of selecting a U.S. Senator.[17]

Instead of discouraging partisanship and chicanery, as intended by the drafters of the U.S. Constitution, indirect election made the senatorial contest the centerpiece of Washington politics. To obtain votes, senate aspirants necessarily paid careful attention to the campaigns of legislative candidates. Watson Squire, for instance, provided substantial funding from his own ample pockets for Republicans in 1889 and again in 1890. Squire, and Allen too, promised federal jobs and contracts in return for support. "It seems strange," longtime Olympia editor John Miller Murphy reflected, "that any considerable number of men who respect their manhood should pin their faith to any man's coattail, and especially to that of such a highfalutin mass of pomposity as Squire."[18] The honor-be-damned rationale was self-evident, since legislators and the senators were locked in symbiotic embrace.

Remarking upon "the great quantity of mud" encountered in wintertime Olympia, a correspondent covering the 1891 senate contest felt the need to explain he was referring to the streets "and not to politics." Watson Squire campaigned upon a single personalized issue—he had been denied "a fair chance" at public service by "drawing the short term." Contesting the gourmet incumbent for the favor of Republican legislators, William Calkins, once an Indiana congressman and briefly a member of the territorial supreme court, recently had moved from Spokane to Tacoma for the specific purpose of becoming the Puget Sound city's self appointed political champion. Squire, who spent more time in New York than in his adopted state, accused Tacoma's Calkins of being "a carpet-bagger pure and simple," a Northern Pacific toady and a professional office seeker. The equally overwrought, though substantially more truthful, Calkins forces maintained that the senator was "a cipher except at the dinner table." Devoid of content, the election turned upon a familiar point, the Seattle-Tacoma rivalry.[19]

A Calkins supporter, though biased against the outcome, nevertheless accurately assessed the three January weeks devoted to the election as "one of the most disgraceful episodes that ever disgraced a legislative body." Both sides maintained round-the-clock free liquor rooms, which one evening resulted in a drunken brawl among legislators in the lobby of the Olympia Hotel, the capital city's finest residential and dining establishment. Squire's cynical manager, John McGraw, managed on another occasion to summon a Republican caucus without the knowledge of opposition members, who arrived just in time to stave off a rump victory for the incumbent. The undignified end came when Squire supporter J. Metcalfe reported that Calkins had attempted to bribe him to change sides. Suitably horrified by what was in fact an ingenious falsehood, the legislature elected Seattle's gentleman senator to return to his eastern pleasure haunts by a slim margin of two votes.[20]

John Allen's reelection attempt in January 1893 likewise resulted in further embarrassment for the state. Once again legislators acted, a political observer noted, "not as law-makers but as Senator-makers." Spokane Republicans had complained since statehood about the eastern Washington seat being filled by a Walla Walla resident, rather than going to a more deserving citizen of their own much larger city. Allen's recent support of federal funding for the proposed Lake Washington canal, a project likely to divert money from desired Columbia River navigation improvements, also cast him in the hapless role of traitor to the Inland Empire. The incumbent was "distinctly a King County man," disgruntled Spokaneites claimed. Seizing an opportune moment, Spokane supporter George Turner declared his candidacy as a genuine patriot of the interior. An unusually complex situation developed. Seattle emerged as the leading supporter of Walla Walla's Allen. Countering their Puget Sound rival, Tacomans sided with Spokane's Turner. U.S. Representative John Wilson, however, realizing that the victory of another Spokane man would sidetrack his own senatorial ambitions, worked covertly for hometown enemy Allen.[21]

Balloting occupied virtually the entire legislative session. "Two factions of one party," noted a report from the Olympian halls, "are fighting each other as bitterly as if they belonged to two contending parties that had never known anything else but war to the knife." Spokane's Turner had no real chance, but Allen at his strongest fell five votes short of victory. Neither would compromise, causing the legislature to adjourn at the end of its allotted 60 days without a successful election. John McGraw, now the governor, attempted to appoint Allen to fill the vacancy, an action of highly questionable legality under the state constitution. When the senate refused to seat him, the state was left for two years—through the worst of the Panic of 1893—with only a single U.S. Senator.[22]

Anything but edifying, the Squire and Allen spectacles badly interfered with the conduct of governmental affairs. "The senatorial contest did not take up many minutes of the session each day," a Seattle newspaper noted of the 1893 crisis, "but it was a disturbing element during the whole 60 days, taking the minds of the members from their work." The time left over was insufficient to properly address serious issues. Bills that did pass were often poorly drafted, hastily considered and likely to be overthrown by the courts. Calling for an effective means of forcing responsible attention to business, unhappy citizens demanded a constitutional amendment denying legislators their pay until after the election for senator.[23]

❦

Regional political humor, though falling below Mark Twain or even Bill Nye standards, nevertheless fully conveyed the all too evident public disdain for Washington's legislature. "It is too bad the legislators are all over age," a journalist pointed out in reporting the creation of the state reformatory, for they otherwise fully met all qualifications for confinement to the "school for defective youth." The typical member supposedly skipped the daily chaplain's prayer, preferring instead to imbibe a "morning toddy" in the lobbyist supplied vestibule. Taxpayers "at last found out" what "law-makers are good for" when senators and representatives formed a "bucket brigade" to extinguish a cigar-ignited fire in the capitol building. According to the Portland *Oregonian*, "two-thirds" of the membership hoped for the longest possible fully paid sessions, because they had no desire, much less prospect, for private employment. Citizens across the state, another less-than-kind wit claimed, declared an impromptu "fourth of July holiday" upon adjournment of the biennial session. A final humorist commented that people might at least "congratulate themselves" on one byproduct of legislative irresponsibility: "It will not take long…before the laws passed can be printed, and the book will not require much postage."[24]

Except for the initial session at statehood, which had no time limit, the legislature met every odd numbered year for 60 days. Business was conducted in out-of-the-way and much maligned Olympia, the capital since 1853. Originally the location had made perfect sense, being the point where the overland trail from the Columbia River struck navigable waters on Puget Sound. Settlement and economic development, however, had long since shifted to other places, relegating Olympia to forlorn status as "a side-track on the routes of travel." Washington's capital was "about as near the center of the state," an eastside editor complained, "as the handle of a jug is to the center of the jug." Politically interested citizens, even when coming only a short distance from other towns on the Sound, had to spend a day coming and a day going in order to visit by train or steamer. In session, legislators and visitors alike often were victimized by inflated prices and inferior restaurant fare and hotel accommodations.[25]

Capturing the out-of-time nature of the place, unfriendly assertions arose claiming rain fell in greater amounts and for longer periods of the year in Olympia than elsewhere in the state. Even visitors meaning to deliver praise unintentionally made the point that the capital failed to measure up to other urban areas. One tourist described Olympia as "quaint," another considered it a "good sort of town, with a lot of very excellent people" and a third reported that the capital's ambition was to become "the fourth largest city in the state." Communities of the same or smaller size had cable and electric railways, but local folk still relied upon horse drawn cars. All the municipal, and many of the mercantile, buildings were "shanties" on the verge of "tumbling down with old age." In conceding another defect—the severe ebb and flow of Budd Inlet's tides—longtime booster Hazard Stevens wrote that Olympia "fronts on…a fine harbor at least half the time." The place, detractors and defenders agreed, had far too many attorneys and few, if any, industrialists and capitalists.[26]

Hardly expecting any sudden influx of new investment capital, Olympians were the only people in Washington favoring a shift from biennial to annual legislative sessions. The business provided by state government was, all too clearly, the key to local prosperity. Olympia barely retained the capital in 1889, when principal challengers Ellensburg and North Yakima split the eastern Washington vote. The site location issue came before the statewide electorate again in 1890, with the choice limited to the three top finishers from the previous year. Unity east of the Cascades presumably would have deprived Budd Inlet of its vital asset. The Yakima River towns, however, lacked the money and energy for a second campaign, factors contributing significantly to Olympia's one-sided victory. Hoping to preempt further elections on the subject, local Olympia interests lobbied without success for prompt construction of expensive and permanent state buildings. The "shack now occupied" by the legislature, an unsympathetic Seattle newspaper suggested, ought to suffice for many years to come. All that was needed, another naysayer noted, was a fireproof safe for proper storage of the public records.[27]

Much had been anticipated during the inaugural Olympia session, convened in cramped quarters in November 1889 and lasting through early spring of the following year. "Everything depends upon the way in which the start is made,"

Ellensburg in August 1890, shortly before the community's hope of gaining the state capital was dashed in a statewide vote selecting Olympia. *University of Washington Libraries (UW11912)*

one political analyst pointed out, "for whatever is done in the first legislature will be taken as a precedent for all others." Several obstacles to the sound conduct of public business, however, soon became apparent. The senate and the house were unwieldy institutions, with far too many legislators and temporary patronage clerks for efficient operation. "It is not alone the cost of such a large body," a reporter advised, "but the imperfect work done and the time wasted in consideration of the cranky propositions of some of the members that harrows the soul." Inexperienced legislators approached the task of setting a government in motion with what one paper charitably described as "considerable bewilderment." The expense was more than expected, especially after senators and representatives shocked a parsimonious citizenry by awarding themselves full pay and benefits while on a two week holiday recess.[28]

Working along customary political lines, Washington's largest business enterprises easily manipulated the legislative process. A cooperative Republican leadership made sure that "corporation men" dominated key committees. Lobbyists supplied free liquor and after hours services of "ladies not recognized by respectable people." The Oregon Improvement Company and the Northern Pacific formed an alliance with leading Puget Sound timber firms to procure passage of favorable bills, and rejection of unfavorable ones. The OIC alone budgeted $6,000 for the cause, one manager providing a confidential addendum that "payments…made to boodlers [were] to be added."[29]

Fiscal concerns of a public nature also influenced the legislature. The initial state budget, covering everything from the $9,000 salary for the governor to the wages of the night watchman at the library, provided for expenditures in excess of

$700,000. Responsibility for the $300,000 territorial debt also was assumed by the state. Legislators intended to spend "a good deal of money," warned one advocate of prudence, "but where the money is to come from remains undecided." The magic revenue device, public land sales, turned out to be a delusion. Washington could only take actual legal possession of surveyed land, but over half of the public domain was yet unsurveyed by federal authorities and limited congressional appropriations meant that the necessary work would remain uncompleted for many years. By that uncertain time, moreover, the most valuable tracts would have been taken by citizen preemptors. Members of the legislature ignored these sobering facts, "rushing ahead far too rapidly in the matter of using up the public money," as more than one observer noted of the spend-happy doings in Olympia.[30]

Still expecting the federal land grants to somehow pay much of the bill, legislators lost no time building the literal structure of government. "A great number of propositions," one onlooker reported of the daily audacity displayed in the capital city, "are under discussion…looking to the establishment of state institutions here, there and everywhere, in such numbers and to such an extent that if all the proposed institutions should be properly endowed and maintained the state, if possessed of five times its present resources, would be bankrupted." With every member demanding something for his district, the mutual exchange of support among colleagues became standard conduct. A critic of the shameless trading noted that state agencies and facilities were created and located without concern for the public interest, but rather "by barter between different points or in payment of political service."[31]

To absolutely no surprise among the politically sophisticated, sectionalism figured prominently in the establishment of offices and institutions. Western Washington already had an asylum at Steilacoom, so the east side had to have one too, a calculation leading to placement of a mental hospital at Medical Lake in Spokane County. Similar logic lay behind the ultimately unsuccessful campaign for a penal institution west of the Cascades to balance against Walla Walla's penitentiary. Eastern Washington residents were satisfied with the single reform school at Chehalis only because of the assumption that sinful Seattle and Tacoma produced virtually all of the state's troubled young people. Every town with sidewalks, from Spokane to Cathlamet on the lower Columbia, meanwhile attempted to secure a teachers college.[32]

Education, the state's prime constitutional responsibility and the designated beneficiary of much of the federal land grant, was the particular focus of barter in early legislative sessions. Careful readers of the constitution insisted that the document actually required establishment of only an elementary school system. "The needs of the many," claimed the *Tacoma Ledger*, "rather than the indulgence of the few should be the fundamental object." Anything else, high schools and colleges included, was a luxury best left to private benefactors. A large segment of the population professed particular disdain for universities. The use of taxpayer money to support "pedantry" and professorial "dead timber" outraged common sense and the philosophy of self reliance. The collegiate experience, moreover, left the graduates unfit for the practical conduct of business affairs. "They enjoy the still air of studies," the *P-I* observed in dismissing undeserving students and faculty alike, and "they enjoy…chattering about books with their fellows."[33] Fortunately for the pedantic and the effete, however, colleges also generated jobs and income for their host communities.

If public colleges must be provided, most people favored the option of normal schools. Such institutions at least had a serious purpose, the training of teachers for the elementary system. They could be located in various accessible places, were cheaper to operate than universities and, in true democratic style, offered genuine educational and career opportunities for the poor and ambitious youth of the state. Ignoring advice to go slow on account of the land grant problem, the legislature quickly provided for geographically diverse normal schools at New Whatcom, Ellensburg and Cheney. The *Oregonian* suggested that, as a result, there ought to "be a great development of learning in the northwest," but the initial performance was hardly encouraging. The Ellensburg campus, opening in 1891, was the only one to perform up to remote approximation of expectations. Whatcom delayed opening the doors, due to lack of facilities. Cheney moved from building to building, remaining in business only when local citizens approved a bond issue to supplement state funding.[34]

Encouraged by the availability of 90,000 federally dedicated land grant acres for an agricultural college—plus another 100,000 federal acres for a school of science—legislators moved to establish a major educational institution in eastern Washington, balancing against Seattle's University of Washington (founded 1861). Though a separate school of science could have been planned, the legislature chose to incorporate it with the land grant institution. Numerous eastern Washington communities put in bids; however, the heated site selection process narrowed to a contest between North Yakima and Pullman.

Mounting a strong effort, Yakima residents stressed their town's central location and the rising importance of irrigation as a subject worthy of technical study. Besides, they claimed, a proper boundary survey, if ever undertaken, would likely reveal that Pullman actually was in Idaho. Willing to risk this scandalous eventuality in a locality thoroughly platted by federal surveyors, the selection committee voted two-to-one in favor of the Palouse in early 1891. Many of the disappointed ridiculed the decision as a product of "influence of the most corrupt sort," the most popular and plausible theory being that Whitman County Republicans had secured the college in return for supporting Watson Squire's reelection to the senate. Yakima went to court contending that the commission itself had been improperly constituted, thereby hoping to render the hateful vote null and void. This legal maneuvering—conducted in one of the state's power centers, Pierce County—eventually proved unsuccessful.[35]

To head off attempts by opponents to relocate the institution, the regents and Pullman advocates moved quickly to open "The Agricultural College, Experiment Station and School of Science of the State of Washington"—mercifully shortened in normal parlance to the Washington Agricultural College, or WAC. Founded in controversy, the college initially suffered from mismanagement. By 1892, 200 students found accommodation in a less-than-impressive brick-and-mortar structure. The five story dormitory, the most elegant building on campus, featured all "the gloom of a prison cell" and was, according to an early visitor, "a practical firetrap." On the management side, the five regents appointed from across the state supposedly "used" the institution "as a means of getting professorships for their friends" and "perquisites for themselves." Faculty and staff engaged in extravagance, the administration going so far, in the horrified view of one critic, as to employ a stenographer. Farm country editors complained that use of the word "agricultural" was fraudulent, since little of actual value to genuine tillers of the soil came out of Pullman's liberal arts classrooms and academic demonstration barns.[36]

Matters came to a melodramatic head in December 1892 when students on campus, protesting the early dismissal of the college's first president, sent a regent and the new president-elect reeling toward downtown Pullman under a barrage of snowballs, vegetables, and eggs. Respectable residents of the Pacific Northwest expressed revulsion over this act of effrontery. One editor advised John Heston, the Seattle high school principal newly appointed to the presidency, to take up a whip and "wield it artistically upon that portion of the Pullman student's anatomy thought…to contain the brains of the callow youths there present." The *Oregonian* demanded closure of the institution, forcing the "alleged students" to return to "more fitting" occupations, such as "potato-digging and dish-washing." The legislature launched an investigation and concerned parents refused to send offspring to out-of-control Pullman, leading to a sharp drop in enrollment. The arrival in mid-1893 of the third president in 2½ years, Harvard alumnus Enoch A. Bryan, together with wholesale replacement of both faculty and regents, finally allowed for a "new start" at WAC.[37]

Trouble in the Palouse diverted attention from the state university in Seattle, for many years the target of higher, or possibly lower, education critics. Elliott Bay's favorite, if often embarrassing, institution also possessed a new state land grant, replacing the original federal tract squandered away, under suspicious circumstances, during the Civil War. More out of luck than design, the school still possessed an invaluable asset, ten acres from Arthur Denny's pioneer claim that now occupied prime real estate in the midst of the downtown business district. "The present property is by far too valuable for the use to which it has been assigned," the *P-I* pointed out after the 1889 fire. The university itself, moreover, could never expand beyond glorified "high school" status unless provided with a much larger campus. The obvious solution, representing to the fullest the Seattle

Spirit in action, was relocation, with proceeds from disposition of much of the old site to be used for an endowment at the new property. The legislature disappointed local promoters by failing to take action at its founding session, but finally approved the transaction in March 1891.[38]

Perpetuating a decades long trend of mismanagement, university administrators made a dreadful botch of matters. Clearing at the new site, facing upon Lake Union and Lake Washington, began promptly in August 1891. Officials soon got into legal trouble, however, by attempting to transfer state funds appropriated for maintenance of the old campus to construction. The initial plans drew widespread criticism for gross extravagance, causing further delay. "The first requisite for a university," one of the Seattle dailies observed in detailing the attempted wastage of taxpayer funds, "is brains and scholarship, not empty edifices of brick and stone, with marble staircases, tesselated ceilings, and a spacious theatrum." Due to such controversies, the cornerstone of the first building was not laid until July 1894, two years after the school was supposed, according to statute, to have been opened to students.[39]

Only part way through creating a state system of higher education, the first legislature adjourned, having convinced most Washington residents that it was an "overwhelmingly stupid and…incompetent" body. In addition to unnecessarily prolonged deliberations, the legislators had, according to wide belief, robbed the treasury. "As nearly as we can make out," a Walla Walla Valley editor reflected, "they have…be[en] influenced by a few loud-mouthed advocates of 'grab' who look upon the state as a buzzard's roost." Attempting too much at the outset of statehood, the assembly inevitably approved hastily conceived legislation, poorly written measures that read, said one legalistic critic, as if they had been drafted by "Falstaff's recruits." Costly efforts to rectify this shortcoming through the "Hill Code," a disorganized compendium of leftover territorial statutes and new state laws, compounded the confusion.[40]

For all their attention to budget busting detail, senators and representatives somehow managed to neglect a crucial mandate. The state constitution required the legislature to redistrict itself prior to the next election, scheduled for November 1890. Failing to do so, legislators placed that polling, and under strict reading of the law all subsequent ones as well, in jeopardy. Confronting the challenge of a future without elected officials, and ignoring public complaint over the cost of a new Olympia gathering, Governor Elisha Ferry summoned a special session in September. Utilizing preliminary census data and operating under ironclad rules to prevent consideration of other matters, the members accomplished the necessary work in eight days, thereby saving Washington's electoral process.[41]

Although the legislature continued to be dominated by Republicans, many incumbents either declined or were denied renomination in 1890. The next regular session, when not dealing with the Squire-Calkins senate contest or the further dispersion of state agencies, focused on railroad regulation, a subject previously neglected in the interest of attracting capital. Emerging from the travails of the wheat "blockade," grain farmers were ready to crack down on transportation firms. Spokane merchants, aggravated by a long haul-short haul freight rate schedule allowing tidewater competitors to secure goods at lower cost, also expressed hostility toward the transcontinental lines. Company management, in somewhat brazen contrast, opposed even the mildest form of regulation as a virtually un-American attempt to "cripple" the "great enterprise" responsible for regional growth and prosperity. Public opinion was, as usual, divided according to section. Unlike the more closely impacted eastside, western Washington still believed that the state was "too young to fight railroads" and ought to postpone any action tending to discourage additional investment and construction.[42]

Two approaches to regulation appeared feasible in January 1891, at least east of the Cascades. The legislature could, as authorized by the state constitution, establish a railroad commission. Post admission experience with the mysterious operations of Olympia lobbyists, however, caused reformers to worry that such a panel would likely fall, somehow, under the effectual control of the rail lines. The better and more immediately effective choice appeared in the form of the Wasson bill, a measure mandating a 15 percent reduction in grain rates. Unfortunately, Governor Ferry, with physical and mental health in ruin, departed early in the session for lengthy recuperation in sunny California. Acting in Ferry's stead, Lieutenant Governor Charles Laughton vetoed the legislation on instructions from the Northern Pacific.[43]

Elevated to brief prominence, Laughton, until recently a resident of Nevada, had relocated to the Okanogan just in time to be ticketed for the lieutenant governorship as a concession to Republican mining interests. Drinking companions considered him a jovial and entirely untrustworthy schemer. No one familiar with Washington politics doubted that he was "a corporation man," a libertine and crook. Governor Ferry had to be desperately ill, journalists speculated, otherwise he never would have gone off to California and left such a loathsome creature in charge. Compounding an existing reputation for blatant amorality, Laughton made himself "odious" to most residents of the state by vetoing the Wasson bill. The measure, after all, was endorsed by both parties and would have saved farmers several hundred thousand dollars a year in freight expenses. Returning to Olympia in April 1891, Elisha Ferry was greeted by demands from east of the Cascades for a special legislative session to override the veto.[44]

Ferry still suffered from "extreme nervousness," however, and, unable to sleep at night, lacked the energy and desire to reopen a contentious issue. Pro-corporation Republicans, meanwhile, fretted over "what might happen if the members of the last legislature were ever legally called to life again." Astutely undercutting their critics, the railroads voluntarily reduced grain rates to almost the level required by the failed Wasson bill. Together with an increased supply of locomotives and railway cars, the eve-of-harvest reduction made a special session superfluous. In Washington politics, good short-term news trumped aggravation over past events and concern about future developments.[45]

~~~~~~~

When not provoking "boodle" alarms, Washington's legislature was, according to a regular commentator on regional affairs, intent upon approving measures "that will attract the brainy and energetic to make their homes within her borders, and not the riffraff and scum of eastern cities." Republicans, at least, must have been sorely disappointed with the result, for immigration in each passing year represented a demographic challenge to their domination of state politics. Dismissed in respectable homes as the party of "the 'Great Unwashed,'" the Democrats could, of course, hardly avoid improvement upon their dismal performance in the 1889 election. A new political dynamo, the foppish and diligently self promoting Seattle lawyer, J. Hamilton Lewis—the man even claimed, one editor joked, to have been leader of the Lewis and Clark Expedition—demonstrated undeniable appeal to workers. Republican divisions, along with public disgust over unsavory senate elections and Charles Laughton, provided made-to-order opportunities for Democratic exploitation.[46]

Rural Washington posed an especially daunting challenge for Republicanism. Membership in the Farmers' Alliance, already on the rise in the Palouse, mounted significantly after the 1890 wheat blockade. The "movement" was "here to stay" according to a supportive editor, eager to fight for lower railroad rates, better storage facilities and favorable credit policies. Pursuing its original mission as something of a nonpartisan pressure group, the alliance sent members to the nation's capital in 1891 to petition the Interstate Commerce Commission for relief on grain freights. Increasing in scope, the organization also became directly involved in politics, initially at the county level and usually in alignment with Democrats. Politicians must henceforth, one of the Walla Walla papers observed of a growing trend, "wear hay seed in their hair" in order to get elected in eastern Washington.[47]

Labor also became politically active and, among other public affairs initiatives, convened a statewide convention at Yakima in July 1891. Attempting to cope with the new America of railroads, capitalism and distant market relations, workers and farmers found they had common interests and enemies. A national People's, or Populist, party already had been organized. In Washington, the Farmers' Alliance called for the formation of a third state party, uniting urban and rural toilers. The alliance platform now featured, in addition to palliatives for rural problems, demands for the abolition of Pinkertonism and the wage undermining effects of free immigration. Meeting in Ellensburg in December 1891, city and farm delegates established a Washington Populist organization.[48]

Most Democrats at this time opposed fusion on a statewide basis with the often ideologically compatible Populists, resulting in a three-way election contest in 1892. The Democrats and Republicans, however, nominated "bankrupts" for governor, conceding the moral high ground to the Populist ticket. Democrat Henry J. Snively, a Yakima attorney, failed in hapless attempts to deflect accusations that he had stolen money from orphan wards in his native West Virginia. Balding and outfitted with a world-class soup strainer mustache, Republican John McGraw of Seattle looked like a bartender gone-to-seed. A poorly educated son of Maine, McGraw indeed had been a saloonkeeper and a police officer in preparation for dubious service as King County sheriff. More recently, a second career in banking allowed him to plant one muddy foot in the semi-respectable camp, the other remaining mired in underworld society.[49]

Upon initial perusal, the 1892 returns appeared to justify Republican claims to continued political domination. Incumbent President Benjamin Harrison, though defeated nationally, carried the state and its four electoral votes by a healthy margin over Democrat Grover Cleveland and Populist James Weaver. Despite his unsavory reputation as the venal personification of Seattle, John McGraw carried 21 of 33 counties, easily besting the Democrat's Snively and People's party candidate C.W. Young for the governorship. Republicans John Wilson and William Doolittle experienced no difficulty in winning Washington's two congressional seats. Legislative majorities were, to be sure, down from the 1889 standard, but Republicans retained substantial strength in Olympia, holding three-fourths of the senate and two-thirds of the house.[50]

Examined more closely, the results actually revealed a Washington that had, within three years of admission, become politically competitive. Regional populism gained appeal as a response to the wheat blockade, the Wasson bill veto, Squire's reelection and management's resort to the National Guard in the coal mines. If combined, the Democratic and Populist candidates' presidential tally would have decisively shifted Washington's electoral votes from the Republican column. In the governor's race, if either Democrat Snively or Populist Young had dropped out, McGraw would have been defeated by 20,000 votes and carried only two counties, King and San Juan. The Republican congressional candidates might also have been rejected.[51] Nothing better points to the rising degree of social discontent manifested in the first years of statehood than the endangered status of the Republican party.

⤜⤛⤜

The most controversial public issue of the early 1890s was never directly addressed by the voters. Upon admission, Washington assumed title to its tidelands, previously in the legal possession of the federal government. Extensive tracts of valuable frontage were involved, including 100,000 acres on Puget Sound and 70,000 acres on Grays Harbor. The constitutional convention had devoted a great deal of time to the subject, with one group of delegates arguing for permanent public ownership, and another faction, representing sawmills and railroads, demanding that corporations be allowed, at minimum, to purchase their existing

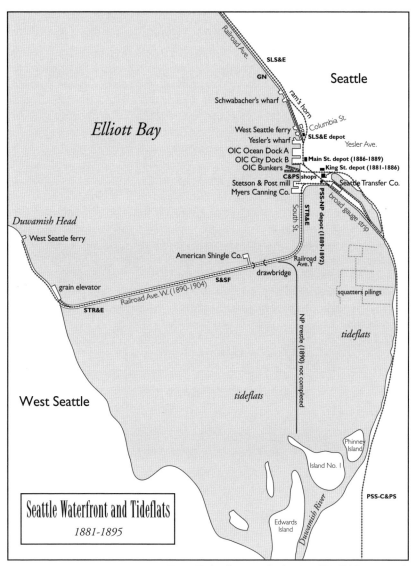

From K. Armbruster, *Orphan Road* (WSU Press, 1999).

improvements. In a provision literally purchased by business—the Oregon
Improvement Company paid $6,500 in bribes and the Northern Pacific "over
four times the…amount"—the constitution, as finally approved, deferred final
decision to the legislature.[52]

Tidal acreage was an essential component of commercial life in western Washington. Timber companies manufactured lumber and loaded cargoes at sawmills

built on tidewater wharves. Transcontinental lines connected with oceangoing steamers, exporting grain and coal over the docks. According to local legend, a beneficent "Creator" had "fixed up" the dry land, throwing "the flats in for good measure" to be used for manufacturing and railroad purposes. Ambitious development plans backed by outside investors could, when fully implemented, seriously impinge upon waterfront tracts. The Northern Pacific anticipated spending $6 million at the mouth of the Puyallup River, dredging navigation channels and depositing the spoil on the banks for the support of warehouses and factories. Seattle promoters focused on exploitation of Ballard's Salmon Bay, a new center of industrial activity in the aftermath of the 1889 fire.[53]

As expected by all of the competing interests, the state supreme court approved the constitutional language claiming original public title. According to the prevailing view in western Washington, ultimate disposition should be based upon calculation of local commercial advantage. Beyond the Cascades, in contrast, public opinion considered tidal acreage the property of the entire state, belonging as much to Spokane and Walla Walla as to Seattle and Tacoma. Decisions regarding sales, leasing or other forms of development must be taken, as a consequence, with the general welfare uppermost in mind. "They belong to the people," the *Spokane Falls Review* maintained in succinct summary of the interior Washington case.[54]

In practical terms, the legislature had to devise a means of reconciling private utilization of the tidelands with the concept of public ownership. Expecting to dictate a solution, corporate lobbyists made sure that their supporters dominated the relevant committees. "Boodle" was freely distributed, according to one inside account, to make sure that "people who have improved their water front properties" somehow secured "the preference right to buy at an approved valuation." Passed by one vote in both the senate and house in March 1890, the legislation authorized sales based on a locally controlled appraisal process. "There is no doubt but they did big work to get it through," sawmill boss Cyrus Walker wrote of the sectionally controversial measure, "considering the big fight the Grasshopper Members made against the bill."[55]

On the eastside of the mountains, the tideland bill was derided, before and after passage, as "a gigantic defrauding measure." Barely a half dozen railroad-beholden legislators from eastern Washington voted in the affirmative. Calling upon the governor for a veto, interior residents condemned the legislature for giving away the state's birthright at minimal cost to eventual purchasers. Instead, tide flat leases based upon honest value would have generated sufficient public revenue to relieve regular property owners of "the necessity of more than local taxation for years and years to come." Port facilities also might have been developed in such a manner as to insure the efficient export of grain.[56]

Before the flats could be appraised and sold, a commission created by the legislature had to first locate the harbor lines in all navigable waters. To the chagrin of waterfront interests, Governor Ferry took his time appointing members—in fact, several prominent persons proved unwilling to become embroiled in controversy and declined to serve—and selected, as a concession to critics, commissioners from both eastern and western Washington. The panel finally commenced work in the summer of 1890, proceeding with little contention at the old milling ports. Problems quickly developed, however, in commercially active locations. On Grays Harbor, for instance, the commissioners defied corporate wishes by extending boundary lines into the Hoquiam and Wishkah rivers. "I suppose they would do so if the water was but a foot deep and ten feet wide," lumberman George Emerson scornfully remarked, "as it still would be navigable for a skiff and if the tide would raise and fall in it, they would call it an estuary." Long denied direct access to the waterfront, the townspeople of Hoquiam and Aberdeen welcomed the action, despite sawmill company threats to abandon Grays Harbor should the surveys be finalized. Emerson's clumsy attempts to suborn the commission by "metallic argument," meanwhile, also failed.[57]

The Harbor Line Commission's work at Seattle proved to be an especially contentious undertaking. As initially surveyed in October 1890, the inner line outraged most local residents as tantamount to "confiscation" of the Elliott Bay waterfront. "It would take the whole or nearly all of Railroad avenue," the *P-I* exclaimed, "cut off the outer fifty feet of the Yesler dock...both the City and Ocean docks, the coal bunkers, part of Hatfield's dock, part of Harrington's docks, practically all the Colman property...[and] most of the Commercial Mill property." The commissioners, Seattle business leaders complained, had ignored the "whole spirit" driving the convoluted tideland process by failing to protect "the rights of those whose enterprise has improved these lands and given value to them." Nor would the panel, particularly the eastern Washington representatives, listen to reason. "We exhausted influence, arguments, newspaper criticism and everything else in trying to have the line thrown beyond the improvements," one exasperated executive reported to his absentee employers.[58]

Led by Seattle, threatened tide flat users secured injunctions against implementation of the surveyed lines. Development work was, as a consequence, halted until the cases could be definitively resolved. Time favored the plaintiffs, however, since the commission had only a modest budget and was due, by statute, to expire in January 1893. The panel's demise opened the way to private tideland wealth. A bill approved near the end of the 1893 legislative session assigned completion of the task to the State Land Commission, a body composed of the elected land commissioner and three gubernatorial appointees. "This Act passed without being noticed," a corporate lobbyist noted, and was subsequently "the subject of a good deal of bitterness" on the part of bamboozled eastern Washington legislators.[59] John McGraw, Seattle's tarnished favorite son, was now governor, so the new setup all but guaranteed belated victory for waterfront industries.

Money spent frustrating the Harbor Line Commission and securing creation of the new land board turned out to be, Hoquiam's George Emerson confided, "a most excellent investment." The 1893 law granted limited freedom of action to sympathetic commissioners. Little more than a year transpired before new lines favorable to tidewater corporations were drawn and certified at all points, Seattle included. Culminating in acceptable appraisals and below market sales, the entire process had generated enormous controversy.[60] The tidal flat issue again demonstrated the behind-the-scenes power of special interests in the capital-oriented affairs of Washington state. The continuing importance of sectionalism, a divisive force to be reckoned with in political maneuvers, once more was brought clearly into focus.

❧❦❧

Upon admission to the Union, Washington at last drew sustenance from the presence of senators and representatives in the nation's capital. Provided with only a single non-voting delegate, the territory always had been at a serious disadvantage in the quest for appropriations. Spending measures, as a Seattle editor pointed out, were, after all, the product of "trades, combinations and iniquitous and unworthy deals" among members of congress. Oregon, a state since before the Civil War, invariably secured "the lion's share" of federal money allotted to the Pacific Northwest. "This condition," an east-of-the-mountains observer lamented, "has ruled so long that it seems to have been firmly established by precedent." Until 1889, irresponsible authorities with nothing to lose had "utterly neglected" the superior commercial qualifications and strategic importance of Washington.[61]

Statehood, in a fortunate bit of good luck for local interests, coincided with America's bumptious rise to world power. Expanding trade, along with construction of a modern Navy, focused attention upon coastal defenses, works previously neglected in the Pacific Northwest. The few ancient artillery pieces guarding the mouth of the Columbia River were, in the bemused opinion of one onlooker, "about as harmless in case of war as a lot of Quaker guns." Except as a site for picnicking, the rusting emplacements served no conceivable purpose. Puget Sound had no defenses at all, leading fearful residents to worry that a single hostile merchant vessel, if minimally armed, "could demolish every city" from New Whatcom to old Olympia.[62]

Now with votes to barter in the U.S. Congress, Washington addressed this defect and in the process eventually secured an infusion of federal funding to complement the flow of private investment. "The United States is not safe from aggression," the *Seattle P-I* pointed out in justification, "merely because 3,000 miles of water roll between us and any formidable foe." The choice of a proper enemy to defend against nonetheless proved to be a tricky matter. Some defense advocates posited an attack by China. "A mighty flood of yellow-faces could be rolled against the Pacific coast," a Spokane newspaper warned, "and, if hurled back into the sea, replaced by another and another indefinitely." Others were convinced, more or less, by threats from Japan or South America. Chile alone, Tacomans claimed to worry, was capable of exacting tens of millions of dollars in tribute from undefended coastal cities.[63]

Happily for fear mongers, Great Britain maintained an important naval base at Esquimalt on nearby Vancouver Island. Regular visits by English war vessels, though intended to promote good will, unintentionally contributed to a developing sense of menace. Generations might have passed since the American Revolution and the War of 1812, but periodic diplomatic imbroglios still roiled Anglo-American relations. Nothing, Washington state residents insisted, could prevent the Royal Navy from descending upon Puget Sound and, within days, destroying all commercial life. Occupation troops would then arrive by the Canadian Pacific or aboard transports from India to incorporate the 42nd state into the British Empire. "It is just such 'might be's,'" the *P-I* advised doubters, "that a wise and prudent government should guard against."[64]

Despite the apparent emergency, congress was slow to approve large scale appropriations for Puget Sound. Though General Nelson A. Miles, America's most prestigious living officer, considered Esquimalt a genuine threat, fortification planning proceeded at a frustrating pace. Better attuned from professional training to seaborne dangers, the Navy took action in advance of the Army's coastal artillery corps. Following intensive surveys and over heated objections from competing points, the government selected Port Orchard in December 1890 as the site for a federal dry dock and all purpose repair yard. Across the Sound from Seattle, the 2,000 acres of Sinclair Inlet's water frontage featured enough secure and sheltered anchorage, enthusiastic naval officials reported, for "at least fifty men-of-war."[65] Coastal defense ranked high on the agenda east of the Cascades as well because of the importance of grain exports. If Puget Sound was "leveled by shot and shell," the *Spokane Review* explained, "we should find ourselves bottled up here."

Eastsiders were more interested, though, in securing enough federal funding to transform hundreds of miles of the Columbia into an "open river to the sea" for exporting products from the interior. However, "Like the Congo," the River of the West was "broken by dalles and cascades, which interpose an almost insurmountable barrier to navigation." With rapids and other obstacles removed from this natural highway, wheat shippers would be able to choose between "two magnificent harbors," i.e., the Columbia and Puget Sound. When reintroduced to region wide river service, steamboats could be expected to provide relief from what one experienced observer called "the thralldom of the railroads." A competitive environment was the ultimate goal. "With an open way to the sea the railroads will no longer control freights and fares," an Inland Empire editor asserted, "but must meet the competition."[66]

In spite of significant expenditures in recent years, no final progress had been achieved in improving Columbia navigation. Army engineers had, to be sure, installed jetty works at the river's outlet, somewhat reducing hazards for ships crossing the bar. "But until the river is made navigable from its headwaters," a critic noted of the apparent backward approach to development, "little benefit can be derived from improving the channel at the mouth." Canal excavation had begun in 1877 at the Cascade Rapids in the Columbia Gorge, but still was a long way from completion. "The money that has been appropriated for the locks," a wheat country writer complained, "has been frittered away." Mismanagement and railroad interference accounted for the mortifying delay, according to the eastern Washington view. Nothing at all, meanwhile, had been attempted at the other great mid-river obstruction, The Dalles. Barring construction of a set of locks at this site, any proposed expenditures of money above this point was dismissed as "utterly worthless" by the resident military expert on the Columbia, Captain Thomas Symons.[67]

Choosing to ignore sound advice, eastern Washington interests procured sufficient congressional funding to begin work on the mid-Columbia just upstream from the mouth of the Snake, a particularly rock infested, hazardous section of the great river that never proved adaptable to steamboat navigation. Between 1891 and 1893, the unhappy Captain Symons spent, or in his view wasted, $62,000 on "chimerical" improvements at Priest and Rock Island rapids. At Wenatchee and above, however, an existing and thriving local sternwheeler trade with the Okanogan provided a less dubious rationale for government compliance with "the wish[es] of the steam-boat people." Supplied with a new appropriation, the corps of engineers in 1895 blasted away dangerous rocks and installed "deadmen" and "other suitable anchorages" for use in lining vessels through turbulent water. Although much of this apparatus soon was destroyed in a flood, a significant, if very localized, enhancement was manifest in this more navigable stretch of the Columbia between Wenatchee and the Okanogan River.[68]

Thoroughly disgusted with the "folly" of the overall federal effort, open river advocates blamed several factors for the limited success of their campaign, particularly at the great Columbia Gorge rapids along the Oregon border. "It is alleged that he prostitutes his position for personal ends," the *Walla Walla Statesman* said of engineer Thomas Symons in suggesting that the railroads had bribed military officers assigned to the region, not to mention selected members of congress. Despite frequent announcements of support coming from west of the mountains, eastsiders were convinced of deadly opposition from Puget Sound. According to a widely held, and undeniably credible, belief, Tacoma and Seattle feared that cheap river transportation would result in reduced profits at tidewater. Massive federal spending on interior projects, moreover, reduced the money available for navigation works on the Sound. "It is annoying," an eastern Washington journalist reflected, "how local selfishness will warp the judgment and distort the view."[69]

Puget Sound's rising commercial importance certainly resulted in a good deal of work by the Army engineers. Government employees devised plans for development of the Commencement Bay tide flats and deep water navigation at the mouth of the Snohomish River. Flush with cash, however, the Northern Pacific and the Everett Land Company preferred to proceed at Tacoma and Port Gardner Bay upon a basis of private resources. The view was that travails of the annual congressional appropriations process, compounded by the inevitable aggravations to be expected from the military bureaucracy, wasted too much time and delayed timely return upon investment.[70]

Seattle promoters were, in grubby contrast, more than willing to grow rich at the expense of taxpayers. Thomas Burke, Daniel Gilman and other influential persons had invested heavily in property adjacent to Salmon Bay, acreage that would increase in value should navigability of the constricted tidal harbor be improved. Proposals for a canal linking the fresh and salt waters east, north and west of downtown dated to the earliest years of Seattle's history. "Revived" following the 1889 fire, the scheme conceived of opening up vast new harbor frontage for shipping and industry. On Lake Washington and Lake Union, wooden vessels and docks required no protection against marine organisms. "The ravages of the teredo are so great," one canal advocate wrote of this by no means insignificant consideration, "that in thirty-five feet of water a pile eighteen inches thick is completely honeycombed, and becomes a mere shell within twelve months."[71]

Early assertions that "the canal can be cut without the expenditure of a great deal of money" proved to be wildly over optimistic. Supporters briefly, and naively, thought that James J. Hill or John D. Rockefeller might finance excavation. The hope initially was to avoid federal involvement. "We may all be dead in from ten to fifteen years," a Seattle paper reflected of the delays to be expected from government undertakings. For lack of an alternative, however, the Burke-Gilman forces turned to congress in the end. Working from surveys authorized in 1891, the corps of engineers designed a $3 million canal connecting the lakes with Salmon Bay and Smith Cove on the main Seattle waterfront.[72]

News of the Lake Washington project aroused opposition throughout the Pacific Northwest. Tacomans, by habit against anything of conceivable benefit to their Puget Sound rival, immediately denounced the "ditch." Grays Harbor residents complained that they would be denied truly necessary navigation works, "because Seattle insisted on the luxury of a canal." Eastern Washington dismissed the scheme as an entirely inconsequential promotion, of value only to its immediate sponsors. The Sound, outraged editorialists insisted, already afforded "enough harborage for all demands that may be made within the next thousand years." Of more practical concern, the millions of dollars to be spent on an artificial waterway could only be appropriated at the expense of the open Columbia River, the favored goal on the east side of the mountains. "Every dollar wheeled out of congress for this local job," the *Spokane Review* warned, "will be taken away from…vastly more important improvements of a public nature."[73]

Despite the out-of-character best effort of Senator Watson Squire, a Lake Washington canal was deleted from the 1892 rivers and harbors bill by an economizing congress. The project remained of vital local interest and would, after surviving a series of subsequent setbacks, eventually be constructed years later.[74] For the moment, the defeat indicated that Washington, though now able to actively seek expensive federal improvement projects, still was not strong enough to overcome opposition from other regions. The continuing potency of interstate sectionalism also was again demonstrated. Without compensatory expenditure, half the state, at the least, could be expected to fight propositions favored in the other half. United in statehood, Washington nevertheless remained a political house partially divided, more often than not unable to agree upon, much less pursue, common goals.

✧

Only recently admitted to the Union, fast growing Washington—populated largely by newcomers—possessed no real sense of history. "Few even of the residents," a Seattle newspaper observed, "have anything like a correct idea of the state." In 1893, an owner demolished Arthur Denny's pioneer Alki cabin, the birthing place of the Elliott Bay metropolis, without sentiment and to little public complaint. That same year in eastern Washington, a surveyor literally stumbled upon the site of the 1847 Whitman "Massacre" while laying out an irrigation ditch. The unmarked graves of Marcus Whitman and the other victims were overgrown in weeds and topped by the weather beaten remnants of a broken down picket fence. "It is indeed a sad commentary," a Walla Walla editor declared in reporting the derelict condition of a long neglected historical landmark.[75]

The rediscovery of Marcus Whitman sparked fresh interest in regional history. So also did the passing of once familiar personalities of the territorial era. Captain William Renton, for decades the resident partner of the Port Blakely Mill Company, expired in July 1891. Henry Yesler, Seattle's most famous citizen, died the following year. Edward Eldridge, the only person to serve as delegate to both the 1878 and 1889 constitutional conventions, also passed from the scene in 1892. The Reverend Cushing Eells, the last of the Whitman missionaries, and Columbia Lancaster, Washington Territory's first representative in the federal congress, were among the pioneers dying in 1893.[76]

Washington's past was, according to widely expressed conviction, overdue for celebration and proper recollection. The existing Hubert Howe Bancroft histories of the Pacific coast—the Washington Territory volume appeared in 1890—drew some scorn as the "machine made" productions of "a good master mechanic" and his "shopful" of researchers and writers. Attempting to fill the void in the partial record, pioneer attorney and orator Elwood Evans prepared, and then failed to publish or preserve, a thousand page tell-all manuscript. Meanwhile, the Seattle journalist and politician, Edmond S. Meany, promoted the writing of county histories for display at the 1893 Chicago World's Fair. Washington's first close-to-legitimate historian, however, turned out to be an improbable New York based author, Julian Hawthorne. A hack whose literary career rested entirely upon his status as the son of Nathaniel Hawthorne, the New Yorker published a heavily subsidized and soon forgotten study in 1893.[77]

Local organizers worked, in the meantime, for a new appreciation of the region's story. Membership in the Washington Pioneer Association was open to all persons who had taken up residence prior to 1860. Organized in 1891, with headquarters in Tacoma, the Washington State Historical Society assumed a broader public mission. "Our history covers so brief a period," one of the founders noted, "that there should be no difficulty in securing a complete…record in full detail." In one of its first endeavors, the society celebrated the centennial of Captain Robert Gray's discoveries along the Northwest coast in the early 1790s. A special train carried dignitaries to Aberdeen, naval gun boats steamed with care over the Grays Harbor bar and the festivities concluded, rather unaccountably, with a "war dance" performed by Yakama Indians from eastern Washington.[78]

These considerable, sometimes confusing efforts produced little in the way of vigorous historical analysis. The Seattle newspapers commended Henry Yesler's "intense loyalty to the city of his adoption," but ignored the man's many years of contentious eccentricity. A similar wave of hagiography swept over other pioneers, living and dead. "They hewed pathways through the forest," a Puget Sound editor exclaimed, "established sawmills, opened coal mines, made a beginning at agricultural development, established towns, erected churches and school houses, and carried forward the great work of civilization." Soon, the *Spokane Falls Review* asserted, "they will pass away forever from the fair land of their discovery, leaving to their children and the newcomer the magnificent heritage of an empire that was wrested from savage foes."[79] Thus did history—a heroic, romantic and somewhat falsified view—serve a contemporary purpose, linking the past with the new Washington of capitalized growth and commercial push.

Notes

1. *Spokane Review*, April 26, 1892.
2. *Seattle Press-Times*, Oct. 22, 1891; *Spokane Falls Review*, Dec. 1, 1889; *Seattle Post-Intelligencer*, April 5, 1890. On California developments, see Glenn S. Dumke, "The Real Estate Boom of 1887 in Southern California," *Pacific Historical Review*, 11 (Dec. 1942), 425–38.
3. *Spokane Falls Review*, Dec. 1, 1889; March 5, 1890.

4. *Tacoma Daily News*, Jan. 22; April 2, 1890; *Seattle Post-Intelligencer*, April 10, 1890.

5. Wilson and Turner originally came to Washington as patronage appointees of President Chester A. Arthur, the former as a revenue official in Spokane. The five Spokane wards were badly, and one presumes deliberately, unbalanced, ranging in size from barely 300 to well over 2,000 registered voters. Wilson won easily statewide, with 29,153 votes to 22,831 for Democrat Thomas Carroll. Capitalizing upon the Wilson-Turner "malice," the Democrats did carry Spokane County. *Seattle Telegraph*, Sept. 10, 1890; Aug. 7, 1893; *Seattle Post-Intelligencer*, Aug. 15, 1890; March 10, 1891; Aug. 12; Nov. 26, 1892; *Olympia Tribune*, Aug. 9, 1890; George Turner to E.P. Ferry, Nov. 4, 1889, Elisha P. Ferry Papers, University of Washington Library; *Spokane Review*, Aug. 6–8, Sept. 7, 1890; Aug. 30, 1892, rep. from Portland *Oregonian*, Feb. 22, 1893; Dayton *Columbia Chronicle*, Sept. 3, 1892; *Yakima Herald*, Aug. 14, 1890; Claudius O. Johnson, "George Turner: The Background of a Statesman," *Pacific Northwest Quarterly* [hereafter cited as *PNQ*], 34 (July 1943), 252; *Tacoma Daily News*, Aug. 30, 1892.

6. "The last census," a Columbia River paper reported in late 1890, "has completely changed the political aspect of the state of Washington…Eastern Washington now stands five to nine in favor of the Sound, whereas previously the portion was five to six." *Tacoma Daily Ledger*, Aug. 6, 1890; *Seattle Morning Journal*, Oct. 26, 1889; *Seattle Press-Times*, Nov. 8, 13, 1894; *Seattle Post-Intelligencer*, Sept. 13, 1890, rep. from Vancouver *Independent*, Jan. 28, 1891; Aug. 12, 1892; Nov. 17, 1894; *Spokane Falls Review*, Jan. 30, 1891.

7. According to reports from the Atlantic coast, Washington was the "one state in the West which gives Republican leaders no uneasiness." Spokane, which received the single house slot in 1889, complained that it also should have been assigned the eastern Washington senatorship. *Tacoma Morning Globe*, Oct. 11, 1890; *Seattle Press-Times*, July 26, 1892; Olympia *Washington Standard*, Nov. 15, 22, 29, 1889; June 26, 1891; *Olympia Tribune*, July 15, 1891; *Tacoma Daily Ledger*, Dec. 7, 1889; *Spokane Falls Review*, Nov. 13, 15, 1889; Robert E. Ficken, *Washington Territory* (Pullman: Washington State University Press, 2002), 212.

8. *Tacoma Daily Ledger*, April 6, 1897; *Everett News*, Feb. 26, 1892; *Spokane Falls Review*, Jan. 17; June 6, 1890; *Seattle Telegraph*, April 20, 1893; *Tacoma Daily News*, March 14, 1890.

9. To lawfully register, a person must have resided in the state for one year and in the voting district for 30 days. The usual Seattle-Tacoma rivalry figured into stories of election fraud. When Seattle cast a total of 8,294 votes in the 1892 municipal election, compared to only 6,909 in Tacoma's local polling, residents of the latter claimed that "the registration in that city was very loosely conducted," while, all evidence to the contrary, "rigid scrutiny" had prevailed on Commencement Bay. Seattle *Argus*, Sept. 1, 1894; *Spokane Falls Review*, Nov. 9, 21, 1889; *West Shore*, 15 (Dec. 14, 1889), 418; *Seattle Morning Journal*, Jan. 27, 1890; *Tacoma Morning Globe*, Sept. 17; Oct. 22, 1890; *Seattle Telegraph*, Sept. 3, 1890; Jan. 15, 25, 1892; *Tacoma Daily Ledger*, March 3; April 6, 1892; *Seattle Post-Intelligencer*, Aug. 26; Nov. 1, rep. from Whatcom *Reveille*, 1890.

10. *Seattle Post-Intelligencer*, Nov. 18, 1892; George H. Emerson to E.J. Holt, Aug, 13, 22, 1891, George H. Emerson Letterbooks, University of Washington Library; *Seattle Times*, Sept. 20, 23, 1897; *Tacoma Morning Globe*, Oct. 5, 1891.

11. *Spokane Review*, Oct. 6, 1891; Jan. 1892; *Seattle Press-Times*, Sept. 29, 1891; *Tacoma Daily News*, Oct. 17, 1891, rep. from Pomeroy *Independent*.

12. *Seattle Post-Intelligencer,* Aug. 7; Dec. 14, 1890; Waterville *Big Bend Empire,* Aug. 20, 1891; *Spokane Review,* May 3, 8, 1891; *Tacoma Morning Globe,* Dec. 27, 1891; Portland *Oregonian,* Sept. 26, 1891. For county-by-county apportionment of taxes, see Olympia *Washington Standard,* Oct. 6, 1893.

13. Portland *Oregonian,* Sept. 24, 27, 1891; *Seattle Post-Intelligencer,* Sept. 24, 1890; Jan. 8, 1891; *Tacoma Morning Globe,* Oct. 5, 1891; *Aberdeen Herald,* Oct. 15, 1891; *Seattle Telegraph,* Sept. 22, 1891.

14. *Seattle Post-Intelligencer,* Nov. 1, 1889; *West Shore,* 17 (Jan. 3, 1891), 11; *Seattle Telegraph,* Jan. 10, 14, 1893; *Tacoma Daily Ledger,* July 20, 1894.

15. "While Washington may have an abundance of large sized timber of all other kinds," one editor quipped, "her senatorial timber never seems to grow bigger than 2 x 4." Olympia *Morning Olympian,* Aug. 26, 1891; *Tacoma Daily Ledger,* Nov. 6, 1890; *Tacoma Daily News,* May 19; Dec. 30, 1892; *Seattle Telegraph,* Jan. 27, 1893; *Seattle Press-Times,* Nov. 13, 1894.

16. Squire insisted that he had spent "thousands of dollars" of his own money promoting Washington at social functions, without credit and "with very little enjoyment to me personally." Congress did not meet until after Allen's elevation to the senate, so he never actually served in the house. The senators had the same day of birth, May 18, Squire in 1838 and Allen in 1843. Ficken, *Washington Territory,* 146–47, 196; *Seattle Press-Times,* Feb. 17, 1891; *Spokane Review,* Oct. 6, 1893; *Tacoma Morning Globe,* Sept. 8, 1890; *Olympia Tribune,* Jan. 16, 1891; *Tacoma Daily Ledger,* Oct. 1; Nov. 20, 1890; Watson C. Squire to S.C. Hyde, July 12; Aug. 8, 1890, Watson C. Squire Papers, University of Washington Library; *West Shore,* 15 (Nov. 30, 1889), 357–60.

17. Olympia *Washington Standard,* Dec. 6, 1889; *Seattle Morning Journal,* Dec. 6, 1889; J.R. McDonald to Squire, Dec. 18, 1889, Squire Papers; *Tacoma Daily News,* Feb. 5, 1897.

18. Squire supposedly financed Democrats in races where the Republican legislative candidate supported a rival for the senatorship. Thomas E. Ewing to Squire, Jan. 9, 1890; Squire to G.H. Heilbron, March 1, 1890, both Squire Papers; *Tacoma Daily Ledger,* Nov. 17, 1890; *Aberdeen Herald,* Dec. 18, 1890; Olympia *Washington Standard,* Jan. 9, 1891; *Tacoma Daily News,* Jan. 17, 1893.

19. *West Shore,* 17 (Feb. 7, 1891), 88; Squire to C.B. Bagley, April 19, 1890; to Hyde, July 12; Aug. 8, 1890; to C.H. Hanford, March 1, 1890, Squire Papers; to D.H. Gilman, Jan. 9, 1891, Daniel H. Gilman Papers, University of Washington Library; *Seattle Post-Intelligencer,* Sept. 26; Dec. 2, 1890; March 13, 1891; *Tacoma Daily Ledger,* Jan. 7, 8, 12, 20, 1891; Jan. 30, 1894; *Tacoma Daily News,* Jan. 8, 1890; *Tacoma Morning Globe,* Sept. 8, 10, 1890; *Spokane Spokesman,* Sept. 12, 1890.

20. An investigating committee controlled by Squire supporters exonerated Metcalfe of any wrongdoing. The senator's law abiding helpmate received rewarding appointment as a U.S. treasury agent. Other pro-Squire legislators also received federal jobs. Office holding friends and relatives of Calkins were dismissed. Calkins himself died at the age of 52 in January 1894, continuing to the end to seek office, appointive or elective. *Tacoma Daily News,* Feb. 26, 1891; *Seattle Press,* Jan. 24, 1891; Olympia *Washington Standard,* Jan. 23, 1891; *Tacoma Daily Ledger,* Jan. 21, 22; Feb. 26, 28, 1891; *Spokane Falls Review,* Jan. 22, 25, 29, 1891; *Yakima Herald,* Jan. 22, 1891; Portland *Oregonian,* April 18, 1891; *Tacoma Morning Globe,* Feb. 10; Sept. 20, 1891.

21. *Tacoma Daily News*, Jan. 16, 1893; *Spokane Review*, Aug. 4, 7, 1892; *Seattle Post-Intelligencer*, June 30, 1892; *Seattle Press-Times*, July 25, 1892; *Seattle Telegraph*, Jan. 6, 1893.

22. The senator's rejection supposedly left the state "in the position of the boy who lost one of his rear suspender buttons." Confirming the suspicions east of the Cascades, Allen moved to Seattle after his rebuff in the nation's capital. *Spokane Review*, Jan. 21; Feb. 24; March 10; Aug. 24; Oct. 2, 1893; *Anacortes American*, Jan. 26, 1893; *Seattle Post-Intelligencer*, Jan. 22, 25, 1893; Jan. 20, 1895; *Ellensburgh Capital*, Jan. 26, 1893; *Tacoma Daily News*, Feb. 15, 1893; Davenport *Lincoln County Times*, Oct. 20, 1893; *Seattle Telegraph*, Sept. 1, 1893, rep. from Spokane *Chronicle*.

23. *Seattle Telegraph*, Jan. 7, 1891; Jan. 18; March 22, 1893; *Tacoma Daily News*, Jan. 16, 1893; *Spokane Review*, Dec. 26, 1892; *West Shore*, 16 (Feb. 15, 1890), 195.

24. *Spokane Falls Review*, Feb. 21, rep. from Portland *Oregonian*, 25, rep. from Oakesdale *Sun*, 1890; March 11, 1891, rep. from Portland *Telegram*; *The Dalles Times-Mountaineer*, Feb. 1, 1890; *West Shore*, 16 (Feb. 8, 1890), 162.

25. Hostile public reaction sidelined an early proposal to extend the limitation to 100 days. Such a change, one newspaper noted, would "invariably lead to long debates on questions of no public importance whatever." *Tacoma Morning Globe*, Feb. 18, 1890; *Tacoma Daily Ledger*, Jan. 27, 1891; *Spokane Review*, March 9, 1893; *Seattle Post-Intelligencer*, Oct. 29, 1890, rep. from Ellensburgh *Localizer*; *Seattle Times*, Feb. 5, 1897.

26. The editor of the *Oregonian* thought Olympia "charming." A Budd Inlet journalist insisted that the town would eventually, tortoise-like, bypass Seattle and Tacoma because its citizens knew how to be "moderate in prosperity." *Seattle Post-Intelligencer*, Oct. 30, 1890; *Tacoma Daily News*, Feb. 17, 1891; *Seattle Telegraph*, March 11, 1893; *Seattle Press-Times*, Aug. 6, 1891; Sept. 29, 1892; Portland *Oregonian*, Jan. 1, 1890; *Olympia Tribune*, Aug. 12, 1890; July 18; Oct. 16, 1891; *Tacoma Morning Globe*, Sept. 5, 1891; Olympia *Washington Standard*, July 18; Sept. 19, 1890; Sept. 11, 1891.

27. Olympia citizens also stood alone in calling for special sessions. Yakima advertised its qualifications with stickers affixed to fruit boxes. *Olympia Tribune*, Nov. 18, 1891; *Tacoma Daily Ledger*, May 8; Oct. 14, 24, 1890; Jan. 3, 1891; *West Shore*, 15 (Nov. 9, 1889), 283; *Tacoma Daily News*, June 2, 1890; *Northwest*, 8 (Dec. 1890), 35; Olympia *Washington Standard*, Nov. 28, 1890; Feb. 3, 1893; *Seattle Telegraph*, Jan. 31, 1891; *Seattle Post-Intelligencer*, Feb. 26, 1891; *Spokane Review*, March 9, 1893; Arthur S. Beardsley, "Later Attempts to Relocate the Capital of Washington," *PNQ*, 32 (Oct. 1941), 423–24.

28. *Seattle Morning Journal*, Nov. 4, 20; Dec. 21, 1889; H.W. McNeill to Elijah Smith, Nov. 20, 1889, Oregon Improvement Co. Records, University of Washington Library; Olympia *Washington Standard*, Dec. 6, 1889; *Seattle Post-Intelligencer*, Dec. 3, 1889; Feb. 2, 1890; Pomeroy *Washington Independent*, Jan. 9, 1890.

29. Prostitutes also served as an effective means of blackmailing legislators. "Two or three of them have been working the Olympia gathering with exceptional success," a Spokane paper reported during the 1891 session, "and not a few members will return to their homes wiser and poorer than upon the day when their fond and devoted wives…kissed them good-bye at the home door." Coal mine operators spent $2,500 in February 1890 to secure, by two votes, rejection of a bill harmful to their interests. *Seattle Times*, July 19, 1889; E.H. Morrison to Smith, Sept. 1, 1889; McNeill to Smith, Nov. 20, 25, 1889; Jan 21; Feb. 3, 10, 1890, all Oregon Improvement Co. Records; Ficken, *Washington Terri-*

tory, 209–10; *Seattle Morning Journal,* Nov. 29, 1889; *West Shore,* 16 (Feb. 1, 1890), 130; *Spokane Falls Review,* Feb. 4, 1891.

30. The state did not assume title to the first acre of its federal land grant until a year and a half after admission. Well over two million acres were devoted to the support of schools, but fewer than 100,000 acres were obtained and sold by 1892. *Seattle Post-Intelligencer,* Nov. 22; Dec. 7, 1889; Feb. 24; Aug. 20; Dec. 7, 1890; *Walla Walla Statesman,* Nov. 23, 1891; Ferry to J.H. McGraw, Oct. 1, 1892, Ferry Papers; *Seattle Morning Journal,* Dec. 4, 1889; *Seattle Telegraph,* Oct. 5, 1890; April 12, 1891; Olympia *Washington Standard,* Jan. 8, 1892.

31. "If the state must be looted," a Bellingham Bay editor forthrightly asserted, "we want our share of the loot." *Seattle Post-Intelligencer,* Feb. 1, 1890; March 29, 1893, rep. from Whatcom *Reveille; Seattle Morning Journal,* Dec. 5, 1889; Spokane Falls *Spokesman,* May 27, 1890.

32. "With the accession of statehood and the attendant bestowal of political honors throughout this state," one newspaper noted of the intense competition, "animosities have been engendered and faith in human nature shattered to an extent that time can never heal." *West Shore,* 16 (Feb. 22, 1890), 232; Olympia *Washington Standard,* July 17, 1891; *Tacoma Morning Globe,* Dec. 19, 1891; *Seattle Telegraph,* Feb. 2, 1891; Jan. 8, 1892; *Seattle Post-Intelligencer,* April 27, 1890; *Seattle Press-Times,* March 15, 1892; *Spokane Falls Review,* Jan. 17, 1890.

33. In 1892, Washington had just three accredited four-year high schools, located in Seattle, Tacoma, and Spokane. Neighboring Oregon and Idaho had but one each. *Tacoma Daily Ledger,* Nov. 16, 1889; May 11, 1890; *Spokane Review,* Jan. 3, 1892; *Seattle Post-Intelligencer,* March 18, 1892; Enoch A. Bryan, *Historical Sketch of the State College of Washington, 1890–1925* (Pullman: Alumni Association, 1928).

34. A Tacoma newspaper suggested that normal schools be set up in every county, feeding teachers directly into local educational districts. The normal schools, whatever their eventual number, were due the revenue from a combined 100,000 state acres. *Seattle Post-Intelligencer,* March 15, 1893; Spokane *Spokesman-Review,* Oct. 16, 1895; Sept. 19, 1897; *Tacoma Morning Globe,* Feb. 3, 1890; *Seattle Telegraph,* Feb. 16, 1891; *Tacoma Daily News,* March 18, 1893; *Spokane Review,* Nov. 26, 1891, rep. from Portland *Oregonian;* Jan. 24; May 2, 1893; *Ellensburgh Capital,* June 18, 1891; March 13, 1893; Portland *Oregonian,* Sept. 7, 1891.

35. In 1890, an initial college site selection committee ended in deadlock, voting for North Yakima, Colfax, and Spokane. Unwilling to compromise, the three commissioners "adjourned permanently." Reflecting the standard focus on geographical distribution of state institutions, the second site commission in 1891 was required to select a location in an eastern Washington county not having a state institution. This consideration eliminated Spokane County (with the Cheney normal school and Medical Lake mental hospital), Kittitas County (with a normal school in Ellensburg), and Walla Walla County (retaining the penitentiary). Yakima boosters also pointed out that Pullman was only eight miles from Moscow, the site of Idaho's land grant college. Pullman champions dismissed the legal challenge as "a piece of mean, selfish, belittling spite work." *West Shore,* 17 (Jan. 3, 1891), 11; John Fahey, *The Inland Empire: Unfolding Years, 1879–1929* (Seattle: University of Washington Press, 1986), 80; *Spokane Falls Review,* May 27; July 12; Aug. 3, 1890; April 14, 1891; Olympia *Washington Standard,* June 20, 1890; *Tacoma Daily Ledger,*

May 31; June 4; Oct. 4, 1890; March 10; May 1, 11, 19, 1891; *Yakima Herald,* May 22, 1890; April 30, 1891; *Tacoma Morning Globe,* Jan. 16, 1892; Portland *Oregonian,* May 11, 1891; *Seattle Telegraph,* June 13, 1891; *Spokane Review,* Dec. 1, 1891; *Tacoma Daily News,* June 29, 1891, rep. from Wilbur *Register.*

36. The dormitory, indeed, did burn down in 1897, with the inhabitants escaping at night-time without injury. Tuition was free, but students paid $10 a month for room and board. The regents, in turn, complained of outsider interference in the matter of academic appointments. *Seattle Post-Intelligencer,* Dec. 18, 1892; Feb. 17, 1893; *Seattle Press-Times,* March 26, rep. from Palouse *News,* May 31, 1894; *Tacoma Daily News,* Feb. 16, 1893; Olympia *Washington Standard,* Dec. 16, 1892; *Seattle Telegraph,* Dec. 19, 1892; March 8; Oct. 7, 1893; *Yakima Herald,* Feb. 23, 1893; *Walla Walla Statesman,* May 11, 1893; George A. Frykman, *Seattle's Historian and Promoter: The Life of Edmond S. Meany* (Pullman: Washington State University Press, 1998), 48–51. For WAC's early years, also see William L. Stimson, *Going to Washington State* (1989), and George A Frykman, *Creating the People's University* (1990), published by WSU Press, and Bryan, *Historical Sketch of the State College.*

37. Student demonstrators again assaulted the regents in February 1893. *Spokane Review,* Dec. 15, 16, 1892; April 21; Aug. 29, 1893; *Seattle Post-Intelligencer,* Dec. 18, 22, 24, 26, rep. from Portland *Oregonian,* 1892; Jan. 3, rep. from Yakima *Republic,* May 12, 1893; *Seattle Telegraph,* Dec. 19, 23, 25, 1892; Feb. 18; Oct. 7, 1893.

38. The university's original federal land grant consisted of 46,000 cares. After statehood, the institution received 100,000 acres of state land, a little more than half as much allotted to the land grant college. *West Shore,* 15 (Dec. 21, 1889), 453; 17 (Jan. 3, 1891), 11; *Seattle Telegraph,* Jan. 21, 30; March 12, 1891; Charles M. Gates, "Daniel Bagley and the University of Washington Land Grant, 1861–1868," *PNQ,* 52 (April 1961), 58–64; Ficken, *Washington Territory,* 73–74; *Seattle Press,* Jan. 23, 1891; *Seattle Post-Intelligencer,* Nov. 11, 1889; July 11, 1890; *Tacoma Daily News,* March 20, 1891; Frykman, *Seattle's Historian,* 33–35; Neal O. Hines, *Denny's Knoll: A History of the Metropolitan Tract of the University of Washington* (Seattle: University of Washington Press, 1980), 15–16; Jeffrey Karl Ochsner, "The University That Never Was: The 1891 Boone and Wilcox Plan for the University of Washington," *PNQ,* 90 (Spring 1999), 59.

39. Two hundred students enrolled at the downtown site for the 1892–1893 school year. Public ire also was directed at such budgetary frills as $3,000 for telephones and $12,500 for a president's house. *Seattle Press-Times,* Oct. 10, 13, 19; Nov. 16, 1891; *Tacoma Daily Ledger,* Oct. 15, 1891; Frykman, *Seattle's Historian,* 53–54; *Olympia Tribune,* Oct. 21, 1891; Ochsner, "University That Never Was," 59–66; Spokane *Spokesman-Review,* Feb. 2, 1895; *Tacoma Daily News,* March 20, 1891; *Seattle Post-Intelligencer,* July 5, 1894.

40. *Seattle Morning Journal,* Jan. 21, 1890; Pomeroy *Washington Independent,* Jan. 23, 1890; *Tacoma Daily Ledger,* March 28, 1890; *Spokane Falls Review,* March 28, 1890; *Seattle Telegraph,* Sept. 15, 1890; Oct. 17, 1892; *Tacoma Daily News,* Nov. 30, 1892; Arthur S. Beardsley, "The Codes and Code Makers of Washington, 1889–1937," *PNQ,* 30 (Jan. 1939), 14–27.

41. The districts used in 1889 were devised by Miles Moore, the last territorial governor. The legislature was not implicated in the state's first political scandal, the June 1890 attempt by a textbook company to bribe the board of education. *Tacoma Daily News,* March 30, 31, 1890; *Spokane Falls Review,* Feb. 5, 1890; *Seattle Telegraph,* Sept. 5; Oct. 2, 1890; May

30; Sept. 22, 1891; Pomeroy *Washington Independent*, Sept. 25, 1890; J.F. Roush, "Legislative Reapportionment in Washington State," *PNQ*, 28 (July 1937), 265–67; *Olympia Tribune*, Sept. 6, 11, 1890; *Tacoma Daily Ledger*, June 12; July 11; Aug. 2, 26, 1890; Jan. 8, 1895; Olympia *Washington Standard*, June 13, 1890; Spokane *Spokesman-Review*, Jan. 5, 1895.

42. At this time, most railway critics opposed public ownership as an impractical intrusion upon private property. *Tacoma Daily Ledger*, Oct. 21, 1890; May 26; Aug. 3, 1891; Douglas Smart, "Spokane's Battle for Freight Rates," *PNQ*, 45 (Jan. 1954), 19–20; C.H. Prescott to Ferry, April 17, 1891, Ferry Papers; *Tacoma Daily News*, April 17, 1891, rep. from South Bend *Journal*; *Seattle Press-Times*, Jan. 27, 1892; *Spokane Falls Review*, Jan. 14, 1891; *Spokane Review*, June 28; Nov. 19, 1892; Davenport *Lincoln County Times*, Oct. 27, 1893.

43. As drafted, the constitution actually created a railroad commission, in a provision deftly altered by corporate lobbyists. Cynics aware of sponsor Samuel Wasson's connection to Senator Squire worried that the bill might contain some hidden benefit for the railroads. Suspicion deepened when Squire secured Wasson's appointment as federal customs collector at Port Townsend. The Wasson bill was one of several railroad opposed measures vetoed by the acting governor. *Seattle Times*, Aug. 7, 1889; *Seattle Press*, Jan. 29, 1891; *Spokane Falls Review*, Feb. 7; March 12, 1891; *Tacoma Morning Globe*, Aug. 30; Sept. 20, 1891; *Seattle Press-Times*, Oct. 26, 1891; *Tacoma Daily Ledger*, Nov. 19, 1890; March 18, 20, 1891; *Seattle Post-Intelligencer*, Dec. 1, 1890; *Seattle Telegraph*, Dec. 1, 1890; March 18, 1891; *Ellensburgh Capital*, March 19, 1891.

44. In addition to being implicated in the 1890 textbook scandal, Laughton supposedly kept, according to salacious report, two unmarried female private secretaries on his official payroll and dispensed pardons for under-the-table payment. Wheat raising counties promised to pay the cost of a special session. *Ellensburgh Capital*, March 19, 1891; I.A. Navarre to Ferry, Sept. 18, 1889, Ferry Papers; *Seattle Press-Times*, March 24; April 20; June 26, 1891; *Seattle Telegraph*, March 18; April 27, 1891; *Seattle Press*, Jan. 9, 1891; *Tacoma Daily Ledger*, Dec. 19, 1889; *Spokane Review*, April 4, 21, 25, rep. from Portland *Oregonian*, 1891; *Tacoma Daily News*, Nov. 20, 1890; Jan. 12, 1893; Olympia *Washington Standard*, Nov. 13, 1891; Portland *Oregonian*, March 26, 1891; *Spokane Falls Review*, April 3, 1891.

45. Never regaining strength, Ferry died in 1895 after catching cold on the deck of a Puget Sound steamer. The rail lines mollified Spokane by lowering charges to merchants shipping goods to the Palouse and the Coeur d'Alenes. In a legally meaningless gesture, the 1893 regular session voted to set aside Laughton's veto. Ferry to Daniel L. Dawley, Nov. 24, 1891, Ferry Papers; *Tacoma Daily Ledger*, April 7; May 9; July 31; Aug. 2, 1891; *Spokane Review*, May 5; July 29; Aug. 4, 11, 1891; *Seattle Press-Times*, Aug. 4, 1891; *Olympia Tribune*, Oct. 22, 1891; *Tacoma Daily News*, Feb. 2, 1893; Spokane *Spokesman-Review*, Oct. 15, 1895; *Seattle Times*, Oct. 14, 1895.

46. *West Shore*, 15 (Dec. 7, 1889), 387; 16 (Jan. 25, 1890), 98; *Tacoma Morning Globe*, Oct. 11, 1890; *Everett News*, Feb. 12, 1892; *Tacoma Daily News*, March 12, 1890; April 24, 1891; June 18; Aug. 8, 1892; *Yakima Herald*, July 28, 1892; *Seattle Post-Intelligencer*, Aug. 5, 1892; *Walla Walla Statesman*, Sept. 4, 1891; *Spokane Review*, May 5, 1892.

47. Colfax *Palouse Gazette*, April 25; Nov. 14, 1890; Portland *Oregonian*, Aug. 19, 1891; Pomeroy *Washington Independent*, Nov. 20, 1890; *Seattle Morning Journal*, Jan. 3, 1890;

Spokane Falls Review, July 30; Dec. 17, rep. from Waitsburg *Times*, 1890; Jan. 14, 1891; Thomas W. Riddle, "Populism in the Palouse: Old Ideals and New Realities," *PNQ*, 65 (July 1974), 100–1; *Seattle Post-Intelligencer*, Jan. 6, 1891.

48. Olympia *Washington Standard*, July 10; Dec. 4, 1891; Carlos A. Schwantes, *Radical Heritage: Labor, Socialism, and Reform in Washington and British Columbia, 1885–1917* (Seattle: University of Washington Press, 1979), 52–54; Keith Murray, "Issues and Personalities of Pacific Northwest Politics, 1889–1950," *PNQ*, 41 (July 1950), 216–17; *Walla Walla Statesman*, Nov. 21, 1891; *Seattle Post-Intelligencer*, May 22, 1891; *Spokane Review*, May 21, 1891; *Tacoma Daily News*, May 26; Dec. 14, 1891; Riddle, "Populism in the Palouse," 97.

49. The election might also be considered a four-sided affair, given the presence on the ballot of credible Prohibition party candidates. *Seattle Telegraph*, Nov. 12, 1891; Oct. 6; Nov. 2, 1892; *Seattle Press-Times*, Dec. 23, 1891; Oct. 25, 1892; *Tacoma Daily News*, March 19; Aug. 12, 29; Sept. 1, 1892; Olympia *Washington Standard*, Sept. 2, 1892; *Seattle Post-Intelligencer*, Aug. 12, 30; Nov. 6, 1892; *Yakima Herald*, Sept. 29, 1892; Robert T. McDonald, "Photographs of Washington Governors," *PNQ*, 34 (Oct. 1943), 400.

50. The usual Seattle-Tacoma rivalry was reflected in the returns, McGraw leading Snively two-to-one in King County, but getting only one in five votes in Pierce County. Dropped from the statewide ticket, Charles Laughton was defeated in an Okanogan County legislative race, ending his brief career in Washington politics. *Seattle Press-Times*, Nov. 30, 1892; *Seattle Post-Intelligencer*, Dec. 9, 1892; Olympia *Washington Standard*, Dec. 16, 1892; *Tacoma Daily News*, Nov. 14, 1892; *Spokane Review*, Nov. 12, 1892; Schwantes, *Radical Heritage*, 54; *Ellensburgh Capital*, Dec. 15, 1892.

51. *Tacoma Daily News*, Aug. 8; Dec. 13, 1892; *Seattle Post-Intelligencer*, Dec. 9, 1892; Olympia *Washington Standard*, Dec. 16, 1892.

52. *West Shore*, 16 (Feb. 15, 1890), 203; C.A. Dolph to Smith, April 26, 1889; Morrison to Smith, Sept. 1, 1889; John L. Howard to Smith, July 25; Aug. 19, 1889, all Oregon Improvement Co. Records; Haines & McMicken to Cyrus Walker, June 29, 1889; H.G. Struve to Walker, Aug. 9, 1889, both Puget Mill Co. Records, Ames Coll., University of Washington Library; *Seattle Times*, May 16, 1889.

53. A territorial statute, rendered null and void by the constitution, had allowed upland owners to build wharves to deep water. *Seattle Post-Intelligencer*, Feb. 20, 22, 23; Sept. 25, rep. from Bellingham Bay *Express*, 1890; *Seattle Times*, May 16, 1889; *Tacoma Daily News*, Jan. 21, 1890; *West Shore*, 15 (May 1889), 273–74; 16 (Feb. 1, 1890), 138; (March 1, 1890), 271; *Tacoma Daily Ledger*, March 11; May 6, 1890; March 21, 22, 1892; Robert E. Ficken, *The Forested Land: A History of Lumbering in Western Washington* (Seattle: University of Washington Press, 1987), 60.

54. *Tacoma Daily Ledger*, Jan. 21, 1890; *Seattle Post-Intelligencer*, Nov. 30; Dec. 2, 1890; Jan. 24, 1891; *Spokane Falls Review*, Feb. 12, 14, 16, 20, 28, 1890; Jan. 27, 1891; Olympia *Washington Standard*, March 20, 1891; Eugene Semple to G.A. Miller, March 25, 1890, Eugene Semple Papers, University of Washington Library; *Tacoma Morning Globe*, Jan. 7, 24, 1890; *Tacoma Daily News*, Jan. 21, 1890.

55. Walker to C. Talbot, Nov. 20, 1889; to W.H. Talbot, March 31, 1890, Cyrus Walker Letterbooks, Ames Coll., University of Washington Library; McNeill to Smith, Jan. 21; Feb. 4; March 29, 1890, Oregon Improvement Co. Records; *Seattle Post-Intelligencer*, Feb. 17, 26; March 12, 22, 1890; *Tacoma Morning Globe*, March 24, 1890; *Tacoma Daily*

Ledger, Feb. 19; March 4, 1890; *Tacoma Daily News*, March 12, 22, 1890; Alan Hynding, *The Public Life of Eugene Semple: Promoter and Politician of the Pacific Northwest* (Seattle: University of Washington Press, 1973), 123–24.

56. Colfax *Palouse Gazette*, March 21, 28, 1890; *Yakima Herald*, March 13, 1890; *Spokane Falls Review*, March 4, 25, 1890.

57. *Olympia Tribune*, Oct. 24, 1891; *Tacoma Daily Ledger*, May 23, 1890; *Spokane Falls Review*, July 8, 1890; *Seattle Post-Intelligencer*, July 12, 23, 1890; Hynding, *Public Life of Eugene Semple*, 124; Walker to W. Talbot, Sept. 21, 1892, Puget Mill Co. Records; Emerson to George W. Bullene, Oct. 28, 1891; to Harry C. Heermans, Oct. 2, 1891 to A.M. Simpson, Oct. 8; Sept. 26; Dec. 21, 1891; to Holt, Sept. 28; Oct. 16; Dec. 11, 1891, Emerson Letterbooks.

58. Controversy also marked the establishment of harbor lines on Bellingham and Commencement bays. The commission's work at Salmon Bay, on the northern limits of Seattle, was widely criticized by Ballard manufacturers. Olympia *Washington Standard*, July 31, 1891; *Tacoma Daily Ledger*, March 27, 1891; *Tacoma Daily News*, Jan. 6, 1892; Semple to W.J. Prosser, July 23, 1891, Semple Papers; *Seattle Post-Intelligencer*, Oct. 25, 29; Nov. 30; Dec. 2, 1890; *Seattle Telegraph*, Oct. 25, 29, 30; Nov. 13, 18, 24, 1890; Thomas Burke to J.J. McGilvra, Nov. 30, 1890, Thomas Burke Papers, University of Washington Library; C. Smith to Smith, Oct. 29, 1890; to W.H. Starbuck, Jan. 28, 1891, Oregon Improvement Co. Records; Maurice McMicken to Walker, Oct. 29, 1890, Puget Mill Co. Records; Hynding, *Public Life of Eugene Semple*, 126–27.

59. Burke to McGilvra, Nov. 30, 1890, Burke Papers; Semple to Prosser, July 23, 1891, Semple Papers; Emerson to Simpson, Oct. 8; Dec. 2, 1891; Feb. 8, 1892; to Holt, Dec. 11, 1891; Feb. 9, 1892, Emerson Letterbooks; *Seattle Post-Intelligencer*, Oct. 29, 1890; Jan. 24; March 9, 1891; March 11, 1893; Hynding, *Public Life of Eugene Semple*, 123–24, 127–30, 139; *Seattle Press-Times*, April 17; Nov. 19, 1891; *Tacoma Daily Ledger*, Nov. 20, 1891; *Spokane Falls Review*, Jan. 27, 1891; Portland *Oregonian*, March 28, 1891; C. Smith to Starbuck, Sept. 18, 1891; Jan. 14; June 8, 1893, Oregon Improvement Co. Records; *Spokane Review*, March 12, 1893.

60. Emerson to Simpson, May 31; June 1, 1894; to E.W. Cowan, Dec. 9, 1893; to Thomas Reed Jr., Dec. 9, 1893; to M.P. Callender, Dec. 14, 1893, Emerson Letterbooks; C. Smith to Starbuck, June 8, 1893, Oregon Improvement Co. Records; Hynding, *Public Life of Eugene Semple*, 139–40; *Seattle Post-Intelligencer*, June 20, 1894; April 2, 1897; Walker to W. Talbot, April 23, 1894, Walker Letterbooks; Spokane *Spokesman-Review*, April 10, 1897.

61. *Seattle Press-Times*, June 22, 1892; *Spokane Falls Review*, May 29, 1890; *Tacoma Morning Globe*, Sept. 15, 1890.

62. *Spokane Review*, March 19, 1892; *Spokane Falls Review*, Feb. 19, 1891; *Seattle Post-Intelligencer*, Jan. 30, 1892.

63. *Seattle Post-Intelligencer*, Feb. 2, 1892; *Spokane Falls Review*, Dec. 24, 1890; *Tacoma Morning Globe*, Feb. 15; Nov. 1, 1891; *Seattle Telegraph*, Dec. 27, 1892; Spokane *Spokesman-Review*, Oct. 15, 1895.

64. *Seattle Morning Journal*, Dec. 1, 1889; *Seattle Post-Intelligencer*, July 27, 1890; Feb. 2, 1892; *Seattle Telegraph*, Dec. 27, 1892; *Tacoma Daily Ledger*, July 25, 1890; *Spokane Review*, March 19, 1892. On Esquimalt, the English fleet headquarters in the eastern Pacific since the Civil War, see Barry M. Gough, *The Royal Navy and the Northwest Coast*

of North America, 1810–1914: A Study of British Maritime Ascendancy (Vancouver: University of British Columbia Press, 1971), 186–96, 233–35.

65. Senator Watson Squire sponsored legislation for a Puget Sound "gun factory," but Democratic critics of Republican fiscal extravagance considered the spending of more than "a few thousand dollars" to be unnecessary waste. "A few sunken mortars and a few strings of torpedoes across the Sound," one editor suggested, "would make Seattle, Tacoma and Olympia as safe as Spokane." *Tacoma Daily Ledger,* July 25, 1890; Feb. 12, 1891; *Seattle Post-Intelligencer,* May 19, 1894; *West Shore,* 16 (Feb. 8, 1890), 162; *Seattle Telegraph,* Dec. 15, 1890; A.B. Wyckoff to B.F. Tracy, June 11, 1892, in "Establishing the Navy Yard, Puget Sound," *Washington Historical Quarterly* [hereafter cited as *WHQ*], 2 (July 1908), 358; *Seattle Press-Times,* July 16, 1892; *Tacoma Daily News,* Feb. 12, 1891.

66. "Close up the Columbia river and leave Puget sound the only ocean outlet for the millions of bushels of Washington wheat," one analyst noted, "and wheat rates from the grain fields to deep water will be double and treble what they now are." *Spokane Falls Review,* Feb. 27, 1890; Jan. 4, 8; Feb. 19, 1891; *Walla Walla Statesman,* Sept. 8, 1891; *West Shore,* 16 (Dec. 6, 1890), 258; 17 (March 7, 1891), 152; *Spokane Review,* March 24; April 15, rep. from Vancouver *Independent;* May 29, rep. from Waterville *Democrat,* 1892; Pomeroy *Washington Independent,* Jan. 30, 1890; Thomas W. Symons to Thomas L. Casey, July 17, 1891, in *Annual Report of the Chief of Engineers, 1891,* 3212; Portland *Oregonian,* April 10, 1891, rep. from Spokane *Chronicle;* Richard White, *The Organic Machine* (New York: Hill and Wang, 1995), 36–37. On the important role of Oregon in the open river campaign, see William G. Robbins, *Landscapes of Promise: The Oregon Story, 1800–1940* (Seattle: University of Washington Press, 1997), 193–96.

67. The Cascades canal was finally completed in 1896. *The Dalles Times-Mountaineer,* Oct. 28, 1889; Pomeroy *Washington Independent,* May 5, 1892; *Spokane Falls Review,* Jan. 8, 17, 1891; *Spokane Review,* Aug. 9, 1891; May 13, 1893; Symons to Casey, July 17, 1891, in *Annual Report of the Chief of Engineers, 1891,* 3213; D.W. Meinig, *The Great Columbia Plain: A Historical Geography, 1805–1910* (Seattle: University of Washington Press, 1968), 279–80, 282; Ficken, *Washington Territory,* 118–19.

68. J.G. Holcombe to Symons, June 30, 1891, in *Annual Report of the Chief of Engineers, 1891,* 3231; April 1, 3; June 30, 1892; F.R. Shrunk to Symons, April 16, 1892; G.H. Mendell to Symons, Jan. 11, 1895; Harry Taylor to James C. Post, Oct. 28, 1895; W.R. Prowell to W.L. Fisk, June 2, 1896, all Seattle District Records, U.S. Army Corps of Engineers, RG 77, Federal Records Center, Seattle; *Spokane Review,* Aug. 5, 6, 1891; *Walla Walla Statesman,* Aug. 15, 1891; *Wenatchee Advance,* Jan. 26, 1895; Symons to W.P. Craighill, May 22, 1895, in *Annual Report of the Chief of Engineers, 1895,* 3534–37; to Casey, Jan. 17; May 3, 1895, Portland District Records, U.S. Army Corps of Engineers, RG 77, Federal Records Center, Seattle.

69. *West Shore,* 17 (Feb. 28, 1891), ; *Spokane Review,* Aug. 5, 6, 11; Dec. 27, 31, 1891; July 7, 1892; Feb. 2, 1893; *Walla Walla Statesman,* Sept. 8, 1891; *Spokane Falls Review,* Nov. 2, 1889; Jan. 16, 1891; *Seattle Press-Times,* Sept. 28, 1891; May 4; July 4, 1892; *Seattle Telegraph,* June 23, 1892.

70. Previously working out of Portland, the corps of engineers established an independent Seattle office in 1890. *Tacoma Morning Globe,* Feb. 14, 1891; A.J. McMillan to Symons, Oct. 28, 1890, in *Annual Report of the Chief of Engineers, 1891,* 3257; Taylor to John M. Wilson, Dec. 27, 1897, Records of the Office of Chief of Engineers, 1894–1923, RG 77,

National Archives; Feb. 16, 1898, in *Annual Report of the Chief of Engineers, 1898*, 3099; *Seattle Telegraph*, Jan. 25, 1893; Symons to Casey, Oct. 12, 1892, in *Annual Report of the Chief of Engineers, 1893*, 3467; July 9, 1894; Thomas Handbury to Chief of Engineers, April 24, 1890, both Portland District Records; *West Shore*, 16 (July 26, 1890), 927.

71. Gilman to Burke, Feb. 24; March 2, 1892; Burke to Carrie Burke, Oct. 27, 1889, all Burke Papers; *West Shore*, 15 (Nov. 2, 1889), 252; 16 (March 8, 1890), 311; Robert C. Nesbit, *"He Built Seattle": A Biography of Judge Thomas Burke* (Seattle: University of Washington Press, 1961), 256–57, 404; Robert E. Ficken, "Seattle's 'Ditch': The Corps of Engineers and the Lake Washington Ship Canal," *PNQ*, 77 (Jan. 1986), 11; Neil H. Purvis, "History of the Lake Washington Canal," *WHQ*, 25 (April 1934), 117–18; *Seattle Morning Journal*, Oct. 27, 1889; *Seattle Press-Times*, Sept. 26; Oct. 2, 1891.

72. The engineers favored Smith Cove over a line west to Shilshole Bay because the former route would more effectively connect the segments of Seattle's harbor system. *Seattle Morning Journal*, Oct. 27, 1889; *Seattle Telegraph*, Sept. 2, 3; Oct. 4, 1892; *Seattle Press-Times*, Aug. 27, 1891; Mendell, Handbury and Symons to Casey, Dec. 15, 1891, in H.E.D. 40, 52d Cong., 1st sess., 5–9; Ficken, "Seattle's 'Ditch,'" 11–12.

73. "Local jealousy does not seem to have got in its deadly work up there," a Seattle editor quipped of canals supposedly observed by astronomers on the surface of Mars. "When canals were needed they built them, and the next town didn't pout and sniffle." *Tacoma Daily Ledger*, Jan. 8, 1892; July 20, 1893; *Tacoma Daily News*, June 25, rep. from Pendleton *East Oregonian*; Aug. 1; Sept. 19, 1892; *Seattle Post-Intelligencer*, Oct. 30, 1892; *Spokane Review*, May 12; June 18, 23, 29; July 29; Aug. 20, 24, 1892; *Seattle Telegraph*, May 3, 24; July 2, 1892.

74. Seattle residents denounced Representative John Wilson of Spokane for "very apathetic" work on behalf of the project. The Lake Washington canal was completed in 1917. Gilman to Burke, Feb. 21; May 20, 1892, Burke Papers; Thomas B. Hardin to Gilman, May 5, 1892; John B. Allen to Gilman, July 8, 1892; Squire to Gilman, July 28, 1892, all Gilman Papers; *Seattle Post-Intelligencer*, July 2, 1892; *Seattle Press-Times*, July 2, 1892; *Seattle Telegraph*, July 2, 1892.

75. *Seattle Telegraph*, March 3, 1893; *Seattle Post-Intelligencer*, Nov. 13, 1893; Portland *Oregonian*, Nov. 14, 1893; *Walla Walla Statesman*, Aug. 1, 1893.

76. The early decade death toll also included George Allan, onetime Hudson's Bay Company employee and "the oldest white settler in Washington," John Flett, a translator at the Isaac Stevens Indian treaty councils, Horace Hart, a survivor of the "Whitman Massacre" and S.M. Wait, the founder of important towns in the Walla Walla Valley. *Seattle Telegraph*, July 20, 1891; Dec. 17, 1892; Walker to W. Talbot, July 21, 1891, Walker Letterbooks; *Seattle Post-Intelligencer*, March 13, 1890; Dec. 17, 1892; Feb. 17, 1893; *Tacoma Daily News*, Oct. 13, 1892; *Seattle Press-Times*, Aug. 9, 1892; Olympia *Washington Standard*, Jan. 1; Dec. 23, 1892; March 31, 1893.

77. "It seems to us," a Portland critic complained of Hawthorne's selection, "that a man who has no thorough personal…knowledge of the Pacific northwest is not the man to do this important work as it ought to be done." *Tacoma Morning Globe*, Aug. 29, 1890; *Seattle Telegraph*, Nov. 29, 1890; Feb. 11, 1893; *Seattle Post-Intelligencer*, March 13, 1890; Frykman, *Seattle's Historian*, 40–41; Julian Hawthorne, ed., *History of Washington: The Evergreen State* (New York: American Historical Publishing, 2 vols., 1893); *Spokane Review*, May 13, 1892, rep. from Portland *Telegram*.

78. Since the 1860 cutoff severely restricted membership east of the Cascades, Spokane old timers formed a rival pioneer society. Olympia *Washington Standard,* June 6, 1890; May 6, 13, 1892; *Tacoma Daily Ledger,* June 6, 1892; *Spokane Review,* Oct. 6, 1891; June 9, 1893; *Seattle Telegraph,* Jan. 7, 1894; Edmond S. Meany, "The Pioneer Association of the State of Washington," *WHQ,* 8 (Jan. 1917), 3–6; *Olympia Tribune,* Oct. 7, 1891; *Tacoma Morning Globe,* Feb. 20, 1892; Spokane *Spokesman-Review,* April 14, 1897.

79. *Seattle Post-Intelligencer,* Dec. 17, 1892; *Seattle Telegraph,* July 20, 1891; *Spokane Falls Review,* July 20, 1891; *Spokane Review,* Oct. 6, 1891; June 9, 1893; *Tacoma Daily Ledger,* June 6, 1892; Spokane *Spokesman-Review,* April 14; Oct. 6, 1897; *Tacoma Daily News,* April 21, 1898.

John H. McGraw, elected to a four-year term as the state's second governor in 1892.
University of Washington Libraries (La Roche 10017)

Chapter Four

Every Necessary of Life

*[Washington] has been compared to Pennsylvania, and justly, in that a wall
could be constructed around it without serious detriment to its population. Every
necessary of life being available within its borders.*—Moses P. Handy, "The
State of Washington," *Lipincott's Magazine.*[1]

S EATTLE RESIDENTS CHORTLED and Tacomans wept tears of utter humiliation
  when President Benjamin Harrison, touring the Pacific coast in the spring
of 1891, visited Elliott Bay for six hours and spent barely two in the rival City of
Destiny. Even in Seattle, however, the visit fell far short of being an inspirational
experience. A bushy dullard on the best of days, Harrison insulted his hosts by
complaining, without end, of the inclement weather. Overcast skies and persistent
drizzle concealed the Olympic Range and Mount Rainier and transformed the
glorious waters of Puget Sound into dank fogs and gray wavelets. Ignoring the
president's foul mood, local organizers insisted that he proceed with a planned
carriage procession from the bayfront to the dreary and dripping shores of Lake
Washington. Glum onlookers stood here and there along the rain swept route,
witnessing the passage of a damp and visibly sullen political dignitary.[2]

  Benjamin Harrison was neither the first nor the last outsider to condemn the
Sound country's infamous precipitation. During the early 1890s, the inhabitants
themselves developed a fixation upon the myths and realities of rainfall. Although
visitors went away convinced that local weather conditions consisted of "three
months winter and nine months blamed late in the fall," actual citizens expressed
a nuanced point of view. The rain might descend from the skies in prodigious
fashion—stylish ladies supposedly adopted "abbreviated skirts" as a means of
coping with muddy streets—but Washington remained a misunderstood climatic
"paradise." While the East suffered from "fogs, floods, frozen rivers, cyclones,
blizzards, [and] devastation in every conceivable shape," the infant state avoided
all extremes. "The fruit trees and vines blossom in October," a happy immigrant
reported, and the people wore the same clothing in both July and January.[3]

  To be sure, predicting the weather, from season to season and year to year,
was "always a puzzle" for Washingtonians. Despite the fact that the state had
"more climate to the square inch…than any other region on the globe," certain

patterns were clear to experienced settlers. The first scientific study, only recently published, confirmed the existence of substantial local variances in precipitation, from over 100 inches yearly at Neah Bay to approximately 20 for Port Townsend at the eastern end of the Strait of Juan de Fuca. Rather than a curse, rain was "heaven's gift to the northwest coast," a "blessing" responsible for vast green forests and swift flowing rivers. The heavy mountain snows of winter were another "of our greatest allies," for they meant abundant crops later in the year.[4]

Eastern Washington was visited by cleansing rains in the spring and again in the fall. "The days are full of sunshine," a Spokane editor noted of the pleasant aftermath, "and the air possesses a tone that is…invigorating." Summers were undeniably hot, with temperatures exceeding 90, or even 100, degrees for weeks at a time. Low humidity, however, made the daylight hours bearable in comparison to conditions east of the Rockies. Refreshing nocturnal breezes produced, according to regional boosters, nights "cool enough to require bedclothing." All in all, climate on both sides of the Cascades was yet another reason for the state's deserved ranking as America's most attractive point for settlement and investment. "It is the ideal longed for by countless millions," one commentator exclaimed, "the conditions fancied in the gardens of the gods, the theme around which poets have woven their imagery."[5]

❦

A good portion of everyday life in Washington took place far from logging camps and grain fields. "Cities do exist," an eastern tourist discovered in the winter of 1894, "and to the bewildered traveller who visits the sound with a hazy notion that its shores are still wilderness, broken here and there by rude frontier settlements, they seem to have sprung into being full fledged, with all the metropolitan adjuncts of electric lights and cars, luxurious club-houses and palace hotels, spacious parks, superb business blocks, and miles of handsomely built-up residence streets." Coming into one of the metropolitan centers, the first thing noticed by the passengers on a train or steamer, however, was the pungent odor, a noxious gas arising from a mixture of environmental and artificial pollutants. Though even medium sized towns had cable driven or electrified transit facilities, teamsters relied upon horses. Animals stood for hours at street side and in alleyways, depositing what one editor delicately referred to as a substance "very offensive to the smell." The dismaying sanitary habits of transients, and of much of the resident population for that matter, caused the larger communities to at least plan for installation of public lavatories.[6]

Sewer systems were either lacking or primitive in nature. Concerns over cost and proper technology usually trumped public health and comfort. In Olympia, "noisome affluvia" bubbled "from the concealed gutters under many of the sidewalks into which the sewerage…is allowed to accumulate." Despite the deepest of pockets, the developers of Everett neglected to provide for any means of drainage, at or below street level.[7]

Rapid population growth everywhere overtaxed the modest abilities of local government. The 13 miles of Seattle sewer line were, to general disgust, "worse than nothing." According to the *P-I*, foul "ooze" regularly flowed into "cellars, back yards and by-ways." The existing mains emptied, without treatment or filtration, onto the bayfront. "Perhaps the tide washes the filth away; perhaps it does not," another of the local dailies reflected. "Most persons whose smelling facilities are normal will incline to the latter proposition." Tacomans made fun of Seattle as "a very unhealthy place...on account of the odors," but their own sanitary arrangements were totally ineffective. Shallow cesspools sufficed until 1890, when the first sewers utilized Commencement Bay as a convenient outlet. Spokane installed a limited and insalubrious system in the same year, dumping waste into the city's namesake river just below the once pristine falls.[8]

Garbage presented another challenging problem for towns large and small. Everett residents deposited refuse in the Snohomish River. "A large part of the foul matter," one onlooker noted of the unsavory result, wound up "deposited on the banks...in the lower parts of the city, or returned on the incoming tide." Ellensburg ranchers, meat packers and rendering plants piled animal carcasses and offal within "smelling distance" of the best residential streets. To the disgust of refined citizens, most inhabitants of Waterville, the Big Bend seat of Douglas County, tossed food scraps and other "swill" out their front doors to become yardbound "fly breeders." Walla Wallans became so fed up with profusely littered streets and lots that the town installed the state's first "garbage crematory" in 1893.[9]

Once again, the big cities were overwhelmed by a growing threat to the public welfare. In Seattle, garbage was dumped in back alleys or into Elliott Bay. A modest reform was instituted in 1891 when the community's much celebrated new fireboat, constructed as a means of combating the next great urban conflagration, was instead pressed into regular service towing fully laden scows to the open waters of the Sound. Untroubled by esthetic concerns, Tacoma made use of Commencement Bay as a handy repository, without heed to whether the tide was outgoing or incoming. Beyond the Cascades, the Spokane River—already providing drinking water, power and sewage treatment—assumed yet another uncertain metropolitan function, garbage disposal. The few persons willing to risk downriver strolls reported finding all manner of disgusting trash "lodge[d] in bends of the stream, there to fester beneath the rays of the midsummer sun."[10]

Washington's fast growing cities were as noisy as they were unwholesome. Out-of-tune bands passed down the boulevards on a near daily basis, loudly touting local businesses and traveling shows. Adults and children alike claimed to have reason on their side when pelting insufferable Salvation Army processions with rotten eggs and fruit. "It is a disgrace to any town," a Tacoma editor asserted, "to permit a lot of buxom women and lusty men to parade the streets…sounding their wind instruments to the discomfort of every decent man and woman." From disturbed dawn to exhausted dusk, peddlers and "nomadic fakirs" obstructed the sidewalks, noisily proclaiming the problematic virtues of medicinal and religious nostrums.[11]

Rube newcomers in particular also found cities to be dangerous places. Disembarking steamboat passengers had to negotiate "a veritable death trap" over several transcontinental lines running along Railroad Avenue, to reach hotels and mercantile establishments in downtown Seattle. The Northern Pacific and the Great Northern bisected Spokane's business and professional district. The guards stationed at some, but far from all, street crossings often failed to sound "the least warning to approaching footmen and conveyances."[12]

Much of the danger came from street railways. Few Washington communities lacked at least a rudimentary commuter system. Port Townsend, for instance, installed five miles of track in 1891. Cars ran along the Willapa River front at South Bend. Ellensburg, Yakima and Walla Walla operated lines at the time of statehood. Electrified interurbans carried passengers between Hoquiam and Aberdeen, Tacoma and Steilacoom—some passengers carried rifles in anticipation of plinking away at deer along the route—and New Whatcom and Fairhaven.[13]

Street car lines were especially important in the major metropolitan areas, allowing workers and business owners to take up homes at a distance from places of employment. Using electricity generated at the falls, Spokane was well served, particularly by the four-mile Ross Park route, a $300,000 undertaking outfitted with heated and "beautifully upholstered" Pullman cars. Thanks to recent construction efforts, Tacoma claimed in early 1890 to have more "railroads complete and under way than any other city of its size in the country." Until a mid-1890s consolidation, the situation in Seattle was notably chaotic. Electric lines served the downtown streets parallel to Elliott Bay, ran to Ballard and Green Lake on the north and snaked across the Duwamish flats to the fast developing suburb of West Seattle. Three cable roads carried commuters and recreationists over the hills to Lake Washington. According to a survey, half the population rode the cars on a regular basis. Unlike Tacoma, where a "complete transfer system" prevailed, passengers paid new fares when changing from one to another of the dozen or so distinct operations.[14]

Greedy fare policies were but an irritation compared to the hazardous nature of street travel. Mechanical malfunction and conductor incompetence produced the occasional "runaway," a real danger in hilly portions of Tacoma and Seattle. On double-tracked avenues, careless debarking passengers were sometimes run down by cars approaching from the opposite direction. "The fact that it happened to be a Chinaman who was injured," a Seattle editor noted in reporting one such incident, "does not lessen the offense." Railway companies ignored speed limits and schedules, and invariably failed to display destination signs. Compounding the risk and inconvenience, some loutish male passengers smoked and refused to surrender their seats to women, displaying contempt for proper modes of societal behavior.[15]

Electric railways drew power from wires suspended overhead on poles, causing a further danger to urban life. "The big naked trees that encomber our streets," a Tacoma critic affirmed, "are not only disagreeable to the eye but a menace to life and property." In addition to being a prime fire hazard "when the current is a powerful one," the wires, together with those installed by telegraph and telephone companies, restricted firefighter access and reduced opportunities for occupants to escape from burning structures. Such concerns led to regular campaigns for mandatory "under-grounding," efforts strongly and successfully resisted by corporate interests opposed to making the necessary expenditures.[16]

In addition to street cars, brothels, gambling dens and, except where prohibited by voters under the old territorial local option statute, saloons were prominent aspects of everyday existence. Spokane maintained a heavily patronized red light district near Riverside Avenue, the city's most fashionable street. Reporting on several dozen prostitutes appearing at the courthouse to pay their "quarterly fines," one of the Tacoma dailies exclaimed that "houses of ill-fame," were for all practical purposes, "openly licensed" by the municipality.[17]

Outsiders claimed that Seattle was home to 3,000 "fallen women," an assertion that, while surely exaggerated, reflected the city's historical reputation as "a vast brothel." Elliott Bay was "next to hell upon earth," according to a scandalized visiting minister. The sin ridden community, another offended tourist claimed, "would outrank for vice the vilest precinct of the old New York 'Five Points' in its rottenest days." A local editor, normally engaged in promoting family oriented Seattle delights, conceded that "the imagination of a Zola…could not draw a picture which would be as extravagant in its corrupting details" as the daily portrait on display in the streets of Washington's largest city.[18]

Whitechapel, a two block district south of Yesler Avenue named for Jack the Ripper's London hunting ground, was the focal point of Seattle's sin trade. Respectable folk condemned the neighborhood as "a melancholy reflection upon the depravity of human nature," and as "the cancer which corrupts the city." Customers of all classes, along with prostitutes, landlords and most politicians, thought otherwise. Giving in to the bleatings of ministers and their housewifely allies of both sexes, the town council moved against Whitechapel in February 1891, ordering the establishments closed and outlawing use of the name. The outcome, after brief churchly elation over the freedom of genuine ladies to again appear in public "without hearing sounds and seeing sights that bring the blush to their cheeks," was to worldly on-lookers predictable. Previously confined to one demented center, "harlotry" spread far and wide, becoming more firmly embedded in the social fabric.[19]

Liquor, another source of pleasure and profit for the morally bankrupt, also was impossible to eradicate. The social impact of uncontrolled alcohol consumption was difficult to ignore. "When drunken ditch men and cowboys," a Yakima newspaper protested, "swagger around the city streets...loudly cursing and threatening in abusive language what they will do with the police if they will interfere, it is time to call a halt." Saloon license fees, though, provided a substantial portion of the municipal revenue in medium sized and small towns, reducing the tax burden on fiscally sober residents. Tacoma, meanwhile, claimed fame for having more saloons than churches, a self awarded status reflecting the position of big city people on temperance. Washingtonians supposedly consumed on a per capita basis only one-sixth of the volume of beer imbibed by New Yorkers. This apparent sign of refinement only partly obscured a sodden truth—the state, rural areas excepted, was awash in alcoholic drink.[20]

Liquor establishments and houses of ill-fame often shared the same premises. Seattle nonetheless boasted in 1892 of having 200 stand-alone saloons. "No one need walk far," a resident claimed, in order to find a place "where he may quench his thirst for malt and alcoholic beverages." Aside from the most demented ministerial types, public opinion opposed all prohibition measures. The bar room, according to wide agreement, was "a necessity as society is at present constituted." Most people did favor, as in the case of prostitution, enforcement of the 1888 municipal ordnance restricting public consumption to the central business district. Regular attempts by the liquor interests and their political affiliates to extend the saloon limits into residential neighborhoods went down in defeat.[21]

Tacoma trailed Seattle in the number of saloons open for trade, but otherwise drank hard to maintain a cherished ribald reputation. "If the people of this city," a preacher complained, "would devote a tithe of what they are willing to spend in gratification of their appetites to the support of enterprises that seek the...moral good of the city every...church...would have treasuries running over." License fees paid for a good portion of the local government. When the religious element briefly secured enforcement of the state Sunday closing law, a statute usually ignored on behalf of commerce, saloon owners adroitly frustrated the campaign by organizing Sabbath liquor cruises on the Sound and by paying the police to raid grocers, cigar stores and ice cream parlors. Spokane's politically connected alcohol vendors also openly violated day-of-rest closure attempts. The city's residents "cannot get shaved on Sundays, but they can still get a drink," an outlying paper noted. "This shows that in an extremity, however great, there is still room for hope."[22]

Gambling, the third essential urban vice, presented distinctive social features to public view. The habit, by more than one account, was "indulged in only by the two extremes of society—the very high and the very low." In big cities and small towns alike, a contemporary witness lamented, "men of standing" patronized "resorts for gaming without the faintest blush of shame." Police and prosecutors conveniently ignored "gentlemen's clubs," the private reserves of the affluent and the influential. Factory and mercantile workers, on the other hand, somehow had to be denied access to the evil practice. If not, employees would more than likely become addicted, leading to thievery as a means of covering losses. The problem was to find an effective means of control, because games of chance, as one editor sagely intoned, "will continue to the millenium."[23]

East, west, north and south, Washingtonians demonstrated by their habits that wagering was, in truth, close to a universal enterprise. By one account, 200 professional and amateur gamblers practiced their craft in the Palouse River town of Colfax. "Stud poker and crap games are running," Prosser's inhabitants stressed when reporting the signs of progress to be encountered in their Yakima Valley community. Card room operators expelled from Roslyn quickly went into business in nearby Cle Elum, running "a line of free busses between the cities for the accommodation of the devotees of the fickle god chance." A Bellingham Bay journalist claimed that "at least a dozen" stylish practitioners of the trade were "in sight almost any minute" on the streets of Whatcom and Fairhaven.[24]

Seattle, as usual, provided the greatest number of opportunities for the pleasure seeker to waste his or her money on ill conceived gratification. "Gambling houses are running freely and openly…on almost every officer's beat," one of the newspapers reported, despite state supreme court decisions validating municipal anti-wager statutes. Hundreds of addicts supposedly labored for no greater purpose than the gathering of their wages "to pass into the dealers' itching palms." The leading gamblers were recognized members of society, meeting in public with city officials, attending political conventions and raising cash for state and county election campaigns. Although charges were occasionally filed against individuals momentarily out of governmental favor, judges usually dismissed defendants upon one or another convenient technicality.[25]

Public wagering was also an everyday fact of life for Seattle's urban rivals. "There is a boss gambler, or factotum," a Commencement Bay daily noted of the Tacoma situation, "who collects a large percentage of the winnings of each house, under the pretence that he uses it with somebody in authority to prevent interference with the games." Card and dice enterprises diverted, in one estimate, several thousand dollars a day from legitimate business. Spokane struggled to reconcile sanctimony with the take-a-chance attitude encouraged by historical mining investment. An alliance of merchants and churches actually secured a gambling shutdown in early 1890. By the end of the year, though, the games of chance were back in full if somewhat more circumspect operation, ably protected by well compensated local police.[26]

Vice flourished by becoming an integral component of government and law enforcement. The owners of saloons, brothels and gambling parlors organized "every hobo and scalawag" to obtain voter registration certificates, legitimate and fraudulent, to control conventions and dominate primaries. The result usually was a general election contest "between two bad or indifferent candidates," both committed openly or covertly to the continuation of immoral activity.

Police department rosters changed on a yearly basis with the victors in the annual municipal pollings often literally selling the money making positions to eager applicants. Periodically appointed, dismissed and reappointed as Seattle chief, depending upon the partisan tenor of the present city administration, Bolton "Baksheesh" Rogers frankly displayed his corruption in the form of a diamond encrusted badge, the gift of underworld admirers.[27]

Dependent upon a compromised political process for their over and under the table income, officers of the law acted as dual public and private employees. Cynical commentators praised the capacity of otherwise sophisticated police-men to become "as unsuspecting as an infant" when assigned to the detection of immoral behavior. A Fairhaven editor concluded that weak eyesight must be a job requirement, since every member of the local force could "wander into a gambling den where four or five games are running full blast and...only catch a single gambler." Police raids usually coincided with the approach of election day to appeal to naive social reformers. The targets selected were, for some reason, invariably supporters of the opposition slate. Happily, all participants in such charades could look forward to the resumption of unrestrained business once the votes had been cast and counted.[28]

~~~~~~~~~

Fast paced development and the increasing demand for modern services meant that the traditionally informal methods of local governance could no longer be tolerated. Merchants, professionals and responsible politicians now believed that the ideal city was "only a business corporation on a larger scale." Government must therefore be so organized as to attract "the very best men available"—pub-lic spirited individuals willing and proud to declare themselves "free from all unsavory and degrading connections." To make way for true citizens, communi-ties must first devise and implement workable charters. In early 1890, the state supreme court invalidated the incorporation documents left over from territorial times, close to 50 in number. Washington's new constitution authorized cities of the first class, those with permanent populations in excess of 20,000, to proceed with up-to-date replacements. Seattle, Tacoma and Spokane, though qualified on the basis of unofficial statistics, hesitated to act prior to completion of the federal census. Passing a more detailed statute on the subject in March 1890, the legisla-ture enabled urban residents to finally take definitive action.[29]

Washington's three big cities supposedly held "elections once every three months," a bemused east-of-the-Cascades editor claimed, "in a vain endeavor to make workable their elaborate city charters." Seattle, in particular, earned a statewide reputation for being "fearfully and wonderfully governed" under the complicated arrangements approved by voters in the fall of 1890. The fun-damental document, according to perplexed critics, provided "wheels within wheels" and was "larger than the constitution of the United States." The mayor's office was weak and the city council divided into two unwieldy adversarial bodies—the aldermen and the delegates. Independent boards and high salaries compounded the confusion, promoted inefficiency and increased the burden upon taxpayers. "No other city of this size in the world," one dumbfounded observer exclaimed, "is paying so much for its whistle." Within weeks of implementation, critics mounted a serious campaign for outright replacement at best or wholesale amendment at the least.[30]

Spokane and Tacoma avoided Seattle's administrative incoherence, while also failing to devise acceptable forms of permanent government. Under the charter adopted in April 1891, the Inland Empire metropolis was plagued by never ending conflict between entrenched town councilors and a relatively powerless mayoralty. Gerrymandered wards allowed persons elected by a third of the population to control the council and determine the course of public affairs. Tacomans, meanwhile, approved a contentious and extravagant governing system.[31] Like their Seattle counterparts, residents of the two cities vocally demanded substantial changes in municipal administration.

More than willing to take part in repeated drafting of new charters, the better elements of society trusted that diffuse and carefully circumscribed responsibilities would frustrate the corrupt designs of the politicians in charge of day-to-day business. The cost of government was without doubt burdensome. The regular 1893 Seattle city budget, for instance, provided for an expenditure of nearly $700,000, with two-thirds of this sum to be covered by tax receipts and the remainder from license fees and utility payments. Large scale urban necessities required that public officials, like private developers, seek outside investment. Seattle and other municipalities, the *P-I* pointed out, needed to devise a proper "financial policy." Credit became, in fact, a vital metropolitan enterprise. Warrants were regularly issued to cover short term lapses in revenue flow. The state constitution allowed cities and counties to assume debt up to 5 percent of assessed property valuation, provided three-fifths of the electorate voted in the affirmative. Under the charters, oldtime "village fashion" reliance upon pay-as-you-go governance gave way to a modern faith in borrowing.[32]

Other levels of government also dealt with new and increasing fiscal requirements. County officials desired, along with their municipal counterparts, to refinance existing obligations at lower rates of interest. In addition, the counties had to construct roads and bridges, expensive farm-to-market projects generally considered the responsibility of local citizens. Population growth severely strained the school districts. Only half of eligible children sought a public education, but over 50,000 pupils attended Washington's schools in 1891. Two hundred schoolhouses were erected that year, an impressive rate that nevertheless failed to relieve overcrowding. Tacoma averaged 50 students to the teacher. An accelerating pace of immigration, of course, translated into substantial future increases in enrollment.[33]

Horrified by borrowing and spending, old fashioned Washingtonians resisted the appeal of public capital. If roads were truly needed, traditionalists argued, construction ought to be funded from either current revenues or special tax assessments. Residents occasionally defeated bonding proposals at the polls, or filed legal actions to thwart implementation of voter approved fiscal measures. Plans to build a new Adams County courthouse on credit ignited a bitter dispute between the inhabitants of Ritzville and their offended rural neighbors. Angry Whitman county commissioners withdrew a bond issue from the market when insulted by the below par bids submitted by eastern financial houses.[34]

Republicans, the dominant political force at the local level, ignored critics. Bonding was a "wise and economic" policy claimed the *Seattle Post-Intelligencer*, Washington's leading establishment paper. This approach to urban finance was "based upon the very soundest principles of modern government." Cities and towns had needs that could most easily and fairly be met by allocating the burden between the taxpayers of today and tomorrow. "The principle...is just," another stalwart party organ, the *Tacoma Ledger*, affirmed. "That future generations shall in part pay for the permanent improvements of which they receive the benefit, is undisputed." Also beyond argument, the advocates of big spending insisted, was the economic stimulus provided by infusions of cash, an important consideration given the periodic disruptions in the national and regional economy.[35]

Great cities and small towns alike engaged in a flurry of debt accumulation. Sprague, the old Northern Pacific division headquarters in the Spokane country, issued bonds in early 1890 to fund past due warrants and pay for the installation of sewers. With only 27 of the 800 votes cast in the negative, the residents of Fairhaven approved a bonding proposition consolidating old obligations and funding new public works. Confronting bankruptcy in 1892—"she has not a dollar in her treasury which can rightfully be expended," the local newspaper confessed—Aberdeen survived by selling securities to eastern banks. Many of the counties also utilized infusions of capital to retire warrants. Citizens organized by Bellingham Bay saloon owners, for instance, turned out in large numbers to ratify a refinancing scheme in Whatcom County.[36]

Larger benefits went, as might be expected, to the premier cities. After a heavy spending year in which public debt increased to well over a million dollars, the Elliott Bay electorate approved an aggressively promoted "business proposition" in early 1892. The $1.2 million thus secured supposedly confirmed that Seattle's "credit" was "second to that of no other city in the country." Tacoma owed less money than its Puget Sound rival, but appeared, according to some accountants and attorneys, to have exceeded its constitutional debt limit. By an overwhelming margin of 3,000 votes for and 80 against, the residents obtained a solution in the form of a bond issue saving $30,000 a year in interest. Spokane took similar action, abandoning "village management" to refund a quarter million dollars in unpaid warrants.[37]

After the 1889 fire, Spokane rebounded with over extravagance when rebuilding the down-town commercial area. *Museum of Arts & Culture, Spokane (L87-1.267)*

Bonding delivered other rewards to a credit happy citizenry. Jefferson County voters approved funding for a road network in the Port Townsend vicinity. Chehalis County secured a $320,000 issue in May 1891 to build all weather connections between backcountry farms and steamer landings on the Chehalis River. Aberdeen and Hoquiam sold bonds to pay for new schools. On the Sound, taxpayers in Mount Vernon, Sedro and Snohomish City took on debt for the same purpose. East of the Cascades, old Walla Walla and the growing college town of Pullman borrowed money for educational projects.[38]

Capital, in the form of private money loaned for public purpose, was of particular importance in funding large scale municipal improvements. The expense required for the excavation and laying of sewer mains exceeded the capacity of even the largest city. Fairhaven and Olympia on the west and Yakima on the east side of the mountains were among many urban areas paying for systems with borrowed money. The demand for street lights and commuter railways was large enough, and the financing available, to justify involvement in the electricity business, either by supplanting or competing with private firms. Between 1890 and 1893, Hoquiam, South Bend, Ellensburg, Waterville and Sprague built or purchased generating plants, issuing bonds for the necessary funds.[39]

Pure water was an obvious source of concern as growing populations abused and exhausted springs and streams. Making use of the new fiscal methods,

Olympia, Shelton, Ellensburg and Pasco installed modern systems, reservoirs and hydrants included, in 1890. The eastern Washington community of Goldendale sold $40,000 worth of bonds in Chicago to pay for its new waterworks. Over the next two years, westside towns building or acquiring plants included Whatcom, Aberdeen, South Bend and Kent in the valley south of Seattle. Beyond the mountains, Dayton, Colfax, Palouse City, Waterville and Kettle Falls, the latter recently founded on the upper Columbia, went into the public water supply business. Walla Walla voters twice approved an expensive municipal venture, but the existing private company took legal action to thwart construction.[40]

Debt and water combined in potent manner in the principal cities, revealing both the crucial importance of capital and the general incompetence of local government. The Spring Hill Company, pumping water from Lake Washington to 3,000 homes, and the smaller Lake Union Water Company, served Seattle at statehood. The system leaked badly, a shortcoming exposed to sobering effect when low pressure seriously impeded attempts to extinguish the 1889 fire. Capacity lagged well behind population growth. The effects of industrial and residential development would soon spread to the lakes, threatening the public health. Already, one inhabitant complained, "the stuff which runs through the pipes literally stinks."[41]

Negotiations begun in the aftermath of the fire resulted in the city's purchase of the Spring Hill works in 1890. Realizing too late that demographic growth would substantially increase the value of their stock, investors vainly attempted to nullify the transaction in the courts, citing various technical objections to the necessary bond sale. Seattle officials initially intended to spend most of the borrowed money on an ambitious new project, supplying future requirements while shifting from dependence upon the soon-to-be-polluted lakes. The plan developed by consulting engineer Benezette Williams involved construction of a dam on the Cedar River, two dozen miles southeast of the city, diversion of water into a high capacity reservoir and distribution by gravity mains. For an estimated expenditure of little more than $2 million, Seattle would attain security against fire and danger to the public health until at least the turn of the century.[42]

Avoiding explicit abandonment of the Benezette Williams scheme, which remained the focus of intense debate, the city council soon reverted to makeshift reliance upon Lake Washington. "It is at its worst," defenders of the traditional source of supply contended, "better than the water supplied to San Francisco at its best." Besides, the alternative would cost too much money, leaving Seattle without the capacity to borrow for other public purposes. "Shall we have Lake Washington water for the next few years at a price we can afford," the *P-I* posited, "or Cedar river water at a price three times greater than we can afford." Acting in accordance with such concerns, the city spent close to a million dollars on improvements to the old Spring Hill apparatus without, unfortunately, producing significant improvement in service. The new pumps were defective, maintenance was lax to non-existent and the overall management, one critic asserted, was so "incompetent" that the entire system was "in daily danger of breaking completely down." Adding pocketbook insult to potential catastrophe, the municipal authorities used the annual profits to finance other programs, rather than to reduce rates or provide essential enhancements.[43]

On Commencement Bay, water matters roiled about the distant personage of Charles Wright, sometimes called, with minimal affection, the "father" of Tacoma from longtime investments in railroading, real estate and utilities. The Philadelphia financier's Tacoma Water & Light Company, drawing its supply from springs and lakes on the municipal outskirts, had become, according to vocal complaint, more of a "curse" than a benefit. Portions of the community were completely without service, forced to rely upon shallow wells one slimy step removed from cesspool status. In the better neighborhoods, well founded concerns over water quality supposedly accounted for the booming patronage of saloons. "A man would rather run the risk of delirium tremens," a resident explained, "than typhoid fever." Snakes and other forms of squiggly reptilian life apparently infested the system, ready to emerge from the pipes at inopportune moments. "That something should be done," one editor summed up, "is a fact as self-evident as Mount Tacoma on a clear day."[44]

Intent upon making Tacoma "the largest city of the upper Pacific coast," Charles Wright conceded that present arrangements sufficed for a community of no more than 10,000 inhabitants. His firm therefore announced, in the spring of 1890, a $1.7 million improvement designed to bring vast supplies into the city from American Lake and the Green River. A group of influential Tacomans, worried about continued outsider control and the likelihood of high rates, responded with a proposal for a publicly financed and owned water system. Both approaches foundered upon obstruction, including legal challenges from right-of-way property owners. Wright soon determined that the Green River route was too expensive, a conclusion substantially reducing the scope of his effort. The public ownership alternative, meanwhile, was frustrated by mounting cost projections and widespread conviction that Wright ought to be indulged in his eagerness to spend money, thereby allowing the city to devote funds to other necessary ends.[45]

Exercising superb insider connections—a direct telephone line supposedly ran from the mayor's office to water company headquarters—Wright manipulated the debate to personal advantage. At his covert bidding, the council abruptly canceled an 1891 bond election for the city owned waterworks. When a committee of experts eventually recommended a public system, Wright offered to sell his plant at an appropriately outrageous price. Prolonged and occasionally nasty negotiations ensued, with the local representatives of the Philadelphian haggling from a position of strength. "All available supply of pure water, excepting Green river, has been obtained by the company," one of the newspapers stressed in detailing the lack of options, "and a Green river system would cost at least three or four millions and take several years to build." In early 1893, pro-Wright city officials twice postponed public votes on the bonding proposition necessary to fund the transaction, adding to the pressure upon a half-dry community. Except for modest improvements implemented under the original 1890 plan, Tacoma was no better served than at the time of the state's admission to the Union.[46]

Spokane also suffered from greed and misfeasance. The city's existing plant pumped water from the Spokane River—upstream at least from the main sewer outlets—through eight miles of main pipes to business blocks, homes and fire hydrants. Flowing from Lake Coeur d'Alene, the river, in spite of extensive mining activity in the north Idaho mountains, was supposedly "as pure and almost as cold as the snow itself." Entering the city, however, the stream was at once "contaminated with the filth exuded from reeking cesspools," and thereby "inoculated with elements akin to poison." Cautious residents boiled water "before drinking," and even then "swallow[ed] it with a fear of the consequences." Rebuilding from the 1889 fire, property owners worried, too, that water pressure was insufficient and the aging pipes likely to burst in the event of a new emergency.[47]

Legitimate urban needs were, unfortunately, ignored in favor of a politically connected real estate speculation. According to the best informed opinion at statehood, a new Spokane works should be based upon development of springs and lakes on the far outskirts of the city. "Otherwise," the *Review* pointed out in July 1890, "the rapid growth of…suburbs would soon pollute the water supply and necessitate a change almost before the new system had been placed in operation." Captain Thomas Symons, actively involved in a series of consulting contracts with the city while ostensibly on active duty with the Army Corps of Engineers, prepared a construction plan on the basis of this rational concept. The result was voter approval of a half million dollar bond issue, the proceeds to be used for initial building and temporary improvements to the existing facilities.[48]

At this personally opportune moment, local developer F. Lewis Clark came forward with an alternative proposal to build an upstream dam on the Spokane River, with diversion works leading into town. Coincidentally, the project depended upon usage of land owned by Clark, acreage he was willing to sell to the city for $100,000, 20 times the assessed valuation. Supported by the municipal authorities, the scheme outraged believers in transparent public enterprise. "Dams have a fashion of washing out," critics warned in calling attention to the lack of solid foundation rock at the construction site. Reversing the trend of previous thought on the subject of pollution, an inventive opposition now insisted that the downtown riverfront was, after all, a reliable and unmistakably cheap source of drinking water. "It looks pure, it tastes pure, and analyses show that it is pure," enemies of the dam-focused monetary grab managed to contend with straight faced determination.[49]

Clark's gambit prevented any serious enhancement of Spokane's water supply. The promoter lost his carefully cultivated, not to mention well compensated, city council majority in the 1892 municipal election. In a separate polling, the voters rejected the dam scheme. Aside from the small amount of money expended upon improvement of the existing works, receipts from the bond issue were still on deposit in the banks, drawing no interest. Unfortunately, the funds were insufficient to undertake more than preliminary work upon the comprehensive project contemplated prior to Clark's disruptive appearance upon the utility scene. In 1893, Spokane residents had unmet water needs and, if possible, less respect than ever before for politicians.[50]

Borrowing was as vital to government as to private business due to near revolutionary economic changes and the new forms of transportation and communication. Through their access to the world of capital, growing cities paid for utilities, roads and education and assumed contemporary debt in order to retire old obligations. Public debtors, like their commercial counterparts, expressed implicit faith in the future, convinced that unrestrained progress would enable repayment upon favorable terms. Only a few truly conservative sorts dared suggest that booms might unexpectedly come to a disastrous end. Speaking for traditionalist Democratic fogeys in April 1893, the *Seattle Telegraph* wondered about the effects of a "depression." In such a case, would urban taxpayers be willing or even able to pay for both current expenses and the interest and principle due upon pre-collapse debt?[51]

❧❧❧

Washington was partway along in the abandonment of its crude frontier societal habits. Anti-spitting ordinances, posted on walls and telegraph poles in most cities, were directed at an egregious and outmoded practice. "Tobacco-masticating loafers," a Spokane editor complained of a time honored facet of urban life, "gather on the street-corners and put the pavement in the condition of the floor of a low doggery." Until the new rules were obeyed, ladies had to continue dragging their skirts through disgusting drool, while small children risked exposure to disease and loathsome behavior.[52]

Men of a certain type, and some women too, also insisted on carrying firearms. Unconcerned observers insisted that Washington was no worse off in this regard than any other parts of the country, and the actual enforcement of the state ban on concealed weapons would correct gun toting abuses. Police blotters and newspaper crime columns told a more compelling story. "Nearly every difference of opinion, petty dispute or common brawl," the *P-I* reported, "is terminated by one party whipping out a revolver and pouring more or less lead into the other." In a by-no-means unique 1892 Seattle incident, an angry drunkard shot his friend, then committed suicide in remorse, needing on account of his liquor impaired aim three bullets to accomplish the close range task. Numerous alcohol and gambling related shootings gave Spokane an "unenviable reputation" for violence. Bloodshed was hardly limited to the big cities. Well fortified by his own product, a bartender in the farm country town of Garfield deliberately and permanently silenced an obnoxious customer. Gun play was a regular feature in the railroad construction camps, making the nights as dangerous as the days.[53]

Respectable folk condemned the open display of weaponry as "an anomaly of nineteenth century civilization." The gunslinger, professional or amateur, was "a disgrace to the land," the practitioner of a "murderous, unmanly and cowardly habit." Literally a loose cannon, he or she would sooner or later kill and maim innocent citizens. Private ownership of handguns must therefore be prohibited as a true measure of public safety. "The privilege of bearing arms guaranteed by the constitution," *West Coast* magazine noted in a representative screed upon the subject, "never included or intended such a state of affairs as exists today."[54]

Part, at least, of the concern over guns reflected a sense that crime was out of control in the Pacific Northwest. Washington proclaimed yet another triumph in 1891 with news that the state had fewer than 300 prison inmates, compared to 400 in Oregon and over 2,000 in sinful California. Seasoned commentators suggested that these figures indicated only that lax Evergreen State authorities had failed to apprehend a higher percentage of genuine lawbreakers. "The sole work of the police department," a Seattle paper claimed, "seems to be confined to the arresting of drunks and collecting licenses under the form of fines, from the women of the town." Preoccupied with such lucrative and relatively unhazardous and energy efficient ventures, the officers of the law apparently did little, if anything, to prevent real offenders from running amok.[55]

Old fashioned crime retained favor among underworld denizens. Stand-and-deliver highwaymen worked the Ellensburg-Wenatchee road like regular employees, holding up stages and terrorizing lone travelers. Masked outlaws ransacked the Port Townsend post office in March 1891. Olympia was infested by a "murderous gang," arriving with the railroad and staying on once the track laying was complete. "Hardly a night passes," a publisher advised of conditions in his eastern Washington community, "that some one is not knocked down and robbed of money or watch, after being beaten almost to death." Baggage was "stolen if left in the depot waiting rooms, and nothing is safe outside."[56]

New style criminal activity also flourished. Counterfeiters passed money on a virtual circuit from one to another of the smaller Puget Sound towns. Scam artists, such as the proprietors of the Tacoma based "Secret Marriage Bureau," which promised a list of willing brides for $5, prospered in cities of all sizes. Truly perverted behavior also reflected modernity, often drawing responses of a more traditional sort. Walla Walla Valley farmers tarred and feathered a neighbor for allegedly teaching "disgusting practices" to their sons. Residents of Snohomish City delivered similar chastisement to the local priest, charged with encouraging parish youth to "participate in every form of vice that a wanton and utterly depraved nature could devise." Pasco wife beater J.W. Larkin emerged triumphant from court in August 1891 after the victim refused to testify. Larkin, however, was seized by outraged citizens, beaten with a fence post "until he shrieked with pain" and literally ran, or at least was compelled to stagger, out of town.[57]

Youthful rebellion was another unwelcome product of modern times. "Little tads, not more than ten years old," a Fairhaven resident reported, "are numerous in the vilest purlieus of the city at all hours of the night, where they are simply vegetating into the worst kinds of criminals." Older boys and their equally footloose female compatriots loitered outside, or even inside, "bad saloons," learning vile habits and lawless trades. Bored teenagers engaged in random acts of destruction, including an 1893 Colfax incident in which "hoodlums" rolled a flatcar into the Palouse River, destroyed the foundation of the municipal pumping plant and overturned piles of lumber. Many communities imposed curfews on minors, with little expectation that such measures would be successful. The only truly effective means of addressing delinquency, a Bellingham Bay observer suggested, was to somehow prevent unfit adults "from having families."[58]

Unpunished killings, another feature of the new order, were to a certain extent a Washington tradition. "It has grown into a proverb," one of the Seattle papers asserted, "that no white man has ever been hung for the murder of an Indian." The shocking thing for many people was that the truism now appeared applicable to all elements of the population. "Since Whitman County has been organized," a self styled expert on the subject declared in 1898, "more than thirty murders and lynchings have taken place and no legal hanging has resulted." Sensational cases provided the public with never ending diversion. Prominent New Whatcom resident D.H. Long murdered his wife and son-in-law in 1891. Ed Hill "plunged a knife into poor Langford Summers" at the climactic point of a Colfax street altercation. The well attended trial of a Seattle woman for shooting her lover featured the public reading of salacious correspondence between the accused and the "Jekyll and Hyde" victim.[59]

Low expectation of punishment in such cases fostered a revealing contemporary anecdote. "Hell and damnation," a Puget Sound man supposedly shouted upon being convicted of murder. "I suppose this means another year in jail." The problem, for most citizens, was that "sentimental juries" and "skilled" attorneys able to "twist and misconstrue the words uttered" by prosecution witnesses invariably would prevent convictions. Killers actually found guilty resorted, with astonishing rates of success, to appeals or gubernatorial pardons, the latter an especially attractive option during the leniency-for-hire terms of Elisha Ferry and John McGraw. "The people," one editor declared in summing up popular contempt for the judicial system, "are getting tired of seeing the woman with the sword and balances flim-flammed on every corner."[60]

Two years had passed, amateur students of crime lamented in 1892, since the state's last legal execution. The time was therefore at hand, an increasing number of residents believed, for the public to take justice in rope wielding hand. The citizenry, an eastside journal demanded, ought to "rise up in righteous wrath and give a few terrible though effective examples such as confronted the wrongdoers of this Coast in the [18]50's and later." Reporting upon the organization of vigilantes in Wenatchee, another newspaper noted that "lynch law is to be deplored, but if judiciously applied…it would no doubt result in great good to the town." Adding to its many claims of superior performance, Washington far outdistanced Oregon and Idaho in the frequency of lynchings.[61]

Arriving by water in April 1891, vigilantes shot the two occupants of an Oysterville jail awaiting retrial on murder convictions overturned by the state supreme court. The assassinations doubled as a form of tax protest, one observer suggested, since the original trial had wasted half of Pacific County's yearly budget. A month later, the townspeople of Issaquah in the foothills east of Seattle seized a person suspected of setting fires in the community. Fortunately for the arsonist, who somehow survived the ordeal, his captors were less than fully competent executioners. "When let down the last time," an account of the botched lynching reported, "the victim was so far gone that he was considered dead." East of the Cascades, officers of the nearby Army garrison at Walla Walla stood by while enlisted personnel murdered an incarcerated gambler. In 1895, an Ellensburg mob lynched a local father and son arrested on charges of murder. Whitman County's reputation for wheat growing respectability was badly compromised by Colfax hangings in 1894, 1897 and 1898.[62]

One more instance of anti-social behavior involved prejudice against the Chinese. Less than 5 percent of the 100,000 immigrants from China residing in the western United States lived in the state of Washington. Much of the rhetoric directed at this small minority was familiar from territorial times. True enough, the Chinese occupied "a niche in the public economy that it would be hard to fill." Except for "cheap labor," the region's vital railroads would, in barely appreciated fact, "still be phantasms of the dim and distant future." Undesirable in spite of this contribution, the Chinese supposedly sent home "every dollar" earned, removing money from local circulation in the course of taking jobs from "deserving" white men and women. The product of "an alien and absolutely unreconcilable civilization," the Asian, moreover, could never be "Americanized."[63]

Based upon such assumptions, many communities adopted customary tactics. Aberdeen drove out its Chinese residents in November 1890, with city officials robbing the expellees in the process. Montesano and South Bend followed the example set by their southwest Washington neighbors. On the Sound, Everett residents prevented the first would-be Asian settlers from coming ashore at the steamer dock. Adopting a somewhat more subtle approach, Olympia authorities accused the Chinese of bearing leprosy, a charge used to forestall the landing of newcomers in the name of public health. To the east of the Cascades, claim jumpers freely evicted Asian miners in the gold country outside Ellensburg. Dayton and Pullman expelled their Chinese populations in the spring of 1892.

Wenatchee rid itself of the sole Asiatic on the scene by detailing, in a town meeting, the few pros and the many cons entailed in his continued presence.[64]

Mounting trade between the Pacific Northwest and Asia mandated a more nuanced approach at commercially oriented points. Bigotry, after all, could not be allowed to interfere with economic growth. Tacomans credited their prosperity to the dramatic 1885 expulsion of the Chinese. "None of our people," one of the Commencement Bay dailies boasted, "are compelled to come into competition with a class who have learned by centuries of contest with famine to live on less than would ordinarily support life." However, the problem was that Seattle's relatively benign attitude regarding Chinese businessmen gave it a distinct advantage as a marketplace for exporting grain. Ignoring "the solemn protest of thousands of good, honest patriotic citizens, who love their city rather than gold," Tacoma authorities therefore decided in 1892 to admit a dozen Chinese merchants in residence. Elsewhere in the state, individuals intent upon attracting capital for private and public projects worked to prevent "repeated outrages" against the Chinese, incidents sure to receive negative press coverage in the East.[65]

Other white Americans complained that porous borders on both sides of the Cascades were responsible for out-of-control illegal immigration. "From one to half a dozen smuggled Chinamen are daily landed upon the shores of Whidbey Island," a report from Puget Sound claimed. Persons turned back merely bided their time north of the Canadian boundary until an opportune moment for a new attempt at entry. Federal exclusionary laws, designed to restrict admission to members of the mercantile class, generated a lucrative trade in fraudulent "merchant certificates." Occasional enforcement attempts focused on major ports-of-entry, producing a shift to secondary locations, which accounted for a sudden and unexpected increase in Olympia's Chinese population.[66]

Drug smuggling afforded another indirect outlet for criticism of the Chinese. The same methods and routes used to bring in illegal aliens were also available for the transportation of contraband substances. According to a widely accepted report, 70,000 pounds of refined opium arrived in Washington via the 49th parallel crossings in 1891. Olympia was the principal distribution point, a local paper noting that "the wary smugglers found the extreme head of the sound just the place at which to operate because there were no inspectors and no customs officers to head them off." A courtesan known as the "Spanish heiress" exercised her sophisticated charms on behalf of the business to "compromise the principal police officers" in the capital city. Federal officials admitted to interdicting one pound in a hundred. "To the door of the Chinese," the *Spokane Review* insisted in a standard scapegoating commentary, "is to be laid the introduction of this terrible vice, which once fostered upon a person never lets go its hold."[67]

Japanese newcomers, rapidly increasing in number, drew off some of the pressure previously focused on immigrants from the Asian mainland. "The same cry is raised against them as against the Chinese," a Spokane newspaper advised.

Railroad contractors and other employers eagerly hired Japanese workers, who accepted lower wages and, by their mere presence, encouraged division in the ranks of labor. The usual discriminations were widely applied. Spokane cooks and waiters organized to "drive out the Japs" in 1891. Opportunistic Sprague police officers assessed an extra $2 tax upon Japanese prostitutes.[68]

Washington's ever closer relationship with the larger American nation caused the old anti-Asian bigotries to be partially subsumed within a new all embracing nativist ideology. In the state, the percentage of the overall population made up of non-Protestant immigrants from southern and eastern Europe hardly came close to the national standard. Washington nonetheless was threatened, or so alarmists contended, by unfamiliar and truly alien cultures. Although the danger was more theoretical than real, the region's citizens came to accept views common in other parts of the country. The rulers of backward Europe, a Bellingham Bay editor claimed, were busily "emptying into our lap the scum, offscourings, and criminals of over-crowded prisons, penal settlements and poor-houses." Most of these newcomers remained in New York and other debauched Atlantic coast ports, but the people of Washington supported restrictions, even an outright ban, on further European importations. "America for Americans," one commentator declared in 1891, "is a good enough platform for the present."[69]

❧❧❧

Living in an increasingly industrialized and urbanized state, many Washingtonians now possessed expendable income and leisure, two things usually missing during territorial times. Spectator sports emerged as a popular fixation. To be sure, boxing, previously an audience favorite, was declining in acceptance. Professional fighters died in matches in Seattle, Portland and San Francisco—horrific incidents responsible for much of the public disgust. The Washington legislature, indeed, outlawed prize fighting, with bouts continuing only under such subterfuges as a legal loophole allowing members of private clubs to engage in "sparring...for exercise." Responding to indignant citizens, Seattle was the first municipality to move against the sport, banning all contests in the winter of 1891. A local promoter was even convicted of complicity in the murder of a competitor killed in the ring.[70]

Baseball—in the past played informally in company towns and among urban weekenders—emerged as the premier athletic spectacle. Seattle, Tacoma, Spokane and Portland organized a professional league in 1890, playing a 97 game season. After a coastal championship series in 1891, the northwest communities joined with California cities to form the first Pacific coast association. Semi-pro and amateur leagues, such as the Palouse country alliance of Colfax, Palouse City, Tekoa and Farmington, also flourished. Players spoke of "setting up in business for themselves," but teams maintained close connections with corporate sponsors. Company agents imported athletes, assigning them to the various "nines."

Rudimentary stadiums were deliberately located at the end of urban railways—Seattle played on the shores of Lake Washington at the Madison Street line's terminus—drawing passengers on fan oriented interurban routes.[71]

Virtually all public and much private business ceased so that ticket holders could flock to crucial daylight hours games. Newspaper sports sections appeared for the first time, featuring box scores and detailed coverage of home teams. Wins and losses assumed importance as another measure of ongoing urban rivalries. "We want to see that the laurels which Tacoma has won in every branch of competition are retained on the ball field," a Commencement Bay editor pronounced. The local Inland Empire club, meanwhile, "maintained the supremacy of Spokane over all other Northwestern cities." Conventional chest thumping aside, the game supposedly possessed intrinsic, socially beneficent merits. Betting on teams was allowed, but the games themselves were "honest," determined by individual skill and teamwork. Fans were exposed to fresh air and wholesome competition, and as "a great leveler of class distinction," the pastime was democratic to the core.[72]

Quite early, certain negative aspects of baseball also became evident. Fans complained and would remain at home when local teams suffered winless streaks, establishing the principle that "people will not go to see their club lose games." Saloon gossip focused on managerial and front office incompetence, and team owners drew additional criticism by threatening to move franchises to other cities. Attempts to control player salaries, leading ostensibly to lower ticket prices, quickly failed, as one or another club violated their solemn pledges in the interest of winning pennants. Purists protested over the introduction of bunting and other unsporting innovations. Outraged religious types demanded that Sunday ball be canceled as an ungodly affront to the Sabbath.[73]

Enthusiasts nostalgic for the violence in boxing found their own peculiar outlet in a new sport, football. "It is a hearty, rollicking, manly game," the *P-I* enthused in a late 1890 appreciation. Pacific Northwest fans followed local town clubs and devoured press accounts about the annual Harvard-Yale match, America's greatest sporting event. Port Blakely bested Tenino in 1891 for the first silver cup championship of the Washington State Association. "A college without a football team," one observer noted regarding the game's growing popularity on campuses, "would be a novelty." Baseball retained wide popular support, but football assumed status among devoted advocates as "the national sport." The newer game, after all, was the perfect outlet for an emerging, expanding new world power, showcasing "courage, persistence, pluck, foresight, and…quickness of thought and action."[74]

Persons more interested in participatory sports adopted another craze, the bicycle, or "wheel." Selling on installment plans for $100, the contraptions drew praise as "the popular vehicle of the future, both for men and women." At the mercy of the fast moving devices, however, less than enthusiastic pedestrians vowed to "tar and feather every wheelman…and ride them out of town on a rail." Outside the cities, residents sometimes blocked roads with logs, brush and boulders, so as not to be endangered by speedsters. Municipalities established 5 mph speed limits, mandated the use of bells and required safety examinations for riders wishing to use sidewalks. On a more positive note, operators became leading advocates for good roads and dedicated pathways, including a proposed wheel-only linkage between Seattle and Tacoma.[75]

Out-of-doors recreational opportunities also attracted energetic members of the populace. Urban sophisticates became tourists in their own land, attracted by previously unappreciated natural wonders on both sides of the Cascades. Blessed by the new American economy, the middle class possessed the means to take excursions. "The time of recreation is at hand," a Seattle newspaper noted. "It is therefore to be decided whether you will spend a few weeks…at a summer hotel, or gather together what of your portable belonging[s] you can, and hie you to some sequestered nook."[76]

Encouraged by the railroads, tourism emerged as a growth industry. Campers and hikers flocked each summer to the mountain girded shores of Lake Coeur d'Alene and Lake Chelan. Boasting rental cottages for "thousands of pleasure seekers," Long Beach on the hard packed sand between the Pacific Ocean and Willapa Bay flourished as a warm weather escape. Places of less obvious appeal also sought visitor dollars. Spokane insisted that "the spirit of reviving nature" was best appreciated by a springtime sojourn in the Inland Empire. Tacomans claimed that their city possessed unique qualities as a "health resort." A trip to any of these places was guaranteed to provide welcome relief from the hurly-burly of commercial and professional existence. In an added bonus, nature served as "an advertising agent for this wonderful country," further encouraging impressed tourists from outside the region to invest money in the Pacific Northwest.[77]

≈≈≈

Affluent Washingtonians inclined toward non-adventurous pursuits devoted their leisure time to cultural refinement. The public library movement drew most of its support from educated individuals. "Provision on a liberal scale for such an institution," argued one bibliophile, "gives high assurance that broad and refined views prevail in the community and indicates an encouraging sense of stability." Libraries, too, encouraged investment by projecting a refined community image to capitalists. Resuming a campaign begun prior to the great fire, Seattle "ladies" made sure that the new municipal charter of 1890 authorized a free library. A special bond issue financed acquisition of reading material and planning for con-struction of a permanent building to replace temporary quarters in the pioneer Yesler mansion. Tacoma and Spokane quickly followed suit, the former with sup-port from local government. Aberdeen, Fairhaven and other westside communi-ties also established libraries. East of the Cascades, the Dayton facility received a $20 monthly public stipend. Yakima commenced operations in the spring of 1891, with 200 books available to borrowers.[78]

Libraries were heavily patronized by an avid reading public. By 1894, Seattle had 12,000 volumes on the shelves and 8,000 card holders. Tacoma patrons checked out "fourteen and a half times the stock of books…every year." A dozen or more persons were to be found in the periodical section at any hour of the day. Municipal prestige was enhanced and social cohesion encouraged by supplying literature to individuals otherwise unlikely to "develop a taste for reading." Certain difficulties also became apparent at an early date. Expenditures frequently exceeded revenue, more often than not by alarming margins, and politicians attempted on a regular basis to shift funding to more profitable public ventures. Refined persons also complained that popularity seeking librarians favored "pablum" in the selection of books and journals.[79]

Urban parks were another newly acquired taste. Tacoma was blessed with Point Defiance, a 700 acre wilderness grant from the federal government. Amidst "the forest primeval," the visitor experienced "nature not art." Standing beneath the firs on the bluff above Puget Sound, day trippers admired "the finest inland salt sea…on the globe," and off to the west, the "ragged, jagged monsters" of the Olympic Range. Funding from private sources, however, was imperative in order for the dramatic vistas to be properly appreciated. Some of the natural wildness would have to be eradicated, Point Defiance supporters asserted in demanding that carriage ways and trails be provided. Fallen timber and underbrush must also be removed, "in order that progress through the park may be easily made."[80]

Park projects, meanwhile, often suffered from neglect by politicians. "Public parks are the breathing places—the lungs of large cities," a Commencement Bay newspaper maintained in arguing that open spaces be "scattered through the densely populated sections." Because of its isolation, Point Defiance was more likely to attract the mobile middle class than the transportation limited families of workers. Tacoma also had the better situated Wright Park, donated by the ubiquitous Charles B. Wright. Failing, apparently, to detect any political or personal advantage from such expenditures, the city council refused to appropriate maintenance funds. Wright Park, the only convenient out-of-doors respite for most Tacomans, as a result resembled "a Yakima coyote farm." The summertime grass turned yellow from lack of watering and the pathways became "as dusty as a country road in the San Joaquin valley."[81]

Seattle's park supporters also experienced frustration. Complaining of "the heavy burdens of enormous taxations" already imposed upon the public, opponents fought off ambitious post-fire development programs. In their limited efforts, municipal officials generated more antagonism than appreciation. Occidental Square, a poorly conceived venture in downtown park making, provided, according to its many critics, little more than a noisome gathering place for "an aggregation…of cranks." City attempts to purchase Woodland Park, a failed private oasis in the north end, for $100,000 were widely, and reasonably, denounced as "jobbery." Seattleites depended instead upon corporate open space developments such as Madison Park on Lake Washington, managed by real estate speculators and commuter railway firms.[82]

Elsewhere, parsimonious local governments relied almost entirely on private undertakings. "Fine parks are almost as essential to fine cities as fine buildings," the *Spokane Review* insisted, to minimal local effect. Property owners opposed the necessary taxes, especially when the funds would likely be used by "a spoils administration" to acquire tracts of "worthless land." Until 1898, when the first true public park, a modest $10,000 project, was opened, Spokane's only open spaces consisted of the occasional bits of greenery set aside by developers of "additions" to attract homebuyers. A similar pattern prevailed in smaller cities. In 1892, for example, the Yakima town council offended "thinking people whose range of vision extends beyond the tip of their nose," but satisfied the majority of the residents by refusing to spend $2,000 for 16 prime acres designated by planners for park purposes.[83]

No one suggested that public money be used for another refined institution of modern urbanized times, the theater. Taking on what one observer called a "metropolitan air," cities of all sizes—Aberdeen, Port Angeles and Colfax ranking among the middling places—opened privately financed opera houses. "The whole new west," a Spokane editorialist proclaimed of the latest cultural fad, has "taken most kindly to the revival of the legitimate drama." Performing companies traveled from town to town on regular circuits. The famous European star Sarah Bernhardt, seemingly on permanent tour in the United States aboard a luxuriously appointed Pullman car, visited Washington on a number of occasions. Bernhardt fans were charged $5 a seat, causing one newspaper to quip, regarding her most popular role, that it be pronounced as "Cleo-pay-tra, with a strong accent on the pay."[84]

Community self-congratulation arose from involvement in the theatrical arts. Sold out plays attended by formally attired couples proved, according to persons genuinely concerned about such matters, that "Tacoma society is composed of the very best people...second to no other city of the union in culture, refinement and discriminating power." A fair amount of pretentious nonsense also was on display, a point suggested by a contemporary observation that "seven out of ten" Sarah Bernhardt ticket holders "will not be able to understand a word she says, as she uses nothing but French on the stage." The theater experience itself was expensive and, more often than not, below the quality promised in advertisements. Seattle socialites actually capable of informed appreciation objected to "the presentation of worn out performances by wretched performers...for prices which ought to be a guarantee of something at least to the level of mediocrity." Even the great Bernhardt garnered snooty criticism for being the personification of "the Parisian demi-monde that is so in conflict with the Anglo-Saxon idea of womanhood."[85]

Class distinctions set the legitimate, if often second rate, theater apart from so called "variety" and "music" halls, entertainment emporiums patronized by the masses. In fact, Tacoma police prevented the "disturbing element" from attending plays frequented by mercantile and professional families. "Many an innocent girl and equally innocent wife," defenders of the prohibition contended on the basis of past unsavory experience, "have had the blush of shame brought to her cheek on taking her seat to discover that the one who perhaps sat next to her was a painted harlot." When a rash promoter opened a music theater north of Yesler Avenue, the unofficial boundary between moral and immoral Seattle, he was quickly bankrupted by non-patronage. Respectable men were willing, even happy, to frequent such places, but only upon expectation that they would not be seen by neighbors and relatives likely to take, or at least pretend, offense.[86]

Though quite literally an "insult to...decency," variety shows provided undeniable entertainment attractions. A visitor to Seattle's popular Tivoli Theater reported that the featured singer—"an old elephant" with "a manly bosom"—made an encore performance "clothed only in her maidenly modesty...and a half dozen hair-pins." Performers at the Coeur d'Alene Theater in Spokane specialized in crowd pleasing displays of "a lewd and lascivious nature." Scantily clad females trolled the aisles, peddling high priced refreshments and negotiable assignations. Private "boxes," the luxury suites of the era, facilitated the conclusion of such forthright transactions. Workers and assorted low-lifes might lack the sophistication and resources, not to mention the phoniness, of the middle and upper classes, but they too had means enough to enjoy themselves in the new state of Washington.[87]

〜〜〜

Visitors to the region's mushrooming cities confronted an immediate and singular problem, the considerable difficulty in locating specific business establishments and residences. "Everything," a Seattleite confessed of the incoherent naming and numbering of streets, "has been at sixes and sevens—a perfectly imperfect system." In Tacoma, the same street name was "repeated seven, eight and nine times," applied to portions of thoroughfares in noncontiguous neighborhoods. Seattle had "two Pine streets, two Thomas streets and...half a dozen others, so duplicated." Attempts to straighten out such confusion met widespread resistance from property owners unwilling to give up long familiar addresses. Campaigns for mandatory house numbers also generated outrage as being akin to "numbering convicts in a penitentiary or counting cattle in a barnyard."[88]

Difficulty in finding addresses was hardly the only problem to be confronted in negotiating Washington's urban boulevards. Olympia's streets were "well nigh impassable" in the aftermath of even a light rain. During the long dry months, Walla Walla residents choked in gritty clouds thrown up by "every passing vehicle." Similar inconveniences were experienced in the big cities. Seattle's streets were "more like navigable streams—navigable by mud scows," the *P-I* claimed, "than public thoroughfares." In Tacoma in the summertime, authorities resorted several times a day to sprinkling water on the streets in vain attempts to control the dust. "Words…failed" to properly convey the filthy nature of Spokane's downtown avenues. A local newspaper reported in nauseous detail: "Late in the fall this filth, comparatively harmless when dry and compact, is taken into solution by the liquid mud which gathers on all the principal streets. There it stagnates and steams under the influence of warm rains until the effluvia become offensive and dangerous."[89]

Most citizens agreed that the time was peculiarly "ripe" for reform in the interest of public health and investment. "Improved streets are the physical sign of thrift, liberality and wealth," editorialists on both sides of the Cascades pointed out. "They enhance the value of real estate and invite the attention of intending purchasers." Cities addressed the issue in a variety of ways, some ingenious and most without much tangible benefit. Oysterville, the colorful pioneer settlement on Willapa Bay, adopted a historically appropriate course, scattering crushed oyster shells as a makeshift pavement. Parsimonious Walla Walla opted for "strawing" in attempting to overcome dust. "We have seen well-kept barnyards which looked neater," one resident noted of the inevitable addition of horse manure to the low cost improvement.[90]

Competing for the dollars of outside investors, the major urban areas were especially concerned about street matters. Expensive regrading, though often controversial, was a necessity in the hilly portions of Seattle, Tacoma and Spokane. Paving also needed to proceed in central business districts and the better residential neighborhoods. No modern city could further rely upon the traditional laying of fir planks. "They will shrink with the one and swell with the other," a critic observed of the transition from dry to inclement conditions, "and will be in a continued state of eruption." Used by "hundreds of teams…daily," planked roadways were slippery and rugged. Cedar blocks were as defective as planking. Asphalt, the best "in point of cleanliness, absence from dust and durability," was by far the most expensive option. Macadam, which was cheaper, failed to hold up in poor weather.[91]

Municipal authorities made limited progress in the early years of statehood. Furthermore, property owners adjacent to street improvements objected to paying for the work through special tax assessments. "The months and the days are drifting by," a Seattle newspaper observed of the widespread refusal to pay the rate, "and with each futile attempt to deal with the subject the hope of collection is receding." Homeowners, too, hesitated in spending money to beautify their homes and properties. Pioneer towns such as Olympia and Walla Walla were famous for having shade trees, but they were rarely found in bustling metropolitan centers. Lawns and gardens usually were lacking in Seattle, Tacoma and

Spokane, and when found were likely to be untended.[92] Washingtonians saw little reason for the expenditure of real money on landscaping frills.

Notes

1. Rep. in *Seattle Post-Intelligencer*, Feb. 16, 1891.
2. *Ellensburgh Capital*, April 30, 1891; *Seattle Telegraph*, May 7, 8, 1891.
3. Richard Maxwell Brown, "Rainfall and History: Perspectives on the Pacific Northwest," in G. Thomas Edwards and Carlos A. Schwantes, eds., *Experiences in a Promised Land: Essays in Pacific Northwest History* (Seattle: University of Washington Press, 1986), 19–20; C.A.H., "Washington's Five Contrasting Climates," *Northwest*, 10 (May 1892), 5–6; *Seattle Press-Times*, Oct. 8, 1891; July 26, 1893; Olympia *Morning Olympian*, Sept. 25, 1891, rep. from Aberdeen *Bulletin*; *Tacoma Morning Globe*, Feb. 17; Sept. 30, 1891; *Seattle Post-Intelligencer*, Dec. 21, 1889; July 15, 1890; Dec. 30, 1894; *Tacoma Daily Ledger*, Jan. 2, 1890; Jan. 29, 1891; *Spokane Review*, Sept. 1, 1893; *Tacoma Daily News*, Nov. 19, 1898. Also see, for a general appreciation of the regional climate, David Laskin, *Rains all the Time: A Connoisseur's History of Weather in the Pacific Northwest* (Seattle: Sasquatch, 1997).
4. "I have lived in Seattle twelve years," one writer noted, "and during that time we have had twelve unusual springs, and the same number of unusual summers, falls and winters." Another observer complained that "when ladies are out in their spring hats they are entitled to at least twenty minutes' notice that they will be called upon to take a sleigh ride." Convinced that there was a reciprocal relationship between trees and rainfall, some Washingtonians worried that the extensive logging underway since earliest territorial times had already resulted in declining precipitation. *Spokane Falls Review*, Jan. 8, 1891; *Tacoma Morning Globe*, Jan. 17, 1890; Brown, "Rainfall and History," 17–19; *Spokane Review*, June 25, 1894; *Ellensburgh Capital*, Feb. 9; April 27, 1893; *Tacoma Daily Ledger*, Jan. 7, 1890; Seattle *Argus*, May 13, 1898; *Seattle Post-Intelligencer*, April 16, 1890, rep. from Snohomish *Sun*; July 8, 1894; *Seattle Press-Times*, Aug. 29, 1891; May 30, 1892.
5. Residents of western Washington also touted their warm weather months as far superior in comfort to summers in the East and South. *Spokane Falls Review*, Feb. 7, 1890; *Spokane Review*, Sept. 9, 1891; March 20, 1892; March 28, 1893; Spokane *Spokesman-Review*, Sept. 2, 1897; Aug. 11, 1898; *Yakima Herald*, July 3, 1890; *Ellensburgh Capital*, July 16, 1891; *Tacoma Morning Globe*, July 3, 1890; July 4, 1891; *Seattle Telegraph*, Aug. 18, 1891; *Seattle Post-Intelligencer*, Aug. 5, 1892. Attempts to put the best face on the regional climate dated to the pioneer era. See Robert Bunting, *The Pacific Raincoast: Environment and Culture in an American Eden, 1778–1900* (Lawrence: University Press of Kansas, 1997), 89; and Robert E. Ficken, *Washington Territory* (Pullman: Washington State University Press, 2002), 32.
6. "There is hardly a district of half a dozen blocks together," the *P-I* admitted of Seattle, "free from conditions which offend the sight and smell." Kirk Munroe, "The Cities of the Sound," *Harper's Weekly*, 38 (Jan. 13, 1894), 35; Park Weed Willis, "A Journey to Seattle, 1883," *Pacific Northwest Quarterly* [hereafter cited as *PNQ*], 34 (Jan. 1943), 22; Seattle *Argus*, Jan. 19, 1895; April 9, 1898; *Seattle Post-Intelligencer*, May 29, 1891.
7. *Yakima Herald*, Sept. 11, 1890; *Seattle Post-Intelligencer*, March 8, 1891; Olympia *Washington Standard*, June 12, 1891; *Everett Herald*, April 7, 1892.

8. Some Seattle schools were befouled by "trickling streams...from the surrounding higher ground." The favored, though witless, solution to Seattle's problem entailed diversion of sewage to Lakes Union and Washington, the two sources of the city's drinking water. Olympia *Washington Standard,* March 27, 1891; *Seattle Morning Journal,* Oct. 15, 27, 1889; *Seattle Times,* May 24, 30, 1889; *Seattle Post-Intelligencer,* Feb. 15; July 29, 1890; April 9, 1896; *Seattle Telegraph,* March 17; April 15, 1893; *Seattle Press-Times,* March 30, 1891; *Tacoma Daily News,* May 19; Aug. 21, 1890; *Tacoma Daily Ledger,* Oct. 17, 1891; Spokane Falls *Spokesman,* March 21; May 23, 1890; *West Shore,* 16 (April 19, 1890), 502; *Spokane Daily Chronicle,* April 27, 1898.

9. *Everett Herald,* March 24, 1892; Portland *Oregonian,* May 1, 1890; Waterville *Big Bend Empire,* Feb. 20, 1890; *Seattle Post-Intelligencer,* June 8, 1891; *Spokane Review,* July 15, 1893.

10. Unaccustomed to negative accolades, Seattle recoiled from its designation as "the dirtiest city on the coast." The Elliott Bay firefighting crew complained of being forced to perform "unfiremanlike work." *Seattle Morning Journal,* Jan. 3, 1890; *Seattle Post-Intelligencer,* July 22, 1890; *Seattle Telegraph,* March 10, 1891; *Seattle Press-Times,* March 13, 1891; June 15, 1892; *Tacoma Daily Ledger,* March 7, 1891; Spokane Falls *Spokesman,* March 12, 21, 1890; *Spokane Review,* Sept. 14, 1892; Seattle *Argus,* April 18, 1896.

11. *Seattle Post-Intelligencer,* Oct. 12, 1890; Portland *Oregonian,* April 19, 1891; *Tacoma Daily News,* Feb. 10, 1890; *Tacoma Daily Ledger,* May 28, 1890; *Tacoma Morning Globe,* Dec. 29, 1891.

12. *Seattle Telegraph,* March 26, 1893; *Spokane Review,* Jan. 2, 1892.

13. Portland *Oregonian,* May 23, 1891; Olympia *Washington Standard,* May 29, 1891; *South Bend Journal,* Nov. 7, 14, 1890; *West Shore,* 15 (May 1889), 280; (July 1889), 405; 16 (June 7, 1890), 726; (July 12, 1890), 885; *Walla Walla Statesman,* Oct. 23, 1891; *Tacoma Morning Globe,* Oct. 9, 1891.

14. The owners of real estate in places opened to development by railways expected their holdings to substantially increase in value. In addition to connecting downtown Tacoma with major residential districts, electric lines ran between new and old settled areas and to Point Defiance at the Narrows. *Seattle Post-Intelligencer,* April 7; May 3; Aug. 27, 1890; March 31, 1893; *Seattle Press-Times,* June 13, 1891; *Tacoma Daily News,* June 27, 1892; *West Shore,* 16 (May 3, 1890), 548–49; *Tacoma Morning Globe,* Jan. 8; Feb. 26; Sept. 23, 1890; *Tacoma Daily Ledger,* Sept. 20, 1890; *Seattle Telegraph,* Nov. 14, 1890; April 1, 1893; Olympia *Washington Standard,* April 7, 1893; *Seattle Times,* Dec. 21, 1895; Portland *Oregonian,* May 9, 1890; Thomas Burke to A.B. Wyckoff, June 4, 1890, Thomas Burke Papers, University of Washington Library.

15. *Tacoma Daily Ledger,* Feb. 23, 1890; *Tacoma Daily News,* March 5; April 11, 1890; *Seattle Press-Times,* Sept. 25, 1891; Seattle *Argus,* March 24; June 16, 1894; March 26; April 16, 1898.

16. *Tacoma Daily News,* Feb. 17; Oct. 7, 1890; *Seattle Morning Journal,* Nov. 17, 1889; Seattle *Argus,* June 30, 1894.

17. Dayton and Colfax were the most consequential towns to adopt prohibition under local option. *Spokane Daily Chronicle,* Jan. 14, 1898; *Tacoma Daily News,* Jan. 10, 1890; Norman H. Clark, *The Dry Years: Prohibition and Social Change in Washington* (Seattle: University of Washington Press, rev. ed., 1988), 36; Ficken, *Washington Territory,* 188–89.

18. *Seattle Telegraph,* Jan. 19, 1892; Seattle *Weekly Intelligencer,* Nov. 18, 1872; Seattle *Puget Sound Dispatch,* April 4; Nov. 14, 1872; *Tacoma Daily News,* Feb. 27, rep. from Fairhaven *Herald;* Nov. 24, 1891; *Seattle Morning Journal,* Oct. 20, 1889; *West Shore,* 17 (March 7,

1891), 152; Murray Morgan, *Skid Road: An Informal Portrait of Seattle* (Seattle: University of Washington Press, 1951, 1982 ed.), 58–61, 80.

19. Seattle *Argus*, Nov. 10, 1894; Morgan, *Skid Road*, 9; *Seattle Morning Journal*, Oct. 20, 1889; *Seattle Press-Times*, Feb. 14, 24, 25, 27, 28, 1891; March 30, 1893; *Tacoma Daily Ledger*, Aug. 9, 1890; Olympia *Washington Standard*, Feb. 27, 1891; *Seattle Telegraph*, Jan. 9; May 3, 1892; *West Shore*, 17 (March 7, 1891), 152.

20. When Goldendale in Klickitat County shifted from prohibition to licensed saloons as a means of generating revenue, one bemused onlooker suggested that the residents had "elected a city council that believes in licensing the sale of liquors, so hereafter they can take their nips from a bottle and not be compelled to go behind the woodshed to get it as in former days." Municipal authorities could not afford to be too onerous in their exactions. Steilacoom's saloons, for instance, closed rather than pay increased license rates, thereby emptying the public coffers. Washington had one liquor seller for every 286 inhabitants, only slightly better on the behavioral scale than the 1 to 249 ratio for Oregon and well below the 1 to 514 figure for Massachusetts. *Yakima Herald*, Aug. 18, 1892; *Ellensburgh Capital*, April 14, 1892; *Tacoma Daily News*, July 21, 30, rep. from Montesano *Vidette*, 1891; Portland *Oregonian*, April 20, 1891, rep. from Yakima *Herald*; Olympia *Washington Standard*, May 29, 1891; *Seattle Press-Times*, Oct. 23, 1891.

21. Olympia *Washington Standard*, Sept. 2, 1892; *Seattle Telegraph*, Aug. 15, 1890; Jan. 16; June 4, 5, 1891; *Seattle Press-Times*, Sept. 15, 1891; *Seattle Post-Intelligencer*, Jan. 16, 1891.

22. A local prohibitionist sheet described Spokane as "venal in public life, rotten in its social relations, and a loafing place for the unemployed." One in three Spokane arrests, according to police department ledgers, was for drunkenness. *Tacoma Daily Ledger*, Oct. 21, 1890; March 7, 1892; *Spokane Review*, June 24; July 1; Sept. 5, 1891; *Seattle Post-Intelligencer*, Sept. 13, 1890, rep. from Sprague *Herald*; *Spokane Falls Review*, Jan. 31, 1891; *Tacoma Daily News*, Aug. 15, 1892, rep. from Spokane *Outburst*.

23. *Tacoma Daily News*, Feb. 2, rep. from Fairhaven *Herald*; Aug. 18, rep. from Walla Walla *Union-Journal*, 1891; *Spokane Falls Review*, Dec. 2, 1889; *Seattle Telegraph*, Jan. 8, 1893; *Tacoma Daily Ledger*, Feb. 26, 1892; *Spokane Review*, Feb. 10, 1893.

24. Fairhaven gamblers defeated a restriction campaign by threatening to withhold subscriptions for the opera house and other civic ventures. Portland *Oregonian*, Sept. 26, 1893; *Spokane Review*, Jan. 7, 1893; Olympia *Washington Standard*, March 31, 1893; *Seattle Post-Intelligencer*, Aug. 30, 1890, rep. from Bellingham Bay *Express*; *Spokane Falls Review*, Nov. 25, 1890.

25. A riot nearly ensued when Seattle police insisted upon burning confiscated gaming tables and equipment. *Seattle Morning Journal*, Jan. 28, 1890; *Seattle Post-Intelligencer*, March 4, 1894; *Seattle Telegraph*, Sept. 29; Dec. 10, 1890; Feb. 24, 1891; Portland *Oregonian*, April 30, 1891.

26. A visiting minister blamed Spokane's apparent preference for sin upon local literary tastes, specifically a preference for reading "dirty, immoral, lewd" French novels rather than the Bible. *Tacoma Daily Ledger*, Feb. 2, 26, 1892; *Tacoma Daily News*, Feb. 4, 1892; *Spokane Falls Review*, Nov. 22, 1889; Jan. 12; Feb. 18; April 8; Nov. 13, 1890; March 5, 1891; *Spokane Review*, Feb. 10; April 13, 1893.

27. *Seattle Telegraph*, Sept. 14; Dec. 9, 1890; June 1; Oct. 6, 1891; Jan. 9, 15, 25; May 25, 26, 1892; *Seattle Post-Intelligencer*, Aug. 26, 1890; Nov. 18, 1892; *Spokane Falls Review*, Oct. 18, 24, 1890; *Tacoma Daily Ledger*, Jan. 19, 1892; *Spokane Review*, March 17; June 28, 1893; *Seattle Press-Times*, March 5, 1892; May 25, 1894.

28. *Spokane Falls Review*, Feb. 8, 1890; *Seattle Post-Intelligencer*, Aug. 30, 1890, rep. from Bellingham Bay *Express*; *Tacoma Daily Ledger*, Feb. 2, 1892.

29. "Seattle is now a large city," the *P-I* commented, "and must not be influenced in future questions of government by what has prevailed in the past." The position of mayor was "not by any means a sinecure or a bed of roses," a Spokane editor noted. "It is purely a business responsibility." Spokane had an additional concern, as past decisions restricting the geographical extent of the municipality in the interest of keeping expenditures and taxes low meant that a good many actual residents lived outside the official boundaries. *Seattle Post-Intelligencer*, Sept. 21; Oct. 6, rep. from Yakima *Herald*, 1890; Feb. 2, 1892; *Seattle Morning Journal*, Oct. 16, 1889; Jan. 9, 1890; *Tacoma Daily Ledger*, Dec. 1, 1889; Jan. 4; March 11; April 19; June 9, 1890; *Tacoma Daily News*, Jan. 3, 4, 6, 1890; *Spokane Falls Review*, Jan. 19; April 13, 1890; *Tacoma Morning Globe*, Jan. 6; Feb. 5, 15, 16, 1890; *Seattle Telegraph*, Jan. 28, 1892; *West Shore*, 16 (Jan. 11, 1890), 37.

30. *Spokane Review*, Feb. 10, 1892; May 7, 1893, rep. from Walla Walla *Union*; *Seattle Telegraph*, Nov. 9; Dec. 3, 1890; Jan. 11, 14; March 23; July 8, 1891; Sept. 25, 1892; *Tacoma Daily Ledger*, Aug. 14, 1890; July 12, 1893; *Tacoma Daily News*, Feb. 6, 1892; *Seattle Post-Intelligencer*, Aug. 10, 1890, rep. from Blaine *Journal*; Jan. 10, 1891; *Seattle Press*, Jan. 3, 1891; *Seattle Press-Times*, Sept. 10, 1891.

31. "One consolation the people of Tacoma have," a Commencement Bay editor claimed, "is that we cannot get up a worse charter than Seattle has got." *Tacoma Daily Ledger*, Aug. 14; Nov. 25, 29, 1890; Jan. 7–9, 1892; *Spokane Review*, April 7; Sept. 30; Dec. 29, 1891; April 6, 1892; April 20, 1893; *Tacoma Morning Globe*, June 29, 1890; *Tacoma Daily News*, Dec. 3, 1890; Jan. 6, 1892.

32. "There are more than 40 cities in the country, all larger than Seattle," asserted one critic of excess spending, "whose municipal expenses are much less per capita." In an important early decision, the state supreme court ruled that the somewhat vague constitutional language required a three-fifths approval by persons actually voting, rather than of all registered voters. *Seattle Post-Intelligencer*, Oct. 16, 1890; July 6, 1892; *Tacoma Daily News*, July 11, 1891, rep. from Port Townsend *Leader*; *Seattle Times*, July 12, 23, 1889; *Spokane Falls Review*, Jan. 19, 1890; Ficken, *Washington Territory*, 210; *Tacoma Daily Ledger*, July 28, 1890.

33. *Anacortes American*, Feb. 16, 1893; *Tacoma Daily News*, Jan. 13; Dec. 19, 1890; Dayton *Columbia Chronicle*, Dec. 31, 1892; Olympia *Washington Standard*, May 15, 1891; Feb. 5, 1892; *Spokane Review*, May 22; Dec. 20, 1891; Spokane *Spokesman-Review*, Oct. 29, 1894; *Pullman Tribune*, July 27, 1895.

34. *Aberdeen Herald*, May 7; July 30, 1891; Portland *Oregonian*, May 10; Sept. 18, 1891; Olympia *Washington Standard*, Jan. 1; Feb. 19, 1892; *Tacoma Morning Globe*, Sept. 11, 1891.

35. "It is not the people of today only who will reap the benefits," a Yakima paper noted, "but those also who will live here twenty or fifty years hence, and bonding the city…is only dividing the expenses up among those who will benefit by them." Much of the money procured from the sale of bonds was deposited in politically-favored banks, which paid no interest and loaned the funds at private profit. *Seattle Post-Intelligencer*, April 8, 1890, rep. from Yakima *Herald*; Feb. 26, 1892; June 7, 1893; *Tacoma Daily News*, Jan. 17, 1891; *Tacoma Daily Ledger*, Jan. 19, 1891; *Seattle Telegraph*, Dec. 13, 1892.

36. *West Shore*, 16 (Jan. 4, 1890), 14; *Ellensburgh Capital*, Sept. 3, 1891; *Fairhaven Herald*, April 28; May 1, 3, 1891; Portland *Oregonian*, April 7; Aug. 20; Sept. 8, 12, 15, 1891;

Olympia *Washington Standard,* May 1, 1891; Sept. 9, 1892; March 31; April 7, 1893; *Aberdeen Herald,* March 31; April 7, 14, 1892; *Anacortes American,* Feb. 16, 1893.

37. In contrast to the rural innocents of Whitman County, who refused to sell bonds below par, Seattle financial sophisticates declared their sale at 98% a great triumph. Tacoma's bonds eventually sold at par, after the proceedings were enlivened by a fist fight between rival bidders. *Seattle Telegraph,* Dec. 19, 1890; March 22; Aug. 15, 16, 1891; Feb. 3, 1892; March 3, 1893; *Seattle Press-Times,* Aug. 13, 1891; *Seattle Post-Intelligencer,* Jan. 30; April 5; May 29, 1892; June 7, 1893; *Tacoma Morning Globe,* Feb. 1, 6; July 12, 1891; *Tacoma Daily Ledger,* Feb. 14; April 11, 13, 1891; *Spokane Spokesman,* June 16, 1891; *Ellensburgh Capital,* Feb. 26, 1891.

38. Under prevailing mud spattered conditions, a farmer living two miles from Montesano on the Chehalis River needed the better part of a day to drive cattle to town. Olympia *Washington Standard,* Sept. 26, 1890; Feb. 6; April 3, 10; May 29; Dec. 4, 1891; *Aberdeen Herald,* Oct. 30, 1890; *Hoquiam Washingtonian,* May 28, 1891; Portland *Oregonian,* March 28; April 22; Sept. 10, 1891.

39. Washington had precisely 41,261 functioning electric street lights in 1893. Olympia *Washington Standard,* March 27; June 12, 1891; Aug. 26, 1892; Jan. 20, 1893; Portland *Oregonian,* April 3, 20, 22; Aug. 14, 1891; *Yakima Herald,* Sept. 11; Nov. 20, 1890; *Seattle Post-Intelligencer,* March 26, 1893; *Tacoma Daily News,* Jan. 20, 1890; *Northwest,* 8 (May 1890), 31; *West Shore,* 16 (Aug. 2, 1890), 970.

40. *Olympia Tribune,* Sept. 18, 1890; *Tacoma Daily News,* July 24, 1890; Portland *Oregonian,* April 9; Aug. 28; Sept. 30; Oct. 3, 1891; *West Shore,* 17 (Sept. 6, 1890), 59; (Nov. 1, 1890), 187; *The Dalles Times-Mountaineer,* Aug. 9, 1890; Olympia *Washington Standard,* March 6; July 31, 1891; Aug. 26, 1892; Jan. 20, 1893; *Spokane Review,* July 23, 1892; July 28, 1893; *Northwest,* 10 (Sept. 1892), 19–20; *Walla Walla Statesman,* May 12; June 7, 8; July 11, 15, 28, 1893.

41. Of 126 million gallons pumped in January 1891, only 59 million actually reached customers, the rest having been lost to leakage. *Seattle Post-Intelligencer,* March 6; May 15; Nov. 26, 1890; *Seattle Press-Times,* Feb. 20; March 17; Aug. 25; Sept. 1, 1891; *Seattle Times,* June 11, 12, 1889; Oct. 8, 1895; *Seattle Morning Journal,* Oct. 11, 1889. On local water issues, see Roger Sale, *Seattle: Past to Present* (Seattle: University of Washington Press, 1976), 70–71; and Richard C. Berner, *Seattle 1900–1920: From Boomtown, Urban Turbulence to Restoration* (Seattle: Charles Press, 1991), 40.

42. Prominent Seattle residents involved in the effort to overthrow the Spring Hill sale included Henry Yesler, David Denny and Dexter Horton. The case produced the definitive ruling on the meaning of the state constitutional three-fifths requirement for bonding authorization. Legal disputation over the transaction continued until at least 1899. Seattle acquired the Lake Union system in 1891. *Seattle Morning Journal,* Nov. 24, 1889; *Seattle Post-Intelligencer,* Dec. 1, 1889; March 6; July 6, 12; Aug. 9, 10, 31, 1890; *Seattle Press-Times,* March 17; Aug. 25; Sept. 1, 1891; Jan. 10, 1895; *West Shore,* 15 (Dec. 7, 1889), 396; *Seattle Times,* Jan. 13, 1899.

43. *Seattle Post-Intelligencer,* March 6, 7, 12, 15; July 6, 7, 18; Aug. 22; Nov. 26, 1890; *Seattle Telegraph,* Aug. 11; Sept. 8, 18, 1891; *Seattle Press-Times,* April 15, 1893; Jan. 10, 1895.

44. *Tacoma Daily News,* June 10, 1890; March 2, 10; April 2; May 28, 1891; April 18; Sept. 28, 1892; April 1, 1893; Murray Morgan, *Puget's Sound: A Narrative of Early Tacoma and the Southern Sound* (Seattle: University of Washington Press, 1979), 181–82, 315; *Tacoma Daily Ledger,* Nov. 24, 1890; March 12; April 13, 1891; *Tacoma Morning Globe,* Jan. 5; July 7, 1890; *West Shore,* 17 (Sept. 27, 1890), 107.

45. *Tacoma Daily News*, May 15, 17; June 7; July 1; Aug. 11, 16, 1890; March 2; May 15; July 28, 1891; *Tacoma Daily Ledger*, April 22, 1890; March 12; April 13, 18, 20; June 30, 1891; *West Shore*, 17 (Sept. 27, 1890), 107; *Tacoma Morning Globe*, July 15, 1891.

46. The Tacoma city attorney was on private retainer from the water company. In an added concern, some observers questioned whether Wright held clear title to all the properties claimed by his firm. *Tacoma Daily News*, June 7, 15; July 27, 1891; Jan. 20; May 16; Aug. 19; Sept. 1, 1892; Jan. 4, 5; Feb. 21; March 1, 8, 10, 1893; *Tacoma Daily Ledger*, July 21, 23, 26; Sept. 2, 1891; March 20; April 7, 1892.

47. "Hair and decomposing flesh" from animals drowned in the river supposedly added "a flavoring to the water." *West Shore*, 16 (May 24, 1890), 661; John Fahey, *The Inland Empire: Unfolding Years, 1879–1929* (Seattle: University of Washington Press, 1986), 171; *Spokane Falls Review*, May 4, 16; July 24; Aug. 1, 1890; J. William T. Youngs, *The Fair and the Falls: Spokane's Expo '74, Transforming an American Environment* (Cheney: Eastern Washington University Press, 1996), 43; *Spokane Review*, Sept. 12, 1891; March 28, 1893, rep. from Post Falls *Post*.

48. Symons was an investor in local real estate. *Spokane Falls Review*, July 24, 25, 1890; *Spokane Review*, Aug. 25, 1891; June 15; Sept. 17, 1892; March 26, 1893.

49. In another reversal, local boosters now claimed that the river somehow cleansed itself of Idaho mine pollutants before reaching Spokane: "No matter how much slickens the Coeur d'Alene may carry into the lake, when the water gets here it shows no trace of the rocky coloring matter." *Spokane Review*, Sept. 16, 17, 1891; March 16, 23; April 8, 9, 16; May 10; July 5; Oct. 2, 3; Nov. 12, 24, 1892; March 16, 24, 1893.

50. *Spokane Review*, May 5; Nov. 26; Dec. 14, 1892; May 12, 13, 1893.

51. *Seattle Telegraph*, April 3, 1893.

52. Spokane *Spokesman-Review*, Oct. 8, 9; Nov. 1, 1897; March 6, 1899; Olympia *Washington Standard*, July 22, 1898.

53. *West Shore*, 16 (June 21, 1890), 770; *Seattle Telegraph*, June 9, 1893; *Seattle Post-Intelligencer*, June 26, 1895; Olympia *Washington Standard*, April 8, 1892; Spokane *Spokesman-Review*, Aug. 1, 1896; Oct. 31, 1897; July 26, 1898; *Spokane Falls Review*, Jan. 15, 16, 18, 1890; *Spokane Review*, Aug. 5, 1891; April 2, 1892; Oct. 19, 1893.

54. *Seattle Post-Intelligencer*, July 31, 1892; Sept. 7, 1893; June 26, 1895; *Spokane Falls Review*, Dec. 25, 1889, rep. from Tekoa *Globe*; *West Shore*, 16 (Jan. 18, 1890), 66.

55. The facts failed to deter Walla Walla legislators from claiming that the penitentiary, with a capacity of 400 inmates, was badly overcrowded. Ignoring the truth, the state provided funds for a new 100 bed wing in 1891. *Seattle Post-Intelligencer*, March 1, 1891; *Seattle Press-Times*, Feb. 18, 1893; *Seattle Morning Journal*, Jan. 31, 1890; *Anacortes American*, Jan. 5, 1893; Olympia *Washington Standard*, July 17, 1891.

56. Olympia *Washington Standard*, March 13, 1891; Aug. 19; Sept. 2, 1892; *Tacoma Daily News*, Dec. 30, 1890, rep. from Olympia *Capital*; *Seattle Post-Intelligencer*, March 29, 1890, rep. from Tekoa *Globe*.

57. Detailed accounts of sexual assault became a press staple. In March 1891, for example, a Tacoma salesman raped "a buxom woman of about 27 years of age." Featuring the victim's name, news accounts noted that the assailant had drugged her with a dose of chloroform concealed in a wine sampler, then "accomplished his vile purpose and fled." Olympia *Washington Standard*, March 27; April 3; Nov. 6; Dec. 25, 1891; July 15, 1892; *Walla Walla Statesman*, Aug. 8, 1891; *Tacoma Daily Ledger*, Aug. 28, 1891.

58. *Fairhaven Herald*, March 25, 1891; Portland *Oregonian*, Sept. 17, 1891, rep. from Walla Walla *Union-Journal*; Sept. 29, 1893; Seattle *Argus*, Jan. 5, 1895; *Spokane Daily Chronicle*,

Jan. 7, 1898; *Tacoma Daily News*, Sept. 16, 1898; New Whatcom *Daily Reveille*, Dec. 21, 1897.

59. Although female spectators were encouraged in advance to vacate the Seattle courtroom prior to the examination of the letters, one reporter wryly noted that a "crowd of filth-hungry women sat through the reading of them all." *Seattle Post-Intelligencer*, Feb. 6, 1890; Dec. 4, 1891; April 25, 1893, rep. from Colfax *Gazette*, *Tacoma Daily News*, Feb. 7, 1890; John R. Rogers to J.B. Winston, Feb. 10, 1898, John R. Rogers Papers, Washington State Archives; *Spokane Review*, June 26, 1893.

60. Respectable Washingtonians, a Seattle paper asserted, "have been maddened beyond control by the failure of judges, juries and prosecuting officers to execute the law upon those who have so indifferent regard for the lives of others." Portland *Oregonian*, Oct. 14, 1891, rep. from Oakesdale *Advocate*, *Seattle Press-Times*, Aug. 17, 1894; Seattle *Argus*, June 27, 1896; *Seattle Post-Intelligencer*, Dec. 4, 1891; June 25, 1893, rep. from Tekoa *Globe*, Aug. 23, 1899; Olympia *Washington Standard*, April 29, 1892.

61. Some commentators, like the Bellingham Bay editor who was sure that "a few officers, judges and juries want stretching," supported the extension of vigilantism to the courts. *Seattle Post-Intelligencer*, April 19, 1892; June 25, 1893, rep. from Tekoa *Globe*; *Ellensburgh Capital*, Dec. 1, 1892; *Tacoma Daily News*, April 29, 1891, rep. from Bellingham Bay *Express*; Michael J. Pfeifer, "'Midnight Justice': Lynching and Law in the Pacific Northwest," *PNQ*, 94 (Spring 2003), 90.

62. *South Bend Journal*, April 10, 17, 1891; *Tacoma Daily News*, April 17; June 29, 1891; July 3, 1897; Jan. 10, 1898; Pfeifer, "'Midnight Justice,'" 83, 85–88; Olympia *Washington Standard*, May 1; June 26, 1891; Feb. 5, 1892; *Tacoma Daily Ledger*, April 26; May 4, 14, 1891; April 20, 1898; *Spokane Falls Review*, Jan. 13; April 25, 1891; *Seattle Post-Intelligencer*, May 13, 1891; June 5, 10, 1894; Spokane *Spokesman-Review*, Aug. 15, 17, 1895; Jan. 9, 13, 1898; *Spokane Daily Chronicle*, Jan. 10, 19, 31; March 18, 1898; William McDonald to Rogers, Jan. 28, 1898, Rogers Papers.

63. The fact that most Chinese resided in California supposedly left that state with another comparative disadvantage. "California is to be pitied," the *P-I* observed. "With these pagan drawbacks she can never hold her own as a competitor…of Washington." *Tacoma Daily News*, March 22, 1893; Olympia *Washington Standard*, Oct. 14, 1892; Sept. 8, 1893; Aug. 6, 1897; Roger Daniels, *Asian America: Chinese and Japanese in the United States since 1850* (Seattle: University of Washington Press, 1988), 73; Ficken, *Washington Territory*, 190–95; *Walla Walla Statesman*, May 18, 1893; *Seattle Telegraph*, Dec. 14, 1892; *Tacoma Daily Ledger*, June 6; Aug. 7, 1890; *West Shore*, 16 (Dec. 16, 1890), 258; *Spokane Falls Review*, Nov. 23, 1890; *Spokane Review*, Feb. 2, 1892; *Seattle Post-Intelligencer*, Feb. 27, 1891.

64. Whidbey Island whites adopted a measure prohibiting the rental of land to Asian farmers. Colfax, Walla Walla and Ellensburg boycotted Chinese business establishments. Colfax residents also blamed a $100,000 1893 fire upon "Chinese cheap labor," failing in the process to cite any credible evidence. Pointing out that the northeast Washington town of Colville "has a China wash house and a restaurant under Mongolian control," a local editor demanded that the "Chinaman" remove "his hideous presence at once." *Aberdeen Herald*, Nov. 13, 27, 1890; March 26, 1891; *Tacoma Daily Ledger*, Sept. 21, 1890; *Seattle Post-Intelligencer*, Nov. 15, 1890; Feb. 20, 1892; Jan. 29, 1893; Olympia *Washington Standard*, Sept. 26, 1890; Feb. 6, 1891; May 6; July 8, 1892; Dec. 22, 1893; *Everett Herald*, June 2, 1892; *Tacoma Daily News*, June 15, 1891, rep. from Island County *Times*; Portland *Oregonian*, Aug. 29; Sept. 5, 1891; *Seattle Telegraph*, May 7, 1892; *Spokane Review*,

March 16, 1892; April 23, 1893; *Ellensburgh Capital,* April 7, 1892; *Tacoma Morning Globe,* March 15, 1890, rep. from Stevens County *Miner.*

65. A Spokane judge sentenced a local pimp to life in prison in 1897 for selling the services of a teenage prostitute to a Chinese customer. "I would not have believed, nor could I have conceived," the jurist pronounced, "that a white man could be so sunken in iniquity as to subject a white girl to the lust of a Chinaman." Tacoma claimed that inclusion of Seattle's Chinese population in the 1890 federal census allowed the Elliott Bay rival to unfairly claim status as Washington's largest city. Seattle had approximately 400 Chinese merchants. Tacoma did not allow the admitted merchants to bring Asian assistants or servants to Commencement Bay. *Tacoma Daily Ledger,* Sept. 22, 1890; Jan. 2; Aug. 11, 1891; Jan. 3, 1896; *Tacoma Morning Globe,* Feb. 20, 1890; Nov. 3, 1891; *Olympia Tribune,* Oct. 29, 1891; *Tacoma Daily News,* July 7, 1890; July 31, 1891; July 26, 27, 1892; March 22, 1893; *Seattle Press-Times,* July 26, 1892; *Northwest,* 10 (Sept. 1892), 18; Seattle *Argus,* Dec. 21, 1895; *Seattle Post-Intelligencer,* Aug. 9, 1892, rep. from Tacoma *Sun;* Spokane *Spokesman-Review,* Jan. 4, 1896; Oct. 17, 1897.

66. Most of the inmates at the McNeil Island federal prison were Chinese awaiting deportation. Of the 25 Chinese persons attempting to legally enter the United States from the steamer *Victoria* in July 1893, only 9 carrying the proper documents were allowed to land. *Seattle Morning Journal,* Nov. 18, 1889; *Spokane Review,* Dec. 26, 1891; Olympia *Washington Standard,* Dec. 2, 1892; Feb. 3, 1893; *Tacoma Daily News,* May 16, 1893; *Seattle Telegraph,* June 9, 15, rep. from Coupeville *News,* 17; Sept. 15, 1891; *Seattle Press-Times,* April 10, 1893; *Tacoma Daily Ledger,* July 13, 1893; Olympia *Morning Olympian,* March 23, 1892. On federal legislation, see Daniels, *Asian America,* 55–58.

67. The supply of opium was so great that Washington consumer prices, in an example of underworld capitalism in action, declined sharply. In a seeming contradiction of purposes, the customs service sold seized opium at public auction, no questions asked, to the highest bidder. *Seattle Morning Journal,* Nov. 18, 1889; *Tacoma Morning Globe,* Sep. 12; Nov. 9, 22, 1891; Jan. 16, 1892; *Walla Walla Statesman,* Nov. 24, 1892, rep. from Olympia *Tribune;* Olympia *Washington Standard,* March 13, 1891; Portland *Oregonian,* March 13, 1896; *Spokane Review,* Dec. 26, 1891.

68. S. Frank Miyamoto, "The Japanese Minority in the Pacific Northwest," *PNQ,* 54 (Oct. 1963), 143; *Spokane Review,* July 12, 1892; June 7, 1893; *Seattle Press-Times,* Dec. 18, 1894; *Index Miner,* April 5, 1900; Olympia *Washington Standard,* May 29, 1891; *Seattle Post-Intelligencer,* May 14, 1893.

69. Seattle, the most cosmopolitan of Washington's cities, had 3,000 Catholic residents attending four churches. *Seattle Post-Intelligencer,* Nov. 28, 1890; Jan. 1, 1891; Portland *Oregonian,* Oct. 6, 1893; Olympia *Washington Standard,* March 20, 1891; *Spokane Falls Review,* Feb. 7; March 31, 1890; *Tacoma Daily News,* April 15, 22, rep. from Coulee City *Times,* 1891; May 25, 1892; *Spokane Review,* Dec. 4, 1891, rep. from Chelan Falls *Leader,* April 24, 1894; *Fairhaven Herald,* March 27, 1891; *Tacoma Morning Globe,* Nov. 25, 1891; *West Shore,* 17 (Jan. 3, 1891), 3; (March 21, 1891), 184; Norbert MacDonald, "The Business Leaders of Seattle, 1880–1910," *PNQ,* 50 (Jan. 1959), 8.

70. A Seattle pugilist, who was a "powerful fisherman" outside the ring, became another casualty, having "gone insane" as the result of a beating at the hands of the legendary John L. Sullivan. *Seattle Press,* Feb. 7, 1891; Olympia *Washington Standard,* Feb. 13, 1891; *Seattle Telegraph,* Sept. 20; Dec. 16, 1890; Feb. 8, 25; March 26, 1891; Olympia *Morning Olympian,* March 15, 1892; *Seattle Post-Intelligencer,* March 15, 1892; *West Shore,* 16 (July 5, 1890), 835; *Seattle Press-Times,* March 13; Aug. 19, 1891.

71. East of the Cascades, a Kootenay-Washington league combined teams from both sides of the 49th parallel. Female players staged exhibitions, drawing large crowds and derision from sports traditionalists. "Attendance fell to a figure giving a net loss on every game played" after a Spokane powerhouse fire shut down a road serving the local ballpark during the 1890 season. James Warnock, "Entrepreneurs and Progressives: Baseball in the Northwest, 1900–1901," *PNQ*, 82 (July 1991), 92; *Seattle Post-Intelligencer*, May 4; July 17, 1890; Portland *Oregonian*, April 24, 1890; *Tacoma Daily News*, Oct. 5, 1891; Jan. 11, 1892; Olympia *Washington Standard*, July 24, 1891; *Spokane Review*, Aug. 21, 1891; Spokane *Spokesman-Review*, April 21; Sept. 13, 1897; *West Shore*, 15 (Dec. 21, 1889), 454; Harry A. Adams to W.S. Norman, Feb. 1, 1892, Washington Water Power Co. Records, Washington State University Library; Seattle *Argus*, April 18, 1896; *Spokane Spokesman*, Sept. 10, 1890.

72. Portland *Oregonian*, May 2, 1891; *Tacoma Morning Globe*, April 27, 1890; *Spokane Falls Review*, Sept. 23, 1890; *Tacoma Daily News*, April 1, 1890, rep. from Port Townsend *Leader*; Spokane *Spokesman-Review*, Oct. 11, 1895; Olympia *Morning Olympian*, March 26, 1892; *Seattle Press-Times*, April 28, 1892.

73. Portland supposedly won the 1891 pennant because it "largely exceeded" the agreed upon salary limit. The highest paid players received $250 a month. Northwest teams complained of attempts by California owners to buy away their best athletes. The amateur Palouse league nearly collapsed amidst charges that Colfax had imported professional ringers. Another innovative move, the 1891 attempt to play night baseball in Tacoma, was premature. *Tacoma Morning Globe*, July 11, 1890; Sept. 3, 1891; *Seattle Press-Times*, April 15; Oct. 5, 1891; June 27, 1892; *Spokane Daily Chronicle*, April 13, 1898; *Tacoma Daily News*, July 7, 1890; Oct. 5, 1891; Aug. 6, 1892; Aug. 10, 1897; *Spokane Spokesman*, Oct. 26, 1890; *Tacoma Daily Ledger*, April 28, 1891; *Spokane Review*, Aug. 20, 1891; March 9, 1894; Olympia *Washington Standard*, Aug. 21, 1893.

74. Football also enlivened urban rivalries. Returning from a Commencement Bay game in 1892, supporters of the Seattle team complained of being subjected to the "grossness of conduct and insufferable insolence…peculiar to Tacoma." The Seattle Athletic Club traveled as far as Butte, Montana, to meet scheduled opponents. North Yakima introduced night football in 1891. *Seattle Post-Intelligencer*, Nov. 24, 1890; *Seattle Telegraph*, Jan. 3, 1893; *Spokane Review*, May 8, 1891; Dec. 2, 1893; *Seattle Press-Times*, Sept. 19, 1891; Nov. 23, 1892; Seattle *Argus*, Jan. 11, 1896; Olympia *Washington Standard*, Feb. 6, 1891; Spokane *Spokesman-Review*, May 1, 1895; *Tacoma Daily News*, Nov. 25, 1893; *Yakima Herald*, Dec. 1, 1892.

75. Despite popular use of the singular "wheel," nearly all bicycles of the time were two-wheeled. Seattle *Argus*, March 7, 14; May 2, 1896; July 17, 1897; *Spokane Review*, June 26, 1892; May 24, 1894; *Tacoma Daily News*, June 10, 1895; April 6; July 7, 1897; Spokane *Spokesman-Review*, Aug. 27; Sept. 13, 16, 1895; April 12; Sept. 3, 6, 8, 10, 1897; *Seattle Post-Intelligencer*, June 24, 1897; *Walla Walla Statesman*, June 23, 1893; *Spokane Daily Chronicle*, April 9, 28, 1898; Olympia *Washington Standard*, March 11, 1892.

76. Earl Pomeroy, *In Search of the Golden West: The Tourist in Western America* (Lincoln: University of Nebraska Press, 1957, 1990 ed.), 205–6; Hal K. Rothman, *Devil's Bargains: Tourism in the Twentieth-Century American West* (Lawrence: University Press of Kansas, 1998), chapt. 2; Seattle *Argus*, Aug. 21, 1897.

77. The Ilwaco Railway, running along the North Beach Peninsula for 16 miles, was the shortest common carrier line in the state of Washington. *Seattle Telegraph*, March 10, 1893; Carlos A. Schwantes, *Railroad Signatures across the Pacific Northwest* (Seattle: University

of Washington Press, 1993), 205–8; and "Tourists in Wonderland: Early Railroad Tourism in the Pacific Northwest," *Columbia: The Magazine of Northwest History*, 7 (Winter 1993–1994), 22–30; *Spokane Review*, April 23, 1891; March 20; May 7, 1892; May 18, 1894; Spokane *Spokesman-Review*, June 28, 1895; April 18, 1899; Nancy F. Renk, "Off to the Lakes: Vacationing in North Idaho during the Railroad Era, 1885–1917," *Idaho Yesterdays*, 34 (Summer 1990), 2–15; *South Bend Journal*, Sept. 12, 1890; *Seattle Post-Intelligencer*, Sept. 18, 1890; *Spokane Falls Review*, Feb. 6; July 6, 1890; Jan. 23, 1891; *Tacoma Daily News*, June 3, 1893; June 24, 1894; July 9, 12, 1897; Seattle *Argus*, Aug. 7, 1897; *Tacoma Daily Ledger*, Sept. 1, 1891.

78. The Seattle city charter allowed women to take part in library management. *Seattle Post-Intelligencer*, April 8; May 4; July 8; Oct. 24, 1890; Dec. 1, 1891; Sept. 26, 1894; *Tacoma Daily Ledger*, Feb. 9, 1890; March 22; May 25; July 30, 1891; *West Shore*, 16 (May 10, 1890), 597; *Seattle Telegraph*, Jan. 6, 1891; *Seattle Times*, Sept. 7, 1899; *Spokane Falls Review*, Sept. 25, 1890; *Aberdeen Herald*, Oct. 15, 1891; Olympia *Washington Standard*, April 24, 1891; Portland *Oregonian*, April 26, 1891.

79. The local library proved, according to a Commencement Bay editor, that "Tacoma is socially descended from the best elements of the northern states of the union." *Seattle Post-Intelligencer*, Sept. 26; Oct. 2, 1894; *Tacoma Daily Ledger*, Feb. 24, 1890; March 22, 1891; Feb. 22, 1892; Sept. 13, 1893; *Seattle Telegraph*, Jan. 6, 1891.

80. *Tacoma Daily News*, March 21, 1890; July 5, 1893; *Tacoma Morning Globe*, March 1, 1890; *Tacoma Daily Ledger*, Jan. 11, 1892.

81. *Tacoma Daily News*. April 21, 1890; June 27, 1892; *Tacoma Daily Ledger*, Jan. 11, 1892.

82. The city of Seattle refused to allow beer sales in private parks, a ban credited with reducing attendance. Tax wary interests made sure that the 1890 Seattle charter severely restricted the ability of park officials to acquire land. *Seattle Post-Intelligencer*, Dec. 31, 1892; May 30, 1897; *Seattle Telegraph*, Nov. 24, 1891; Seattle *Argus*, May 25; Oct. 19, 1895; May 6; Aug. 5, 1889; *Seattle Times*, July 13, 1897; Oct. 17, 1899; Berner, *Seattle 1900–1910*, 101–3; Sale, *Seattle 82–84*; *Seattle Press-Times*, July 27, 1893.

83. *Spokane Review*, Aug. 17, 1893; June 11, 1894; Spokane *Spokesman-Review*, Aug. 28, 29; Sept. 9, 1897; Feb. 20; July 12, 1898; *Yakima Herald*, Sept. 22, 1892.

84. *Tacoma Daily News*, Sept. 26, 1891, rep. from Walla Walla *Union-Journal*, Aug. 6, 1892; Portland *Oregonian*, April 26; Sept. 2; Oct. 14, 1891; Spokane *Spokesman-Review*, March 16, 1899; *Tacoma Morning Globe*, Sept. 17, 1891; *Seattle Press-Times*, Sept. 25, 1891. On construction of the Spokane and Seattle opera houses, see *West Shore*, 15 (Dec. 21, 1889), 456; 17 (Jan. 17, 1891), 41.

85. *Tacoma Daily Ledger*, Sept. 29, 1890; *Tacoma Daily News*, Aug. 6, 1892; Nov. 4, 1897; Portland *Oregonian*, Sept. 18, 1891, rep. from Vancouver *Independent*; *Seattle Telegraph*, Jan. 5, 1893; April 6, 1894; *Olympia Tribune*, Jan. 23, 1891; Olympia *Washington Standard*, Dec. 9, 1892; *Seattle Post-Intelligencer*, April 13, 1899; *Spokane Review*, Sept. 26, 1891.

86. Spokane residents complained that one of the city's most heavily patronized music theaters was located adjacent to the public library, forcing "young girls and boys applying for books…to pass through…dirty waters, to reach the clear forest of better knowledge." *Tacoma Daily News*, July 9, 1890; *Seattle Post-Intelligencer*, April 13, 1899; Spokane *Spokesman-Review*, April 4, 1899.

87. According to one account, 97 women worked as music hall "attendants" in Tacoma at the time of statehood. *Seattle Post-Intelligencer*, April 1, 1892; Seattle *Argus*, April 25, 1896;

Spokane *Spokesman-Review*, April 8, 1899; *Seattle Telegraph*, Jan. 12, 1891; *Seattle Press*, Jan. 13, 1891; Morgan, *Skid Road*, 12–31; *West Shore*, 15 (Nov. 9, 1889), 260.

88. *Seattle Press*, Feb. 7, 1891; *Tacoma Morning Globe*, July 28, 1891; *Tacoma Daily News*, Dec. 10, 1890; Jan. 7; Feb. 1, 1892; *Seattle Press-Times*, Oct. 6, 1891; *Seattle Times*, July 13, 1895; *Spokane Review*, May 20, 1891.

89. Seattle residents admitted to embarrassment over the fact that the total mileage of improved street in their city was less than half the figure for upstart rival New Whatcom. *Olympia Tribune*, Aug. 7, 1890; Nov. 17, 1891; *Spokane Review*, Aug. 5; Dec. 8, 1892; *Seattle Post-Intelligencer*, Nov. 2, 1889; *Seattle Morning Journal*, Oct. 24, 1889; *Tacoma Daily News*, May 6, 1890; *Spokane Daily Chronicle*, April 18, 1898.

90. Providing further evidence that it was "putting on metropolitan airs," Oysterville also installed sidewalks. *Seattle Morning Journal*, Oct. 24, 1889; *Spokane Falls Review*, Nov. 22, 1889; *Tacoma Daily News*, July 9, 1891, rep. from Walla Walla *Union-Journal*; *Tacoma Morning Globe*, Feb. 19, 1891; Portland *Oregonian*, May 7, 1890.

91. *Seattle Post-Intelligencer*, Sept. 16, 1890; *Tacoma Morning Globe*, Jan. 12, 1890; July 13; Sept. 9, 1891; *Tacoma Daily Ledger*, July 4, 1893; *Spokane Review*, May 6, 1892; *Spokane Falls Review*, Jan. 19, 1890.

92. Some of the newer cities, among them Yakima and Waterville, saw the value of modest beautification efforts. "The town embowered in the shade," a visitor wrote of Waterville, "would seem a veritable oasis, after crossing the long, dusty, treeless desert between the Grand coulee and the town." *Seattle Post-Intelligencer*, Sept. 16, 1890; Feb. 20; May 13, 1891; April 22, 1892; *Tacoma Daily Ledger*, July 27, 1890; *Tacoma Morning Globe*, July 29, 1890; Sept. 15, 1891; Feb. 18, 1892; *Spokane Falls Review*, Nov. 20, 1890.

Tacoma's Ninth Avenue, spring 1890. *University of Washington Libraries (UW11920)*

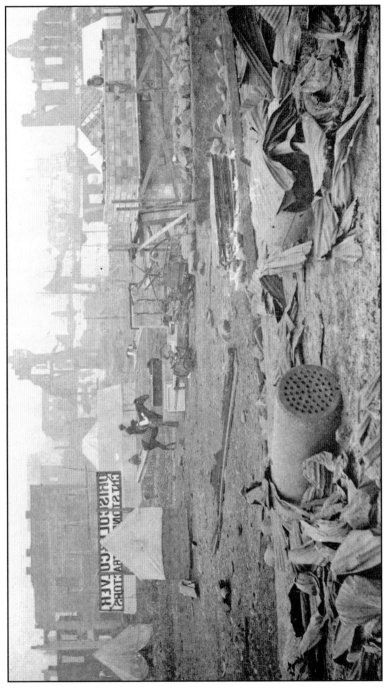

Ruins from the Spokane Falls conflagration of August 4, 1889. Spokane's boosterism resumed immediately after the fire, including the building of an exhibition hall for an 1890 "World's Fair of the Northwest." *Museum of Arts & Culture, Spokane (L86-140)*

Contractor Nelson Bennett's railroad construction equipment, which provided fill for Hoquiam streets, ca. 1893. *University of Washington Libraries (UW26802z)*

Homesteaders
in Grays Harbor
County, ca. 1895.
*University of
Washington Libraries
(UW4368)*

Puget Mill Company docks at Port Gamble, December 19, 1895. *University of Washington Libraries (UW4950)*

By 1899, "The Agricultural College, Experiment Station and School of Science of the State of Washington" in Pullman was expanding under the capable leadership of WAC's third president, Enoch A. Bryan. *University of Washington Libraries (UW26803z)*

Seattle's Pioneer Square at First Avenue and Yesler, where many suppliers and ticket agents occupied storefronts and offices during the Klondike and Nome gold excitement. *Museum of History and Industry, Seattle (SHS 801)*

A new Seattle Electric Railway Company trolley, ca. 1890. By 1892, 48 miles of electric streetcar and 22 miles of cable railway lines served the city. *Museum of History and Industry, Seattle (SHS 7701)*

A Seattle family in the 1890s, when much of what eventually became the Central District was still rural. *Museum of History and Industry, Seattle (SHS 17081)*

Named for being the closest hill to downtown Seattle, the First Hill residential area included homes of Elliott Bay's elite in the 1890s. *Museum of History and Industry, Seattle (SHS 1969)*

Chapter Five

Darkness upon the Earth

Capitalists and laborers will look back upon 1893 as a year of blackness and despair. There were months when even the most courageous heart quailed, when men accustomed to dealing with hard situations lost faith in themselves; it was an accursed year. The toiler worked, but could not get his pay. The business man sold, but could not make collections. Railroads could not meet interest obligations. Banks could not pay depositors...Confidence, the sun which gives life to the world of business, had gone behind a cloud. Darkness was upon the earth...Some cursed God and others lifted up sobbing voices in prayer. May such a year never, never come again.—Tacoma Daily News.[1]

PERSONS ON EITHER SIDE of the Cascade Range looked on in trepidation whenever Mount St. Helens emitted a plume of steam or Mount Rainier an apparent cloud of smoke. "Nothing is more likely than that Mount Rainier should be in a state of eruption," one amateur geologist reported. "It is situated on the line of the great crack in the crust of the earth." The real explosion of the era, however, was economic in nature, the product of an enormous fault in human affairs. The Wall Street crisis of 1890 had been, according to conventional wisdom, of far more importance in New York than in the Pacific Northwest. Money was tight for several months, a regional publication asserted, but the panic had neither "paralyzed trade, nor wrought commercial ruin." Although speculative real estate ventures were hard-hit, well planned developments, such as fruit-bearing Wenatchee on the banks of the Columbia River, suffered only minimal harm. Positive thinkers even detected benefits to the situation, the country needing an occasional disruption to "clear up the financial horizon."[2]

At some inexact point in 1891, the few lingering signs of depression lost force, the end of the panic supposedly being confirmed by "the return of the money lenders" to Washington state. Inflated in numbers by hard times in the East, the "annual spring migration" brought new people and new energy to the coast. Continued irrigation work in the Yakima Valley provided a welcome stimulus to settlement. Improvements in the lumber trade, facilitated by the opening of rail markets, had a similar impact west of the mountains. Expectations of heavy grain output in the fall, plus "the sending of money to the West for the movement of the crops," generated renewed confidence in the grain country and in exporting centers. "We are over the breakers," a Tacoma newspaper concluded from a survey of the regional economy, and "comparatively smooth sailing is before us."[3]

Concealed beneath a placid surface, strong currents nonetheless drove the Pacific Northwest toward dangerous shoals. "So surely as water seeks its level," a cautious observer noted, "does capital...seek employment in those fields...most prolific of return." Domestic and foreign investors were, unfortunately, timid adventurers in the aftermath of the Wall Street fright. The press insisted, for public consumption, that cash was abundant, but insiders knew better. "Money is as tight as ever on the Sound," lumberman Cyrus Walker reported to his San Francisco partners in December 1891. Visiting London and Paris in quest of buyers for his Seattle properties, Thomas Burke found no takers, even when he offered to sell "at 50% on their cost."[4]

For a number of reasons, all related to the continuing financial challenges of the late nineteenth century, the United States was literally "short of money." The national currency itself consisted of a mishmash of gold coins, silver dollars and certificates, leftover Civil War greenbacks, legal tender notes and treasury department securities. Of more importance, the spreading influence of the international gold standard and the development of fast transportation and communications exposed America to the influence of economic developments in the most remote parts of the earth. The Pacific Northwest could no longer avoid the impact of panics and depressions once assumed to be the parochial concern of New York and other bastions of capital.[5]

More money could be provided, a rising chorus of domestic opinion insisted, by the simple expedient of free and unlimited silver coinage. Once in circulation, a substantially enlarged supply of cash would produce increased returns for commodities, wheat in particular, and general economic growth. Under the Sherman Act of 1890, the federal government purchased and issued 4.5 million ounces of silver per month. Inflationists believed, however, that the measure did not go far enough for real effect. Opponents, investors in the forefront, feared the possible impact upon prices and stock values. To a large extent, silver also was a cultural issue, the means for rural and small town America to relieve concerns over the new financial dependence upon New York and London. "The struggle," an Inland Empire editor declared, "is between the money aristocracy of the world and the people." Current profits from the Coeur d'Alene mines, and potential similar earnings from the Okanogan and the north Cascades, gave free coinage additional practical appeal in the state of Washington. Conservative and otherwise non-innovative Republican stalwarts like Senator Watson Squire and Lieutenant Governor Charles Laughton stood out as early advocates of silver.[6]

The underlying fiscal problems escaped general public notice, thanks to positive economic indicators. Despite the Wall Street smashup, statewide property valuations mounted from $217 million in 1890 to $357 million in 1891.

Construction activity continued at an impressive pace, Seattle, Tacoma and Spokane issuing a $1.5 million worth of building permits in the first quarter of 1892. Washington's business enterprises failed at a significantly lower rate in 1891 than for the nation at large or in California. The number of banks in the state increased from 80 in 1891 to well over a hundred in 1892. Deposits were up by a good margin, supposedly an "unfailing sign" that the populace could safely "look backward on the worst times instead of anticipating further distress." The Northern Pacific recorded a $27 million net profit in 1891, followed by $30 million in 1892. Five hundred million tons of freight passed through Spokane in 1892, a two-thirds increase over the previous year. Although mill owners claimed that times were "dull" on account of overproduction, Washington sold record amounts of lumber in 1891 and 1892.[7]

Land prices in the Palouse doubled, reflecting the profitability of wheat ranching. Building upon high springtime prices for grain left in storage from the preceding season, 1891 proved to be the best year yet for eastern Washington growers. Bountiful winter snows "increased acreage in every direction" and enormous per-acre yields produced a record 15 million bushels. Poor returns from Russia and India stiffened prices. Transportation improvements instituted in the aftermath of the infamous "blockade" allowed for more efficient marketing of grain. A third of the state's output, arriving in port at a rate of 200 carloads a day, was exported through Commencement Bay. Farmers reported a 50 percent increase in earnings over 1890.[8]

Though unseasonably hot weather in early summer resulted in a lower than expected output per acre, the 1892 performance was equally impressive. Planting had increased substantially in the Big Bend country, and Whitman County alone shipped over nine million bushels to market. One reporter wrote, "At every station throughout the length and breadth of the land will be seen elevators and warehouses, full to running over, with golden grain, platforms piled high with the overflow, and long lines of loaded wagons waiting their turn to add to the steadily growing mountains of wheat heaped up under the autumn sky." Farmers drove their teams into line before dawn in order to have a chance of unloading by nightfall. At least one railway platform collapsed under the weight of stacked grain.[9]

Optimistic Washington residents had ample reason to expect a continuation of prosperity, especially with another remarkable wheat harvest anticipated for 1893. Between the completion of the Great Northern and the likely purchase of sawmills and timber by the Frederick Weyerhaeuser syndicate, the future of lumbering also seemed "almost beyond computation." Lingering ill effects of the Wall Street panic, if any, were hardly of consequence. "Prospects for Western Washington have not been so bright as now since 1890," an editor based on the sea coast reflected in late winter. "The weeding out of…debtors and weak business institutions" had been completed, giving way to "a gradual return of money to its accustomed channels, a gradual restoration of confidence, [and] a disposition to try new enterprises." Fully manifested in every corner of the state, the conviction would not survive the spring.[10]

⬳⬳⬲

America's 1893 economic collapse—still the second worst depression in the nation's history—began as a repeat of the 1890 crisis. Gold drained from the country at an alarming rate in the first weeks of the year. By mid-February, $15 million had been shipped from New York to European financial houses. "The present condition of affairs," the *Seattle Telegraph* advised, "is simply paralyzing speculative capital." The specie outflow placed an enormous strain on an expanding economy already short of money. "It is true that business is done with credit and not with coin," the *Telegraph* noted, "but credit always presupposes that coin will be forthcoming to defray an indebtedness if it is demanded." Wall Street stock prices slumped, the notoriously loan sensitive Northern Pacific leading the way downward. Private developers and local governments experienced sudden difficulty in finding buyers for essential bonds.[11]

For several weeks, the brunt of the contraction appeared confined to England, where several banks were "obliged...to suspend," and to the London dependent economies of Australia and Argentina. In early May, however, New York investors began dumping stocks wholesale, commencing the full-blown Panic of 1893. Sixteen thousand American businesses failed before the end of the year, along with 600 financial institutions. Reliable statistics are lacking, but one in five workers apparently lost employment according to the most authoritative estimates.[12]

Railroading absorbed much of the damage. James J. Hill canceled the Great Northern's elaborate completion ceremony, expected to equal in grandiosity Henry Villard's 1883 golden spike extravaganza. Thanks to sound management and stern discipline, Hill otherwise suffered little in comparison to his rivals. Construction virtually ceased nationwide, with the miles of track laid in 1893 falling to the lowest figure in 17 years. Unable to borrow money, the Northern Pacific and the Union Pacific declared bankruptcy during the summer. A hundred lines, representing a quarter of the country's mileage, passed into the hands of receivers by Christmas. "It will not be long," an eastern Washington observer suggested in a moment of black humor, "before the whole system will be practically operated by the Government, through the Federal Courts."[13]

Initially, few people in the Pacific Northwest had predicted any of these shattering developments. The Wall Street crash had been widely dismissed as "one of those financial breezes that periodically blow through," ruining "gamblers, and...speculating dupes," leaving America's producing millions unscathed. "The United States is in not as much danger of a financial depression this year," the *Tacoma News* avowed, "as it is in the probability of a visit of cholera." Summoning a special session of congress to repeal the Sherman silver purchase act, for traditionalists the best means of ending the panic, President Grover Cleveland apparently restored prosperity at the stroke of a White House pen. "There is no better time to make investments of all kinds than at the present," the *News* claimed in a June pronunciamento.[14]

These blinkered expressions took on an aspect of insanity only in retrospect. Although the crisis in New York had closed the new railroad lumber trade, most signs suggested that the region would otherwise avoid serious damage. "The prosperity and development of this state," an eastern Washington editor asserted in much repeated language, "is by no means retarded by the recent unfortunate circumstances." Money, or at least credit, was in undeniably short supply for the moment, but wheat ranchers "never promised a more abundant crop" than the impending 1893 harvest. The Great Northern was finished, most sawmills were busy and the markets of China and Japan stood open for exploitation. "The seriously evil consequences of the general pressure of hard times," a Yakima Valley paper reported, "have scarcely been perceptible in this prolific section."[15]

Possibly inclined toward pessimism by the long decline of his hometown, a Walla Walla editor was one of the few onlookers to grasp the true nature of things. "In the pioneer days," the *Statesman* pointed out,

> when the Pacific coast was far removed…from the East, and lived within itself, no ripple of any financial troubles on the Atlantic shores ever disturbed the serenity of its business relations. But now all is changed, and every financial disaster in the Eastern money market causes the very foundation of Pacific business to tremble.

The first signs of real trouble came from California, where San Francisco and Los Angeles banks began failing in late May. Coastal lumbering transactions soon "dwindle[d] down to almost nothing" from a lack of financing. "You had better look out up north," a prominent timber merchant informed his Puget Sound partner, "& not keep…money in unsafe institutions as the panic may extend all over the country." Several Portland banking establishments, representing $3 million in assets, were already in the process of closing their doors.[16]

By mid-summer, one in six Washington banks had suspended operation. Financial houses shut down, or at least refused to make loans, in Ellensburg and Port Townsend and on Bellingham Bay and Grays Harbor. "Senseless panic" seized Spokane depositors in the second week of June. "The public went to bed Sunday night with entire confidence in the situation," the *Review* reported, "but by noon Monday it had lost faith in everybody and everything, and was trembling with alarm at shadows conjured out of its own imagination." Unable to sustain themselves, the city's four principal banks promptly failed. Fearful Tacomans took advantage of a brief opportunity to secure their funds. The money, one witness noted, was "hidden away in safety vaults or buried…in the ground." In response, Commencement Bay banks, the soundly administered along with those driven by "speculative management," ceased operation.[17]

Seattle survived, according to local legend, because of its "Spirit." Depositors were "loyal" to the city and thus unwilling to precipitate the collapse of key Elliott Bay institutions. "No bank failed...during the panic," Seattleites boasted. The reality was not especially heroic. Initial withdrawals were, in fact, heavy, with a million dollars, in one confidential account, being quickly "stowed away in Safe Deposit Boxes." Bankers, merchants and public officials, the latter transferring taxpayer funds from one threatened firm to another, met in continuous private sessions, orchestrating measures of mutual defense. Employers pressed their workers to keep money on deposit, and no loans were made and no checks cashed. "I don't believe I could go to any of the Banks of Seattle today with $50,000. of good securities," sawmilling magnate Cyrus Walker exclaimed, "and raise $1000. on it." Although business hours remained nominally in effect, Seattle's commercial activity had ended as effectually as in communities where financial houses went belly-up in a forthright manner.[18]

Money disappeared, stitched into mattresses and buried in backyards. "There is about as much of it stowed away, in secret places, as there ever was in circulation," one analyst noted, "but to derive benefit from money it must be kept moving." Attempting to devise practical substitutes, shingle manufacturers paid their employees in scrip. "An hour later," a newspaper in Mount Vernon reported of one such issuance, "every store in town had exchanged groceries, etc., for it in precisely the same manner as if it were legal tender." Time checks distributed in lieu of regular pay by the North Western Lumber Company passed "current as currency" in the Grays Harbor country. A single draft issued by a timber firm in Blaine, near the Canadian border, was eventually "returned to the mill after paying sixteen debts and receiving sixteen indorsements." City and county warrants circulated in many parts of the state as a makeshift medium of exchange.[19]

Times were suddenly hard in a Washington deprived of coin and credit. The Evergreen State, the always supportive Portland *Oregonian* crowed, had "no money, no wages, [and] almost no business." Schools outside the big cities closed, one eastside district attempting to generate revenue by turning its vacant building into a dance hall. Lack of funds forced Pullman to cancel a municipal election. A city council candidate in South Bend withdrew his name from consideration, rightly fearing that he would not be paid if elected to office. In Blaine, a boarding house robbery went awry when the residents turned out to have neither cash nor valuables. Seattle and Spokane renters were unable to make their monthly payments, while landlords, burdened with inflated post-fire interest charges, could not afford to reduce rates. Debt ridden wheat ranchers fled in the night with their families, often with pre-harvest crop checks in dishonest hand. Some Palouse farmers even committed an unthinkable act, migrating to California.[20]

On a larger economic scale, disaster was everywhere recorded. Reflecting the financial collapse, Washington bank clearings dropped from $27 million in the first six months of 1893 to $14 million in the second half of the year. The liabilities of failed business enterprises, exceeding $2 million, doubled the 1892 figure. Daily newspapers were reduced to four page editions, after "throwing out...a large number of poor paying advertisements." Finding the placement of necessary bonds "almost impossible," the Washington Water Power Company nearly foundered, putting to temporary end the development of hydro-electric energy at Spokane Falls. Most of the private irrigation firms east of the Cascades were bankrupted. "The East has no money, consequently can't buy them," Cyrus Walker succinctly observed in describing the downfall of shingle manufacturing.[21]

Lumbering experienced a complete collapse. Citing the panic, Frederick Weyerhaeuser abandoned plans for major investment in the Pacific Northwest. The national and international nature of the depression curtailed lumber demand in all directions. Business went from "bad to worse" over the summer, Cyrus Walker confided in a dispatch from Puget Sound, "and I don't believe bed rock has been reached yet." Despite avid cost cutting efforts, George Emerson reported a "loss on lumber manufactured and shipped amounting to about 50 cents per thousand feet." Agreeing with other industry leaders, Emerson concluded in despair that "our only road to better times leads by way of the bitter end in the present condition."[22]

Accentuated by layoffs in the mills and logging camps, unemployment quickly emerged as a source of discontent. Distressed workers protested in Seattle and Spokane, demanding relief and jobs. "If this is not sufficiently serious to compel action of some kind," an Elliott Bay editor remarked after observing a parade of 500 angry men, "we hope to be spared from seeing anything that would be regarded as such." In Tacoma, unemployed persons assembled on street corners to debate the causes and means of resolving their mutual plight. Delegations appeared before the city council, pressing the need for municipal construction projects, the eight hour day and a ban on imported workers.[23]

Public attitudes hardened along lines that would become familiar for the duration of the panic. Democrats supported the issuance of scrip and the acceleration of sewer works and other municipal projects that would provide jobs and put money in circulation. Republicans reacted to such proposals with undiluted horror. Spokane business interests organized a Law and Order League to protect the community and their own pocketbooks from the costly "anarchistic sentiments" of the unemployed. "To demand that the city shall make employment...for those who are in need of it," Tacoma conservatives blustered, "is to ask that additional burdens shall be laid upon those who pay the taxes." In Seattle, the *P-I* railed against "indiscriminate alms-giving" and insisted, in another argument favored by the propertied classes, that most of the self styled unemployed were really "tramps and...professional idlers."[24]

Regardless of partisan affiliation or personal ideology, thinking Washingtonians looked to the fall harvest for salvation. "No matter how hard times many think they are undergoing at present," one eastern Washington paper contended, "everything must turn out all right, for in wheat we have the foundation of the prosperity of the country." Heavy snow followed by plentiful spring rain suggested that the crop would be enormous. Detailing the expanded planting and heavy per-acre yields, early reports from the Big Bend, the Palouse and the Walla Walla Valley confirmed optimistic expectations. "Every field is as full of wheat as possible for it to contain," a late July account affirmed, "and...there is nothing now that can happen to injure it." Supposedly, the annual influx of money for marketing and buying grain would soon bring Washington's despair to an end.[25]

Fall, unfortunately, brought only a final crushing disappointment. Abnormal rainfall at the outset of the harvest produced a "partial loss of the...crop," to the extent of five million flattened and rotted bushels. Turned to muddy obstacle courses, roads became "killers of men and horses and destroyers of wagons," slowing the movement of grain. Increased production in South America, Egypt, India and Australia overstocked the world market. New German tariff policies shifted Russian exports to England. Liverpool wheat prices dropped, as a result, to the lowest point since the early years of the French Revolution. In a matter of weeks, every agricultural trend turned from positive to negative, with no relief in sight. "The day that the producers...will get more than 50 cents a bushel," an eastern Washington resident mourned at the end of the season, "is a long way off."[26]

Stark pessimism prevailed, forcing the remaining positive thinkers to stretch the limits of mental invention. "There need be no thought of starvation," according to one wishful argument, "in a country such as this." Ample stocks of salmon in the Sound and trout in the lakes and streams meant that the unemployed could "in an hour" procure "enough fish...to support themselves and families for two days." Those who had previously condemned Washington's "carnival of credit and speculation" believed that hard times taught much needed lessons. "People must...modify their wants and control their luxurious cravings," avoiding in the future the reckless borrowings of the past. Commercial interests, moreover, derived from bitter experience the wisdom of conducting affairs on a cash only basis. "If we are going to the very hard-pan before we stop," an Everett editor reflected, "there is at least this consolation, that business ventures from now on will have a more solid basis than at any time in the past ten years."[27]

Assuming, as most economists pontificated, that confidence was the key to restoring prosperity, people must somehow manifest a positive attitude. "A busy, cheerful air" was "one of the best business tonics that can be administered in a time like this." Newspapers strained mightily to provide evidence that the worst was over. The slightest bit of favorable information—the reopening of a bank, a rare shingle order, increased passenger traffic on one of the rail lines—became in the final months of 1893 grist for the encouragement mill. "Ground will be recovered almost as rapidly as it was lost," an Olympic Peninsula journal predicted on the basis of carefully selected data. Obscure historical comparisons came into strange play, including a *P-I* claim that "times…are not nearly as hard as they were in 1837," the year of the Jacksonian panic. In a weirdly inverted version of the old booster rhetoric, editors insisted that the depression was "less hardly felt in this, the Evergreen State, than in most other localities."[28]

Usually whistling in the graveyard of lunatic faith, even the stoutest journalistic heart occasionally touched reality. "The new year that has just opened," the *P-I* admitted in a gloomy January 1894 forecast, "is likely…to be a time of industrial stagnation, public despondency and personal hardship."

Outside Olympia, nonetheless, sentiment was all but unanimous against the convening of a special meeting of the legislature to address the economic crisis. "There is no more necessity for holding an extra session," declared a Walla Walla paper, "than there is for adding another tail to a dog." In addition to the expense involved, past performance suggested that the members would only raise taxes and pass measures benefiting corporate, rather than the public, interest. As a result, no state response to the panic could be expected until at least 1895.[29]

Though perfectly valid reasoning justified such feelings, given the dire record of past sessions, the consequences of the pre-1893 "boom idea" had left Washington knee deep in a "quagmire of debt." The state had barely a quarter million dollars in the coffers, with two-thirds of this sum assigned by law to the permanent school fund. In the face of declining revenue, warrant issues more than doubled, to nearly $1 million outstanding, between 1892 and 1894. Creditors had to wait over a year, at minimum, to be paid, a dismal fact causing the market value of state paper to deteriorate. Olympia based officials, moreover, saw no need to mend the extravagant ways of the past. "If there has been any disposition to economy," a Tacoma editor reflected after perusing public employee expense vouchers, "it has not been strong enough to attract notice." The post-crash annual report submitted by the state education superintendent, economizers complained, consisted of "pages and pages of worthless stuff…which the people are taxed to pay for." Preparing for the 1895 meeting of the legislature, most agencies actually intended, in further affront, to ask for increased funding.[30]

More galling to state residents—with Olympians again excepted—Governor John McGraw was planning to proceed with a costly new capitol building. The 1893 legislative session had authorized an expenditure of $500,000 for selecting a design and commencement of work. The shortcomings of the existing outmoded structure were evident to all observers. The woeful "hygienic conditions," for instance, supposedly contributed to the "vicious" nature of laws passed since 1889. Critics nonetheless charged the special governor-appointed commission with paying undue attention to high rolling architects and contractors from outside the state. The million dollar construction budget, opponents also maintained, depended upon revenue from public land sales, a highly dubious source

Proposal submitted for an architectural competition organized by the Washington State Capitol Commission in 1893. This design was never built. *University of Washington Libraries (UW1985)*

of money under the current economic conditions. Besides, the project would, as a practical matter, permanently resolve the contentious capital location issue in Olympia's favor by building, as an east-of-the-mountains editorialist decried, "a temple of Corinthian columns and Moorish minarets" amidst "the oozy abodes of the patient clam." Ignoring protests, plus the fact that available funding was only sufficient to lay a foundation, McGraw, in a victory of sorts, commenced excavation at the site.[31]

Controversial to begin with, John McGraw further undermined his reputation by involvement in Washington's first sex scandal. The state library, the governor demanded in the summer of 1893, must hire Mrs. J.E. Smart as assistant librarian, a "very dear friend" whose professional qualifications did not extend to the management of books. P.D. Moore, the head of the institution, refused to do so, in part because his son currently held the position, and was promptly displaced in favor of a more pliant administrator. Thoroughly flummoxed when Moore aired his grievances in the press, McGraw insisted that he had only meant to perform an innocent service for a "most excellent lady" who had befriended him when he was "a ragged barefoot boy." The public snickered in disbelief, especially when Smart's thoroughly incompetent librarianship became the ribald stuff of patronage legend.[32]

Outside Olympia, attention drawn to local government waste produced all sorts of sensational revelations. "The taxpayers of the state," one newspaper convincingly remarked in a fall 1893 summary of the wrongdoing uncovered, had been "systematically robbed" by public officials. On the northern Sound, the New Whatcom city treasurer turned out to be $40,000 "short" in his accounts, having invested the money in a private logging venture. The holder of the corresponding office in nearby Blaine got into similar trouble, albeit over a mere $900. To the southwest on the Olympic Peninsula, Clallam County's treasurer was unable to provide a convincing explanation for a missing thousand dollars, not to mention a much larger sum deposited in a defunct Port Angeles bank. In an east-of-the-Cascades "sensation," investigators revealed that Lincoln County officers had long been in the habit of pocketing fees and other public payments.[33]

Dishonesty was anything but a surprising development in the larger municipalities. Two members of the Spokane city council were arrested in August 1893 for accepting bribes. The county sheriff was charged with stealing $4,000 a year from the jail, a feat accomplished by diverting two-thirds of the sum allotted for the daily feeding of prisoners. In Tacoma, numerous arrests of city and county officials exposed a network of corruption. Commissioners had long demanded kickbacks from public employees, a practice hardly mitigated by one disgraced individual's claim that he had meant to return the money in the form of Christmas gifts.

Several clerks, meanwhile, practiced the profitable trade of forging warrants. Personnel in the treasurer's office used public funds to make short term high interest loans, expecting the cash to be back in the coffers prior to any outside accounting. "They yielded too readily," one editor wrote of the implicated officeholders, "to the solicitations of friends…who faithfully promised to return within a very short time any part of these funds that they were allowed temporarily to take."[34]

Seattle residents discovered that city and county employees had for years submitted heavily padded expense and travel vouchers. In the most spectacular example of local corruption exposed during the panic, a quarter million dollar shortage was uncovered in the accounts of city treasurer Adolph Krug, that sum having been loaned to friends and business associates. The scandal threatened to ruin several high profile members of the community, the signatories to Krug's bond. Affording "another illustration of…the 'Seattle' Spirit," fellow members of the respectable class covered the defalcation, saving their society friends. Krug himself was arrested in the process of making a belated dash for the Canadian border. After prolonged court proceedings, he was committed, in wretched personal condition, to eight years in the Walla Walla penitentiary.[35]

Behind the headlines devoted to miscreants, the real crisis in local government was the same as at the state level, a lack of revenue to meet expenses. Bonds could not be sold, regardless of the rate. Despite the introduction of incentives, including discounts for timely payment and suspension of penalties on overdue accounts, property owners failed to pay their taxes. Citizens complained, with some logical force, when the same counties and cities busily issuing warrants in lieu of cash refused to accept the certificates to cover tax liabilities. By mid-decade, Pierce County carried a quarter million dollars in delinquencies upon its books. Unpaid street improvement assessments, sums exceeding $400,000 in Spokane and $200,000 in Tacoma, placed an additional burden on strapped municipalities.[36]

Hard pressed to cover current requirements, counties resorted to various stratagems. On the westside, Snohomish County canceled all road and bridge projects. Saddled with nearly $200,000 in debt, Whatcom County followed suit. Thurston County slashed tax requirements by half through such expedients as closure of the county poor farm. "Even the course of justice is delayed," a Grays Harbor editor noted in reporting the Chehalis County response to indebtedness: a ban on jury trials. East of the Cascades, Yakima County slashed public salaries. Okanogan County dismissed most of its employees, the only exception being the elected officials responsible for the draconian action.[37]

Cities also adopted ingenious money saving schemes. South Bend banned wagons from its planked streets, thereby postponing the need for repairs. The community's elective officers exhibited "the finest sort of patriotism" by agreeing to take dollar-a-year salaries. Council members in Ocosta-by-the-Sea resolved to serve an additional 12 months, avoiding the cost of the annual municipal election. Olympia hired out prisoners from the city jail at 50 cents a day. Ballard, still an independent entity immediately north of Seattle, abolished all local taxes. Yakima lopped $3,000 from the town budget by laying off the police force. In common with most urban areas, Pullman extinguished its street lights.[38]

Washington's biggest cities instituted large economies. Burdened with $2 million in debt, Spokane applied "the brakes to municipal and other public extravagance." Employees were ordered to engage in "hard work," apparently an innovation on the local scene, and to quietly accept pay in warrants when cash was short. Seattle citizens, carrying an indebtedness twice the Spokane figure, insisted that their government be conducted as a "matter of business." Efficiency oriented do-gooders, organized as the Municipal League, claimed to represent a renewal of the Seattle "public spirit," that peculiar community loyalty "equal to any emergency." Winning control of the city council in March 1894, the league and its followers put their concepts into action, securing, through substantial reductions in police and fire protection, a 28 percent cut in the municipal budget. With tax cutting their principal aim, reformers also abolished the traditional allocation of free water to the poor.[39]

Tacoma experienced peculiar difficulty in restoring order to public finances. City officials shifted early on to the warrant method of meeting salary and other obligations. A true crisis developed when the Pierce County auditor, intent upon reducing the local tax burden relative to other counties, slashed property valuations by a third without taking into consideration the impact upon constitutional debt limits. Tacomans belatedly discovered in 1895 that they had borrowed in excess of $100,000 beyond the legally authorized amount. In addition to being unable to secure new loans, the city also must deal with the bitter fact that most of its cash was tied up in failed banks. "Our financial condition could not well be worse," one of the daily papers concluded. For all practical purposes out of money, Tacoma relied upon subscription drives to meet interest payments. After lengthy and occasionally emotional debate—many residents forthrightly advocated that creditors simply be ignored—the voters retroactively validated the excess borrowings, along with a refunding proposal putting the municipality back in business.[40]

Despite the prolonged emergency, Tacoma officials insisted upon proceeding with the long discussed acquisition of the local water company. The city had finalized details of the purchase in July 1893, Charles Wright himself financing the transaction as high bidder for the bonds approved by the electorate on the eve of the panic. Relying upon ambiguous contractual language, the firm's agents refused to turn over "the tools and supplies necessary to run" the plant. In bold response, the mayor raided the Wright owned gas works, where the contested items had been stored, in September. Adding to the public sense of aggravation, an early court ruling determined that Tacoma had only acquired "flumes and pipes," the water rights transferred by Wright being invalid. Various legal actions, as complex as they were time consuming, ensued, including actions to invalidate the bonds and compel the Philadelphia financier to pay substantial damages. Until all issues were formally resolved in 1897, Tacoma suffered from both water shortages and sustained financial embarrassment.[41]

Panic related stringencies caused the three big cities to use "a cleaver…not a pruning-knife" upon their forms of governance. Devising entirely new charters, the common objective was to promote efficiency, reduce expenditures and limit the tax burden. "The sooner steps are taken," a reformer declared in the summer of 1893, "to get rid of…the cumbrous, crude and unwieldy combination of aldermen, delegates, boards, commissioners, and all the rest of them…the better for Seattle as an organized community." Changes instituted over the strenuous objections of incumbents in Spokane and Tacoma, as well as on Elliott Bay, shifted power from councils to the mayor's office, reduced the number and authority of independent commissions, applied civil service principles and altered ward boundaries to maximize the electoral influence of the propertied classes. Monetary savings were significant, but the question remained as to whether economizers would be more honest and competent than their displaced spend-happy predecessors.[42]

❧❦❧

An economic crisis of unprecedented dimension was bound to have negative consequences for laboring men and women. An estimated one in five workers lost employment across the nation and in the Pacific Northwest. The earliest reaction to the panic, though, came in the form of wage reductions, as employers failed to grasp the true magnitude of the collapse. Puget Sound's coal mines imposed a 15 percent cut in July 1893. Receivers of the bankrupt railroads slashed pay by 20 percent in the fall, an economizing gesture that was not applied to their own salaries. Palouse wheat farmers reduced harvest wages to 75 cents a day, plus board. In addition to paying mill workers in scrip, shingle manufacturers instituted two cuts before the end of the year.[43]

Western Washington's mainstay industry, lumbering, followed the deflationary trend of the times. Sawmills lowered wages by 10 percent in early August. "There is very little kicking about it," Cyrus Walker reported from Puget Sound, "as at these times there is nothing to do, in any other part of the country." A second round of reductions followed in January. Traditionalist employers briefly rejoiced that the crisis allowed them to once again manage labor "with a taut rein and whip in hand." Although the depression had thus far been "a rich man's panic," Hoquiam's George Emerson reflected, "before spring, it will be a poor man's empty stomach, which is perhaps the only way to teach a large class of our people that they cannot...dictate to capital."[44]

Outright job loss, in an age predating unemployment insurance, social security and other forms of public assistance, was another, more catastrophic, matter. There was, after all, a certain logic to wage cutting. "The men certainly cannot expect us to continue losing money," a prominent lumberman explained, "when they are getting the same wages as they have been getting in the past." Work at any rate of pay was preferable to no income at all. The continuing economic decline, however, soon caused mills, logging camps and mines to shut down, throwing men and women on the street. Increasing numbers of the unemployed assembled in Seattle, Tacoma and other municipalities during the bitter winter of 1894, protesting their plight and maligning former employers.[45]

Though threatened with ruin themselves, middle class Washingtonians expressed little sympathy for the unemployed. Persons marching in the street were "not seeking work at fair wages, but...rather trying to get the government to support them." Democrats and Republicans blamed one another for fomenting the jobs issue out of political expediency. Mainstream party members agreed, though, that sinister foreign agitators were somehow responsible for the demonstrations. Better off urban residents complained of the increasing "hobo" and "tramp" menace. Seattle and a few other places attempted to expedite previously approved improvement projects to provide immediate work, but conventional opinion rejected the concept of depression related public works. "The idea that it is the duty of the government to promote the...prosperity of the individual is, we contend, a mistaken one," the establishment oriented *Seattle Telegraph* affirmed.[46]

So far as the genuinely unemployed were concerned, it was thought that such individuals ought to take care of themselves through the exercise of American initiative. "Hard times," more than one commentator noted, were best regarded as "migrating times." Persons out of work might, as many did, take ship for Alaska, to prospect for gold among the frozen creeks of the American and Canadian possessions. Less adventurous sorts could seek "independent fortune at a single bound" in eastern Washington camps, an option reflected by a notable increase in placer mining activity. Many observers suggested that the jobless be encouraged, and even supplied with tools and seed, to clear vacant land and establish subsistence farms. "A hundred dollars thus spent," a Seattle editor claimed, "would afford more substantial relief than if doled out in small sums in the city."[47]

Out-of-work people, however, favored political and economic action. Local shingle weaver unions mounted strikes at various Puget Sound points from the summer of 1893 through the early months of the following year. Teachers organized on both sides of the Cascades to protest pay cuts and the closure of schools. Still intent upon delivering a sobering lesson to labor, George Emerson staved off a general strike on Grays Harbor in early 1894 by threatening a preemptive sawmill shutdown, "letting the poor devils starve to a sense of their position." Pointing out that lumber could not be sold at a profit anyway, Emerson recognized the strategic weakness of his unionized opponents—if not prolonged or violent, a strike would actually save money for most milling operations, as well as preserve valuable timber for profitable cutting in the future.[48]

Respectable opinion was truly horrified by the union movement. "The time for sympathy with laborers…has passed," the *Tacoma Ledger* declared in condemning the "Chinese yoke" of unionization. Any consideration of strike action in the midst of a depression, other critics maintained, meant that labor was "putting a knife to its throat and…deliberately sawing away with it." Nervous capitalists, their potential investments representing the only means for restoration of prosperity, would be convinced from a perusal of news bulletins that the Pacific Northwest "has gone anarchistic." The few editors willing to admit that workers had both legitimate grievances and the right to organize nevertheless vehemently opposed anti-management action as contrary to the public interest.[49]

Major trouble came first in the mines. Roslyn workers organized in the spring of 1894, commencing a nasty dispute that ended only when the coaling operation's owner threatened, in a reprise of past anti-strike stratagems, to import black replacements from the South. Disorder, meanwhile, flared anew across the Idaho line in the Coeur d'Alene mines. Directed by the unabashedly radical Western Federation of Miners, laborers resisted company attempts to reduce wage scales. The very interested residents of Spokane complained of union intimidation, foreign agitators and the prolonged impact upon production of precious metals. Alarmed citizens demanded that federal troops be sent in, as in 1892, to restore order and protect property. Peace of a sort returned only in 1895, after the lengthy dispute and the continuing depression exhausted all participants in the fight.[50]

Dramatic events, too, took place on the region's railway lines in the spring and summer of 1894. Supporting an ongoing strike against the Pullman, Illinois, sleeping car company, the American Railway Union declared a boycott against western railroads using the well known conveyances. Middle class opinion was once again offended, especially when Spokane demonstrators attacked a Northern Pacific train. The boycott supposedly was a "foreign importation" directed at innocent bystanders and bound to injure "nearly everybody in the United States…excepting the one man it was desired to reach," the widely despised passenger car builder, George Pullman. By interfering with the flow of freight, mail and passengers, the strikers exposed themselves as "treasonable criminals," wanton destroyers of what was left of American economic enterprise. Outside the ranks of labor, few people complained when the federal government intervened, terminating the dispute and arresting union leader Eugene Debs and his associates. Unrelated troubles, meanwhile, also shut down the Great Northern, to the particular chagrin of Seattle business interests.[51]

Unfolding at the same time as the Pullman strike, the Coxey's Army affair added to the public's general fear of incipient revolution. Loosely organized under the leadership of Jacob Coxey, a wealthy Ohio eccentric, thousands of the unemployed from across the country attempted to descend on the nation's capital in quest of relief measures from congress and the Grover Cleveland administration. Some onlookers found little that was threatening in the demonstration. After all, as the *Seattle Telegraph* noted in a perspective-setting commentary, corporate lobbyists "marched on Washington time and again to demand legislation to fill their pockets." Most observers, though, disdained the army as a band of loafers bearing a message sure to sabotage recovery. In attempting to "intimidate" the federal government, the *Spokane Review* declared, Coxey "sails close to treason." To an excited editor in the Okanogan, the movement was "composed largely of the 'scum' of the land," organized by "socialists, anarchists, and all the elements of a revolutionary and treasonable character."[52]

Property owners and business interests worried that the Coxeyite "lunacy" would force capital to "go abroad" for safe investment. Fifteen hundred unemployed Puget Sounders assembled an "army" in Puyallup in early May, causing fearful conservatives to call for the dispatch of the regular military. Governor John McGraw appeared instead, but failed in a manly face-to-face confrontation to persuade the campers to go home. Federal Judge Cornelius Hanford, a jurist whose pro-corporation bias would be difficult to exaggerate, appointed deputy U.S. marshals—recruited from the ranks of railroad goondom—to act against the Coxeyites as a danger to interstate commerce and mail delivery. The first large Coxey party, heading east at mid-month, attempted to seize a train in Yakima, only to be arrested by the unique representatives of the law. The implacable Hanford sentenced the ostensible leaders, under dubious pretext, to prison.[53]

The Coxey's Army incident hardly turned the region upside down. Together with the railroad strikes, the episode nonetheless reflected a worrisome trend. "We have fallen upon evil times," one of the state's oldest newspapers lamented. Labor had somehow become "bold, arrogant, dictatorial, tyrannical." Unwilling to "accept the changed conditions which circumstances have brought about," organized workers made matters worse, stalling any hope of recovery from the depression. The panic experience completed the hardening of social divisions begun during earlier labor disturbances.[54] Henceforth, middle and working classes—the salaried and the wage earning, the propertied and the renter—confronted each other across a chasm of suspicion and miscomprehension. Militancy was arrayed against conservatism, force against law, in a dynamic born of industrialization.

∼∼∼

Sudden in its impact, the panic caught many well known individuals unprepared for public exposure, attacks on their reputations, and financial loss. Convinced that his onetime Tacoma beneficiaries had turned "communist" by suing him over the city waterworks sale, Charles Wright died in 1898. Paul Schulze, a veteran Northern Pacific land agent and more recently the leader of corporate irrigation in the Yakima Valley, committed suicide upon revelation of his secret career as an embezzler. Sued by associates in Seattle real estate ventures and forced to sell his Puget Sound investments, Senator Watson Squire confronted financial ruin. Another prominent Elliott Bay developer, David H. Gilman, absented himself from the city to avoid angry creditors. Anthony M. Cannon and John J. Browne, for years the leading business figures of Spokane, declared bankruptcy. Hazard Stevens, the son of Washington Territory's first governor and himself a longtime figure of importance in political, commercial and social affairs, departed Olympia for Boston after being criticized by former friends for bad pre-panic fiscal advice.[55]

Along with the departure of these compromised individuals, the earlier passing of Henry Yesler and other venerable figures came close to terminating the last connection between frontier and modern times. The depression would give birth to new and inevitably diminished historical personalities.

Notes

1.   *Tacoma Daily News,* January 1, 1894.
2.   Volcanic activity in the mountains may have encouraged the congregation of one Puget Sound church to assemble in expectation that the world would end on March 29, 1892. Reflecting the traditional view that the Pacific coast was immune from eastern economic disturbances, an Olympic Peninsula editor predicted that "Washington people will be wearing diamonds" at a time when New Yorkers must still be content with "sewing buttons on their last year's clothes." *Seattle Telegraph,* June 8, 1891; Nov. 23, 1894; *Tacoma Daily News,* March 3; Nov. 13, 14, 18, 1890; Cyrus Walker to W.H. Talbot, March 9, 1891, Cyrus Walker Letterbooks, Ames Coll., University of Washington Library; *West Shore,* 17 (April 11, 1891), 236; Thomas Burke to Don C. Corbett, June 6, 1892, Thomas Burke Papers, University of Washington Library; *Spokane Falls Review,* Dec. 19, 1890; *Tacoma Morning Globe,* Nov. 29, 1891; *Spokane Review,* Feb. 26, 1892; Portland *Oregonian,* Sept. 2, 1891, rep. from Port Angeles *Times.*

3. The reports of a single month, July 1892, reveal the importance of the timber industry, with 28 lumber carrying ships sailing from Seattle, 18 from Tacoma, 10 from Port Blakely and 4 from Port Gamble. *Ellensburgh Capital*, Feb. 5, 1891; *Tacoma Daily News*, Dec. 15, 1890; Aug. 22, 24, 1891; Feb. 12, 1892; *Tacoma Morning Globe*, Aug. 22; Sept. 28, 1891; Burke to C.H. Lewis, Sept. 3, 1891, Burke Papers; *Spokane Falls Review*, March 27, 1891; *Tacoma Daily Ledger*, March 28; Oct. 5, 1891; *Yakima Herald*, June 28, 1891; *Seattle Telegraph*, June 28; Aug. 29; Oct. 3, 1891; Olympia *Washington Standard*, Dec. 25, 1891; George H. Emerson to E.J. Holt, Sept. 3, 1891, George H. Emerson Letterbooks, University of Washington Library; *Seattle Post-Intelligencer*, Aug. 1, 1892.

4. In a rare reversal of conventional wisdom, a Grays Harbor newspaper delivered a sobering assessment: "The state has probably suffered more from the recent depression than Eastern localities for the reason that its development could not be carried on in the lines as contemplated. Capital and enterprise are indispensable in the opening up…of a new country and the withdrawal of either is necessarily followed by a suspension of progress." *Tacoma Morning Globe*, Sept. 24; Nov. 1, 1891; *Ellensburgh Capital*, Dec. 1, 1892; Walker to Talbot, Dec. 14, 1891, Walker Letterbooks; Burke to D.H. Gilman, Jan. 5, 8; Feb. 3; May 12, 1892, Burke Papers; Feb. 7, 1892, Daniel H. Gilman Papers, University of Washington Library; Portland *Oregonian*, Sept. 27, 1891, rep. from Hoquiam *Tribune*.

5. *Spokane Falls Review*, Dec. 19, 1890; *Tacoma Daily News*, July 19, 1892; William G. Robbins, *Colony and Empire: The Capitalist Transformation of the American West* (Lawrence: University Press of Kansas, 1994), 91. On the transformation of the British gold standard into a "global monetary system," see Niall Ferguson, *Empire* (New York: Basic Books, 2002), 244–45.

6. *Spokane Falls Review*, Jan. 4, 1890; *Walla Walla Statesman*, July 6, 1893; *Spokane Spokesman*, Dec. 17, 1890; *Spokane Review*, Dec. 19, 1891; *Seattle Telegraph*, July 19, 1893, rep. from Cheney *Sentinel*; Thomas Ewing to Watson C. Squire, Dec. 23, 1889, Watson C. Squire Papers, University of Washington Library; *Tacoma Morning Globe*, Feb. 2, 1891.

7. Washington had twice as many banks as Oregon. *Tacoma Daily Ledger*, Sept. 19; Nov. 4, 1891; *Seattle Telegraph*, July 8, 1891; Jan. 14, 17, 1892; Jan. 26, 1893; *Tacoma Daily News*, May 31, 1892; *Ellensburgh Capital*, Feb. 18; Dec. 22, 1892; *Anacortes American*, Jan. 19, 1893; *Seattle Press-Times*, Sept. 21, 1892; *Spokane Review*, Jan. 1, 1893; Walker to Talbot, May 20; June 4, 1892, Puget Mill Co. Records, Ames Coll., University of Washington Library.

8. Portland *Oregonian*, May 1; Aug. 15; Sept. 7, 1891; *Spokane Review*, Aug. 2; Oct. 14; Nov. 21, 1891; April 17, 1892; Olympia *Washington Standard*, April 3; May 8, 29, 1891; *Spokane Falls Review*, March 6; April 2, 1891; *Tacoma Daily News*, June 17; July 23, 1891; *Seattle Press-Times*, April 2, 1891; *Tacoma Morning Globe*, July 1; Sept. 30, 1891; Jan. 1, 1892; *Tacoma Daily Ledger*, Oct. 30, 1891.

9. European crop output again came up short in 1892. Tacoma received 1,000 carloads of grain in the first four weeks of the season. Despite the enormous increases of recent years, however, Washington still trailed Oregon, also the scene of expansion, in overall wheat production. *Spokane Review*, Dec. 29, 1891; May 15; Sept. 24; Oct. 3, 4, 8; Nov. 2, 11, 21, 1892; *Seattle Press-Times*, Sept. 16, 1891; May 25; Sept. 7, 1892; *Northwest*, 10 (May 1892), 41; *Seattle Telegraph*, Jan. 31, 1893; *Tacoma Daily News*, Sept. 28, 1892; *Seattle Post-Intelligencer*, Nov. 15, 1892; William G. Robbins, *Landscapes of Promise: The Oregon Story, 1800–1940* (Seattle: University of Washington Press, 1997), 154–55.

10. A leading Seattle lumber manufacturer expected, as of March 1893, to "have a good season this year." *Seattle Post-Intelligencer*, Feb. 11, rep. from South Bend *Journal*; April 22, 1893; *Spokane Review*, May 22; June 15, 1893; Olympia *Washington Standard*, Jan. 6, 1893;

Fred S. Stimson to T.D. Stimson, March 7, 1893, Stimson Mill Co. Records, University of Washington Library.

11. *Tacoma Daily News*, Feb. 10, 27, 1893; *Seattle Telegraph*, Feb. 11, 13, 14; March 28, 1893; *Spokane Review*, April 23, 1893.

12. *Seattle Telegraph*, May 5, 14; July 7; Sept. 19, 1893; *Spokane Review*, May 21, 1893; *Seattle Post-Intelligencer*, May 5, 14, 1893; *Tacoma Daily News*, May 15, 1893; *Seattle Press-Times*, June 19, 1893; Carlos A. Schwantes, *The Pacific Northwest: An Interpretive History* (Lincoln: University of Nebraska Press, 1989, 1996), 270–71; J. Kingston Pierce, "The Panic of 1893," *Columbia: The Magazine of Northwest History* [hereafter cited as *Columbia*], 7 (Winter 1993–1994), 39.

13. Hill did put on a subdued affair in St. Paul. Barely 40 of the 500 miles of track scheduled for construction in Washington during 1893 were actually laid down. The UP bankruptcy restored the old Oregon Railway & Navigation Company to independent operation. *Spokane Review*, May 23; Aug. 16, 1893; Jan. 3, 8; May 30, 1894; *Seattle Press-Times*, June 9; Aug. 16, 1893; Jan. 29, 1894; *Tacoma Daily News*, June 9; Aug. 16; Dec. 30, 1893; *Ellensburgh Capital*, May 4; June 15; Oct. 12, 19, 1893; Jan. 11, 1894; Albro Martin, *James J. Hill and the Opening of the Northwest* (New York: Oxford University Press, 1976), 396–98; Michael P. Malone, *James J. Hill: Empire Builder of the Northwest* (Norman: University of Oklahoma Press, 1996), 151–52; *Seattle Telegraph*, Oct. 11, 1893; *Tacoma Daily Ledger*, Aug. 16, 17, 1893; *Northwest*, 11 (Sept. 1893), 24–25; *Walla Walla Statesman*, July 21, 1894.

14. *Tacoma Daily News*, May 6, 8, 15; June 2, 30, 1893; *Seattle Post-Intelligencer*, May 5, 14, 1893; *Spokane Review*, May 21; June 12, 1893.

15. Emerson to Samuel Perkins, June 12, 1893; to A.M. Simpson, July 6, 1893, Emerson Letterbooks; Charles D. Stimson to T. Stimson, June 10, 1893, Stimson Mill Co. Records; *Spokane Review*, June 10, rep. from Sprague *Mail*, July 11, 23, 1893; *Tacoma Daily News*, May 15, 1893; *Seattle Press-Times*, June 19, 1893; *Tacoma Daily Ledger*, July 11, 22, 1893; *Yakima Herald*, Aug. 17, 1893.

16. *Walla Walla Statesman*, June 29, 1893; F.C. Talbot to Walker, May 19, 1893; W. Talbot to Walker, June 21; July 1, 18, 25, 1893; A.W. Jackson to Walker, July 25, 1893, all Puget Mill Co. Records; Robert E. Ficken, *The Forested Land: A History of Lumbering in Western Washington* (Seattle: University of Washington Press, 1987), 79; *Tacoma Daily News*, Aug. 1, 1893.

17. Only one suspended Washington bank managed to reopen by the fall of 1893. Seven of Tacoma's 23 banks survived the panic. The Ellensburg closures made money "very scarce" in the Kittitas Valley. Hoquiam mill company executive George Emerson avoided the accumulation of "stock for eastern trade inasmuch as too much coin is required to carry the business." *Ellensburgh Capital*, Aug. 3, 10, 1893; *Tacoma Daily News*, June 1, Oct. 9, 1893; *Spokane Review*, June 6, 8, 13, 1893; Pierce, "Panic of 1893," 40; *Seattle Telegraph*, June 4, 8, 1893; *The Dalles Times-Mountaineer*, June 10, 1893; John Fahey, "When the Dutch Owned Spokane," *Pacific Northwest Quarterly* [hereafter cited as *PNQ*], 72 (Jan. 1981), 4; *Tacoma Daily Ledger*, July 9, 23, 1893; Murray Morgan, *Puget's Sound: A Narrative of Early Tacoma and the Southern Sound* (Seattle: University of Washington Press, 1979), 275–76; Emerson to Simpson, July 13, 1893, Emerson Letterbooks.

18. A Seattle savings bank finally closed in January 1894, and most of the city's banking houses eventually failed. Walker to W. Talbot, July 5, 17; Aug. 3, 1893; to Jackson, Aug. 1, 1893, Walker Letterbooks. *Tacoma Daily News*, Sept. 16, 18, 26, 1893; *Seattle Telegraph*, Aug. 30, 1893; Burke to Gilman, Jan. 26, 1894, Burke Papers; *Seattle Press-Times*, July 31, 1893; Portland *Oregonian*, Nov. 7, 1893; Carlos A. Schwantes, *Radical Heritage: Labor, Socialism,*

and Reform in Washington and British Columbia, 1885–1917 (Seattle: University of Washington Press, 1979), 51.

19. Olympia *Washington Standard*, July 14, 1893; *Spokane Review*, Oct. 19, 1893; *Seattle Telegraph*, July 18, rep. from Mount Vernon *Post*, 20, 1893; Emerson to Simpson, Sept. 23, 1893, Emerson Letterbooks; *Seattle Post-Intelligencer*, Aug. 23, 1893; Jan. 2, 1894, rep. from Whatcom *Reveille*.

20. *Spokane Review*, Sept. 1; Dec. 23, rep. from *Oregonian*, 1893; March 19, 1894; Olympia *Washington Standard*, Dec. 1, 8, 1893; Seattle *Argus*, March 3, 31, 1894; Portland *Oregonian*, Oct. 2, 1893.

21. "Shingle mills are all going to the wall," George Emerson wrote from Grays Harbor, "as fast as the sheriff can get around to close them up." *Seattle Post-Intelligencer*, Dec. 31, 1893; Spokane *Spokesman-Review*, June 1, 1896; *Seattle Telegraph*, Jan. 6, 1894; *Tacoma Daily News*, July 17, 1893; Geo. H. Southard to W.S. Norman, July 29; Aug. 7; Nov. 10, 1893; Wm. Augs. White to A.A.H. Boissevain, May 28, 1897, all Washington Water Power Co. Records, Washington State University Library; Robert C. Nesbit and Charles M. Gates, "Agriculture in Eastern Washington, 1890–1910," *PNQ*, 37 (Oct. 1946), 288; Walker to W. Talbot, July 21, 1893, Walker Letterbooks; Ficken, *Forested Land*, 80–81; Emerson to Simpson, July 6, 1893, Emerson Letterbooks.

22. Cyrus Walker, a longtime critic of overproduction, managed to combine a bit of optimism with his habitual pessimistic outlook, forecasting that the panic would "cause lots of the Mills to quit the business, and when the most of them are closed out, we may look for a better lumber business." Frederick Weyerhaeuser to J.P. Weyerhaeuser, April 11, 1893, Weyerhaeuser Family Papers, Minnesota Historical Society; Ficken, *Forested Land*, 80–81; Emerson to Simpson, July 6; Oct. 23, 1893; to J.W. Sanborn, July 26, 1893; to Perkins, June 12, 1893; to M.P. Callender, Dec. 14, 1893, Emerson Letterbooks; *Seattle Post-Intelligencer*, Dec. 11, 1893; Walker to W. Talbot, July 17, 1893; to Jackson, Aug. 1, 1893, Walker Letterbooks.

23. According to a reliable source, at least 4,000 residents of Spokane, Tacoma and Seattle lost their jobs during 1893. *Spokane Review*, Nov. 25, 1893; Jan. 5, 1894; *Seattle Telegraph*, April 19, 20, 1894; *Tacoma Daily Ledger*, July 18, 24, 25, 1893.

24. *Tacoma Daily News*, Aug. 23, 1893; *Seattle Telegraph*, Aug. 23, 25, 1893; Jan. 1; April 19, 20, 1894; *Spokane Review*, Nov. 24–29, 1893; *Tacoma Daily Ledger*, July 24–26; Aug. 23; Sept. 2, 1893; *Seattle Post-Intelligencer*, Dec. 26, 1893; Jan. 2, 1894; *Seattle Press-Times*, Jan. 5, 1894.

25. *Walla Walla Statesman*, July 20, 1893; *Seattle Post-Intelligencer*, April 22; Aug. 9, 12, 1893; *Ellensburgh Capital*, April 27, 1893; *Tacoma Daily News*, May 3, 1893; *Spokane Review*, May 8, 22; June 15; July 12, 30; Aug. 4, 1893; *Tacoma Daily Ledger*, July 17, 1893; *Seattle Telegraph*, Aug. 3, 21, 1893; Portland *Oregonian*, Oct. 7, 1893; *Northwest*, 11 (Sept. 1893), 37.

26. "Far into the summer it rained," a wheat country journalist lamented in January 1894, "throughout the harvest season the big wet drops pattered unremittingly; all the fall and early winter they kept coming, and…people are wondering if the genuine old Palouse weather will ever be known again." *Seattle Telegraph*, Sept. 3, 4, rep. from Colfax *Gazette*, Nov. 6, 1893; Portland *Oregonian*, Oct. 7, 13, 14, 25, 26, 1893; *Ellensburgh Capital*, Oct. 19, 1893; April 19, 1894; Davenport *Lincoln County Times*, Oct. 20, 1893; *Seattle Post-Intelligencer*, Jan. 26; March 21, 1894; *Walla Walla Statesman*, Dec. 4, 1893; *Spokane Review*, Jan. 19, 1894, rep. from Farmington *Journal*.

27. *Tacoma Daily News*, Aug. 7; Dec. 9, 1893; Spokane *Spokesman-Review*, May 13, 1895; *Pullman Tribune*, May 4, 1895; *Ellensburgh Localizer*, Aug. 11, 1894; *Tacoma Daily Ledger*,

July 1, 1893; *Seattle Telegraph*, Sept. 12, 1839; May 6, 1894; *Spokane Review*, Oct. 18, 1893; March 3; May 15, 1894; *Everett Herald*, Aug. 3, 1893.

28. The Seattle press claimed that prosperity had returned when the city council managed to float a bond issue in October at 94%, a rate that would once have been considered unacceptable. "The great financial strain of 1893," E.V. Smalley declared, "may be said to have begun in June, to have raged hardest in July, to have moderated in August and to have pretty well spent its force by the first of September." An Aberdeen newspaper claimed that times were "less dull" in Washington than elsewhere in the country. "If our people had not read the newspapers," a Walla Walla commentator boasted, "they would not know that there is a panic on." Olympia *Washington Standard*, July 14, 1893; Feb. 9, 1894; *Walla Walla Statesman*, Sept. 15, 1894; *Seattle Telegraph*, Aug. 14, rep. from Aberdeen *Herald*, 26, rep. from Walla Walla *Union*, Sept. 12; Oct. 31; Nov. 6, 1893; *Ellensburgh Capital*, Sept. 14, 21, 28, 1893; *Spokane Review*, Sept. 13, 1893, rep. from Port Angeles *Tribune-Times*; *Seattle Post-Intelligencer*, April 23, 1894; *Tacoma Daily Ledger*, July 11, 1893; Waterville *Big Bend Empire*, Sept. 21, 1893; *Northwest*, 11 (Oct. 1893), 30.

29. The failure to hold a special session also meant that Washington would continue to be represented in the nation's capital by a single U.S. senator. *Seattle Post-Intelligencer*, Nov. 20, 1893; Jan. 1, 1894; *Seattle Telegraph*, Sept. 2, rep. from Walla Walla *Union*, Oct. 30, 1893; Jan. 11, 1894; *Yakima Herald*, Oct. 12, 1893; *Tacoma Daily News*, Feb. 2, 1894.

30. *Seattle Telegraph*, Jan. 29, 1894; Spokane *Spokesman-Review*, Dec. 2, 17, rep. from Kettle Falls *Pioneer*, 1894; Jan. 16; Feb. 24, 1895; Olympia *Washington Standard*, Nov. 10, 1893; *Tacoma Daily Ledger*, Dec. 3, 1894; *Ellensburgh Capital*, Oct. 5, 1893; John R. Rogers to J. Gaston, Feb. 24, 1898, John R. Rogers Papers, Washington State Archives.

31. Opponents also contended that the state constitution required selection of a permanent capital city, a process still technically incomplete, prior to the use of public land revenue for construction of such a building. Olympia residents, meanwhile, opposed any new election for state capital, ostensibly because of the need to avoid depression-time public expense. According to interior critics of the Olympia project, "a foreign vessel" could "lay at anchor and destroy" the structure. Norman J. Johnston, "A Capitol in Search of an Architect," *PNQ*, 73 (Jan. 1982), 2–9; and "The Washington State Capitol Campus and Its Peripatetic Planning," *Columbia*, 13 (Spring 1999), 17; Olympia *Washington Standard*, Jan. 12; Feb. 9; April 6, 1894; *Walla Walla Statesman*, Feb. 9, 1894; *Seattle Telegraph*, Jan. 23, 30; April 27, 1894; *Spokane Review*, March 29, 31; May 20, rep. from Walla Walla *Statesman*, 1894; *Tacoma Daily Ledger*, Jan. 30, 1896.

32. Moore's replacement, one Colonel Gilbert, eventually fired Smart. The post of state librarian seemed hazardous to the holder's health. Gilbert died in office, as did overworked successor George Kennedy. "It was a common remark," one newspaper noted in explanation of Kennedy's physical and nervous breakdown, "that he not only knew the exact location of every book in the library, but the contents of the books." *Spokane Review*, March 2, 1894; *Seattle Telegraph*, Aug. 20, 22, 1893; Olympia *Washington Standard*, March 2, 1894; *Seattle Post-Intelligencer*, Aug. 21, 1893; *Tacoma Daily News*, July 3, 1895.

33. *Seattle Telegraph*, Oct. 3, 23, 1893; Olympia *Washington Standard*, Sept. 15, 1893; *Tacoma Daily Ledger*, March 9, 1894; *Seattle Press-Times*, May 3, rep. from Spokane *Chronicle*, June 6, 1894; Port Angeles *Democrat-Leader*, Jan. 25, 1895; Spokane *Spokesman-Review*, Jan. 30, 1895.

34. *Spokane Review*, Aug. 30; Sept. 19, 1893; Spokane *Spokesman-Review*, Feb. 13, 1895; Chauncey W. Griggs to Charles Foster, Nov. 8, 1895, St. Paul & Tacoma Lumber Co. Records, University of Washington Library; *Tacoma Daily Ledger*, April 1; June 30, 1896; *Seattle Press-Times*, May 26, 1894.

35. Taxpayers also learned that the King County surveyor required employees to kick back two dollars of their daily pay. Construction of the county poor farm produced another scandal. Accountants examining the ledgers of the Seattle school district found that "irregularities, to call them by a mild name, extend over a series of five or six years." Krug's beneficiaries intended to buy up undervalued city warrants, then pay back the "loans" from their profits. The panic, unfortunately, precluded the bond issue that would have refinanced and inflated the price of the warrants. *Seattle Telegraph*, Sept. 25, 26, 29, 30; Oct. 1, 1893; April 5, 7, 9, 10; Oct. 29, 1894; *Seattle Post-Intelligencer*, Jan. 30, 1894; Seattle *Argus*, March 17, 1894; March 2, 1895; Jan. 25; March 7, 1896; *Seattle Press-Times*, Sept. 13–16, 18, 19, 30, 1893; *Tacoma Daily News*, Sept. 13, 1893; Olympia *Washington Standard*, Sept. 29, 1893; R.R. Spencer to Gilman, Oct. 25, 1893, Gilman Papers.

36. Taxes not paid by the first of April were normally assessed a 5 percent penalty and 20 percent interest. Portland *Oregonian*, Oct. 31; Dec. 5, 1893; Davenport *Lincoln County Times*, April 6, 1894; *Seattle Press-Times*, June 5, 1894; *Yakima Herald*, April 12, 1894; *Ellensburgh Capital*, April 26, 1894; *Tacoma Daily Ledger*, April 13, 1896; April 7, 1897; *Spokane Review*, Dec. 28, 1893.

37. "The financial depression must have struck Snohomish," a local editor mused. "The taxpayers are kicking because the county…allowed one of the deputy sheriffs an expenditure of $5.40 for drinks taken during a trip to one of the mining camps." Portland *Oregonian*, Nov. 3, 1893; New Whatcom *Daily Reveille*, Sept. 29, 1897; *Seattle Post-Intelligencer*, March 9, 1896; Olympia *Washington Standard*, Jan. 5, 1894; *Seattle Telegraph*, Aug. 1, 1893, rep. from Aberdeen *Bulletin*; Chehalis *Bee*, June 4, 1897; Spokane *Spokesman-Review*, Dec. 15, 1894; Jan. 31, 1895; *Spokane Review*, Sept. 6, 1893, rep. from Port Townsend *Leader*.

38. *Seattle Post-Intelligencer*, May 17, 1894; Spokane *Spokesman-Review*, Oct. 18, 1895; *Tacoma Daily Ledger*, Dec. 7, 1894; Portland *Oregonian*, Oct. 16; Nov. 1, 1893; *Yakima Herald*, May 3, 1894; *Pullman Tribune*, May 22, 1897; Olympia *Washington Standard*, Oct. 13, 1893.

39. City warrants were accepted by local merchants. Spokane teachers combined their pay certificates and sold them to a speculator for 97 cents on the dollar. In another proposal to save taxpayer money, the Municipal League recommended a shortened Seattle school year. *Spokane Review*, Sept. 23; Oct. 24, 1893; Spokane *Spokesman-Review*, Nov. 30; Dec. 1, 4, 13, 1894; Jan. 4; July 15, 1895; Portland *Oregonian*, Oct. 10, 1893; *Seattle Post-Intelligencer*, March 6, 1895; Feb. 9, 1898; *Seattle Times*, Oct. 3, 1895; *Seattle Press-Times*, Jan. 19, 25; Feb. 6, 24; March 5–7, 1894; March 12, 1895; Seattle *Argus*, March 31, 1894; Sept. 26, 1896; *Seattle Telegraph*, March 21, 1894; Lee F. Pendergrass, "The Formation of a Municipal Reform Movement: The Municipal League of Seattle," *PNQ*, 66 (Jan. 1975), 13–25.

40. Tacoma also attempted to eliminate the $23,000 annual cost of "superfluous," or phantom, employees. The assessment reduction left Tacoma property owners with a 10 mill tax levy, compared to 13 mills in Seattle. Seattle viewed the Commencement Bay fiasco as another triumph in the ongoing interurban competition. "The whole affair is an extraordinary one," a local editor gloated, "and illustrates the scandalously loose way in which business has been done in Tacoma." Portland *Oregonian*, Sept. 30, 1893; Olympia *Washington Standard*, May 5, 1893; *Tacoma Daily News*, June 1, 3, 5, 7, 1895; *Tacoma Daily Ledger*, March 10, 1894; March 2, 1895; April 8, 12, 13, 17, 24, 27, 29, 30; May 2, 9, 17, 31; June 21–23; July 8, 1896; *Seattle Times*, Oct. 3, 17, 1895; Morgan, *Puget's Sound*, 278.

41. A local paper noted that "Mr. Wright must be angry indeed, if he is as mad with us as we are with him." *Tacoma Daily Ledger*, July 14; Aug. 19, 27; Sept. 5, 1893; July 20; Dec. 7, 1894;

Jan. 9, 10; March 2, 1895; Jan. 10, 1896; Aug. 26, 1897; *Tacoma Daily News*, July 15; Sept. 5; Nov. 7, 13, 1893; Feb. 14, 19, 1894; Jan. 2, 1896; Aug. 26, 1897; *Spokane Review*, Nov. 13, 16, 1893; Morgan, *Puget's Sound*, 316–20.

42. Seattle abandoned its bizarre two chambered council system in favor of a single legislative body. The drafters of Spokane's new charter claimed that their handiwork would save the city $75,000 a year, a sum "worth more...than the coming of a new transcontinental railroad." *Spokane Review*, Oct. 17, 1893; Jan. 4; March 1, 3; April 24, 1894; *Seattle Press-Times*, March 14, 1895; Seattle *Argus*, March 9, 1895; Jan. 11; Feb. 8, 15, 1896; *Seattle Telegraph*, June 29; Aug. 20; Sept. 2, 1893; April 30, 1894; Spokane *Spokesman-Review*, Dec. 30, 1894; *Seattle Times*, Dec. 17–19, 1895; *Tacoma Daily Ledger*, March 2, 3, 1894; April 10, 22, 1896.

43. Carlos A. Schwantes, *Coxey's Army: An American Odyssey* (Lincoln: University of Nebraska Press, 1985), 13–17; Pierce, "Panic of 1893," 39; *Tacoma Daily Ledger*, July 8, 1893; *Tacoma Daily News*, Dec. 11, 1893; *Walla Walla Statesman*, Aug. 14, 1894; F. Stimson to T. Stimson, Oct. 24, 1893; C. Stimson to T. Stimson, Nov. 9, 1893, both Stimson Mill Co. Records; *Seattle Press-Times*, May 19, 1894.

44. Walker to Jackson, Aug. 1, 1893; to W. Talbot, Aug. 3, 1893, Walker Letterbooks; W. Talbot to Walker, Aug. 17, 1893, Puget Mill Co. Records; Emerson to Simpson, Sept. 1, 1893; Jan. 18, 25, 1894; to Perkins, Jan. 15, 1894; to William Thompson, Jan. 19, 1894, Emerson Letterbooks; Ficken, *Forested Land*, 79–80.

45. Ficken, *Forested Land*, 80; *Tacoma Daily Ledger*, Feb. 5, 10, 11, 1894; *Seattle Telegraph*, April 19, 20, 1894.

46. *Seattle Press-Times*, June 16, rep. from Everett *Herald*; Nov. 24, 1894; *Seattle Post-Intelligencer*, Dec. 26, 1893; Jan. 2; May 10; June 26, 1894; *Tacoma Daily Ledger*, March 12, 1894; Schwantes, *Coxey's Army*, 16; *Seattle Telegraph*, April 14, 1894.

47. *Spokane Review*, Sept. 2, 1893; June 13, 1894; Spokane *Spokesman-Review*, Feb. 25, 1895; *Tacoma Daily Ledger*, Aug. 28, 1893; Jan. 18, 1894; *Seattle Press-Times*, Jan. 5, 1894.

48. Portland *Oregonian*, Oct. 3, 1893; *Seattle Press-Times*, May 19, 1894; Spokane *Spokesman-Review*, Oct. 5, 1895; Emerson to Perkins, May 31, 1894; to Simpson, June 1, 2, 5, 12, 1894; North Western Lumber Co. to Grays Harbor Commercial Co., June 2, 1894, all Emerson Letterbooks.

49. "Nearly all of them voted for Cleveland and democratic principles," Governor John McGraw sneered of striking workers. "Now they are taking their medicine." *Tacoma Daily Ledger*, July 9, 10, 1894; *Yakima Herald*, July 5, 1894; *Seattle Post-Intelligencer*, Jan. 22, 1895; *Spokane Review*, Sept. 17, 1893; *Seattle Press-Times*, April 30; May 3, 1894; Seattle *Argus*, April 28, 1894; *Seattle Telegraph*, April 18, 1894.

50. Anti-union forces relied heavily upon nativist propaganda, emphasizing that only a quarter of the 300 employees at Idaho's famous Bunker Hill mine were U.S. citizens. *Seattle Press-Times*, May 19, 1894; *Seattle Post-Intelligencer*, April 23; Aug. 3, 8, 1894; *Ellensburgh Localizer*, Aug. 25, 1894; *Spokane Review*, Feb. 20; April 29; May 17; June 26–28, 1894; Spokane *Spokesman-Review*, July 5, 8, 9, 25, 1894; May 14, 15; June 29; July 11, 1895. On the W.F.M., see Schwantes, *Radical Heritage*, 113–14.

51. Though officially a boycott, the A.R.U. action built upon pro-strike sentiment dating to the previous year. Few strike critics defended George Pullman, who was widely portrayed as manifesting "an attitude as high and mighty as that assumed by any tyrant of old." *Seattle Press-Times*, April 14, 1894; *Seattle Telegraph*, April 16, 28, 1894; W. Thomas White, "Railroad Labor Protests, 1894–1917: From Community to Class in the Pacific Northwest," *PNQ*, 75 (Jan. 1984), 14–15; Spokane *Spokesman-Review*, July 6–8, 17, 1894; *Tacoma*

Daily Ledger, Jan. 1; July 1–3, 1894; *Seattle Post-Intelligencer*, July 10, 12, 1894; *Tacoma Daily News*, Dec. 29, 1893; Seattle *Argus*, July 7, 14, 1894.

52. Noting that "considerably less than one-tenth of 1 percent of the people ever joined the Coxey procession," another paper concluded that "this talk about an impending revolution is gibbering idiocy." Schwantes, *Coxey's Army*, chaps. 1, 2; *Seattle Telegraph*, April 16, 25; May 23, 1894; *Spokane Review*, April 25, 28; May 2, 3, 16, 19, 26, 1894; *Ellensburgh Capital*, May 3, 1894; *Seattle Post-Intelligencer*, April 3; May 5, 1894; Conconully *Okanogan Outlook*, May 19, 1894; *Seattle Press-Times*, June 9, 1894, rep. from Chehalis *Nugget*.

53. *Spokane Review*, May 7, 26, 1894; *Seattle Post-Intelligencer*, May 4, 14, 18, 23, 1894; *Seattle Press-Times*, April 30, 1894; *Yakima Herald*, May 17, 1894; *Seattle Telegraph*, May 13, 14, 1894; Schwantes, *Coxey's Army*, 231–45, 276.

54. Olympia *Washington Standard*, April 27, 1894; *Seattle Press-Times*, May 2, 1894; White, "Railroad Labor Protests," 15.

55. *Tacoma Daily Ledger*, Jan. 10, 1896; *Tacoma Daily News*, March 24, 1898; Spokane *Spokesman-Review*, June 2, 1895; Morgan, *Puget's Sound*, 277–78; Pierce, "Panic of 1893," 42; *Seattle Press-Times*, Oct. 16, 1894; *Seattle Times*, Feb. 12; Sept. 22, 27, 1897; July 15, 1898; Burke to Gilman, Nov. ?, 1894, Burke Papers; Fahey, "When the Dutch Owned Spokane," 4–5; Olympia *Washington Standard*, Oct. 8, 1897.

ᕤᘏᕬᘏᕤ

Chapter Six
Somewhat of a Black Eye

*The state received somewhat of a black eye from the failure of many schemes...
widely advertised a few years ago and which were never designed for any purpose
except to enrich their rascally promoters...let there be no more exaggerations, no
more high-colored descriptions, nothing more to lead the immigrant to think
that he can get rich here without working. Rather let it be known that this is no
state for the sluggard to come to. Let it be made known that what riches nature
has here she...surrenders only to those who compel her by patient industry and
intelligent enterprise to give them up. Let it be known that this is no Arcadia, no
place for those who want to live without work, but that what a man gets here he
has to earn.*— Seattle Times.[1]

*W*ASHINGTON STATE, according to a widely endorsed observation, looked
to the East "to see what signs may be visible of the dawn of better times."
Hopeful portents, unfortunately, were rarely sighted. In the fall of 1893, gold
standard advocates waited vainly for repeal of the Sherman silver purchase act
by congress to restore investor confidence and return money into circulation.
President Grover Cleveland's other anti-depression policy, reduced tariff barriers,
hurt the Pacific Northwest by allowing lower priced British Columbia lumber
and coal into the California market. A year into his term, Cleveland was completely discredited, as suggested by a nasty bit of doggerel from the east side of
the Cascades:

> Oh, where are we at, with Grover so fat...? With banks without cash, and
> things going to smash, and wheat that is cheaper than corn, men are prone to
> be rash and drink sour mash and wish they had never been born.[2]

His habitual pessimism for once confirmed by contemporary developments,
Cyrus Walker reported that "times appear to be getting worse all the time." The
entire region, another prominent industry figure confided, was "prostrated."
Despite the opening of new markets in Britain's African possessions, Puget Sound
lumber exports decreased from 113 million board feet in 1891 to 86 million in
1894. The railroads reduced rates, but shipments to the East dropped by a third.
Three out of four Washington shingle mills closed down from lack of trade.

Purchases of timber land, meanwhile, declined, in one informed account to "approximately nothing."[3]

Other economic activities also tallied "hard, cruel, cold, sterile, unproductive and unhappy" returns. Coal production dropped and the Oregon Improvement Company, principal operator of the King County mines, declared bankruptcy for a second, and final, time. The value of Washington's waterborne wheat shipments fell from $3 million in 1892 to $2 million in 1894, in spite of a significant increase in the number of bushels exported. Puget Sound imports also slumped, with little prospect of recovery. Financial institutions continued to close their doors. Bank clearances dropped by two-thirds in Spokane and by half in Seattle. Rental income "diminished at least fifty per cent" for both Inland Empire and Elliott Bay landlords. Assessed property valuation, previously a favorite promotional statistic for real estate speculators, declined statewide from $224 million to $166 million between 1893 and 1895. "The country," an eastern Washington editor succinctly noted on the basis of such figures, "is in distress."[4]

Agriculture shared fully in the pain. Undeterred by lower prices, wheat ranchers increased their planting in 1894, generating a yield larger "than any previous year." Unfortunately, mounting foreign competition overstocked an already weak market. Per bushel rates collapsed to a rate of less than 40 cents, and a fast growing Chinese thistle infestation added to woes in the Palouse. "The shadow of the sheriff looms up high over every farm," claimed reports from eastern Washington. Dispirited producers finally cut crops back in 1895 and 1896, but without any impact upon earnings. "The bonanza days of wheat raising have vanished never to return," mourning onlookers declaimed.[5]

Residents of the Pacific Northwest had been long accustomed to "scanning the horizon for the appearance of new railroads." Sustained disaster, however, now took the place of habitual expectation. Nationally, a hundred railway firms failed between 1894 and 1896, with employment in the industry dropping by 50,000 workers. Regionally, the depression initiated a "rapid process of readjustment" in railroad management. The Great Northern's James J. Hill invested heavily in the Northern Pacific and, after an abortive attempt to secure formal ownership of that cross-country rival, instead devised a mutually supportive alliance between the NP and GN. The NP, meanwhile, lost effectual control of the Spokane connected Washington Central and Palouse systems. The Union Pacific bankruptcy restored, at least for the moment, the old Oregon Railway & Navigation Company to independent and aggressive rate cutting competition. Once vigorous, but now all but moribund, properties originally developed by the Oregon Improvement Company and George W. Hunt lapsed into the uncertain hands of discouraged new investors.[6]

In private correspondence, corporate leaders regularly bemoaned the prolonged failure of the economy to revert to a "natural order of business." The public, though, was treated to ongoing, and generally unconvincing, claims that the depression was "largely a matter of imagination." From the spring of 1894 onward, newspapers insisted that "the lowest notch in the scale…has undoubtedly been reached." Lumber production, even at low prices, was supposedly on the increase, as the timber industry changed its focus from the Great Lakes to the Pacific coast. Mining, too, appeared on the verge of significant expansion. The emerging trade connections with Asia represented a "golden opportunity" for the Northwest. A "growing stream of immigration…from the blizzard-swept, famine-stricken regions between the Mississippi river and the Rocky mountains" added new force to Washington's population base. The only thing missing was confidence in the future. Lamenting the counter productive "tendency to feel 'blue,' to look 'blue' and talk 'blue,'" a Tacoma journalist urged his readers "to be cheerful…in the face of seeming adversity."[7]

The persistent depression instead produced a realistic reaction among the cheerless people of Washington state. "There is," wrote one concerned observer, "a great fiery, swift river of discontent rolling through the land just under the surface through which it is bursting in a few places." It was a development that was difficult, if not impossible, to avoid even by establishment commentators. "Hard times," the Republican *P-I* conceded, "always breed honest discontents and dishonest malcontents." In practical terms, a rival Democratic daily affirmed, the population was "in a decidedly restless state of mind." The Pullman strikers and Coxey's Army had been defeated in 1894, but "the ruling classes in this country have not settled the causes…by clever cartoons with 'keep off the grass'"—a reference to Jacob Coxey's anticlimactic arrest in the nation's capital—"as their inspiration."[8]

Badly offended by faint hearts and social indiscipline, the old lumberman Cyrus Walker huffed that "every body seem[s] to loose their heads when things go bad." A reflection of personal dyspepsia, the observation nonetheless captured a widespread feeling that the panic had generated the makings of profound change. "The Anglo-Saxon race has hitherto gained its triumphs through individual self-reliance," a Seattle editor noted in an analysis of the 1894 disturbances. "It is something new that from all points along the Pacific coast…organized troops of men…seek from the government what their fathers would have scorned to receive from the hands of the state." The labor unions, dramatically if briefly on the offensive, were hardly the only element of society to act upon the conviction that unity provided the best means of dealing with the modern industrial order. On a genuinely compelling, though somewhat naive, note, the depression encouraged the founding of utopian colonies on Puget Sound. Inspired by the writings of Edward Bellamy, Equality Colony, but one example of a regional phenomenon, operated a 600 acre farm on the northern Sound, fully equipped with stock, agricultural implements and a steam driven sawmill.[9]

Following a more conspiratorial and potentially violent line, other depression impacted groups organized in self-defense. Supposedly "officered like an army," debt ridden Palouse farmers pledged bloody resistance to creditor foreclosure attempts. On both sides of the Cascades, unemployed persons joined in what the press quickly termed "Patriot armies." While openly lampooning such entities as the work of "quack doctors, broken-down lawyers, and disgruntled politicians," the property classes nevertheless privately circulated fearful reports about supposed secret weapons purchases and military training exercises by these organizations.[10]

Such claims also were reflected in the propaganda of the growing forces of nativism. These alarmists worried that one-fifth of Washington's population was foreign born, twice the percentage for neighboring Oregon. Labor and political discontent appeared, as the *P-I* asserted, to be the product of un-American "prejudices and imported ignorance." Barely a quarter of the workers in the strike embroiled Coeur d'Alenes, after all, were U.S. citizens. The equally threatened sawmill industry, a trade publication pointed out, employed "about all the different kinds of people that are on earth at the present time, including inhabitants of islands."[11]

This anti-immigrant rhetoric took on additional vitriolic force when claiming that the harsh economic conditions were due to low paid alien workers and the actions of overseas investors. "We cannot hope to assimilate the mass of ignorance, crime, filth and pauperism daily dumped upon our shore," an Olympia newspaper declared. "They are the dregs of Europe's lowest and most vicious orders," a Yakima editor contended in denouncing the employment of "Dagos" by the nation's corporations. Democrats and Republicans alike demanded that immigration be "entirely prohibited, until such time as the present foreign population shall have become entirely Americanized." Pressed by self-appointed patriots, schools in Spokane and other Washington cities added mandatory U.S. history courses to the educational regimen.[12]

Nativist organization and activism centered on the rabidly anti-papist campaigns of the American Protective Association. The movement's members involved themselves in municipal elections, paying particular attention to educational issues. APA tickets won school board elections in Seattle and Spokane—with Catholic schools suffering as a result. While calling the pope "a macaroni-eating Dago," the supposedly sophisticated Seattle *Argus*, a prime APA mouthpiece, attacked local street railway companies for providing "sisters" free passes and accused the city's Catholic hospital of denying medical treatment to Protestants. Church owned property, the journal declared, ought to be subjected to special, and all but confiscatory, taxation. Promoting prejudice whenever possible, the *Argus* and several other like minded publications broadcast pseudo-news accounts, claiming that Puget Sound priests maintained a secret female "prison," forcing the inmates to "work like slaves, clad only in the coarsest raiment" and sending the profits to Rome.[13]

❧

Thanks to the depression, as one troubled commentator noted, Washington's "political situation" was "full of perplexity to every honest man." Even before the panic, a trend toward partisan upheaval was evident. The superficially impressive Republican victory in 1892 was due to a split in the opposition vote between Democrats and the People's party. However, the growing tendency of these disenchanted portions of the electorate to combine against old allegiances, and thereby oust incumbents in the yearly municipal elections, had resulted in numerous local models for a unification of forces to end the GOP's statewide dominance. Factoring in the likely political impact of the economic collapse, the *Seattle Times* reflected that "it would take the seventh son of a seventh son to make even a fair guess as to who'll be who in 1896." Some of the state's most experienced politicians moved to take advantage of the impending, though still uncertain, makeover. John Allen was reported as "toying with the populists" in the interest of regaining his U.S. senate seat. On a more improbable, albeit desperately cynical note, Senator Watson Squire declared his sympathies with populism. The pleasure loving New Yorker-in-the-Northwest even publicly renounced the use of alcohol in an effort to appeal to rural sentiment.[14]

Protest elements in the electorate now had better means to express their views regarding the lack of any effective public response to the economic crisis. The voters confronted a choice in November 1894 that, as one conservative publisher suggested in partisan fashion, was "between anarchy and economic idiocy on one side and law, patriotism and common sense on the other." In a mixed result, the Republicans retained a solid, if much reduced legislative majority. Nineteen Populists, however, joined a half dozen Democrats in the state house. The anti-GOP forces, moreover, had united behind a common candidate in many districts, a harbinger of a fusion effort anticipated for 1896. "The result was better than I thought it would be," Cyrus Walker reported to his sawmilling associates, but the long term prognosis for Republicanism was troubled.[15]

Rather than venture thoughtful responses to the economic collapse, legislators instead chose to act as "blind leaders of the blind." The new 1895 session was immediately sidetracked by the necessary election of a U.S. senator. Three Republicans offered themselves for the honor—Representative John Wilson, his longtime Spokane rival George Turner campaigning on behalf of restoring silver coinage, and the politically influential, though otherwise lightly qualified, Walla Walla banker Levi Ankeny. Fulfilling dread expectation, the contest was prolonged, bitter and corrupt. "Esau, who sold his birthright for a dish of poridge [sic]," an observer of the maneuverings advised, "pales into insignificance before the later day spectacle of one of the highest offices in the land being sold at auction to the highest bidder." After weeks of balloting, Wilson emerged as the victor, becoming for lack of a credible alternative his party's dominant statewide leader.[16]

Washington finally had two senators, presumably a sign of societal benefit and progress. The legislature had little time left, however, for the responsible conduct of public business—one critic said he was looking forward to the session's minimal accomplishments being printed "on the back of a postage stamp, without being crowded for space." Still in control of key committees, Republicans easily stymied railroad regulation measures, which were more than ever a prime goal of rural regions where wheat prices had dropped to half the value of 1893. Wedded by personal and financial connections to corporate lobbyists, GOP leaders would rather, noted a disgusted commentator, "cause a tremendous slide...to the Populist party" than break with their discredited masters.[17]

In city, county and state levels, the "universal demand" of the politically aware public was for major retrenchment in government expenses. Agencies had been created, high salaried workers employed and costly obligations assumed "in the days when dollars looked small and...false ambition carried away the founders of the new commonwealth." Tax revenue, unfortunately, was "down to bed rock level" in the aftermath of the 1893 Panic, and the market for bond issues was virtually nonexistent. Most legislators nonetheless scorned common sense, preferring to cater, in traditional log-rolling manner, to the specific short term interests of their constituents, as well as to "the persistent, insidious influence of the lobby." These discredited methods prevented the state from restoring fiscal discipline, the only real means of once again appealing to outside capital. The public debt soared to new and more dangerous levels, far exceeding constitutional limits in the view of legal and economic analysts.[18]

Going where the legislative branch declined to tread, Governor John McGraw wielded a stern veto pen, supposedly saving "the state from an ugly wound to its reputation." Though admirably parsimonious, the gubernatorial actions— building upon a similar economizing penchant demonstrated after the 1893 session—were insufficiently draconian to change Washington's appeal to outside investors. By ostentatiously favoring King County, moreover, McGraw alienated statewide opinion and widened traditional divisions in the Republican party. The governor vetoed appropriations for the Cheney and Whatcom normal schools, but preserved funding for the Ellensburg institution, located in a community long favored by Seattle residents. The University of Washington somehow wound up with more money than originally requested by the regents. At the stroke of a pen, however, the state historical society in Tacoma lost its public support. The sectionally calibrated vetoes—combined with the library scandal involving Mrs. Smart's hiring in 1893, the capitol commission brouhaha and new reports of corruption in the King County sheriff's office, the governor's longtime political base—all contributed to complete the ruination of McGraw's reputation, a significant development on the eve of the 1896 campaign.[19]

Only one imaginative initiative emerged from the legislative session. Educa-tion normally had been an issue of modest public concern, except for ritualistic taxpayer complaints and local interest efforts to secure institutions of higher learning. The "barefoot schoolboy bill"—proposed by one of the new mem-bers elected in 1894, John Rogers of Puyallup—upset tradition in the course of securing, via intricate and lucky maneuver, legislative approval. When fully implemented, the measure would transfer educational funds from the richer to the poorer counties, thereby widening social and economic opportunity in the state. Tacoma residents, for instance, were assessed $106,000 for schools in 1895, but retained under the formula adopted in Olympia only $78,000. The three big municipalities protested, with one Commencement Bay newspaper insisting that country youth "suffer less from a lack of school facilities than city children," and therefore had no reason to expect better treatment, especially at outside expense. The law stimulated rural-urban rivalry—"the barefoot school boy bill," the *P-I* objected, "might better be termed 'a bill to rob the cities.'" [20]

Populist energy in the towns and farming country was "a sign of awakening" protest against industrialization and the unrelenting depression. "The growth of populism," a Seattle editor pointed out, "is…a symptom of a deep-seated feel-ing of discontent with things as they are." Populism's adherents might well be, a grumpy critic contended, "the funniest people on earth," motivated by "the crudest notions…and the rankest demagogism," not to mention unadulterated opportunism. There was no denying, however, the movement's appeal during the hard times. Although the People's party first attained political success in out-of-the-way rural places such as Klickitat County, by mid-decade the reformist appeal was evident in urban areas as well. Spokane elected a Populist mayor in 1894, and a quarter of the state's 163 Farmers' Alliance chapters were located west of the Cascades, rather than in traditional agrarian locales. [21]

Mounting in popularity, populism drove conservative Washingtonians into a frenzy of denunciations. The barefoot schoolboy bill, proposals to seriously regulate corporations and the mere suggestion that the wealthy ought to pay higher taxes seemingly amounted to an all out assault on the American way-of-life. The Populists, decried the *P-I*, "would have us surrender all we have gained, and substitute for the individualism that has made America great the paternal-ism that has made Europe's…squalid millions anxious to find under our banner a freedom…that is unknown and unattainable under their own flag." Put the malcontents in office and the logical outcome would be confiscation of property, for communism was "the natural child" of interventionist government. "We shall all have pie three times a day and no mistake" about it, another Republican news-paper remonstrated in scornfully mocking state residents who would supposedly exchange their patriotic birthright for delusional promises. [22]

Under challenge in a new age, the great (though conflicting) principles—Jef-ferson's belief in the individual, and Hamilton's faith in business enterprise—must be defended at all cost, proclaimed populism's enemies. The particular circumstances of the continuing depression, indeed, added force and context to the basic struggle. Critics claimed that should Populists come to power in Olympia, not to mention nationally, they would complete the destruction of public credit, forever preventing the return of prosperity. Built upon railroad construction and land development, Washington was "naturally dependent upon capital" stated one Puget Sound editor. "We should never forget," agreed a Big Bend compatriot, "that the money invested in this country is very largely eastern capital." Considered solely in practical terms, a third observer bemoaned the political upheaval's impact by noting that populism "made the capitalists timid, and no new money will be risked," which would continue "so long as there is any doubt that good government will be maintained."[23]

Together, old time thinking, the horrific economic suffering and a fixation upon a key role for capital must explain the otherwise inexplicable tendency to equate the Populist party with bad governance. As set forth in convention and legislative debate, the movement's proposals were actually more responsible than irrational, and reflected widely held public opinions. Railroad regulation advanced the interests of both producers and consumers; many Republicans and most Democrats endorsed a concept that was, in fact, embraced in the state constitution. Educational improvements were certainly in the general public interest. Though denounced by the *P-I* as "socialism," the income tax and other fiscal innovations benefited, according to independent analysts, the average citizen. Honest and economical government may have represented a clear break with the post-1889 Washington standard, but was otherwise hardly a revolutionary proposition.[24]

Silver was the one issue that both unified Populist opposition to the established order and provoked reasonable counter arguments by supporters of the gold standard. In a fundamental sense, the in-state debate over silver was meaningless as one observer correctly pointed out. "The election of a full ticket composed of...the energetic friends [i.e., Populists and others] of free [minting of silver] coinage would not benefit the cause...in the slightest." The nation's money supply was, after all, the sole responsibility of the federal government. Congress, however, had declined to address the question, beyond revocation of the Sherman act back in 1893. In regard to the U.S. Congress, "no measures of importance on anything have been passed," a Tacoma editor would note in the course of an early 1896 diatribe. Thus the rhetorical initiative, at least, had passed from congressional into unofficial public hands.[25]

Absolutely no doubt existed, according to Spokane's *Spokesman-Review*, that "nine-tenths of the people of Washington" favored the free and unlimited coinage of silver at a ratio of 16 ounces of the white metal to one ounce of gold. Few, if any, residents, disagreed with the assessment that "the question of finance... dwarfed all other issues." Prominent Republicans and Democrats joined the fray on behalf of the cause, in such numbers that some commentators expressed doubt over the need for a third party. Seattle's *P-I* continued to equate Republicanism with "sound" gold backed money, but Senator Watson Squire assumed a prominent role in the fight against repeal of the Sherman act and thereafter remained a champion of silver. Stalwart John Wilson briefly extended support, before realizing that George Turner already had secured Spokane's support on the question. Some of the free silver advocates also privately worried that their economic cause would be undermined by too-close identification with populism.[26]

On behalf of gold, the *P-I* insisted that "the mainspring" of the silver argument was nothing more elevated than simply "self-interest." Washington was, in comparison to Idaho and Oregon, a modest producer of precious metals, but, a Spokane editor advised, "times have always risen and fallen here with the rise and fall of the mining industry in the surrounding country." Those in debt to eastern or European creditors, moreover, stood to benefit from an increased supply of money. "An inflated currency," noted one Puget Sound analyst, "means the payment of debts at 50, 60 or 70 cents on the dollar—whatever a silver dollar may be worth."[27]

Far more was involved, however, than the greed of mine operators and debtors. The silver debate revolved around an intense examination into the causes of America's financial crisis. "The 'hard times,'" an east-of-the-Cascades newspaper suggested in reference to this intellectual discourse, "are making more people do their own thinking than ever was known before." Simply put, the reform argument held that the post-Civil War demonetization of silver—immortalized as the "crime of '73"—plus repeal of the Sherman act left the United States with an insufficient circulating medium, especially in a time of mounting world trade and production. "Increasing business calls for [an] increasing supply of money," reasoned a Spokane editor. By restricting that essential supply, the gold standard placed the region at the mercy of outside bankers and speculators. Reestablish silver coinage, though, and "the volume of actual money" would be substantially augmented, to the great good of all Americans. "Instead of the commodities of the world being set off against the supply of gold," one commentator wrote of the expected economic quickening, "they will be set off against the gold and silver supply, and the value of all commodities, as well as of labor, will increase when estimated in the coinage of the country."[28]

Questions regarding financial policy dominated the print media to an unprecedented degree, even though most readers were unable to fully comprehend the fine points of a discussion that often was misinformed and invariably esoteric. Confusion was both inevitable and somewhat beside the point, for the argument proceeded as much along symbolic lines as on dollars-and-cents calculations. Free coinage advocates longed for the bygone days when hard work and individualism mattered, as against the modern times of impersonal industrialism and capital. "Restore silver to its rightful use as a money metal," an eastern Washington paper affirmed, "and the United States would throw off its financial allegiance to the old world and enter upon a new era of independence." Silver, according to the evocative title of one supportive editorial, possessed true meaning as "The Dollar of our Daddies."[29]

Gold supporters made little headway with the chronologically incoherent claim that the low tariff policies of the Cleveland administration had produced and prolonged the panic. Nor was humor an effective response to the challenge from free silver advocates. Since "congress can legislate values into things," a Palouse wit suggested that Cayuse horses might just as easily be used as a circulating medium. The opposition made one valid point, however, reminding Washington residents that prospective investors feared inflation and would invest capital only under a secure gold standard. The question of real import was the best means of again placing cash in circulation. The existing gold oriented mechanism might be English in derivation, the *P-I* reflected, but "so long as any system is a good system it doesn't make much difference whose it is."[30]

Monetary issues provided a common rationale for the unification of forces opposed to the existing political order. Traditionalist Republicans derided the prospective fusion of Democrats and Populists as an illogical, and presumably illicit, pairing of a Jeffersonian "party which declares that the state shall do next to nothing" with "a party which declares that the state shall do nearly everything." One befuddled observer, playing upon the 16 to 1 silver-gold issue, depicted the incongruity in Shakespearean terms:

> To bolt, or not to bolt. That is the question, Whether 'twere better to repudiate a platform, sixteen planks of which just suit us, because there is one plank which does not, and fly to another platform, sixteen planks which do not suit us, because it has one plank which does—that seems to us to be about the size of the problem of the hour.

The fusionist cause already had prospered at the local level in the 1894 municipal and legislative elections, which had not gone unnoticed by many career politicians. Thus, the approach of the 1896 state and national campaigns was an opportunity for some established politicians to act in their own office gaining self-interest. "It is the old story of the Goths and Vandals before Rome," the Portland *Oregonian* observed with respect to the tendency of ambitious politicians to abandon old allegiances for "no common purpose but to get office."[31]

The sense of complete economic devastation added to the appeal of silver and increased the willingness of candidates to avoid the discredited state Republican organization. Business failures in the first quarter of 1896 were "larger than ever known before for a like period." The tardy arrival of spring ruined an estimated one-third of the Palouse wheat crop. Tacoma merchants were "compelled to go down in their pockets," raising money by private subscription to keep the municipal fire department in operation. On the outer coast, fiscally strapped

Pacific County had to pay $1,393 to print its telephone-book length delinquent tax list. "Signs of revolution are in the air," a grain country editor noted in assessing the likely political impact of such developments; "no less a revolution because it will be peaceable and will be carried out on lines only possible in a democracy as this."[32] Thoroughly Republicanized at statehood, Washington was about to undergo a shocking transformation.

The GOP had little, if any, prospect of victory at the state level in 1896. At the summer convention, silverite party members, led by onetime territorial governor Miles Moore and incumbent attorney general William C. Jones, gravitated toward fusion after failing to seize control of the Republican party proceedings. Mainstream attempts, following the line of GOP presidential candidate William McKinley, to finesse the money issue by advocating a highly unlikely international bi-metallic agreement, attracted little support. As for the ticket, Governor John McGraw saw no point in even trying for renomination. John Wilson, who had expressed gubernatorial ambitions earlier in the decade, was preoccupied with the manipulation of federal patronage on behalf of his increasingly dim prospects for reelection to the U.S. senate, two years hence. In addition to being considered a traitor for his serendipitous flirtation with populism, Watson Squire—like Moore, another occupant of the governor's chair in territorial times—found the prospect of residing in Olympia, or anywhere else in the state for that matter, thoroughly offensive. Nothing better suggested the low status of Republicanism than the nomination-by-default of Charles Potter Sullivan, a deservedly obscure and totally unscintillating Tacoma lawyer.[33]

Meanwhile, the fusionist ticket—following a series of preliminary meetings among the component entities—emerged from an August convention in Ellensburg. Many Populists, convinced that the party by itself "was strong enough to… win over all opposition," initially had opposed cooperation with former antagonists. The prospect of guaranteed victory through unification, however, won out over such scruples. Selecting a carefully apportioned ticket, the Ellensburg delegates put forth Seattle Democratic dandy James Hamilton Lewis and silver Republican W.C. Jones for Washington's two seats in congress.[34] The gubernatorial slot went to Populist John Rogers, a figure of some public note from sponsorship of the barefoot schoolboy bill in his single session of legislative service.

In his late fifties and looking somewhat like an antebellum planter, complete with drooping moustache, John Rogers was a thoroughly unique aspirant for high office. He had been, at various times, a farmer, an author of utopian books and essays, a critic of private property and a real estate agent. Widely read, Rogers was more likely to cite Mohammad or Buddhist philosophy than Jesus, the favorite mentor of conventional political orators. Like most Washingtonians, he was a latecomer, having migrated at the time of admission after years of involvement in the Kansas Farmers' Alliance movement. Unlike most contemporaries in state politics, he was personally incorruptible and close to ethical in the conduct of public affairs.[35]

Exhibiting an occasional flair for booster rhetoric, Rogers happily proclaimed Washington "a new Eden prepared for the habitation of man"—a literal paradise promising "all the opportunities in unexampled profusion." Most of his pronouncements, though, were unlikely to be found in promotional brochures. Eschewing pious hypocrisies and organized churches, he was religious only in the generic sense. "There is...at the root and foundation of things," Rogers would inform college graduates in a series of commencement addresses, "a moral and supersensual power...which forces itself upon the attention of men everywhere." Directed by that unnamed universal power, "all the natural rights of man" were encompassed within a pair of fundamental truths: "The right to the soil and the right freely to exchange the products of labor." These principles had been violated by the money interests of the East and Europe, to the extent, claimed Rogers in a blunt statement, that Independence Day had "lost its true significance" for the American people. An imperiled citizenry could save itself only by uniting behind the fusion Populist-Democratic and silver Republican alliance that was supporting William Jennings Bryan for the U.S. presidency.[36]

For Washington's Republicans—overwhelmingly burdened by incumbency during a depression, and assaulted by the three-headed opposition and the straight talking appeal of John Rogers—even the defection by some gold standard Democrats to the ranks of the GOP and the William McKinley camp provided scant consolation. "A crisis is before the people of the state of Washington," Republicans cried in desperation. Party speakers claimed that Rogers wished to remove the American flag from schools, which was the first step, should he be elected, toward an eventual "raising" of the red ensign of revolution "above the stars and stripes." Selected readings from the fusion leader's writings were meant to convey the impression, presuming that voters paid attention, that such tracts were nothing but "anarchy, riot and...rot," unfit for placement on the same bookshelf with the Bible and other genuinely patriotic works of literature. As for the other fusionist nominees, James Hamilton Lewis, with his pink vests and colorful hair stylings, would embarrass Washington if sent to congress. Free silver, moreover, was an out-and-out fraud, an issue financed by mining interests that would ruin the holders of state and local debt, and destroy any chance of new capital infusion.[37]

With "nearly all of the enterprises of any magnitude" dependent "upon the election of the Republican ticket," the bastions of manufacturing, merchandizing and investing worked hard to stave off Bryan and Rogers. The irascible Captain Asa Mead Simpson, a stern talking mercantile veteran of the California gold rush, came north from San Francisco to threaten lumbering employees on Grays Harbor with immediate dismissal should the Republicans be defeated. Other conservative stalwarts preferred more subtle methods. Railroad management provided a special train so that Thomas Burke, a two-time Democratic congressional candidate in territorial days, might conveniently lecture mill workers, on company time, regarding the evil nature of free silver. GOP orators insisted, on the basis of bits and pieces of unconvincing evidence, that the mere prospect of William McKinley in the White House had already caused an economic upswing.[38]

Mixed election day results produced both relief and consternation in the ranks of the established order. "There has been a marked feeling of confidence in business," Cyrus Walker reported from Puget Sound after McKinley's presidential victory. William Jennings Bryan, though, had carried Washington by a substantial margin, with over 50,000 votes to under 40,000 for the national Republican winner. "They wore McKinley buttons, [and] turned out in McKinley proscessions [sic], but voted…for Bryan," Walker groused of the many industrial workers who had, in the end, refused to knuckle under to intimidation. "Popocrat" John Rogers, meanwhile, coasted into the governorship. Fusionist candidates won all statewide races, the two congressional positions included, and secured large legislative majorities, particularly in the house of representatives. Only the presence of Republican holdovers elected to four year terms in 1894 enabled the defeated party to retain a significant minority position in the state senate.[39]

The depression had been the crucial factor in the collapse of seven years of Republican rule since statehood. "We all feel very sorry," wrote prominent Tacoma lumberman Chauncey Griggs, a McKinley Democrat, regarding the fusion triumph, "but could not overcome…the element that believed any change would be better than what we have had for the past four or five years." Incompetence and corruption on the part of GOP officeholders, much in evidence prior to the onset of the panic, added to the conviction that a day of reckoning was in order. Washingtonians were discontented, but many also were apathetic, worn down by economic hardship and apparently unconvinced that politics offered a solution. Despite its larger population, Washington cast fewer votes for president in 1896 than Oregon. Although domestic immigration had continued, voter turnout declined from 1892, a relatively prosperous and less rancorous election year.[40] The most important question to be addressed in the aftermath of the free silver polling was whether the greatest danger to public order came from people who were angry or from individuals who had given up hope for the future.

≈≈≈

Concealed from general view by the political hoopla and monetary arguments, significant changes in the relationship between the people of Washington and their government had emerged from the long depression experience. For many thinkers, locally financed public works seemed a logical response to unemployment, especially because such undertakings also would produce much needed municipal improvements. Horrified conservatives, on the other hand, immediately denounced such propositions as "visionary" in concept, and a "demand" that out-of-work laborers "be allowed to take, in the name of law what others have accumulated." Claiming to represent the middle class citizen fortunate enough to still have a job or a business, the *P-I* burbled in outrage: "When it is urged that money be raised...to give work to the unemployed it is worth remembering that probably one-half the burden of it would fall upon the very class...least able to support it."[41]

Fine minded scruples did not apply, however, to the securing of funds from the federal government. Brief experience had demonstrated the wondrous potential of congressional logrolling, even for a state limited to a single U.S. senator, Watson Squire. Under such happy, if sometimes tawdry, procedure, the nation's taxpayers might be tapped for local projects of some, little or absolutely no benefit at all to the general welfare. Depression era authorities in Spokane, Tacoma and Seattle, for instance, vied with one another for construction of a regional federal building, overlooking the substantial office vacancy rate in all three communities.[42]

That patriotic pork barrel mainstay, national defense, had already procured the Port Orchard naval station and again appeared likely to attract federal largesse. Orating for his political life, Senator Squire reported that "the defenseless condition of Puget Sound" presented "a constant temptation to the nations of Europe." The great waterway, local editors agreed, was "an open door" and "practically defenseless against British aggression." The ongoing Alaska boundary dispute provided invaluable context for those warning of a surprise descent of the English fleet from its Vancouver Island lair. Japan, too, posed a growing threat, as indicated by increasing migration from the Asian empire to Hawaii. "A considerable number of the Japanese on the islands," alarmists contended, "are skilled soldiers." Chilean battle cruisers and Chinese armadas might also, as in past lobbyist fantasies, steam Sound-ward, intent upon bombarding undefended metropolitan economies into rubble.[43]

Amateur naval strategists recommended that two modern battleships be permanently stationed on Puget Sound to counter the British at Esquimalt. Remembering the economic value of Indian treaty era forts, business leaders also favored land installations. "Any old place seems to be able to get an army post these days," one commentator complained of the congressional failure to accord the interests of the Sound fair treatment. Citing past military studies, newspapers broadcast the fact that local shores embraced "numerous sites for defense which give great advantage over any aggressive fleet." A concerted Seattle Spirit lobbying effort culminated in early 1896 with the announcement that fortifications, featuring heavy guns, would be built on Magnolia Bluff, at the northern entrance to Elliott Bay. The project was exhibit number one for claims that prosperity would soon return to the city. Tacomans, in contrast, complained that Watson Squire, the leader of the fight for federal funds, had exhibited habitual bias toward Seattle, neglecting the superior qualifications of Commencement Bay.[44]

The search continued for other forms of government investment as well. Campaigns for river and harbor work, aptly described by one enthusiast as often "a game of grab," offered the best opportunities for communities on both sides of the Cascade Range. While complaining about pro-Oregon governmental favoritism, interests across Washington eagerly sought new Army engineering construction projects. For the members of congress, public favor depended upon the delegation's ability to secure appropriations in the nation's capital. By 1895, navigation was, thanks to recent improvements, "commercially practicable...ten months in the year" on the Columbia River from Wenatchee north to the mouth of the Okanogan River. Below Wenatchee, however, the corps of engineer efforts failed, as all informed parties had anticipated, on account of insufficient funding and the extensive natural obstructions. Partially thwarted along the mid Columbia, proponents lobbied for funds for navigation improvements on the Okanogan River, to benefit adjacent mining ventures. Improvements also were proposed on the Palouse River, thereby facilitating log drives from the Idaho border to sawmills in Colfax.[45]

On the westside, other money generating navigation improvements were suggested. A truly visionary proposal called for the construction of canals linking Puget Sound with Grays Harbor, Willapa Bay and the lower Columbia. Another ahead-of-its-time proposition involved straightening and deepening the Duwamish River in the supposed interest of shipping, but which actually was meant to help control flooding south of Elliott Bay. In terms of actual accomplishments, a corps of engineers plan at the entrance to Grays Harbor was implemented at mid-decade, leading to the investment of $1 million on a government jetty. Extending well out to sea, the rock lined structure was designed to concentrate tidal flows, thus maintaining a stable deep water channel. When completed, a leading business figure claimed the jetty "should result in placing us on a par with the best located points on the Coast."[46]

Puget Sound communities had no intention of allowing the corps of engineers to concentrate on Grays Harbor. Prior to the panic, Everett investors and the NP at Tacoma devised ambitious improvement schemes, intending to proceed via private means. New fiscal constraints, however, caused developers at both locations to abandon anxieties about the assorted negative aspects of federal involvement. Although military officers on the scene expressed concern over the propriety of proceeding with a project "gotten up entirely by the Everett Land Company," congress in 1895 approved the dredging of a dike protected deep draft harbor on Port Gardner Bay. Tacomans, meanwhile, lobbied for navigable channels in the Puyallup River delta, enabling full-scale exploitation of the adjoining tidelands. Agreeing to the need for docks and industrial space, Captain Harry Taylor, the senior Army engineer on the Sound, nevertheless pointed out in a negative report to the war department that the development "would...be [al]most entirely for the direct benefit" of the NP and its Commencement Bay affiliates. Set back for the moment by Taylor, local Tacoma boosters noted that the captain operated out of a Seattle headquarters.[47]

Meanwhile, Elliott Bay promoters aggressively embraced all opportunities to best their long-time Commencement Bay rival. A depression era congress might be in an economizing mood, but skilled lobbying managed to resuscitate a Lake Washington canal. That project, claimed the *P-I*, would make Seattle "within a few years…the first city of the Pacific coast," justifying any incidental profit to well sited property owners. A new federal survey authorized by congressional action in 1894, though a "drop in the bucket" in terms of funding, supposedly guaranteed construction. "Uncle Sam never receeds [sic] from a position that he has once taken," one editor asserted, "and appropriation may be looked for to follow appropriation." More than meeting expectations, so far as planning was concerned, Captain Thomas Symons, recently transferred from his habitual posting on the upper Columbia, recommended a $1.4 million undertaking, featuring locks at both Lake Washington and Ballard's Salmon Bay.[48]

Speculators anticipating "a tremendous boom" in property values were instead frustrated by the emergence of a private competing plan to the federal project. Publicized as the latest manifestation of the "old spirit of Seattle," a proposal offered by Eugene Semple, the next-to-last territorial governor, featured excavation of a canal from Lake Washington to the mouth of the Duwamish River. An additional, and by no means inconsequential, provision of the ambitious plan focused on the dredging of two navigable waterways in the lower Duwamish, with the noxious tide flats to be filled in and made ready for industry and commerce. Provided with the necessary state authorization and ample capital from eastern investors, Semple commenced work in 1895. The former territorial governor also trumped the competition by employing Captain Thomas Symons, the officer in charge of the federal or northern canal, as consulting engineer. Ignoring a too obvious conflict-of-interest, Symons drafted an overall "plan," leant his professional reputation to the cause and allowed Semple to hint that his excavation enjoyed Army Corps of Engineers support.[49]

Thanks in part to the ethically dubious labors of Captain Symons, a Tacoma newspaper pointed out, "Seattle now finds herself embarrassed with the prospect of more canals than it wants." The existence of two projects, one north and the other south of downtown, raised the likelihood of a mutually destructive outcome. "No reason for two Canals to be urged is known to me," a senior Army engineer noted in advising against further federal funding. Government work was delayed by the ineffectual efforts of King County to acquire title to the right-of-way, a task mandated by congress. Semple, meanwhile, faltered on the fund raising front. Although excavation of the Duwamish waterways proceeded, his investors were unable to pay for the Lake Washington-to-saltwater portion of the plan.[50] For the time being, Seattle was left without even one canal.

Either Lake Washington canal plan would be a key component in an ongoing rearrangement of the Elliott Bay waterfront. Pending eventual excavation of one project or the other, Seattle proceeded with implementation of a comprehensive plan for developing the flats at the mouth of the Duwamish River. This portion of Semple's larger scheme drew various forms of assistance, some savory and some not, from the state and city. The two waterways were each a thousand feed wide. "Radiating from these on either side," dry land formed from dredge deposits became the location for terminals, warehouses, mills and the Moran Brothers shipyard. Railroad Avenue, extended across the Duwamish, provided for present and prospective railway access. Partially in place by the turn of the century, the waterfront makeover represented another triumph over a less energetic foe. "For every wharf that Tacoma has," one local booster gloated, "Seattle has a mile of them."[51]

Expenditures for navigation work compensated in part for the private investment lost to the panic. Other aspects of Washington's increasingly close relationship with the federal government also produced controversy. The national movement for conserving natural resources, in particular, appeared to place the state at the mercy of outside and often unsympathetic political currents. In a rare instance of general agreement, Mount Rainer National Park was created in 1899 after several years of regional and congressional deliberation. Prospective benefits from tourism and the lack of commercially accessible timber and minerals on the slopes of the great peak precluded serious opposition. "No important considerations of expediency were involved," the *P-I* noted.[52]

Given the value of the state's merchantable timber, business leaders drawn into the conservationist ethos thought mainly of countering the seasonal visitations of fire in the Pacific Northwest. Forests west of the Cascades experienced widespread devastation during the abnormally dry summer of 1895—the woods burned, logging camps were destroyed and operations ceased due to the smoke. "Enough timber has been…destroyed this year," one account claimed, "to build half the houses in the world." Newspaper editors and other observers demanded greatly improved protective measures, to the extent of even stationing regular Army troops in the forests.[53]

Rather than sending in soldiers, federal authorities reduced the areas open to logging. In 1891, congress had authorized presidential authority to establish forest reserves, thus removing timber from normal public exploitation. Acting on the advice of forestry experts, Grover Cleveland created 13 new reserved tracts— with a third of the total 21 million acres in Washington—shortly before vacating the White House in early 1897. Ironically, the larger lumber manufacturers generally welcomed the move. "It will leave the timber…in one of two positions," Grays Harbor veteran George Emerson pointed out with respect to regional impacts. "The first will be in private hands, and mostly large holders; the second, in hands of the government, but not for sale." The monopoly-encouraging result, therefore, would be "to fix the ownership of timber in such a way that it could be controlled" in the interest of more efficient exploitation and greater long term corporate profit.[54]

However, other voices denounced "the method and manner adopted by Cleveland," who had acted in accordance with the dictates of "sentimentalists and…theorists" bent upon applying academic forestry concepts in "ignoramous fashion." Furthermore, they claimed, the executive orders interfered with mining and settlement to the detriment of economic progress. Mineral exploration in the upper Skagit River basin and around Lake Chelan supposedly would shut down with the creation of the vast Washington Reserve in the northern Cascades. On the Olympic Peninsula, meanwhile, two-thirds of the land suitable for agriculture would henceforth be unavailable. The conservationist ethos, restricting contemporary usage in order to preserve opportunities for tomorrow, seemed to many Washingtonians to defy common sense. "If that logic were to prevail," the *P-I* protested, "we would have very little posterity to leave it to in this state."[55] The conundrum for growth-preoccupied boosters was that they desired assignment of federal funding for local projects, but at the same time a distant national government was interfering in regional matters, which in the local view should be left to the better informed residents of the Pacific Northwest.

⧼⧽

Nevertheless, a hopeful if sometimes troublesome financial dependence upon the U.S. government emerged during the depression years. Another trend that eventually would become an aspect of everyday life in Washington was first manifested in a significant way during the panic. The state possessed undeniable potential for the generation of hydroelectric power at the time of admission, but the prevailing technology severely limited actual utilization. The existing small plants primarily supplied electricity to street railway and municipal lighting systems. Indeed, proper urban illumination was considered an essential "big advertisement" in urban campaigns for investment capital. "It makes things look bright, cheerful and wide awake," a Tacoma promoter advised. By the onset of the depression, $13 million was invested across the state for providing energy for 3,000 arc and 38,000 incandescent street lights. Only at Spokane Falls, however, was a source of water power convenient enough to drive a major industrial enterprise.[56]

Within a few years, technological advances finally made it possible to transmit sufficient energy from remote sites for use in mills and homes. "The electrical force can be transmitted by wire to great distances without serious loss," a Puget Sound newspaper pointed out, while also exclaiming that the potential applications "make one's head swirl with astonishment and awe." However, the construction of dams, generating plants and power lines required large amounts of capital, the raising of which was no easy task in the midst of a depression. "To facilitate rapid adoption of, and hence to cause an early revenue from…electrical energy," one expert also pointed out, financial assistance should be provided to homeowners to encourage them to make necessary changes in "machinery" and appliances. Private interests also faced an early challenge from Populists and others convinced that water power ought to be developed as "a valuable possession of the people."[57]

Attention turned to Snoqualmie Falls, located two dozen miles east of Seattle and already a must-see tourist attraction. The power available at the site, promotional and engineering reports attested, could be "readily utilized" in the same manner as "the great cataract of Niagara." Having exiled himself from the Sound on account of panic related difficulties with creditors, Daniel H. Gilman intended to restore his reputation as "a son-of-a-gun of a rustler" by becoming the first to exploit the falls. Writing from New York in 1894, Gilman advised that there was "a lively prospect, amounting to almost a certainty, of closing out the Snoqualmie property and securing its early development through negotiations with the chief moguls in the…electrical transmission business." Meeting with eastern and European investors, Gilman outlined an ambitious plan that included, in addition to supplying Seattle with electricity, the construction of mills and chemical manufacturing facilities. The scheme, unfortunately, was too audacious for serious consideration during the depression. Gilman failed, but new promoters took up the cause at Snoqualmie Falls, and in 1898 completed the pioneer plant that eventually become one of the region's major utilities.[58]

Expansion, not to mention even survival, of the original hydroelectric facility was threatened by a long and complex struggle over control of Seattle's water and power resources. Shortages severe enough to compel a moratorium on lawn watering and street sprinkling led local voters to approve a $1 million bond issue for constructing the long discussed Cedar River project. Operating through politically well connected corporate entities, Edward Ammidown, an eastern speculator who had previously attempted to preempt the city's rights to the Cedar River, responded with a plan to develop the stream in the interest of both electrical generation and supplying water. If successful, this initiative would thwart public competition and at the same time deprive the Snoqualmie Falls operation of its market. Taking advantage of assorted legal and technical problems, Ammidown managed to subvert a sufficient number of Seattle officials to stall development of any kind. Consequently, with "a new sensation…sprung in regard to Cedar river…almost every day," no substantive work was undertaken.[59] As the nineteenth century turned into the twentieth, contentious issues of public versus private control—a legacy of attempts to build out of the depression—troubled residents of the state. Appropriately, in light of subsequent ideological and economic struggles, Washington entered the age of electricity in full argumentative mode.

Notes

1. *Seattle Times*, Jan. 13, 1896.
2. The last silver dollar would be minted in November 1895. *Seattle Telegraph*, Nov. 1, 1893; Jan. 20, 1894; *Tacoma Daily News*, Aug. 2, 3; Oct. 31; Nov. 4, 1893; *Seattle Post-*

Intelligencer, Oct. 31, 1893; *Walla Walla Statesman*, Dec. 6, 8, 1893; Gordon Hak, *Turning Trees into Dollars: The British Columbia Coastal Lumber Industry, 1858–1913* (Toronto: University of Toronto Press, 2000), 17–18, 25; Robert E. Ficken, *The Forested Land: A History of Lumbering in Western Washington* (Seattle: University of Washington Press, 1987), 81; *Spokane Review*, Sept. 4, 1893, rep. from Waitsburg *Times*; Seattle *Argus*, April 7, 1894; *Seattle Times*, Nov. 1, 1895.

3. "Every thing in the East," a Grays Harbor manufacturer advised in the summer of 1894, "has dried up, been stuck by the strike, washed out by the freshets or discouraged by the Democratic Administration and suspended business." Cyrus Walker to W.H. Talbot, June 15, 1894; Feb. 5; Sept. 12, 1895, Cyrus Walker Letterbooks, Ames Coll., University of Washington Library; Chauncey W. Griggs to C.M. Griggs, July 6, 1896, St. Paul & Tacoma Lumber Co. Records, University of Washington Library; *Seattle Post-Intelligencer*, Jan. 1, 1895; Ficken, *Forested Land*, 80–81; North Western Lumber Co. to W.H. Boner, Aug. 8, 1894; George H. Emerson to John C. Hill, April 17, 1894, both George H. Emerson Letterbooks, University of Washington Library.

4. Wheat exports to England declined from 1.4 million to 839,000 bushels. *Tacoma Daily Ledger*, Sept. 14, 1893; Jan. 1, 1895; *Seattle Post-Intelligencer*, April 7, 1894; Jan. 1, 1895; Robert A. Campbell, "Blacks and the Coal Mines of Western Washington, 1888–1896," *Pacific Northwest Quarterly* [hereafter cited as *PNQ*], 73 (Oct. 1982), 154; *Seattle Times*, Oct. 1, 1896; Feb. 27, 1897; J.J. Browne to Edison Electric Light Co., April 4, 1895, Washington Water Power Co. Records, Washington State University Library; Walker to Talbot, Sept. 12, 1895, Walker Letterbooks; Spokane *Spokesman-Review*, Sept. 21, 1895; Aug. 11, 1896.

5. *Spokane Review*, March 16, 1894; *Seattle Post-Intelligencer*, March 21, 1894; Feb. 26, 1895; *Ellensburgh Capital*, April 19, 1894; Spokane *Spokesman-Review*, July 13; Dec. 8, 1894; Oct. 30; Nov. 5, 1895; Jan. 1, 1896; Jan. 1, 1897; *Tacoma Daily Ledger*, Oct. 6, 1894; *Pullman Tribune*, Aug. 3, 1895; *Seattle Times*, Sept. 16, 1895; Alexander Campbell McGregor, *Counting Sheep: From Open Range to Agribusiness on the Columbia Plateau* (Seattle: University of Washington Press, 1982), 51–52.

6. *Tacoma Daily News*, July 11, 1893; Spokane *Spokesman-Review*, May 24; June 16, 21, 25; July 10; Aug. 15; Sept. 28, 29; Oct. 1, 17, 1895; Feb. 15, 1896; Jan. 5, 22, 1898; *Pullman Tribune*, April 4, 1896; Michael P. Malone, *James J. Hill: Empire Builder of the Northwest* (Norman: University of Oklahoma Press, 1996), 175–84; Albro Martin, *James J. Hill and the Opening of the Northwest* (New York: Oxford University Press, 1976), 453–58; *Spokane Review*, May 30, 1894; *Walla Walla Statesman*, Aug. 14, 17, 1894.

7. Reporting that the value of his holdings had been cut "right in two," Tacoma lumberman Chauncey Griggs complained of a "burden which I am hardly able to stand." Emerson to E.J. Holt, July 11, 1895; to A.M. Simpson, April 10, 1896, Emerson Letterbooks; *Tacoma Daily Ledger*, Jan. 1, 3, 1896; *Seattle Post-Intelligencer*, May 26, 1894, rep. from Port Townsend *Democrat*; March 18, 1895; *Seattle Press-Times*, Jan. 25, 1894; Feb. 14, 1895; *Seattle Telegraph*, April 23; June 25; Nov. 20, 1894; *Spokane Review*, March 20, 22; May 25, 1894; Spokane *Spokesman-Review*, Feb. 21; May 4, 12; Sept. 24; Dec. 31, 1895; Seattle *Argus*, May 11, 1895; *Tacoma Daily News*, June 6; July 1, 1895; *Seattle Times*, Jan. 4, 13, 1896; Griggs to Mrs. F.C. Williams, May 28, 1896, St. Paul & Tacoma Lumber Co. Records.

8. *Spokane Review*, May 7, 1894, rep. from Pomeroy *Independent*; *Seattle Post-Intelligencer*, Nov. 30, 1894; *Seattle Telegraph*, Nov. 17, 1894. On Jacob Coxey's arrest, see Carlos A. Schwantes, *Coxey's Army: An American Odyssey* (Lincoln: University of Nebraska Press, 1985), 181–85.

9. Advocates of hard work and individualism expressed alarm over the utopian experiments. "Of the colony 300 strong that is said to 'nourish' in Skagit county, Washington," the Portland *Oregonian* commented, "it may be said…to be dreaming, in sluggish fashion, dreams of…luxurious living on a basis of four hours' labor out of 24….What to do with the people the rest of the time must be a puzzling proposition, even to the disciple of Bellamy." Walker to Talbot, April 18, 1897, Puget Mill Co. Records, Ames Coll., University of Washington Library; *Seattle Telegraph*, April 26, 1894; Charles Pierce LeWarne, *Utopias on Puget Sound, 1885–1915* (Seattle: University of Washington Press, 1975), chaps. 4–6; and "Equality Colony: The Plan to Socialize Washington," *PNQ*, 59 (July 1968), 137–46; Spokane *Spokesman-Review*, Nov. 21, 1898, rep. from *Oregonian*, May 17, 1899.

10. Davenport *Lincoln County Times*, Nov. 24, 1893; *Spokane Review*, Oct. 23, 1893; *Tacoma Daily News*, Oct. 26, 1893; Seattle *Argus*, May 26, 1894.

11. *Tacoma Daily News*, July 18, rep. from *West Coast Lumberman*, Oct. 26, 1893; *Spokane Review*, March 25, 1893; Feb. 20, 1894; *Seattle Post-Intelligencer*, June 26, 1894.

12. Ironically, nativism mounted at a time of decline in the rate of immigration, with, according to one observer, "the falling off…most marked from those nations"—Russia, Poland and Hungary—"which furnish the least desirable contributions." *Seattle Press-Times*, May 18, rep. from Olympia *Olympian*, June 12, rep. from Yakima *Herald*, 1894; Seattle *Argus*, May 5; July 21, 1894; *Tacoma Daily News*, Jan. 23; April 25, 1893; *Seattle Telegraph*, April 8, 1894; Spokane *Spokesman-Review*, June 17, 1895.

13. The *P-I* denounced the APA as "nothing but an organization of anti-Catholic bigots" intent upon promoting "religious warfare between neighbors." Seattle *Argus*, April 14; May 12; Aug. 24, 1894; Jan. 5; Feb. 2; June 8; Nov. 9, 1895; Feb. 15, 22, 1896; Aug. 28, 1897; *Seattle Telegraph*, June 21, 24, 1894; *Seattle Times*, Nov. 4, 1895; Spokane *Spokesman-Review*, May 27–31, 1896; Oct. 21, 1897; *Seattle Post-Intelligencer*, Feb. 13; March 14, 1894.

14. Stung by the derisive public response to his renunciation, Squire later claimed to have given up liquor because of gout. Charles Laughton also attempted an unlikely political comeback by going "over to the Populists." *Tacoma Daily Ledger*, Jan. 3, 1895; July 14, 1896, rep. from Cheney *Sentinel*; *Seattle Times*, Nov. 6, 1895; *Spokane Review*, Oct. 11, 1893; Seattle *Argus*, Oct. 26, 1895; Aug. 15, 1896; *Seattle Post-Intelligencer*, Feb. 15, 1893, rep. from Sprague *Advertiser*.

15. Lumberman George Emerson declared that he "would willingly suffer all the inconvenience that exists under our present laws, to be assured that they [legislators] would not meet again for the next five years." *Spokane Review*, June 12, 1894; *Seattle Press-Times*, Aug. 16; Nov. 16, 1894; Carlos A. Schwantes, *Radical Heritage: Labor, Socialism and Reform in Washington and British Columbia, 1885–1917* (Seattle: University of Washington Press, 1979), 60; Thomas W. Riddle, "Populism in the Palouse: Old Ideals and New Realities," *PNQ*, 65 (July 1974), 106–7; *Seattle Post-Intelligencer*, Jan. 14, 1895; Walker to Talbot, Nov. 13, 1894, Walker Letterbooks; Emerson to Austin Griffiths, April 30, 1894, Emerson Letterbooks.

16. The victor served the remaining four years of the term that should have been filled by the legislature in 1893. John Allen briefly indicated interest in regaining his seat. The Wilson-Turner feud figured into all aspects of Spokane political life. "The mayoralty hinges on whether the republican aspirant is for…Turner or Wilson for senator," one paper reported. "Ain't it playing the senatorial question pretty fine to pull it down into municipal politics?" *Tacoma Daily Ledger*, March 4, 1894; Jan. 27, 1895; Spokane *Spokesman-Review*, Oct. 3; Dec. 17, 28, 1894; *Wenatchee Advance*, Jan. 19, 1895; *Seattle Press-Times*,

April 10, rep. from Walla Walla *Union*; Nov. 15, 1894; Jan. 31, 1895; Seattle *Argus*, Jan. 12, 26, 1895; *Seattle Post-Intelligencer*, Jan. 31, 1895; Winston B. Thorson, "Washington State Nominating Conventions," *PNQ*, 35 (April 1944), 101.

17. "There is no doubt that some of the senators received a good big wad of money for betraying the people's interest," a wheat country editor contended in the aftermath of regulation's defeat. "Compared to such Judases, the ordinary burglar or horse-thief is a gentleman, and…the people would be justified in hanging them from the most convenient tree." Seattle *Argus*, March 2, 1895; *Pullman Tribune*, Feb. 23, 1895; *Seattle Press-Times*, March 7, 12, 1895; *Seattle Post-Intelligencer*, March 12, 1895, rep. from Pomeroy *Washingtonian*.

18. *Tacoma Daily Ledger*, Jan. 15, 1895; Spokane *Spokesman-Review*, Aug. 28; Nov. 20, rep. from *Big Bend Empire*, 23, 26, 27, 29; Dec. 2, 1894; Feb. 22, 1895; *Pullman Tribune*, Jan. 19, 1895; *Seattle Times*, Oct. 14, 1896; John R. Rogers to J. Gaston, Feb. 24, 1898, John R. Rogers Papers, Washington State Archives. "The increase of interest-bearing indebtedness…has been 283 per cent," Populists charged during the 1896 state campaign. "The general fund warrant indebtedness has increased nearly a million and a half during the last four years." Unidentified newspaper clipping in Scrapbooks, John R. Rogers Papers, Washington State University Library.

19. Thomas Burke to Erastus Brainerd, March 21, 1895, Thomas Burke Papers, University of Washington Library; *Spokane Review*, Feb. 4, 7, 8; March 18, 19, 1893; *Tacoma Daily News*, March 18, 1893; *Ellensburgh Capital*, March 23, 1893; *Seattle Telegraph*, March 19–21; Aug. 27, 1893; *Seattle Post-Intelligencer*, March 29, 1893; July 18, 1894; Seattle *Argus*, March 30, 1895; May 23, 1896; *Seattle Press-Times*, April 3, 1893; March 25, 1895; *Pullman Tribune*, March 27, 1897.

20. Among beneficiary counties, Whitman County received $52,000 after paying $40,000 in school taxes. With its outside contribution, Columbia County was able to more than double educational expenditures. Proposals for the state to provide free textbooks also aroused indignation among taxpayers. *Seattle Post-Intelligencer*, Feb. 12; March 10, 1895; March 27, 1896; *Seattle Press-Times*, March 12, 1895; *Tacoma Daily Ledger*, March 11, 1895; Spokane *Spokesman-Review*, Feb. 14, 27, 1895; *Tacoma Daily News*, Jan. 24, 1893.

21. Cyrus Walker claimed that most Populists were illiterate. *Tacoma Daily News*, Jan. 22, 1898; *Seattle Press-Times*, March 14, 19, 1894; *Spokane Review*, June 3, 1894; *Seattle Post-Intelligencer*, May 9; July 2, 1894; Seattle *Argus*, Oct. 26, 1895; Olympia *Washington Standard*, Feb. 24, 1893; *Seattle Telegraph*, May 3, 1894; Walker to Talbot, Sept. 13, 1896, Puget Mill Co. Records.

22. *Seattle Post-Intelligencer*, May 8, 21, 1894; *Tacoma Daily Ledger*, July 21, 1896; *Tacoma Daily News*, Sept. 19, 1893; *Seattle Press-Times*, Nov. 1, 1894.

23. *Seattle Post-Intelligencer*, May 8, 1894; *Seattle Times*, Jan. 21, 1896; Seattle *Argus*, Oct. 3, 1896; *Everett Herald*, June 21, 1894; Davenport *Lincoln County Times*, Nov. 3, 1893; *Tacoma Daily Ledger*, July 29, 1894.

24. *Tacoma Daily Ledger*, July 21, 1896; Riddle, "Populism in the Palouse," 98; Carroll H. Woody, "Populism in Washington: A Study of the Legislature of 1897," *Washington Historical Quarterly* [hereafter cited as *WHQ*], 21 (April 1930), 108–9; *Seattle Post-Intelligencer*, May 22, 1894. Attempting to secure mass appeal via a focus on economic questions, the Populists downplayed such contentious issues as prohibition and woman suffrage. On the relation between populism and female voting, see T.A. Larson, "The Woman Suffrage Movement in Washington," *PNQ*, 67 (April 1976), 55–56; and G. Thomas Edwards, *Sowing Good Seeds: The Northwest Suffrage Campaigns of Susan B. Anthony* (Portland:

Oregon Historical Society Press, 1990), 157–58. Some regional suffragist leaders nonetheless involved themselves in the Populist crusade. Ruth Barnes Moynihan, *Rebel for Rights: Abigail Scott Duniway* (New Haven: Yale University Press, 1983), 148, 166–67.

25. *Tacoma Daily Ledger,* July 5, 1896; *Tacoma Daily News,* Feb. 4, 1896.

26. "No man," an eastern Washington paper asserted, "whose views on the financial question are not in harmony with the free coinage of silver principle will be awarded a position of any importance on any of the tickets." Spokane *Spokesman-Review,* Oct. 11, 1893; Sept. 22; Oct. 3; Nov. 30, 1894; July 18, 1896; *Tacoma Daily News,* July 8, 1896; Seattle *Argus,* May 18, 1895; *Seattle Post-Intelligencer,* March 10, 1896; *Walla Walla Statesman,* Sept. 21, 1894; *Pullman Tribune,* May 4, 1895; *Tacoma Daily Ledger,* July 17, 1896, rep. from Okanogan *Outlook.*

27. The *P-I* claimed that mine owners bankrolled the Populist party. *Seattle Post-Intelligencer,* June 29, 1895; March 15, 1896; *Seattle Times,* Jan. 5, 1897; Spokane *Spokesman-Review,* Jan. 3, 1895; Aug. 10, 1896; Seattle *Argus,* Sept. 22, 1894; Aug. 8, 1896.

28. A pro-coinage Seattle paper pointed out that the big Puget Sound sawmills exported "almost exclusively to 'silver countries,'" with little apparent ill effect or consternation to the mostly Republican management. *Spokane Review,* July 1; Aug. 2, 26; Sept. 2, rep. from *East Oregonian;* Oct. 3, 1893; Spokane *Spokesman-Review,* Jan. 3, 1895; July 23, 28, 1896; *Tacoma Daily News,* July 6, 15, 16, 1896; *Seattle Times,* Oct. 13, 16, 1896.

29. "That the financial question…is not understood by one voter out of fifty is generally conceded," one political analyst contended. "The struggle," a silver supporter suggested, "is between the money aristocracy of the world and the people." Seattle *Argus,* July 25; Aug. 8; Oct. 17, 1896; Spokane *Spokesman-Review,* Oct. 2, 1894; *Tacoma Daily News,* July 22, 1896; *Seattle Telegraph,* July 19, 1893, rep. from Cheney *Sentinel.*

30. "Congress can by legislation alter the size, shape or composition of the silver coin called a dollar," a free coinage opponent agreed. "It can by legislation direct that coins containing 53 cents' worth of silver shall be struck at the mint and stamped 100 'cents.' But neither the congress of the United States, nor the parliament of England…can create or destroy or regulate values. These are determined absolutely by the laws of trade." *Seattle Post-Intelligencer,* April 16; June 8, rep. from Chehalis *Nugget,* 23, rep. from *East Washingtonian;* July 19; Sept. 6, 8, 10, 1896; *Tacoma Daily Ledger,* July 11, 20, 1896; *Seattle Telegraph,* June 9, 1894.

31. *Tacoma Daily News,* July 6, 1896; *Seattle Post-Intelligencer,* Aug. 22; Oct. 14, 1894; April 16; July 3; Aug. 1, rep. from Chelan *Leader,* 1896; Spokane *Spokesman-Review,* Feb. 4; Aug. 19, rep. from *Oregonian,* 1896; *Spokane Review,* June 5, 1894; *Seattle Telegraph,* June 6, 1894; *Seattle Press-Times,* Aug. 16; Oct. 6, 8, 1894.

32. Olympia *Washington Standard,* April 24; May 8, 1896; *Tacoma Daily News,* July 1, 1896; *Pullman Tribune,* Aug. 8, 1896.

33. "The man always was a transparent humbug," one regular Republican editor declaimed of Squire, "and we are heartily glad to see him go over to the enemy." *Tacoma Daily Ledger,* July 2, 5, 16, 1896; *Pullman Tribune,* July 27, 1895; Walker to Talbot, Aug. 23, 1896, Puget Mill Co. Records; Seattle *Argus,* Aug. 8, 15, 1896; *Seattle Post-Intelligencer,* Aug. 12, 1892, rep. from Everett *Herald.*

34. The unions were acknowledged by the selection of Robert Bridges, prominent in the Knights of Labor ranks, for state land commissioner. Bridges dramatized his candidacy by walking from Seattle to the Ellensburg fusion convention, eschewing the railroad passes accepted by most politicians, including Populists. Spokane *Spokesman-Review,* July 30; Dec. 18, 1896; Riddle, "Populism in the Palouse," 107; Schwantes, *Radical Heritage,* 60–61.

35. Robert T. McDonald, "Photographs of Washington Governors," *PNQ*, 34 (Oct. 1943), 400. Biographical details are taken from clippings in Scrapbooks, Rogers Papers, Washington State University Library, supplemented by Russell Blankenship, "The Political Thought of John R. Rogers," *PNQ*, 37 (Jan. 1946), 4–6; and Karel D. Bicha, "Peculiar Populist: An Assessment of John R. Rogers," *PNQ*, 65 (July 1974), 110–13. Also see the thoughtful observations in Schwantes, *Radical Heritage*, 62–64; Thomas W. Riddle, *The Old Radicalism: John R. Rogers and the Populist Movement in Washington, 1891–1900* (New York: Garland, 1991); and Norman H. Clark, *Washington: A Bicentennial History* (New York: W.W. Norton, 1976), 110–11.

36. *Seattle Times*, Jan. 9, 1897; Address to Pullman graduates, June 24, 1897; Fourth of July Address, New Whatcom, July 5, 1897; Rogers to George Grantham Bain, May ?, 1897, all Rogers Papers, Washington State University Library. On the Rogers philosophy, see Bicha, "Peculiar Populist," 111–17; and David B. Griffiths, "Far-western Populist Thought: A Comparative Study of John Rogers and Davis H. Waite," *PNQ*, 60 (Oct. 1969), 183–92.

37. *Seattle Times*, Oct. 5, 13, 1896; Griggs to F.A. Weiblin, Sept. 21, 1896; to F.W. Miller, Aug. 10, 1896, St. Paul & Tacoma Lumber Co. Records; Robert C. Nesbit, *"He Built Seattle": A Biography of Judge Thomas Burke* (Seattle: University of Washington Press, 1961), 354–59; Seattle *Argus*, Oct. 10, 24, 31, 1896; *Seattle Post-Intelligencer*, July 17; Sept. 14, 23, 1896; *Pullman Tribune*, Sept. 19, 1896.

38. Griggs to J.W. Graff, Oct. 20, 1896; to J.L. Farwell, Sept. 25, 1896; to Miller, Nov. 9, 1896, St. Paul & Tacoma Lumber Co. Records; Emerson to Samuel Perkins, Oct. 19, 1896, Emerson Letterbooks; *Seattle Times*, Oct. 5, 1896; Walker to Talbot, June 29, 1896, Walker Letterbooks.

39. "We are ashamed of our State," lumberman George Emerson said of the Bryanite victory. Bryan won Idaho by a four-to-one ratio, a reflection of that state's close interest in silver, but narrowly lost Oregon and California. Walker to A.W. Jackson, Nov. 14, 1896, Puget Mill Co. Records; Dec. 19, 1896, Walker Letterbooks; *Seattle Times*, Jan. 1, 2, 1897; Emerson to Harry C. Heermans, Nov. 9, 1896, Emerson Letterbooks; *Seattle Post-Intelligencer*, Nov. 5, 1898.

40. "The campaign was not one so much in favor of free silver," the *P-I* reflected, "as it was of general discontent due to hard times." Griggs to Edward C. Gale, Nov. 7, 1896; to L.R. Royce, Nov. 11, 1896; to Mark Hanna, Nov. 16, 1896, St. Paul & Tacoma Lumber Co. Records; *Seattle Times*, Jan. 1, 1897; *Seattle Post-Intelligencer*, June 30, 1897.

41. *Tacoma Daily News*, Jan. 4, 5, 1894; *Seattle Telegraph*, April 21, 1894; *Tacoma Daily Ledger*, Sept. 2, 1893; *Seattle Post-Intelligencer*, Jan. 3, 1894.

42. *Seattle Post-Intelligencer*, June 19, 1898.

43. *Seattle Times*, Oct. 30, 1895; *Tacoma Daily News*, Sept. 28, 1897. Jan. 17, 1898; Seattle *Argus*, March 16, 1895.

44. Seeking a consolation prize, Tacoma lobbied for relocation of the Port Orchard naval station to Commencement Bay. Spokane *Spokesman-Review*, Oct. 15, 1895; *Seattle Post-Intelligencer*, May 19, 25, 1894; March 13; April 3, 8, 1896; Seattle *Argus*, April 4; June 6, 1896; *Tacoma Daily Ledger*, Jan. 20, 1896; *Tacoma Daily News*, Nov. 22, 1898.

45. Eastern Washington shared a common interest with Oregon in the construction of canals at the Cascades and The Dalles, and in the furtherance of jetty work at the mouth of the Columbia. In addition to hazardous rock outcroppings, the Columbia downstream from Wenatchee dropped 22 feet in two miles at Rock Island Rapids, and 72 feet in 10 miles at Priest Rapids. Seattle *Argus*, March 31, 1894; *Seattle Post-Intelligencer*, March 25,

1899; *Seattle Press-Times*, Feb. 2, 1895; *Spokane Daily Chronicle*, Jan. 22; Sept. 7, 1898; *Wenatchee Advance*, Jan. 26, 1895; Thomas W. Symons to W.P. Craighill, May 22, 1895, in *Annual Report of the Chief of Engineers, 1895*, 3534–35; to Thomas L. Casey, Jan. 17, 1895, Portland District Records, U.S. Army Corps of Engineers, RG 77, Federal Records Center, Seattle; Colfax *Palouse Gazette*, May 16, 1890; Spokane *Spokesman-Review*, Dec. 9, 1896; Aug. 6; Sept. 28; Oct. 6, 1898.

46. Inland Empire residents complained that appropriations for river and harbor works in western Washington were 10 times the amount allotted to projects east of the mountains. The grandiose westside canal scheme also had politically useful national defense implications, as the system would provide an alternate means of access to Puget Sound should Great Britain place "a few guns...at the entrance to the Straits of Fuca." Technical difficulties resulted in completion of a Grays Harbor jetty that was neither as long nor as high above the water as originally planned. Army engineers urged local business leaders to "stir up your representatives" as a means of securing additional appropriations. *Seattle Telegraph*, Nov. 21, 1894; Symons to Casey, Sept. 6, 1894, Portland District Records; May 22, 1895, in *Annual Report of the Chief of Engineers, 1895*, 3528–33; Harry Taylor to Craighill, July 14, 1896, Records of the Office of Chief of Engineers, RG 77, National Archives; to Emerson, Dec. 31, 1896; A.A. Mackenzie to Taylor, June 10, 1897, both Seattle District Records, U.S. Army Corps of Engineers, RG 77, Federal Records Center, Seattle; Emerson to Simpson, June 4, 1896; to I.N. Goodhue, March 19, 1896, Emerson Letterbooks; Olympia *Washington Standard*, Feb. 4, 1898; Spokane *Spokesman-Review*, June 14, 1896; *Seattle Times*, Feb. 3, 1900.

47. Tacoma protested the diversion of funds, supposedly explained by Senator Watson Squire's personal interest in the Everett project. Symons to Casey, July 9, 1894, Portland District Records; Sept. 15, 1894; Taylor to John W. Wilson, Feb. 13, 1900, both Seattle District Records; Dec. 27, 1897, Records of the Office of Chief of Engineers; *Tacoma Daily Ledger*, Nov. 25; Dec. 2, 1894; Jan. 11, 28; May 21, 1896; April 3, 1898; Gardner Colby to Watson C. Squire, Aug. 12, 1895, Watson C. Squire Papers, University of Washington Library.

48. Great Northern influence was reflected by the limitation of the survey, under the 1894 legislation, to "the existing waterway." Symons therefore did not examine a previously favored Ballard-Smith Cove canal line to Elliott Bay, a route that would have interfered with railroad development plans. Olympia *Washington Standard*, Feb. 16, 1894; *Seattle Post-Intelligencer*, Aug. 3, 1894; Seattle *Argus*, Aug. 11, 1894; Symons to Casey, Nov. 1, 1894, Records of the Office of Chief of Engineers; to Craighill, Aug. 29, 1895, in *Annual Report of the Chief of Engineers, 1896*, 3356–63, 3372; Robert E. Ficken, "Seattle's 'Ditch': The Corps of Engineers and the Lake Washington Ship Canal," *PNQ*, 77 (Jan. 1986), 13.

49. "His duties as an employee of the private corporation," one offended Seattleite remarked of Symons, "are certainly most inconsistent with his duties and obligations to the government." The captain was soon transferred to the Atlantic Coast, but remained involved from afar in the south canal project. Gilman to Burke, March 2, 1892; April 26, 1896, Burke Papers; *Seattle Press-Times*, March 26, 27, 19, 1895; Alan A. Hynding, "Eugene Semple's Seattle Canal Scheme," *PNQ*, 59 (1968), 77–81; Seattle *Argus*, Jan. 12; March 30; June 15, 1895; *Seattle Post-Intelligencer*, Feb. 9, 1895; *Seattle Times*, July 2, 1895; Ficken, "Seattle's 'Ditch,'" 12–13.

50. Semple supporters joined Tacoma in lobbying against government funding for a Seattle canal. Legal complications, however, regarding the south canal's impact on the shoreline

of Lake Washington amounted to what the casually racist *Argus* called "a large-sized colored gentleman in the woodpile." *Tacoma Daily Ledger*, April 23, 1896; G.H. Mendell to chief of engineers, Sept. 19, 1895, Records of the Office of Chief of Engineers; Gilman to Burke, April 26, 1896, Burke Papers; *Seattle Times*, Oct. 25, 1895; Ficken, "Seattle's 'Ditch,'" 13–14; *Seattle Post-Intelligencer*, Aug. 17, 1898; Seattle *Argus*, April 20; Aug. 31, 1895.

51. Great Northern Railway Co. petition, Feb. 22, 1898; Mackenzie to secretary of war, March 11, 1898, both Records of the Office of Chief of Engineers; to Taylor, April 19, 1898, Seattle District Records; Ficken, "Seattle's 'Ditch,'" 14; Spokane *Spokesman-Review*, April 10, 1897; *Seattle Post-Intelligencer*, Dec. 10, 1894; April 15; June 22, 1897; Seattle *Argus*, March 24, 1894; April 3, 1897; *Seattle Times*, Sept. 30; Oct. 17, 1895; Jan. 13, 1900.

52. The prime sponsors of the national park legislation were Watson Squire and John Wilson, individuals seldom suspected of anti-corporation independence. Tacoma protested usage of the name Rainier in place of the measure's original "Washington National Park." *Seattle Post-Intelligencer*, March 3, 5, 1899; Olympia *Washington Standard*, Nov. 26, 1897; Theodore Catton, "The Campaign to Establish Mount Rainier National Park, 1893–1899," *PNQ*, 88 (Spring 1997), 70–81.

53. *Seattle Times*, July 16, 1895; Walker to Talbot, Aug. 15, 26, 1895; to Jackson, Sept. 9, 1895, Walker Letterbooks; Emerson to Simpson, Aug. 18, 1895, Emerson Letterbooks; Spokane *Spokesman-Review*, Sept. 9, 1895; *Seattle Press-Times*, Sept. 9, 1893; *Seattle Post-Intelligencer*, Jan. 12, 1895. The concept of soldiers fighting forest fires was, at the time, not unusual. See Stephen J. Pyne, *Fire in America: A Cultural History of Woodland and Rural Fire* (Princeton: Princeton University Press, 1982), 227–29, 295–96; and, in general, Harvey Meyerson, *Nature's Army: When Soldiers Fought for Yosemite* (Lawrence: University Press of Kansas, 2001).

54. Cleveland's "Washington's Birthday" proclamations doubled the acreage so far set aside under the 1891 act of congress. "Not a man interested in the lumbering interests," one newspaper report affirmed, "cares a cotton hat" about the reserves. Harold K. Steen, *The U.S. Forest Service: A History* (Seattle: University of Washington Press, 1976, 2004 ed.), 26–34; *Seattle Times*, March 8, 1897; Emerson to Simpson, March 17, 1897; to John L. Wilson, March 18, 1897, Emerson Letterbooks; *Seattle Post-Intelligencer*, March 11, 1897; Ficken, *Forested Land*, 124–25.

55. A Tacoma editor recommended—with a widely repeated suggestive reference to the conservationists' lack of masculinity—that "scientific preservers" be required to "come out to this state and ride in a man's saddle for a few weeks." *Pullman Tribune*, April 10, 1897; *Seattle Post-Intelligencer*, March 1, 5–7, 23, rep. from Whatcom *Blade*, April 7; June 8; Sept. 6, 1897; Sept. 14, 1899; *Tacoma Daily Ledger*, April 30; May 20, 1898; *Seattle Times*, March 8, 1897; Spokane *Spokesman-Review*, March 10, 24, 1897.

56. In Spokane, the Washington Water Power Company supplied energy for street lights and railways. By the mid-1890s, the United States had 13,000 miles of electric railroads, with 30,000 "motor cars." As a practical matter, according to many contemporary accounts, the urban "lighting service," in addition to being expensive, tended to be so dim that "it would take two of the ordinary electric incandescent lights…to furnish an acceptable light for a room twelve feet square." Suggesting an additional application, an eastern Washington orchardist used an electric motor to pump irrigation water from the Snake River and for lights installed to attract insect pests to traps set among trees. C. Edward Magnusson, "Hydro-Electric Power in Washington," *WHQ*, 19 (April 1928), 97; Robert C. Wing,

"Washington Lights Up," *Columbia: The Magazine of Northwest History*, 2 (Fall 1988), 36–37; Spokane *Spokesman-Review*, April 18, 1899; *Tacoma Daily News*, March 26, 1897; *Seattle Post-Intelligencer*, May 18, 1890; March 26, 1893; March 7, 1895; *Tacoma Daily Ledger*, Dec. 7, 1890; Seattle *Argus*, Feb. 25, 1899; *Seattle Press-Times*, March 5, 1891; Feb. 19, 1895; *West Shore*, 16 (Feb. 8, 1890), 171–73; Bailey Avery, "Spokane Falls," *Northwest*, 8 (April 1890), 22–24; Portland *Oregonian*, July 30, 1888.

57. An Olympia editor called for full development of the falls at the nearby Deschutes River, arguing that the industrial applications of electricity would "drag" the capital city out of its depression-induced "Slough of Despond." The *P-I* pointed out that "cheap power…can only be had through an enormous outlay, which can afford a profit only after years of development." Wing, "Washington Lights Up," 37; *Tacoma Daily Ledger*, May 8, 1896; R.H. Thomson to Gilman, Nov. 6, 1894, Daniel H. Gilman Papers, University of Washington Library; Spokane *Spokesman-Review*, Feb. 18, 1897; Olympia *Washington Standard*, July 23, 1897; *Seattle Post-Intelligencer*, July 9, 1898.

58. "He over-capitalized his proposed company," one newspaper concluded of Gilman's venture. Wanting "to make too big a stake out of it," he "was crushed by the depression and went down." *Seattle Press-Times*, March 26, 1894; *Seattle Post-Intelligencer*, Feb. 6, 1894; Jan. 3, rep. from Snohomish *Eye*, 6, 1895; Gilman to Burke, Sept. 26; Nov. 5, 24; Dec. 1, 1894; Feb. 23, 1895; June 2, 1896, Burke Papers; Nesbit, *"He Built Seattle,"* 376; Wing, "Washington Lights Up," 37; *Tacoma Daily News*, Jan. 26, 1898.

59. General Electric, Seattle's first street light vendor, attempted to frustrate competition from Snoqualmie Falls by persuading the city council to impose arbitrarily expensive franchise requirements. Seattle had previously exhausted its constitutional debt capacity, necessitating a complicated procedure under which future water earnings were dedicated to repayment of the bonds. Mired in the depression, local taxpayers had neither the ability nor the inclination to directly finance the Cedar River project. Criticizing the "folly" of the bonding expedient, opponents maintained that Seattle's present water was "as pure as when old Chief Sealth was monarch" of the region. Seattle *Argus*, Oct. 2, 1897; Jan. 1; March 5; July 9, 1898; Jan. 14; Feb. 25; April 15, 22, 1899; *Seattle Times*, Oct. 8, 30; Dec. 11, 16, 1895; Sept. 10, 15; Nov. 24, 1898; May 5; Sept. 15, 1899; *Seattle Post-Intelligencer*, June 26, 1898; April 18; Oct. 16, 1899; Spokane *Spokesman-Review*, Oct. 19; Dec. 12, 1895.

Washington's third state governor, John H. Rogers, elected on the Populist ticket in 1896.
Washington State University Libraries (85-023)

Chapter Seven

As the Flood-tide Follows the Ebb

It is folly...to lament the past and to chase rainbows of hope that seem to lead to a restoration of good times gone by. Times will assuredly be better than they now are, because the uncertainties concerning the currency...have been removed, and there is a hopeful feeling which will stimulate new enterprises and increase business activities. We should bear constantly in mind, however, the fact...that normal times are times of patient industry and slow accumulations. Speculative periods, when rapid money-making is possible to the shrewd and daring, come only at long intervals, and they are sure to leave behind many wrecks and much bitterness. We believe that we are now at the beginning of a long period of normal business activity, which will as naturally follow the years of depression we have just gone through, as the flood-tide follows the ebb.—Northwest.[1]

$\mathcal{W}$ASHINGTON'S THIRD GOVERNOR assumed his official duties in an unpretentious and, for that matter, unprecedented manner. When writing about earlier inaugural celebrations, one onlooker recalled that the "champagne flowed like water and gold was scattered like hailstones by ambitious office-seekers." Patronized by high spending party leaders, saloons and "sporting houses" prospered "and the devil had no impediment." In simple Jeffersonian contrast, John Rogers strolled like an ordinary citizen, unaccompanied by marchers, music or slogan emblazoned banners, from his boarding house to the "odd, rambling, old-fashioned white building" still in tumbledown service as the state capitol.[2]

"Times are hard," the state's new executive proclaimed in his blunt address. Washingtonians fortunate enough to have employment in January 1897 were earning wages "not adequately remunerative." Heavy mortgages burdened land owners, causing "the hearts of strong brave men [to] sink within them as they view with moistened eyes the needs of helpless children for whom they are called to provide." Resurrecting the great national issue of the previous year's campaign, Rogers blamed the suffering on "the constantly appreciating value of money consequent upon the demonetization of silver and the establishment of the gold standard." His equally forthright response was sure to alarm the investing class. "The great plain people"—farmers, laborers, small business owners and middling professionals—must "unite against the organized aggressions of the privileged few, or they are to become helpless servants of a poorly concealed plutocracy."[3]

For good reason, conservative John McGraw refused to meet with his successor, or to participate in the official ceremonies. Fleeing Olympia before the arriving fusionist horde, the former governor dealt instead with personal troubles, including bankrupt banking ventures and frustrated senatorial ambitions due to the lapse of a Republican legislative majority. Long delayed audits of the King County sheriff's department uncovered a series of early-decade accounting peculiarities, as well as several thousand dollars in cash left in a locked cabinet since the time of McGraw's service in that office. "It is no wonder," one observer wryly suggested, that "'the late executive moustache' kept handy a large sized whitewash brush."[4]

Supporters of the new governor stressed an all-too-obvious contrast with the departed and widely unlamented Republican. Rogers was "an honest theorist" with genuine plans for the "future," while McGraw was "a political trickster, who has ruined his party." Governor Rogers also was a less-than-enthusiastic supporter of private property rights, a non-user of alcoholic spirits and, if not quite a professed atheist, a willing unbeliever in the "buncombe and balderdash" favored by pulpit hypocrites. "He dragged Adam and Eve from their quiet resting place in the good Book," the *P-I* claimed in mock horror, "and announced that…they were never real, living…personages."[5] Though undeniably besmirched, John McGraw, meanwhile, believed in the sanctity of land ownership, accepted the Bible as the word of God and worshipped at the long polished altar of 100-proof beverages.

Both men, though, were ambitious politicians, with McGraw differing in the brutal and unsophisticated manner utilized in the pursuit of his native craft. Contemporary perception of Rogers as a turn-of-the-century Thomas Jefferson greatly exaggerated his intellectual depth, but accurately reflected his self-chosen role as a thinking individual intent upon construction of an enduring partisan organization. Rather than a temporary political expedient, fusion was, for the governor, the starting point in building "the dominant political party" in the state of Washington. Democrats and silver Republicans, he believed, must be encouraged to remain within the fold by a fair distribution of patronage, making for a permanent alliance and denying the old majority organization any opportunity for a comeback. The major obstacle to this scheme lay in the counterproductive fact that many Populists, or "pops," thought primarily in terms of immediate advantage. "There was scarcely a pop in the whole state," Rogers privately lamented, "who did not think that…he was fully entitled to whatever there might be in the line of…favor lying around loose." Giving a job to one supplicant necessarily induced "heart-burnings and envyings" among disappointed rival aspirants. Although the governor waited until after the 1897 legislative session to fill the most important positions at his disposal, internal disputes threatened from the beginning to wreck his victorious coalition.[6]

Populists and their allies emerged from the dramatic national and state campaigns of 1896 with optimistic spirits fully intact. McKinley's election to the presidency was a setback, though hardly, or so things seemed, a definitive loss for free coinage. "Its cause is just and right," a west-of-the-Cascades editor insisted in assessing the long term prospects, "and just so sure as just and right always prevail in the end, so sure will silver be given her rights along with gold." Silver continued to stir emotions, as in the nasty Spokane County argument over adoption of "notoriously…unfair" goldbug textbooks by the local schools. Reform leaders urged William Jennings Bryan himself to relocate to Washington and accept election to the U.S. senate in 1897. As for a legislative agenda, fusionists favored a modest unity-protecting program featuring railroad regulation, a "common-sense" approach to taxation and a "return to the severe economy and primitive simplicity of early days."[7]

Old guard alarmists worried that Washington, under fusion, would be "classed as a freak state," to the detriment of reputation and investment. Election returns and legislative majorities aside, however, thoughtful analysts suggested that the commonwealth was "populist in name only." In private, intelligent business leaders saw no reason for alarm, much less for hysteria. Describing the fusionist alliance as "a mixed and many headed uncongenial mass," George Emerson advised distant associates that "capital has nothing to fear in the state of Washington from adverse legislation." Chauncey Griggs, the McKinley supporting Tacoma lumber manufacturer, considered John Rogers a major improvement, in capacity and honesty, over his Republican predecessor and believed that the legislature would have "enough good men," out-and-out Populists included, "to prevent anything that would be detrimental to the general interests of our state."[8]

Silver, to the considerable relief of persons interested in attracting capital, could not, of course, be addressed at the state level. This fact alone substantially reduced the probability of drastic action in Olympia. Leaving nothing to chance, surviving Republicans took advantage of their long experience in the means of doing business in the legislature. Party leaders, behind-the-scenes political power George Emerson noted, intended to "load" undesirable bills "with venom and malice," greatly increasing the likelihood of subsequent court action invalidating such extreme legislation. Recognizing in Governor Rogers a potent danger to the old order, Republican legislators even considered supporting his election to the U.S. senate, thereby removing him from the scene.[9]

From their near complete lack of governmental experience, fusionists gave the Republicans good reason to anticipate a successful outcome. Of the 61 alliance members responding to a survey, three-quarters were in their thirties and forties. Only four—three attorneys and a medical doctor—were professional persons. Eleven claimed to have attended some sort of college. Fifteen, including

George Turner, a silver Republican from Spokane, was selected U.S. senator on the 29th ballot by the 1897 fusionist state legislature. Sketch from J.F. Gilbert, *Greater Spokane's Builders* (1906).

seven Canadians, admitted to foreign birth. Only two of the American born were natives of the Pacific Northwest. Twenty-three, plus an avowed spiritualist and one follower of the "Do Good" church, conceded that they belonged to no organized religious denomination. Of the 85 fusionist members in the legislature, 57 were Populists, 15 were Democrats and 13 were silver Republicans.[10]

Matters quickly bogged down in the usual senatorial election brawl. Numerous self-nominated Populist aspirants entered the contest, "most of these of…uniform mediocrity" in the unkindly view of one pro-fusion editor. Two serious candidates eventually emerged. Incumbent Watson Squire, though seriously afflicted by the panic, was still "in pretty fair shape" so far as capacity to barter cash, liquor, women and patronage for tainted support. Honorable fusionists considered Squire a disreputable charlatan, a past-his-prime hack who was "in everything but the silver question…a Republican." Challenger George Turner of Spokane, also a longtime GOP leader, had in genuine contrast "worked like a trojan for the cause of silver and the people's ticket" during the 1896 campaign. Winning on the 29th ballot, Turner became one of six silver Republican members of the U.S. senate. In retiring Squire, however, fusion legislators upset an unwritten rule of state politics—the allocation of one senatorial seat to the west and the other to the east of the mountains, a violation bound to have negative political repercussions in tidewater areas.[11]

Poorly led and—with silver off the table—often at odds with one another, the legislative majority struggled to implement at least some of the election season platform. Railway regulation, the key issue in the original rise of Washington's Populist movement, remained a major demand. In one newly prominent complaint, state residents paid passenger fares averaging 5¢ a mile, compared to 4¢ in Oregon. "Even during the depression which followed the panic of 1893," the Spokane *Spokesman-Review* exclaimed, the transportation lines "made no move to abate any part of the high rates…they had established during the boom days." Wheat ranchers and exporters, along with shipping interests in general, expected passage of a measure implementing the constitutionally authorized railroad commission, the only point worth debating being whether the members should be chosen by popular vote or appointed by the governor.[12]

Taking full advantage of traditional regional differences and inexperienced fusionist legislators, the railroads thwarted naive aspirations with an ease reminiscent of the glory days of outright Republican control. Lobbyists supervised the organization of vital committees, encouraged greed and jealously between regions and dispensed the standard number of free railway passes. To the dismay and disgust of the general public, the legislature failed to establish a regulatory commission. As a false consolation prize, the rail lines agreed, after a good deal of feigned hemming and hawing, to allow passage of a misleading and economically dangerous measure mandating a modest reduction in wheat freights.[13] Mishandling a long contentious issue, the fusionists alienated constituents and demonstrated thorough ineptitude.

Various other attempts at positive legislating also ended in grotesque embarrassment. A new mortgage statute was supposed to reduce foreclosures through the establishment of inventive procedural hurdles. Alarmed investors were partially mollified when the courts quickly ruled that the measure did not apply to preexisting financial arrangements, thus thwarting the legislators' original intent. All new buyers of homes and land would end up suffering, however, after the state supreme court allowed the law to otherwise stand. "Thanks to…the pop. legislature," one analyst noted of the dire unintended consequence, "Eastern capitalists cannot be induced to loan money on real estate mortgages…excepting on absolutely prohibitive terms."[14]

Similar damage resulted from an ill conceived reform of taxation, doubling the property exemption to $1,000. The wealthy protested the "outrage" and the supposed inducement to fraud, but many, if not most, Washington residents welcomed an apparent shift in the fiscal burden. Fortunately for the well-propertied, the state supreme court, a last ditch bastion of old time Republicanism, took emergency action, ruling by a partisan and a seriously flawed four-to-two vote that the concept of exemption itself was unconstitutional. The effect was to make taxpayers of nearly all adult Washingtonians, including those previously exempted under the defunct $500 limit. The only remedy was for a special legislative session to repair the technical defects cited by the jurists as an excuse for their decision. Governor Rogers, though, refused on the grounds that his incompetent and irresponsible fusion colleagues would, if again allowed to lay hands on the public business, "damn us to all eternity—politically."[15]

Fiscal responsibility was the one area in which reformist legislators performed at a higher level of competence than their Republican predecessors. "The cost of running the state government should be put down to bedrock," fusionists contended upon taking over in Olympia. "Not one new institution, office, commission or other fixed charge should be added at this time to the…expense list." Serious and all but draconian reductions—the Steilacoom and Medical Lake asylums lost a quarter million dollars in funding and the University of Washington's allocation declined by 75 percent—resulted in a two year budget authorization of less than half the figure approved by the previous legislature in 1895. State warrants, badly depreciated for years, sold at par by summer. According to one news account, agencies were able "to buy as much with 90 cents as the outgoing administration was able to buy with 100 cents." GOP stalwarts denounced the economizing as false, destructive and even illegal. By restoring investor faith in public credit, however, the legislature did much to attract capital back to the Pacific Northwest.[16]

Governor Rogers took a personal role in the cost cutting, restraining legislators when necessary and convincing business leaders that he had "no intention of driving Eastern capital out of the State." Rogers vetoed further expenditures for the new capitol building, leaving only a bare foundation to remind onlookers of John McGraw's supposed folly and, in the process, earning good will in the many communities hoping to relocate the state offices from Olympia. In line with his predecessor's approach, the governor also eliminated appropriations for the Cheney and Whatcom normal schools. Except in the impacted towns, the action was popular, there being wide belief that the state was "top-heavy" in higher education, diverting money better and more fairly spent on the primary grades. Suggesting that old, local oriented rivalries died hard, an editor in Ellensburg, blessed with the surviving institution, pointed out ostensibly on behalf of good government that "in states of greater population than Washington, one normal school is all that is required."[17]

Horribly inept as legislators except when slashing expenditures, fusionists also proved to be inefficient and controversial administrators once the governor began restaffing state agencies in the interest of building a permanent third party. The Walla Walla penitentiary soon was embroiled in another controversy over the corrupt disposition of grain sacks. Prison management followed tradition by expecting the guards and other employees to pay for campaign expenses across the state. The physician in charge of the Steilacoom mental hospital for the past 16 years gave way, news accounts asserted, to "a much younger man who admits that he has made no special study to fit him to…care for the insane." East of the mountains at Medical Lake, attempts by "spoilsmen" to "'clear out' the old force" provoked protests at the asylum and in surrounding communities. Regents appointed by Governor Rogers interfered in various questionable ways with the proper conduct of affairs at the Washington Agricultural College. In a genuinely egregious example of manipulation, the city of Pullman secured a new municipal water system, courtesy of the collegiate budget. Even the normally supportive local newspaper condemned this "ignorant attempt to cinch the institution which is the backbone of the town."[18]

Fusion management of the University of Washington fortified the school's long tradition of academic misfeasance. The regents avidly sought positions of great and small importance, down to the janitorial level, for friends and relatives. One member of the board managed to secure a side appointment for himself as registrar. Successive presidents were dismissed, one after being publicly exposed as an agnostic by an ignorantly outraged Seattle minister. Populists attempted to establish a chair of spiritualism, eliminated Greek and Latin from the curriculum, reduced the credits required for graduation and founded the first formal athletic department. Many students protested against mandatory exercise and an apparent attempt to make the UW a football powerhouse. Governor Rogers periodically replaced offensive regents, but contributed to the mess by instructing the board to reject the employment application of Republican partisan Edmond S. Meany, the founder of Pacific Northwest historiography, on grounds of insufficient scholarly expertise. The small number of persons genuinely interested in higher education resigned themselves to believing there was "no likelihood" of the sorry institution ever ranking with California's new Stanford University.[19]

Beset by woeful performance and "friction in the ranks," fusion governance turned out to be a short lived phenomenon. Once fervid supporters were disappointed, while alarmist detractors expressed grateful relief. From its earliest moments in Olympia, the three-headed party of the future marched toward the exit door. The defeat of silver at the national level removed from consideration a much needed unifying issue. Pro-coinage Republicans soon began considering the means of returning to their old party. Democrats scuttled toward safe refuge once the alliance with populism lost office-seeking viability. Incumbent fusionist tickets went down to defeat in the local 1897 and 1898 elections, signaling the approach of definitive statewide rejection.[20] Crippled by internal contradictions and the perils of responsibility, the reformers also suffered when the late-century economic depression came to a belated end.

⊱≋⊰

Grover Cleveland had given way to William McKinley, with no immediately discernible impact upon the economic crisis. Gold was triumphant and silver vanquished, yet "a decided scarcity of the circulating medium," as Republicans conceded, continued into the early months of 1897. A Grays Harbor editor contrasted the campaign literature touting the Republican candidate as the "advance agent of prosperity" with the reality of the latest 15 percent reduction in local sawmill wages. "Gall and wormwood must be sweeter than honey," the *Aberdeen Herald* suggested, "compared with the taste of the ashes which these men are receiving in place of the apples promised before election to all laborers if McKinley won." If the new president was, as advertised, the prophet of recovery, another observer offered, "then he is a long way ahead of his country."[21]

Though buoyed up in spirit by McKinley's victory, Washington's leading lumbermen still experienced another hard winter. "The whole outlook" continued to be "dark," especially in badly overstocked San Francisco. One of the last surviving saltwater operations from the early territorial era, the Washington Mill Company, finally closed down at Seabeck on Hood Canal. A popular comedy of the Puget Sound theater circuit, "A Run on the Bank," testified to public preoccupation with the persistent weakness of the state's financial institutions. Padlocked since the first stage of the panic, the Bank of Tacoma concluded its official life when a court appointed receiver disposed of the paper assets, including a quarter million dollars in public deposits, for less than $10,000. East of the Cascades, absentee investors vainly sought purchasers for dozens of foreclosed Palouse farmsteads. In the lower Yakima Valley, a few hundred disconsolate settlers longed for better times among the partially completed canals of the Sunnyside irrigation project. On a genuinely ominous note, many analysts concluded that another round of state and federal elections, those scheduled for 1898, might be necessary for restoration of business confidence.[22]

Humbled by the economic collapse, the once mighty Tacoma Land Company was unable to pay $265,000 in back taxes owed Pierce County. Spokane property owners refused, or were unable, to cover a half million dollars in delinquent street improvement assessments. Governments large and small suffered from the long term fiscal strain. Whatcom County admitted to having no prospect of repaying $197,000 in debt, "incurred when the people had their eyes wide open" in demanding modern roads and bridges. Chehalis County, south of Olympia, labored under a similar problem, though the sum owed was a relatively modest $75,000. Whitman County warrants circulated in the grain country at less than 50 cents on the dollar.[23]

By one contemporary estimate, Tacoma had lost 10,000 inhabitants since 1893. Stores stood vacant on the hillside streets. "For ten miles round about," rotting survey markers and frayed promotional banners provided stark reminders of long-ago real estate booms. Seattle, too, had empty mercantile establishments and dwellings. The King County council devoted two days a month to pleas for food from impoverished residents. Spokane had suffered because of overbuilding in the aftermath of the 1889 fire. Offices were unoccupied, especially in the upper stories of major buildings, and landlords had long since given up the fight to maintain mortgage payments. Much of the downtown was in the hands of creditors, notably the Northwestern and Pacific Hypotheekbank, an institution headquartered in the Netherlands. Local fusionist officeholders looked out for themselves, installing family members and friends in makeshift free-of-charge courthouse apartments.[24]

Certain signs of improvement nonetheless became evident toward the end of winter, confirming the Republican claim that recovery began with McKinley's election. Merchants recorded an upswing in trade, their ledger books proclaiming the long anticipated "general revival which is always certain to follow a…period of depression." A federal government announcement revealed that Tacoma was the nation's second busiest port, behind only New York City. More building permits were issued in Spokane in March 1897 than for any month since the beginning of the panic. "Traveling men" returning from east of the mountains reported that sales were "better than they have been in five years." A half dozen new canneries prepared to process salmon on Puget Sound.[25]

Reorganized by the end of Cleveland's term, the railroads fully participated in the general economic revival. Bankruptcies among transportation lines declined sharply in 1897, with barely 1,000 miles of track involved, compared to nearly 30,000 in the first year of the panic. Across the nation, railroad employment increased by 100,000 workers as of mid-summer. Although James J. Hill had failed to bring about "unification" between the Great Northern and the Northern Pacific, a mutually beneficial alliance between the transcontinental rivals emerged from the process. The firms joined with the Union Pacific in securing operational control of the Oregon Railway & Navigation Company, providing all three concerns with direct access down the Columbia River to Portland. On its own, the NP assumed ownership of the old Hunt railroad system in eastern Washington. The equally decrepit Seattle, Lake Shore & Eastern—lampooned for years on Puget Sound as the "Seattle and Elsewhere"—also wound up in Northern Pacific hands. Building again to tap mining regions across the 49th parallel, D.C. Corbin's Spokane Falls & Northern was incorporated into the Great Northern network.[26]

In part because of the railroads, lumbering recovered from what one manufacturer termed the "unhealthy competition" of traditional California business. Shipments, by rail in particular, commenced a long term upward trend in 1897, reflecting the new status of the Pacific Northwest as America's premier forest products region. "Indirectly," a trade journal noted in pointing out the importance of this development, "every other person in Western Washington is dependent on the lumber and shingle business." Personally encouraged by James J. Hill and attracted by the investment potential of NP land grant timber, only recently put on sale, the first Great Lakes capitalists since the panic visited the state. Escorted by Hill himself, Frederick Weyerhaeuser, who privately admitted to having lost $1 million during the depression, arrived in early summer to resume his stalled investigation of the Washington woodlands.[27]

Another long distressed activity, wheat ranching, exhibited signs of life in the early months of 1897. Even during the worst of the depression, visitors marveled at the "wonderful soil" of eastern Washington, "the like of which no farmer born and bred east of the Appalachians has ever seen." Years of low prices, unrelenting expenses and foreclosed mortgages took a heavy toll on residents of the region. "So great were the discouragements," noted a report on the experiences of Big Bend growers, "that not a few even among the more determined among them gave up all." Those who held on did so by shifting energy and time to the production of butter, eggs and other perishable items for sale in country market towns.[28]

Despite increasing output east of the Cascades, grain prices improved a bit in the fall of 1896, a promising indication that better times were on the way. Crops failed over the winter in Argentina, Australia and India, and drought in California sidelined a major competitor in the rapidly expanding Asian market. Revived confidence among farmers brought land back into cultivation, and abundant rains generated mounting expectations of heavy per-acre yields. Early season quotations approached 80¢ a bushel in the Walla Walla Valley, a rate unheard of since the earliest months of statehood. Railroads scrambled to assemble enough rolling stock to haul away what appeared likely to become the greatest output in regional history. Looking ahead to the harvest and regardless of other developments, the economic impact was bound to be breathtaking. "The boom in wheat alone," said one editor in mid-summer, "would go far to dispel the clouds of depression which have so long hung over the land."[29]

Mining, too, appeared in a new positive light. A good deal of activity was, to be sure, promotion oriented and disappointing in terms of profit. Reports of a "rich mineral belt" along the lower Columbia turned out to have no basis in fact. Depression conditions, along with persistent flooding along the rail outlet to Everett, caused the Rockefeller syndicate to lose interest in its Monte Cristo mining development. Elsewhere in the northern Cascades, prospectors failed to make discoveries of consequence. Seattle based promoters nonetheless eagerly peddled stock in any number of gold and silver ventures. Most of these brokers, the visiting railroad writer E.V. Smalley noted in a revealing aside, had been "real estate men in the time when lots bought one day could be sold at an advance the next." Desperate boosterism trumped common sense, as suggested by far circulating reports that 10 mineral exploration firms were incorporated per day in the state of Washington.[30]

East of the mountains, development actually justified the excitement. Older diggings along the stark ridges above the Kittitas Valley and the Okanogan River produced profitable returns, at least for some prospecting enterprises. After years of pressure from Washington's congressional delegation, the government opened the northern half of the vast Colville Indian Reservation to mining in 1896. "Frontiersmen" had for years insisted that the tract contained enormous mineral wealth, including placer deposits in the streams. The more intrepid, or foolish, mounted occasional trespassing forays, only to be roughly expelled by the native inhabitants and government officials. Now, a full scale invasion took place, with the best claims going to opportunists sneaking across the boundary in advance of the official opening date. The Indians supposedly grew "rich at a rate that would make a Palouse wheat rancher green with envy" by selling fresh produce in the camps. Spokane merchants also prospered, becoming the principal providers of equipment and non-perishable supplies.[31]

Profit came, as well, from north of the 49th parallel. "Not since the mining days of early California…has fortune been so free with her favors," an Inland Empire editor wrote in celebrating the rushes of 1896 and 1897 to the Kootenay country in southeast British Columbia. The population of Rossland, at the center of the boom five miles above the border, increased to 7,000 as dozens of new mines were opened over the winter. Taking advantage of convenient rail and ferry connections, Washington residents participated fully, with Senator George

Turner, for one, securing a $100,000 return in the early months. Proximity and access also made Spokane the center of supply and investment. "The whole town is as excited about mining as Denver was after the Leadville discoveries," E.V. Smalley noted during an April 1897 visit. Crowds gathered about bulletin boards, perusing the latest prices of 50 or more stock offerings. "All the talk" in the hotel lobbies and corridors was of "the money being made by Tom, Dick or Harry." Already, these happy individuals, and their equally fortunate colleagues, had become the new Spokane elite. "The great mansions" built "in the real estate boom-times by men who 'went broke,'" Smalley reported, "are now the homes of men who 'struck it rich' on Trail Creek" in Canada. Sudden urban prosperity accounted for record bank deposits and the highest rate of construction in six years.[32]

By early summer 1897 at the latest, Washingtonians were convinced that prosperity had returned. "The grain growers and the business community," a Walla Walla Valley editor exclaimed, "need not be told that a condition of better times is already upon them." Thanks to the ripening wheat crop, "the discouraged looks on the farmers' faces have been dispelled and their countenances bespeak... contentment." Lumberman Chauncey Griggs celebrated "the general improvement throughout the country." Writing to a California friend, George Emerson agreed that "here in the north we feel a change in the times." Something of the old time swagger returned, a boosterish revival in keeping with restored spirit and drive. Beneficent resources and climate, a Tacoman claimed, had enabled Washington to avoid "the extreme wretchedness" prevailing since 1893 "in the big cities of the east." The state was now properly, "the earliest to recover from the worst effects of the great depression."[33]

〜〜〜

On July 15, 1897, the steamship *Excelsior* docked in San Francisco with $400,000 in Alaskan and Yukon gold, inspiring the dispatch of "startling reports" to all points on the Pacific coast. Steaming into the Strait of Juan de Fuca two days later, the *Portland* was met by chartered tugboats carrying reporters from Puget Sound cities. Before the vessel tied up at Seattle that evening, newspaper extras broadcasted the basic details to an excited public—$700,000 in gold dust, maybe more, lay under armed guard in the *Portland's* storeroom. Individual passengers carried unknown extra amounts, concealed in baggage or on their unkempt persons. "There has never been," declared the *P-I* in its first gold rush edition, "anything like the strike in the Klondike since the famous days of California nearly fifty years ago."[34]

Debarking miners told dramatic tales at dockside. Nils Anderson, who had borrowed $300 to go north in 1895, returned with dust worth $100,000. Anacortes resident William Stanley had $20 when he abandoned home and wife at

Steamship *Portland*. *University of Washington Libraries (Hester 10609)*

mid-decade, a stake turned into a forgiveness-inducing $90,000 fortune. "Seattle," an eastern journalist wrote of the response to these and other equally sensational accounts, "has gone stark, staring mad on gold." Viewing the hectic scene, Eugene Semple described the waterfront streets as "crowded with knots of men so worked up over the news that they can scarcely avoid being run over by the cars." The sudden golden effusion was even credited, in the following weeks, with ending the depression, a claim that ignored the impressive economic progress of the previous months. Supposedly, the *Portland*'s glittering cargo also brought Alaska to the attention of Puget Sounders for the first time, enabling Seattle to become the leading city in the Pacific Northwest.[35]

In reality, post-statehood Washington always had been closely linked to Alaska. Under one early proposal, the former Russian possession—larger than England, France and Germany combined—would have become a gigantic county in the new state of Washington, administered at great distance from Olympia. More realistic perceptions viewed the wilderness territory as an economic colony of Puget Sound. The U.S. post office facilitated an emerging connection by routing all mail for the north through Tacoma or Seattle. Beginning in 1890, five steamers provided regular Alaskan service from Commencement Bay alone. The prefabricated buildings used by the Alaskan customs service were, in symbolic fashion, constructed by a Port Townsend company.[36]

Washington residents knew, as an Inland Empire editor declared in 1890, that "from a financial standpoint the purchase of Alaska was a good investment." The apparent lack of "vacant land" on the diminished western frontier meant that "enterprising young men and women" could go north in search of opportunities for settlement and development. By reason of "comparative proximity," the new beacon for American settlers could hardly avoid becoming a "naturally tributary" to Puget Sound commerce. Salmon canneries already were well established, employing thousands of persons on a seasonal basis. Scheduled steamship connections enabled the fisheries interests to export frozen halibut and cod to Washington ports, for rail shipment to eastern consumers.[37]

At an early date, Alaska also became a "Mecca for sight-seers and tourists." Each summer, Sound-based vessels carried excursionists through the Inside Passage to view the fjords, glaciers and other wonders of the panhandle coast. "Every visitor," a Seattle newspaper noted in 1891, "has returned an enthusiastic missionary, so that the…journey from Puget Sound to Alaska promises to become [the] most popular of all American recreative sports." Coming and going, travelers filled hotels and patronized outfitters, to the immediate profit of tidewater business enterprises. In great part due to exposure courtesy of "the Alaska trip," Washington was, one commentator asserted, "fast becoming known all over the civilized world."[38]

Persons more interested in wealth than in scenery had long been drawn to the north. Two hundred Yukon River prospectors, supplied by steamer, spent the winter of 1890 among the placer diggings of Forty Mile Creek. "The miners were well scattered," according to an account published in a British Columbia newspaper, "prospecting up and down the river, and in many of its tributaries." Returnees reported "astonishing" discoveries, even though the most fortunate gold seekers averaged "but $12 per day" and the total production for the season failed to exceed $100,000. "Enough good claims have been located," an on-the-scene booster asserted, "to convince the most sceptical that Alaska is one of the most extensive mineral sections in existence."[39]

Returning Yukon miners revealed "the secrets of that hitherto strange country" to a receptive Pacific Northwest audience. Individuals responded in sufficient numbers to populate the Forty Mile camps in succeeding seasons. "The old cry of 'Westward ho!'" one observer enthused in late 1890, "will soon become 'Ho for Alaska!'" The basic routes to the mines quickly became well known, and so too did the many obstacles to success. "The summer lasts only about sixty days," one veteran of the early diggings advised, "and the ground is so frozen that the summer heat has but little effect upon it." Back in Seattle after an uncomfortable tour, a wealth hunter passed on the unsettling intelligence that the mosquitoes "would kill a naked man inside of an hour." Supplies could easily run short, especially if river boats were delayed by accident, ice or unfavorable stream flows.[40]

Visions of gold trumped concerns for practicality, not to mention personal survival. By 1893, Forty Mile Creek was, a letter from the Yukon informed residents on Puget Sound, "thoroughly prospected from one end to the other." Nearby streams were "staked and worked at all places where pay was found." Something of a mature exploitative environment—a reminder of earlier days in California, British Columbia and Idaho—appeared to have been implanted among the remote half-frozen camps. "A few persons will grow rich, very rich," reflected one Seattle editor, "a few will amass a small competency, many will be furnished employment, and many will be ruined." Low steamer fares, however, attracted new argonauts each spring. The panic, too, provided ample incentive for the unfortunate—"the overflow of the Pacific Northwest"—to test their luck among unfamiliar challenges.[41]

New discoveries in 1893 focusing on Circle City, another point accessible by Yukon River steamer, commenced a "rush to Alaska…in dead earnest." By 1896, over 1,000 miners worked the bars and stream banks. An eyewitness on the docks noted that oceangoing vessels were departing Puget Sound in the spring "loaded" to the "gunwhales with prospectors." Exploration also began for a more direct land route to the Yukon, perhaps by way of the White or Chilcoot passes, looming above the lower Alaskan coastline.[42]

Large numbers of persons went north again in the spring of 1897, attracted by, among other inducements, "highly colored posters…displayed in the depots along the northern transcontinental lines." The latest reports were "of a nature to stir the blood of the '49er," causing 1,000 fortune seekers a month to sail from Puget Sound ports. Trade rivalries were by now well established, with the sale of "outfits" to Alaska-bound prospectors being an obvious and highly lucrative enterprise. As early as 1890, the Tacoma chamber of commerce sent agents north to investigate potential business opportunities. Displaying the customary "spirit," Seattle soon took the lead, as even Tacomans conceded. Prior to July 1897, however, the city hardly ranked as the principal jumping-off point for Alaska. All points south of the 49th parallel, for example, expressed concern that British Columbia might secure the advantage, especially if rumors about the best deposits being in Canadian territory turned out to be true.[43]

Thus, news of a great find at Dawson—a recently opened camp on the upper Yukon River—was more of a long anticipated culmination that a stunning surprise. Cautious observers worrying about the dislocation of Washington's recovering economy, however, advised against an emotional response to the *Portland's* arrival. "Those who know when they are well off will stay where they are," a Tacoma editor advised. Similar expressions appeared in the Seattle press. "All who go in search of fortunes do not make them," the *P-I* asserted, proverb-style, in a special edition welcoming the *Portland* to Elliott Bay.[44]

"Don't let anybody lose his head because of the discovery of the new gold fields," the *Seattle Times* pronounced in another example of wariness. The Klondike diggings near Dawson, after all, were many hundreds of hard miles distant via water and land. Would-be prospectors leaving immediately would arrive before the first deep snowfall, but still too late to locate claims before the onset of winter. Those departing in August could only expect to get stalled on the coast, with river navigation having ceased for the season. The new direct trails, by White Pass from Skagway and Chilkoot Pass from Dyea, would have long since been closed, at least for sensible travelers. "While those who are acustomed to out-door life…may be able to keep comfortable," an experienced hand noted, "75 percent of those who are talking about going will find a 'wintery grave' if they start out at this time." Individuals planning the trip ought to "think twice" and remember that ample wealth would be readily and safely available in the spring of 1898. "There is gold in Alaska—lots of gold," a common sensical Seattleite reflected. "But in order to get it you must go after it intelligently."[45]

This sober advice was, to minimal surprise, ignored. The entire Pacific Northwest, indeed much of the country, promptly fell victim to the "Klondicitis" epidemic. "Everybody here are crazy to get to Klondyke," Cyrus Walker wrote from Seattle in uncharacteristically bad grammar. All kinds of supplies and equipment, the useful together with the nonessential, cluttered the Elliott Bay wharves. Smaller Washington towns all but shut down, with the more energetic male residents decamping, cash in pockets, for the Puget Sound embarkation points. According to official passenger manifests, 2,000 miners sailed aboard the first outbound steamers. All were convinced that the Yukon was the greatest thing since the Sierra Nevada strikes of 1849, better than the Fraser River, richer than the Clearwater mines and more promising than the Coeur d'Alenes. The Pacific Northwest in turn was California's true successor, a region sure to fatten upon nature's newly revealed bounty.[46]

Easterners also considered Alaska and the Yukon to be "the new California." Western Union operators in Seattle transmitted 50,000 words of golden news within 48 hours of the *Portland's* docking. Exaggerated reports that $2 million in gold dust already had been received stimulated interest. Ten thousand fortune hunters arrived in Washington by the end of August, most going to Elliott Bay, where mail from home was conveniently received. In local opinion, the initial horde represented the barest preview of incredible numbers to come, with most forecasters expecting 100,000 prospectors to pass through before spring. "You may expect to see throngs of enthusiasts taking the roads to Seattle," Eugene Semple informed a distant friend, "very much as the religious fanatics did in the first crusade." Instead of crosses, most carried hastily printed and invariably unreliable guidebooks. The California bard Joaquin Miller, for one egregious example, fooled many innocents by claiming, before nearly starving himself outside of Dawson, that "American energy" was the only thing required to endure supply related obstacles.[47]

A phenomenon common to all gold rushes explained the failure to heed well intentioned as opposed to lunatic advice. "The more reports [that] are circulated about the hardships and perils of the country," one onlooker pointed out, "the more intense the desire of adventurous men and women to go to the front." For some, the "poetry and romance" of wilderness adventure trumped rational analysis. Worn out by depression induced "fretting," many sought financial redemption. "They have been pronounced fool-hardy by some but nothing can be further from the truth," a Yakima journalist wrote of those local residents leaving for Alaska in 1897. "None of them have thrown up situations by which they could hope to gain a comfortable competency…while some were steadily loosing [sic] the little they possessed." The majority undoubtedly would fail, but a few could expect to attain wealth, a lottery-like calculation sure to overwhelm reason. A Seattleite noted the conflicting emotions experienced by persons welcoming the *Portland*: "They see men laden with bags of gold who insist they should turn around and refrain from entering the land of nuggets."[48]

Since prospectors were determined to make the journey in 1897 regardless of the obstacles, Washington businessmen felt they might as well make money off the hysteria. Arguments stressing the trip's dangers and the wisdom of waiting for spring were, henceforth, treated as expressions of commercial disloyalty. The hazards, as the *P-I* now belatedly revealed, were after all "astonishingly small." The northern working season was much longer than previously believed and might even extend year-round in the most promising places. The only genuine threat to life and limb came from possible pirate attack on southbound gold ships, a potential experience that only added to the romantic aspect of the Yukon adventure. "Wintering," in a further measure of good tidings, was "not as unpleasant as might be supposed." Difficulties remained, of course, but "they may be overcome by individual effort, requiring neither capital, machinery or organized labor."[49]

Mercantile enterprises of all kinds moved to profit from the exodus. A South Bend firm sent fresh Willapa Bay oysters, tightly packed in five gallon cans, to Alaska for transit across the mountain passes to delicacy craving Dawson gourmands. Skagway and Dyea, like San Francisco in the days of '49, required large quantities of lumber for constructing wharves and buildings. Puget Sound and Grays Harbor sawmills were in the best position to send the much needed cargoes. Senior partners of the old California lumber firms met in the Bay Area to organize a joint exploitative effort, complete with steamers and on-the-scene agencies. By the time the first consignment arrived, however, upstart Seattle sawmills had shipped in enormous quantities, overstocking all markets and greatly diminishing the prospects of substantial profit.[50]

Outfitting was the easiest means for Washingtonians to benefit from the gold rush. "When it is considered that an outfit includes sufficient necessaries to last at least one year," one commentator noted, "it will be seen that the business…will increase enormously." Self-appointed experts advised that each miner take, in addition to appropriate clothing and tools, 1,000 pounds of provisions, including 400 pounds of flour, 200 of bacon, 100 each of beans and sugar and 10 of coffee. Though prone to quarrelling among themselves, all Washington supply points insisted that the lowest-priced and highest-quality goods were to be found on Puget Sound, not in Alaska or the Canadian Yukon. Many merchants took advantage of the gullible whenever possible, a tendency personalized by the many duded-up strangers strolling about in "the most unique Klondike outfits imaginable." Local residents took unending delight in the wide brimmed Texan hats, hip-high rubber fishing boots and finely pressed shirts and trousers sported by prospectors waiting for steamer berths.[51]

Chauncey Griggs reported "doing about two or three thousand dollars of Klondike business daily" at the St. Paul & Tacoma company store. The attention devoted to the Alaska trade was an easily comprehended development. Through its advertising notices, a single issue of a Port Townsend newspaper concisely conveyed this preoccupation. The Waterman & Katz emporium claimed to "make it a specialty fitting out Klondike gold seekers." Grocers and bootmakers proffered food and footwear "for the Klondike!" Wright's Racket Store held in stock 1,000 "complete and accurate guides, giving the distances between points and maps of the Klondike and Yukon." The Townsend Awning Company had tents "and all kinds of Canvas" available for sale "at short notice" to departing "Klondikers." Establishments selling items of little or no use in the north also used gold rush themes in their ads. "Some Say 'Ho!' for Klondyke!," proclaimed a bicycle seller. "We Say 'Ho!' for a Good Bike—Cheap!"[52]

Because no miner could find gold without actually going to Alaska, transportation was another obvious source of profit. Old memories of the California trail apparently stirred a number of poorly informed souls. Forty covered wagons passed through Seattle in early August carrying overland trekkers north by unknown, and indeed non-existent, pathways. Technologically up-to-date promoters sought capital for equally dubious ventures. One inventor announced a plan for a gasoline fueled airship, a balloon capable of taking passengers from Puget Sound to the Yukon at a speed of 25 mph. Another developer proposed sending insulated cars, mounted on runners and drawn by steam engines, across the wintertime passes. Various speculators promised, should investors be forthcoming, to construct a railroad from Spokane to the diggings, as well as shorter lines from Alaskan and British Columbian ports.[53]

Seaworthy shipping provided a more realistic option. Enough vessels eventually were placed in service to afford travelers "a steamer for every day of the month," driving down fares and earnings alike. In the early months, however, the "tremendous demand for passenger and freight room" created truly golden opportunities for ship owners. Coastal mill companies eagerly disposed of their "old hulks" at unexpectedly lucrative prices. The same lumbering firms also secured huge fees from charters, with the Port Blakely Mill Company earning $40,000 from a single voyage to St. Michael at the mouth of the Yukon River. Schooners and other sailing craft, decks piled high with unstable cargo, also were pressed into use despite the danger of severe ocean storms. Puget Sound yards, meanwhile, set-to in earnest constructing steamships and riverboats for the Alaskan trade.[54]

Under these money making circumstances, dreadful abuses were difficult to avoid. The Seattle owners of the *Humboldt* sold passage to inexperienced easterners for an August 1897 voyage to St. Michael, requiring the ticket holders to work the sub-standard vessel up the Yukon and to assume liability for accidents and injury. The passengers at least arrived safely, a luxury often enough denied to other Alaska bound compatriots. "Steamers which have for years been in the 'boneyards,'" a news account reported of a lamentably widespread practice, "have been repainted and hastily refitted." Tidewater interests insisted that federal inspectors guaranteed the "safe condition" of all vessels, but these officials were all too ready to engage, for a price, in thoroughgoing non-diligence. The ancient *Eliza Anderson*, rotting on the flats after four decades of heavy duty on Puget Sound, sailed in September without lifeboats, eventually running out of coal and winding up on a beach short of its destination. Three ships were wrecked on uncharted rocks, a fourth exploded and a fifth was abandoned by its fearful crew. "The Klondiker...literally takes his life in his hands," one newspaper noted, "from the moment his steamer leaves the docks."[55]

Ignoring such perils in the interest of maximizing trade, Seattle merchants secured the leading role in economically exploiting the gold rush. Recognizing that "it is a difficult task to divert the trade when it once sets strongly in one direction," local leaders capitalized on advantages, including Seattle's existing northern commercial connections, linkage to three transcontinental lines—the GN, NP and Canadian Pacific—and possession of the main Puget Sound post office. Seattle's chamber of commerce spent $2,000 a month promoting Elliott Bay in eastern newspapers and magazines, and 100,000 copies of special Yukon editions published by the city's newspapers were distributed to train stations, libraries and city halls across the nation. Laying claim, as a result, to three-quarters of the business, outfitters credited "the old-time spirit of Seattle push." Competitors grumbled instead about "the old arbitrary spirit which long sought to rule the entire state of Washington."[56]

Other major urban ports along the Pacific coast were equally adept, though not as fully successful, in "blowing their Klondike horns." In the Bay Area, where the populace went "crazy" over the Yukon excitement, San Francisco adopted a number of stratagems in attempting to gain business, including the publication of maps suggesting that Alaska was but a few hundred miles north of the Golden Gate, with no ports in between. Portland boasted of having the lowest prices and a superior representation in Skagway. Tacoma's chamber of commerce also was promotion oriented. "The opportunity that is presented is one that very seldom comes," a Commencement Bay editor affirmed in demanding an activist approach, "and it behooves this city to make the most of it." Victoria and Van-couver engaged in competition as well, even sending agents to Elliott Bay to meet incoming trains and divert miners to outfitting places north of the border.[57]

An energetic commercial scheme also was attempted in the Inland Empire. Initially, though, regional leaders argued against wealth seekers going north, insisting that "Spokane's Klondike" was "at home" in the mines of northeast Washington, southeast British Columbia and the Idaho panhandle. Local news-papers stressed the extreme dangers of the trip and the no less daunting obstacles to success. A "food famine" loomed in the Yukon because of the impossibility of shipping in provisions during the winter, and mass starvation undoubtedly would ensue. There was, according to a discouraging theme broadcast from Spokane, "only one journey more intense than the desire of the man with the Klondike fever to be in Dawson City—the longing of the man already in Dawson City to return to the land where square meals are sold for 25 cents."[58]

Inland merchants soon concluded, however, that by exhibiting a bit of dash and hyperbole, they too might profit from the rush north. Upon reflection, Spo-kane claimed to be a "natural starting point for American prospectors." Heavily promoted by the city's imaginative chamber of commerce as the old Hudson's Bay Company trail, an overland wagon and packing route supposedly led to the upper Yukon drainage, where miners could easily construct boats for the final stage to Dawson. The trail supposedly was open in deepest winter, avoided all mountain ranges and crossed regions abounding in water, fish and game. "It is the poor man's route," Spokane business interests declared. "He need not pay a dol-lar for transportation or freight." Expeditions sent out to locate the exact route, unfortunately, were thwarted by harsh weather and impenetrable wilderness. Spokane fell back, in the end, upon predictions that the Yukon's inevitable failure would benefit the local economy, with scores of returning prospectors augment-ing eastern Washington's population.[59]

By the fall of 1897, the "frozen truth" about the Klondike became fully evi-dent to all but the most irresponsible profiteers. Food would, in fact, be dear and prices high, at least over the winter. Accounts from Dawson reported that the provident and the improvident—those who had come with and those who had come without adequate supplies—already were preparing for weeks of conflict, perhaps even bloodshed, over provisions. "The speedy rule of the hard law of survival of the fittest" prevailed in the passes, claimed a traveling Oregonian. Apocryphally, preachers supposedly swore like enraged teamsters on the rugged trails and pack animals committed suicide rather than be driven into the mountains. The federal government prepared a relief expedition, only to cancel the enterprise amidst the general public conviction that famine stories were a ploy devised by merchants intent on supplying the soldiers.[60]

Few questioned that the crisis, whatever its exact magnitude, was but a temporary setback. "There is little doubt that in the spring there will be a great exodus in that direction," most observers agreed. An unhappy fact—conceded even by persons inclining to believe that the Alaska-Yukon boundary was improperly located—was that Dawson lay in Canada, which therefore posed a genuine dilemma. Canadian authorities had promptly established a licensing and taxation system, and at the same time imposed customs duties and special fees. Americans on the scene, and Washington's commercial towns at a distance, protested these "outrageously oppressive" acts on the part of a foreign government. "Unable themselves, through lethargy and inertness," the *P-I* blustered of the Canadians, "to prospect, discover and develop a region so inhospitable, they suffer others to do it unhindered until something is found, and then greedily sweep down like the robber barons of old to gather plunder." Patriotic, or inebriated, miners threatened to mount an "uprising" against arbitrary rule. Other voices, among them commentators usually inclined to sane reflection, demanded that the U.S. Army be sent to the diggings to protect hard working American citizens against this imposition.[61]

As those experienced in the seasonably limited nature of Yukon mining had predicted, gold returns for 1897 fell short of the frenzied expectation. The north was "a land of gold and mystery…sweeping…to the shores of the Arctic sea," but the wealth could not easily be removed by poorly equipped prospectors arriving at the end of a brief summer. When newspapermen spent $6,000 on tugboat charters to meet another return of the fabled *Portland* off Cape Flattery, they learned that the steamer carried only a small amount of gold and there were no reports of new discoveries. Army officers stationed in Alaska noted that a mere 7 percent of the miners reaching the Klondike found enough precious metal to cover expenses. The excitement nonetheless was expected to resume, under far better conditions, in the spring of 1898. "Nine out of ten persons going to the Klondike will make a failure," a Seattle newspaper noted in explaining the continuing rationale for chance taking. "Unfortunately…it cannot be determined in advance who are to form the lucky one-tenth."[62]

In summing up events, observers of the Pacific Northwest scene concluded that the most significant impacts had been in "waking up of our people" and restoring confidence, regionally and nationally, among a populace long in "apathetic" mode. "California gold was the wonderful magician in 1849," a Puget Sound daily suggested. "Klondike gold was the magician in 1897." Merchants and shipowners, in truth, had earned a great deal of money, but the conviction that the gold rush ended the hard times was more of a dramatic fable than economic reality. The "work" of two mill laborers "knocking down…a ton of ore worth $200 seems commonplace in contrast with the picturesque spectacle of two men washing that value of gold nuggets from a creek bed," an east-of-the-mountains editor wrote in comparing the importance of sustained, if mundane, local industrial enterprise to the Yukon legend. Recovery derived as much from the production of grain fields, coal mines and Douglas fir forests, economic activities already on the advance at the time of the *Portland*'s ballyhooed arrival in Seattle. Instead of publishing another Alaska special number at the beginning of 1898, the *P-I* crafted a "Greater Washington" edition. "The interests of the people of Washington are one," the paper maintained of the substantive Pacific Northwest commercial order, "for prosperity cannot come to any city, county or section without making its effects felt throughout the whole state."[63]

❧❧

"Everybody is in luck this year," a Big Bend weekly observed in celebrating the general economic situation across the state in the fall of 1897. Returning to Tacoma from a tour of coastal towns, Chauncey Griggs reported that "everything" was "looking better all over the country." The Tacoman's special interest, lumbering, generated positive returns. Increasing demand in the railway and overseas markets, and high tariff policies instituted by the McKinley administration, accounted for an upswing in prices of between $2 and $4 per thousand feet, depending upon grade. Mills on the eastern shore of Puget Sound with efficient domestic and water connections ran on a "night and day" schedule. The many employees departing for Alaska were easily replaced from among the mounting ranks of immigration to the Pacific Northwest, limiting the short-term pressure on wage scales and keeping pay increases to a level tolerated by management.[64]

East of the Cascades, the wheat harvest more than fulfilled springtime expectations, emerging as the "Klondike product" of Washington's interior. In an awesome combination, the largest crop on record was marketed at prices not seen since the pre-panic years. Field hands, machinery and rolling stock were barely sufficient, at substantially increased costs, to handle and haul grain in timely fashion. Farmers earned between $3,000 and $5,000 in net profit for the season, allowing them to pay off debt and add acreage. Land prices surged in the Big Bend, the Palouse and the Walla Walla Valley. Homesteads previously ignored at $15 an acre attracted ready cash buyers at rates in excess of $30.[65]

Flush times, by any measure, were back in all parts of the state. The influx of newcomers generated rental income for landlords and encouraged a resumption of building in cities and towns. Bank deposits continued at a sharp upward trend. With stores, homes and schools under construction, grain coming in at two dozen bushels to the acre and merchants restocking shelves, a local newspaper reported that "Big Benders have nothing in particular to complain of at present." On the coast, "the tide" had, appropriately enough, "certainly turned at last in the affairs of South Bend." Sawmills and shingle plants ran full time, canneries doubled capacity and dilapidated housing underwent repair.[66]

Together, general prosperity and the Alaska excitement meant, as a leading timber industry figure suggested, that "the eyes of the whole world" once again focused upon the Pacific coast. With good reason Washington looked forward to "a tide of immigration…unprecedented since the boom days of 1889." Some would go to the Yukon and some would settle on farms or begin new lives in the fast growing cities. Regardless of the eventual gold production from the northern mines, the region, according to no less a figure than James J. Hill, had an all-but-guaranteed future. "Aside from Alaska," the railroad magnate reflected, "Washington has within itself an abundance of wealth, in the water, in the fields, in the mines, and in her forests; and the permanent and great prosperity of the State will come through the development of these resources."[67]

Notes

1. *Northwest*, 15 (Jan. 1897), 28.
2. A Republican witness described the governor elect's inaugural stroll as "a case of Jeffersonian simplicity being carried to a point approaching fanaticism." Unidentified newspaper clippings in Scrapbooks, John R. Rogers Papers, Washington State University Library; *Northwest*, 15 (Jan. 1897), 24.
3. Inaugural Address, n.d., Rogers Papers, Washington State University Library; Carroll H. Woody, "Populism in Washington: A Study of the Legislature of 1897," *Washington Historical Quarterly* [hereafter cited as *WHQ*], 21 (April 1930), 108–9.
4. The ex-governor's explanation, that he had simply forgotten about the money innocently left behind in his old Seattle office, was widely dismissed as "a little fishy." McGraw's remaining defenders insisted that "none but a fool" would have engaged in "willful [mis]appropriation" and then abandoned "in a public office…open to public inspection, the positive proof of such act." The moustache reference was to McGraw's famously luxuriant chops. Unidentified newspaper clipping in Scrapbooks, Rogers Papers, Washington State University Library; *Seattle Times*, Feb. 27; March 22, 24, 1897; June 17, 1898; *Seattle Post-Intelligencer*, March 21, 1897; Seattle *Argus*, March 27, 1897; Spokane *Spokesman-Review*, March 28, rep. from Whatcom *Reveille*, 29, rep. from Lincoln County *Populist*, 31, 1897; *Pullman Tribune*, March 27, 1897.
5. *Pullman Tribune*, Jan. 23; April 17; July 3, 1897; *Seattle Times*, Jan. 11, 1897; *Tacoma Daily Ledger*, April 8, 1897; *Seattle Post-Intelligencer*, Sept. 8, 1897.
6. In addition to subsidizing press outlets, Rogers exhibited a forward looking interest in the general use of public relations. "The man who might possibly have made a janitor

wished to be Prime Minister," the governor observed of a related problem. "Incompetents, impracticables and men criminally inclined were alike strenuous in their demands." Russell Blankenship, "The Political Thought of John R. Rogers," *Pacific Northwest Quarterly* [hereafter cited as *PNQ*], 37 (Jan. 1946), 3–4; John R. Rogers to W.W. Langborne, Feb. 26, 1898; to A.J. Blethen, June 28, 1898; to George Turner, Feb. 16; May 4, 1898; to P.O. Chilstrom, March 7, 1898; to F.V. Adams, Feb. 3, 1898, John R. Rogers Papers, Washington State Archives; Letter on Patronage, Nov. 27, 1896, Rogers Papers, Washington State University Library.

7. *Aberdeen Herald*, Nov. 5, 1896; Spokane *Spokesman-Review*, Jan. 5; Oct. 30, 31, 1897; *Spokane Daily Chronicle*, April 15, 1898.

8. "The distinctive features of the populist movement," a commentator sympathetic to reform pointed out, "have not been in any degree indorsed by the democrats or silver republicans." *Seattle Post-Intelligencer*, Sept. 15; Nov. 8, 1898; Seattle *Argus*, Nov. 14, 1896; George H. Emerson to A.M. Simpson, July 28, 1896; to Harry C. Heermans, Nov. 9, 1896, George H. Emerson Letterbooks, University of Washington Library; Chauncey W. Griggs to L.B. Royce, Nov. 11, 1896, St. Paul & Tacoma Lumber Co. Records, University of Washington Library; Cyrus Walker to A.W. Jackson, Nov. 14, 1896, Puget Mill Co. Records, Ames Coll., University of Washington Library; *Tacoma Daily News*, Jan. 18, 1897.

9. Gold standard advocates joked about the fusionist "oversight" in neglecting the monetary issue at Olympia. At the local level, ousted Republicans slashed their salaries once the election returns were in, intending to force fusion successors to either live on low pay or attempt politically risky restoration of the old rates. Emerson to Heermans, Nov. 9, 1896; to H.C. Henry, Jan. 27, 1897, Emerson Letterbooks; *Seattle Post-Intelligencer*, Feb. 27, 1897, rep. from Ilwaco *Journal*; Unidentified newspaper clipping in Scrapbooks, Rogers Papers, Washington State University Library; Spokane *Spokesman-Review*, Dec. 20, 1896.

10. *Seattle Times*, Jan. 2, 19, 20, 1897; *Seattle Post-Intelligencer*, March 13, 1897.

11. A number of pundits suggested that the senate seat be "sold" on the first day of the session to the "highest bidder, thereby avoiding wasted time & energy & rewarding the individual who would win in the end anyway." Twenty-two persons received at least one vote in the early balloting. Dismissing Senator Squire's supposed conversion to populism, an eastern Washington editor observed that the incumbent would "admit of almost anything" to win a new term. Senator John Wilson, fully aware of the implications for his own 1899 reelection prospects, worked behind the scenes to thwart Turner. Spokane residents chuckled that with Wilson and Turner in the senate and W.C. Jones in the house, U.S. Representative J. Hamilton Lewis of Seattle need only move to the Inland Empire to give their city a monopoly of the congressional delegation. *Pullman Tribune*, Jan. 16; Feb. 6, 1897; *Seattle Times*, Jan. 6, 23, 29, 30, 1897; Seattle *Argus*, Dec. 26, 1896; Jan. 9, 1897; *Aberdeen Herald*, Jan. 14, 1897; Spokane *Spokesman-Review*, Jan. 9, rep. from Pasco *News*, 30, 31, 1897; *Ellensburg Localizer*, Feb. 13, 1897; *Seattle Post-Intelligencer*, March 5, 1897; Claudius O. Johnson, "George Turner: The Background of a Statesman," *PNQ*, 34 (July 1943), 256–62.

12. The fusionists, a dismayed Populist noted, "have no definite organization, no chosen leaders, and are bushwhacking among themselves." The railroad commission, one enthusiast asserted, would "be to the all and more than the interstate commerce commission is to the United States." Unidentified newspaper clipping in Scrapbooks, Rogers Papers, Washington State University Library; *Ellensburg Localizer*, Feb. 20, 1897; Spokane *Spokesman-*

Review, Dec. 16, 20, 1896; Feb. 12, 13, 1897; Aug. 3, 1898; *Tacoma Daily News,* Jan. 20, 1897; *Seattle Post-Intelligencer,* Nov. 22, 1898; *Aberdeen Herald,* March 4, 1897.

13. Critics complained that the railroad legislation applied only to grain shipments and had no impact on the Oregon Railway & Navigation Company, an interstate carrier, thereby encouraging the roads to divert traffic from Puget Sound to Portland, which threatened fiscal ruination to such important feeders as the Washington Central. *Tacoma Daily News,* Jan. 25, 1897; *Seattle Post-Intelligencer,* Feb. 25, 1897; Feb. 26, 1899; Spokane *Spokesman-Review,* Jan. 3; Feb. 16, 1897; Aug. 9, 1898; March 4, 1899; *Aberdeen Herald,* March 4, 1897; *Seattle Times,* March 22, 1897.

14. *Northwest,* 15 (May 1897), 24; *Seattle Post-Intelligencer,* Sept. 25, 1897; *Spokane Daily Chronicle,* Feb. 18, 1898; Seattle *Argus,* Dec. 11, 1897.

15. According to one estimate, passage of the exemption bill briefly reduced the number of taxpayers by one-third. In another fiscally controversial move, the legislature addressed an enormous local government administrative burden—King County alone had 90,000 delinquent tax cases—by reducing, and in some cases eliminating, interest and penalties on overdue taxes, the idea being to promote voluntary payment on such accounts. *Seattle Post-Intelligencer,* April 6, 13; June 25, 1897; Oct. 28, 1898; March 17, 1899; *Seattle Times,* March 5; June 24, 1897; Spokane *Spokesman-Review,* April 15, 1897; *Chehalis Bee,* March 19; May 21, 1897; *Spokane Daily Chronicle,* April 7; Sept. 9, 1898; *Tacoma Daily Ledger,* April 2, 1898; *Tacoma Daily News,* Sept. 27, 1898; Seattle *Argus,* March 19, 1898; Rogers to Blethen, March 26, 1898, Rogers Papers.

16. The fusionists continued the traditional risky policy of depositing state funds in "certain favored banks." The UW reduction was considered an overdue efficiency move, since the state had been spending $200 a year per student at the Seattle campus, compared to $100 at the University of Minnesota, supposedly a comparable institution. *Tacoma Daily News,* Jan. 20, 29; Oct. 12, 1897; Aug. 27, 1898; *Seattle Times,* Oct. 14, 1896; Feb. 5; March 1, 25, 1897; Sept. 22, 1898; Spokane *Spokesman-Review,* April 4, 1897; Feb. 28, 1898; *Tacoma Daily Ledger,* May 23, 1898; *Spokane Daily Chronicle,* Aug. 31, 1898; *Seattle Post-Intelligencer,* Oct. 29, 1898.

17. Olympia residents alone condemned the capitol veto as "venomous" irresponsibility. Elsewhere, the public tended to regard inhabitants of the city as "very greedy and very intolerant" for attempting to foist the structure upon an impoverished state. A Seattle wit suggested that the "foundation" be converted into a makeshift asylum, with the assorted commissioners, architects and contractors committed as the first inmates to atone for their "foolishness." The fusion era University of Washington regularly lobbied against funding for Cheney and Whatcom, fearing the diversion of money from its budget. The town of Cheney raised money to look after the shuttered buildings until the campus reopened for the 1898–1899 school year. The structures at Whatcom, only recently completed, remained closed. *Northwest,* 15 (March 1897), 25; *Seattle Times,* Feb. 5, 9; March 10, 17, 23, 1897; Spokane *Spokesman-Review,* Feb. 7, 14; March 14, 17, 21, 1897; May 15; Aug. 28, 1898; Feb. 26; March 1, 9, 1899; Olympia *Washington Standard,* July 23, 1897; Seattle *Argus,* Feb. 13, 27, 1897; Norman J. Johnston, "A Capitol in Search of an Architect," *PNQ,* 73 (Jan. 1982), 9; *Tacoma Daily News,* March 20, 1897; *Pullman Tribune,* March 27, 1897; *Ellensburg Localizer,* March 20, 1897; Richard Winsor to Rogers, July 16, 1898, Rogers Papers, Washington State Archives.

18. *Tacoma Daily Ledger,* April 5, 7, 21, 1897; Seattle *Argus,* April 10, 1897; Spokane *Spokesman-Review,* April 21; Sept. 12, 16, 1897; May 7, 1898; John Yeend to Rogers, April 11, 1898, Rogers Papers, Washington State Archives; *Chehalis Bee,* Oct. 8, 1897; *Pullman*

Tribune, March 20; Aug. 28, 1897; *Seattle Times*, June 30, 1897; *Seattle Post-Intelligencer*, Sept. 10, 16, 1897; *Tacoma Daily News*, Sept. 20, 1897.

19. A veteran observer accused the university of "prostituting and ruining the…educational interests of our fair State." On the basis of contemporary events, one editor detailed the necessary qualifications of a fusionist UW president: "The successful applicant must be a nonentity in every sense of the word. He must have no ideas of his own…He must know nothing, do nothing, see nothing. He must be a mere figurehead…He must wink at all irregularities, turn his back religiously on all jobs, and bow and scrape to all fakirs and confidence workers." *Seattle Post-Intelligencer*, May 30, 1897; Aug. 12, 13; Sept. 16, 1898; Seattle *Argus*, April 24; May 1, 15; June 5; Oct. 2, 9, 1897; New Whatcom *Daily Reveille*, Oct. 19, 20, 1897; *Seattle Times*, Oct. 1, 4, 1897; Aug. 13, 15, 1898; *Tacoma Daily News*, Oct. 19, 1897; Edmond S. Meany to Rogers, July 6, 1897; Rogers to L.D. Godshall, May 23, 1898, both Rogers Papers, Washington State Archives; George A. Frykman, *Seattle's Historian and Promoter: The Life of Edmond Stephen Meany* (Pullman: Washington State University Press, 1998), 74–75, 78–80; Olympia *Washington Standard*, Oct. 8, 1897.

20. *Tacoma Daily News*, Sept. 12, 1898; Woody, "Populism in Washington," 103–19; *Seattle Post-Intelligencer*, Aug. 20, 1898; Seattle *Argus*, Aug. 20, 1898; Spokane *Spokesman-Review*, April 21, 1897; *Tacoma Daily Ledger*, April 6, 1898; H.N. Belt to Rogers, May 8, 1897; George H. King to Rogers, March 11, 1898; Rogers to King, March 10, 1898, all Rogers Papers, Washington State Archives.

21. *Seattle Post-Intelligencer*, Feb. 26, 1897; *Aberdeen Herald*, Feb. 25, 1897; *Ellensburg Localizer*, March 13, 1897.

22. George Emerson fell ill from the prolonged strain of hard times. "It seemed to have wheels in it," he wrote of one migraine bout, "and those wheels all revolving saw mill appliances." Emerson to Heermans, Feb. 9, 1897; to L.S. Dyar, March 1, 1897; to Simpson, March 16, 1897, Emerson Letterbooks; Griggs to Charles Foster, Feb. 23, 1897, St. Paul & Tacoma Lumber Co. Records; Walker to Jackson, May 13, 1897, Puget Mill Co. Records; Seattle *Argus*, May 29, 1897; *Tacoma Daily Ledger*, May 2, 1897; *Northwest*, 16 (Feb. 1898), 31; E.V. Smalley, "Four Weeks in a Car," *Northwest*, 15 (June 1897), 6–7; *Tacoma Daily News*, Nov. 11, 1896; W.A. White to Henry M. Richards, Oct. 26, 1898, Washington Water Power Co. Records, Washington State University Library.

23. *Seattle Post-Intelligencer*, July 29, 1898; Spokane *Spokesman-Review*, April 9, 1897; New Whatcom *Daily Reveille*, Sept. 29, 1897; *Chehalis Bee*, June 4, 1897; Portland *Oregonian*, May 8, 1898.

24. Smalley, "Four Weeks in a Car," 5, 7–8; Seattle *Argus*, May 29, 1897; John Fahey, "When the Dutch Owned Spokane," *PNQ*, 72 (Jan. 1981), 2–10; Spokane *Spokesman-Review*, March 6, 7, 1897.

25. Smalley, "Four Weeks in a Car," 3; *Seattle Post-Intelligencer*, April 10, 17, rep. from Tekoa *Times*, 18, 1897; *Northwest*, 15 (Jan. 1897), 30; (Feb. 1897), 38; (April 1897), 24.

26. Also interested in service upgrades, the NP switched its entire track between Tacoma and Seattle from narrow to broad gauge and completed the long delayed Grays Harbor extension from Aberdeen to Hoquiam. "The increased earnings of Western railways," transportation expert E.V. Smalley recorded, "are a very gratifying sign of the times." Spokane *Spokesman-Review*, Feb. 4; April 17; Sept. 1, 1897; Jan. 3, 5, 1898; *Seattle Post-Intelligencer*, June 12; Aug. 21, 1897; *Seattle Times*, Feb. 5, 1897; *Tacoma Daily News*, March 8, 1897; *Northwest*, 15 (March 1897), 24–25; (Nov. 1897), 33; (Dec. 1897), 22; 16 (March 1898), 30–32; (Sept. 1898), 30; Seattle *Argus*, Nov. 20, 1897; John Fahey, *Inland Empire: D.C. Corbin and Spokane* (Seattle: University of Washington Press, 1965), 188–91.

27. South Bend *Willapa Harbor Pilot*, May 27, 1898; *Northwest*, 15 (Jan. 1897), 13; (Feb. 1897), 15; (Oct. 1897), 30; Walker to W.H. Talbot, Dec. 7, 1896, Puget Mill Co. Records; Emerson to C.F. White, May 25, 1897, Emerson Letterbooks; *Seattle Post-Intelligencer*, July 26, 1897; *Seattle Times*, July 12, 1897; Frederick Weyerhaeuser to J.P. Weyerhaeuser, Aug. 18, 1896, Weyerhaeuser Family Papers, Minnesota Historical Society; Robert E. Ficken, "Weyerhaeuser and the Pacific Northwest Timber Industry, 1899–1903," *PNQ*, 70 (Oct. 1979), 147.

28. Israel C. Russell, "The Wheat-Lands of Washington," *Harper's Weekly*, 41 (July 24, 1897), 735; Portland *Oregonian*, Aug. 28, 1897; Spokane *Spokesman-Review*, May 2, 1897, rep. from Garfield *Enterprise*.

29. Some commentators warned that publication of optimistic planting accounts would cause an unwarranted market collapse. *Tacoma Daily News*, Feb. 2, 1897; *Seattle Post-Intelligencer*, Aug. 15, 21, 1897; Spokane *Spokesman-Review*, Jan. 1; April 12, 26, 1897; *Ellensburg Localizer*, Feb. 6, 1897; *Northwest*, 15 (May 1897), 12; Portland *Oregonian*, Aug. 22, 25, 27, 1897; Olympia *Washington Standard*, July 30, 1897; *Pullman Tribune*, Aug. 14, 1897.

30. Spokane *Spokesman-Review*, Feb. 22, 1897, rep. from Vancouver *Independent*; *Seattle Times*, Sept. 20; Dec. 14, 1897; Sept. 22, 1898; *Northwest*, 15 (Jan. 1897), 41; 16 (Jan. 1898), 30; Norman H. Clark, *Mill Town* (Seattle: University of Washington Press, 1970), 33; New Whatcom *Daily Reveille*, Sept. 22, 1897; Smalley, "Four Weeks in a Car," 8.

31. Inland Empire mercantile and banking institutions took in gold from 300 Colville Reservation claims by the end of 1896. The energetic Native American profiteering cited in the press ironically contrasted with pre-1896 newspaper claims that Indian refusal to exploit farming and other development opportunities made the reservation "a blot upon the state and a barrier against progress." *Seattle Post-Intelligencer*, Sept. 15, 1897; Spokane *Spokesman-Review*, March 1; July 15, 1898; March 10, 1899; *West Shore*, 16 (Jan. 25 1890), 108; *Spokane Falls Review*, July 9, 1890; *Spokane Review*, April 24; Nov. 20, 1891; March 2; Aug. 9, 1892; *Seattle Times*, Feb. 20, 1896; *Northwest*, 15 (Jan. 1897), 32; (March 1897), 8; *Spokane Daily Chronicle*, April 11, 1898.

32. Despite having to pay Canadian tariff duties, U.S. merchants still were able to undersell competitors by shipping over the Canadian Pacific transcontinental line. Spokane *Spokesman-Review*, April 23, 24; Oct. 15, 1897; Fahey, *Inland Empire*, 166; *Northwest*, 15 (Jan. 1897), 30; (March 1897), 8–10; (April 1897), 29; Smalley, "Four Weeks in a Car," 5–6.

33. "There is hardly a line of business represented in Seattle," an Elliott Bay weekly advised in May, "that is not in better condition today than it has been for five years." *Walla Walla Union*, Aug. 12, 1897; *Walla Walla Statesman*, Aug. 28, 1897; *Yakima Herald*, July 15, 1897; *Seattle Post-Intelligencer*, April 10; July 18, 1897; Griggs to F.W. Miller, July 17, 1897, St. Paul & Tacoma Lumber Co. Records; *Northwest*, 15 (Feb. 1897), 20; Smalley, "Four Weeks in a Car," 3; Emerson to Edwin Woodward, Aug. 18, 1897, Emerson Letterbooks; *Tacoma Daily News*, Feb. 11; July 26, 1897; *Seattle Argus*, May 1, 1897.

34. *Seattle Post-Intelligencer*, July 16, 17, 1897; J. Kingston Pierce, "River of Gold," *Columbia: The Magazine of Northwest History* [hereafter cited as *Columbia*], 11 (Summer 1997), 24–25; William R. Hunt, "Goldfield Gateway," *Columbia*, 4 (Winter 1990–1991), 36–37; *Seattle Times*, July 19, 1897.

35. C.A. Snowden, "Another Account," *Harper's Weekly*, 41 (Aug. 7, 1897), 791; Hunt, "Goldfield Gateway," 37; Eugene Semple to Daughter, July 17, 1897, Eugene Semple Papers, University of Washington Library; *Seattle Post-Intelligencer*, July 20, 1897. The eastern journalist is quoted in Pierre Berton, *Klondike: The Last Great Gold Rush, 1896–*

1899 (Toronto: McClelland and Stewart, 1958, 1987 rev. ed.), 101. According to a recent article, Seattle had exhibited little interest in Alaska prior to 1897. Pierce, "River of Gold," 24–25. "The rush flared, faltered, and faded...within the space of roughly a year," claims a well regarded survey of western mining history. Paula Mitchell Marks, *Precious Dust, The American Gold Rush Era: 1848–1900* (New York: William Morrow, 1994), 126.

36. Proponents of Alaska's political incorporation conceded that "the tail would...be many times bigger than the dog." *Tacoma Daily News*, Nov. 8, 1892; Jan. 27, 1893; Kathryn Morse, *The Nature of Gold: An Environmental History of the Klondike Gold Rush* (Seattle: University of Washington Press, 2003), 169–70; Jonas A. Jonasson, "Portland and the Alaska Trade," *PNQ*, 30 (April 1939), 132; *Tacoma Daily Ledger*, June 15, 1890; *West Shore*, 16 (Jan. 18, 1890), 78; Olympia *Washington Standard*, Sept. 18, 1891.

37. Cheaper costs allowed the marketing of Alaskan salmon at $1 per dozen cans, compared to $1.35 from the Columbia River. *Spokane Falls Review*, Dec. 31, 1890; *Spokane Review*, Dec. 12, 1891; Feb. 4, 1893; *Tacoma Daily Ledger*, Aug. 19, 1890; Feb. 20, 1891; *West Shore*, 16 (March 29, 1890), 386; 17 (Feb. 7, 1891), 97; Portland *Oregonian*, March 17, 1896.

38. Some deckchair adventurers combined practical concerns with sight seeing. Frederick Weyerhaeuser, for instance, spent a good portion of his 1891 trip "examining the...lumber forests of Alaska." *Tacoma Daily Ledger*, Aug. 19, 1890; *Northwest*, 8 (Nov. 1890), 5–9; *Seattle Press-Times*, Feb. 11; Aug. 3, 1891; *Tacoma Daily News*, July 6, 1891; June 12, 1895; *Seattle Post-Intelligencer*, Aug. 4, 1891; *Seattle Morning Journal*, Nov. 6, 1889; *Spokane Review*, Aug. 12, 1892.

39. Early mining camps were named for river distance markers, which tended, from the difficulties of wilderness measurement, to be wildly inaccurate. *Seattle Post-Intelligencer*, Oct. 22, 1890, rep. from Nanaimo *Free Press*; *West Shore*, 15 (May 1889), 276; 16 (April 26, 1890), 533, rep. from Juneau *Mining Record*; (Nov. 8, 1890), 204; *Spokane Falls Review*, March 28, 1891; *Seattle Press-Times*, Aug. 14, 1891; Clarence L. Andrews, ed., "Some Notes on the Yukon by Stewart Menzies," *PNQ*, 32 (April 1941), 201.

40. The first female gold rusher traveled to the Yukon in 1892. Less adventurous prospectors preferred to work the coastal beaches. *Spokane Review*, Dec. 3, 1891; March 24; Dec. 5, 1892; *Spokane Falls Review*, Sept. 11, 1890; March 28, 1891; *Tacoma Daily News*, March 14, 1890; *Tacoma Daily Ledger*, May 7, 1890; *West Shore*, 15 (May 1889), 276; *Northwest*, 11 (Dec. 1893), 13; *Seattle Post-Intelligencer*, Oct. 22, 1890; Sept. 16, 1892.

41. A returnee from the Yukon reported that gold "is found in greater or lesser quantities in all of the creeks." *Seattle Post-Intelligencer*, Dec. 12, 1893; March 3, 1895; *Seattle Press-Times*, June 4, 1894; March 9, 1895; *Seattle Telegraph*, June 27, 1894; Spokane *Spokesman-Review*, Feb. 25, 1895; *Seattle Times*, Jan. 9, 1896.

42. One historian dates the beginning of the gold rush proper to 1893. In the first week of March 1896, the *City of Topeka* carried 300 passengers and 100 dogs north, while the *Willapa* sailed "with a cargo of humanity, dogs and freight." Portland *Oregonian*, March 6, 9, 1896; Stephen Haycox, *Alaska: An American Colony* (Seattle: University of Washington Press, 2002), 201–3; Caspar Whitney, "The Stampede to Alaska for Gold," *Harper's Weekly*, 40 (April 4, 1896), 318; *Seattle Times*, Feb. 14, 20, 1896.

43. Many miners traveling with insufficient funds were stranded on the Alaska coast when steamer fares for the return voyage increased from $15 to $32. Juneau merchants accused Puget Sound competitors of burning all Alaskan newspapers found on incoming vessels, thereby preventing north-bound prospectors from discovering that supplies cost less on the scene. Spokane *Spokesman-Review*, Jan. 25; Feb. 22; April 22, 1897; Seattle *Argus*,

March 20, 1897; *Seattle Times*, Jan. 20, 1896; March 15, 1897; *Tacoma Daily News*, June 27, 1890; July 19, 1897; Hunt, "Goldfield Gateway," 36; Portland *Oregonian*, March 5, 1896; *Tacoma Daily Ledger*, May 4, 1897; *Seattle Post-Intelligencer*, March 17, 1896.

44. *Tacoma Daily News*, July 19, 1897; *Seattle Post-Intelligencer*, July 17, 1897.

45. "The present eldorado is all staked," a veteran Puget Sounder claimed in the summer of 1897, "and it may require an exhaustive and prolonged search to discover another." *Seattle Times*, July 17, 19, 1897; *Aberdeen Herald*, July 22, 1897; Seattle *Argus*, July 24, 1897; Olympia *Washington Standard*, July 30, 1897.

46. "Probably no place on the Pacific coast of over a thousand people," a Yakima resident wrote, "is without its personal interest in the Klondyke excitement." A practical minded editor warned that "if this mad rush for the Klondyke continues there will be more dead than living men up there before spring." An eastern Washington paper made the same point about the impractical nature of the journey: "There is one advantage in prospecting at Clondyke over prospecting in South America. Dead bodies do not fall into decay at Clondyke, being preserved by the cold." *South Bend Journal*, Sept. 3, 1897; Berton, *Klondike*, 101; *Seattle Times*, Sept. 16, 1897; Walker to Talbot, Aug. 15, 1897, Puget Mill Co. Records; Semple to Daughter, Aug. 17, 1897, Semple Papers; *Seattle Post-Intelligencer*, Aug. 5, 1897; *Tacoma Daily News*, Aug. 2; Oct. 4, 1897; Olympia *Washington Standard*, Aug. 13, 1897; *Northwest*, 15 (Aug. 1897), 24; Seattle *Argus*, July 31, 1897; Portland *Oregonian*, Aug. 26, 1897; *Yakima Herald*, Aug. 12, 1897; *Hoquiam Washingtonian*, Aug. 5, 1897; *Pullman Tribune*, Aug. 7, 1897.

47. Debunking early reports on gold shipments, an Inland Empire observer insisted that "more gold has been lost in daily newspapers in Portland, Seattle, Tacoma and Spokane than has come out of the Klondike." Alaskan gold production for all of 1897 barely exceeded $2 million, substantially below the California figure. A Seattle critic quipped that the city's gold related population growth was mainly in the form of "crooks, pickpockets, sneak-thieves and common burglars." A rare useful guidebook provided such revealing bits of wisdom as the supposed fact that "the man who travels in Alaska only when the weather is good will make about a mile a month, on an average." *Harper's Weekly*, 41 (July 31, 1897), 750; Spokane *Spokesman-Review*, Aug. 29, Dec. 18, 1897; *Seattle Times*, July 20; Dec. 13, 1897; *Tacoma Daily News*, Aug. 16, 1897; Griggs to John L. Farwell, July 24, 1897, St. Paul & Tacoma Lumber Co. Records; *Walla Walla Union*, Sept. 9; Dec. 10, 1897; *Seattle Post-Intelligencer*, Aug. 25, 1897; Olympia *Washington Standard*, July 23, 1897; Seattle *Argus*, July 31; Aug. 28, 1897; Walker to Talbot, Dec. 14, 1897, Puget Mill Co. Records; Semple to Edgar Ames, Sept. 6, 1897, Semple Papers; Haycox, *Alaska*, 205; Terrence Cole, "One Man's Adventure in the Klondike," *Columbia*, 11 (Winter 1997–1998), 20–26; J. Kingston Pierce, "Words of Gold," *Columbia*, 12 (Spring 1998), 5–6.

48. Only a small number of the argonauts were, in fact, successful farmers, professionals or merchants. Spokane *Spokesman-Review*, Nov. 19, 1897; Jan. 5; Feb. 13, 1898; Olympia *Washington Standard*, July 23, 1897; *Yakima Herald*, July 29, 1897; *Seattle Post-Intelligencer*, Sept. 15, 1897; James H. Ducker, "Gold Rushers North: A Census Study of the Yukon and Alaskan Gold Rushes, 1896–1900," *PNQ*, 85 (July 1994), 89.

49. *Seattle Times*, Dec. 21, 1897; *Seattle Post-Intelligencer*, July 21; Aug. 17, 22, 1897; Snowden, "Another Account," 791; Portland *Oregonian*, Aug. 18, 1897.

50. Places far from the seaboard also took advantage of the potential economic opportunities. Walla Walla, for instance, promoted itself as an ideal winter resort for Klondike miners in need of rest and relaxation. *Northwest*, 16 (April 1898), 33; Emerson to Jas. McCabe, Feb.

16, 1898, Emerson Letterbooks; Walker to Talbot, Jan. 14, 20; March 3, 1898; Talbot to Walker, Jan. 12, 17, 26, 1898, G.L. Evans to Puget Lumber Co., Jan. 25, 1898, all Puget Mill Co. Records; Robert E. Ficken, *The Forested Land: A History of Lumbering in Western Washington* (Seattle: University of Washington Press, 1987), 87–88; Olympia *Washington Standard*, Dec. 17, 1897.

51. *Walla Walla Union*, Aug. 6, 1897; Spokane *Spokesman-Review*, Feb. 22, 1898; *Tacoma Daily News*, Jan. 12, 1898; Seattle *Argus*, Feb. 19, 1898.

52. The word "Klondike" quickly became, as one Puget Sounder recounted, "very generally used over the country to denote the superlative degree of almost any idea." Griggs to Miller, Feb. 15, 1898, St. Paul & Tacoma Lumber Co. Records; Port Townsend *Weekly Leader*, Sept. 2, 1897; Olympia *Washington Standard*, Dec. 3, 1897.

53. In another ill conceived plan, New England gold hunters proposed sending a fishing schooner around Cape Horn and up the Yukon River to the furthest practicable site, beaching the craft on a sandbar to serve as cabin, cookhouse and base of exploration. *Northwest*, 16 (Sept. 1898), 16; *Tacoma Daily News*, Oct. 1, 1897; Spokane *Spokesman-Review*, Oct. 20, 1897; *Seattle Post-Intelligencer*, Sept. 4, 18, 1897; *Seattle Times*, Sept. 18, 24, 1897.

54. "Never," one observer wrote, "has there been such a demand for water craft…Were the tonnage increased ten-fold the steamers of the Pacific could do no more than comfortably accommodate the traffic." According to another report, "no better illustration of the fact that the Klondike fever has reached the mental stage of aberration could be given than the case of the schooner *Moonlight*, at Seattle. The inspector found the old craft overloaded, listing with a heavy deck load of lumber, and crowded into her hold without proper accommodation of any kind, sixty men." The timber firms also profited by hiring out their steam tugs to tow schooners to Alaska. Olympia *Washington Standard*, Jan. 14, 1898; *Seattle Post-Intelligencer*, Aug. 18, 1897; Walker to Talbot, Jan. 31; March 19, 1898; to E.G. Ames, March 14, 1898; Talbot to Walker, July 28; Aug. 21, 1897; March 9, 1898, all Puget Mill Co. Records; *Seattle Times*, Dec. 13, 1897; Spokane *Spokesman-Review*, Jan. 31, 1898; Portland *Oregonian*, Aug. 25, 1897; Emerson to McCabe, Feb. 16, 1898; to Simpson, Feb. 17; April 18, 1898, Emerson Letterbooks.

55. Seattle *Argus*, Aug. 14, 21; Sept. 18, 1897; *Seattle Post-Intelligencer*, Aug. 18, 1897; Feb. 3, 1898; Spokane *Spokesman-Review*, Jan. 31; Feb. 28, 1898; *Spokane Daily Chronicle*, Feb. 5, 24, 1898; Olympia *Washington Standard*, Sept. 17, 1897.

56. *Seattle Post-Intelligencer*, July 18, 20; Aug. 28, 30; Sept. 2, 8, 1897; *Seattle Times*, July 20, 1897; *Tacoma Daily News*, Aug. 9, 1897; E.V. Smalley, "Seattle in 1898," *Northwest*, 16 (July 1898), 24–25; Morse, *Nature of Gold*, 170–81; Hunt, "Goldfield Gateway," 37–38; Jeannette Paddock Nichols, "Advertising and the Klondike," *WHQ*, 13 (Jan. 1922), 21–23; Spokane *Spokesman-Review*, March 4, 1898; Seattle *Argus*, Dec. 18, 1897; Sharon A. Boswell and Lorraine McConaghy, *Raise Hell and Sell Newspapers: Alden J. Blethen and the Seattle Times* (Pullman: Washington State University Press, 1996), 109.

57. San Francisco merchants unable to profit from the Alaska trade made much of a stay-at-home argument that California still possessed twice the gold available in the Yukon. Seattle business leaders demanded that the city council impose prohibitive taxes on commerce poachers from British Columbia. *Tacoma Daily News*, Aug. 2, 9, 1897; Jan. 14, 21, 1898; Walker to Talbot, Jan. 25, 1898; F.C. Talbot to Walker, Aug. 4, 1897, both Puget Mill Co. Records; *Seattle Times*, Dec. 14, 1897; Spokane *Spokesman-Review*, Jan. 12, 1898; Portland *Oregonian*, Aug. 31, 1897; May 6, 1898; Jonasson, "Portland and the Alaska Trade," 136; *Seattle Post-Intelligencer*, Feb. 1, 2, 1898; Seattle *Argus*, Aug. 21, 1897;

Norbert MacDonald, "Seattle, Vancouver and the Klondike," *Canadian Historical Review*, 49 (Sept. 1986), 234–46.

58. "The Big Bend," a small town editor contended, "must not allow the flattering promises of the Klondike to distract its attention from the realities of the great mineral belt at its own doors." *Spokane Daily Chronicle*, Jan. 28; Feb. 5, 24, 1898; Spokane *Spokesman-Review*, Sept. 7, 11, 12, 20; Oct. 5, 31; Nov. 29, 30; Dec. 8, 1897; Jan. 31; Feb. 28, 1898; *Wilbur Register*, Dec. 24, 1897.

59. Despite the failure to open a viable trail, commercial groups continued to cite "experienced mountaineers," who claimed that this "almost ideal route" from Spokane was "feasible, desirable, attractive and cheap." Spokane *Spokesman-Review*, Oct. 8, 20, 26; Nov. 21, 23, 28, 29; Dec. 4, 24, 1897; *Seattle Post-Intelligencer*, Sept. 11, 1897; *Spokane Daily Chronicle*, April 6, 1898.

60. Two-thousand pack animals perished on the trail, their frozen carcasses ready to release "contagion in the air with the spring thaw." *Tacoma Daily News*, Feb. 5; March 3, 1898; *Seattle Post-Intelligencer*, Aug. 31; Sept. 5, 1897; Feb. 3, 1898; Olympia *Washington Standard*, Sept. 10; Oct. 1; Dec. 31, 1897; Portland *Oregonian*, Aug. 20, 1897; Berton, *Klondike*, 143; *Seattle Times*, Dec. 18, 23, 1897; New Whatcom *Daily Reveille*, Dec. 21, 1897; *Spokane Daily Chronicle*, March 2, 1898; *Wilbur Register*, Dec. 3, 1897. For details on the journey, see Morse, *Nature of Gold*, chapt. 1; and Don McCune, *Trail to the Klondike* (Pullman: Washington State University Press, 1997).

61. *Seattle Post-Intelligencer*, July 29; Aug. 21; Sept. 7, 22, 1897; *Tacoma Daily News*, Aug. 3, 6; Sept. 22, 1897; *Spokane Daily Chronicle*, Jan. 3, 1898; Spokane *Spokesman-Review*, Feb. 24, 1898.

62. According to one historian, only 4,000 of the 40,000 individuals traveling to Dawson in 1897 and 1898 found any significant quantity of gold. Spokane *Spokesman-Review*, Nov. 13, 1897; Feb. 2, 5, 1898; *Seattle Post-Intelligencer*, Aug. 29, 1897; Feb. 4, 1898; Portland *Oregonian*, Aug. 30, 1897; Port Townsend *Weekly Leader*, Sept. 2, 1897; *Spokane Daily Chronicle*, March 14, 1898; Haycox, *Alaska*, 205.

63. *Tacoma Daily News*, Sept. 22, 1897; *Seattle Post-Intelligencer*, Sept. 5, 1897; May 15, 1898; Spokane *Spokesman-Review*, Oct. 31, 1897; Seattle *Argus*, March 12, 1898.

64. "All industries in this section of the country," wrote Hoquiam's George Emerson, "are active with the prospect of a very decided step forward in the near future." *Wilbur Register*, Oct. 1, 1897; Griggs to C.M. Griggs, Oct. 1, 1897; to S.L. Levy, Aug. 3, 1897; to Royce, Aug. 12; Nov. 14, 1897; to Miller, Jan. 27, 1898, St. Paul & Tacoma Lumber Co. Records; R.D. Merrill to T.D. Merrill, Aug. 2, 1898, Merrill & Ring Lumber Co. Records, University of Washington Library; Walker to Talbot, Jan. 17, 1898; to Jackson, Dec. 11, 1897; Talbot to Walker, Jan. 10, 1898, all Puget Mill Co. Records; Emerson to Woodward, Aug. 18, 1897, Emerson Letterbooks.

65. Waterville *Big Bend Empire*, Oct. 14, 1897; *Northwest*, 15 (Aug. 1897), 35; 16 (Jan. 1898), 35; *Wilbur Register*, Sept. 3, 1897; *Walla Walla Statesman*, Sept. 11, 1897; Portland *Oregonian*, Aug. 25, 27, 1897; Spokane *Spokesman-Review*, Dec. 20, 1897; *Tacoma Daily Ledger*, April 12, 1898.

66. "A glance through the columns of Washington newspapers," a business publication advised, "shows that more new buildings are under construction and improvements in progress than at any time in several years." Seattle *Argus*, Oct. 23, 1897; *Seattle Times*, Oct. 5; Dec. 11, 24, 1897; July 28; Sept. 13, 1898; Spokane *Spokesman-Review*, Dec. 9, 11, 1897; *Spokane Daily Chronicle*, Jan. 6, 8; Feb. 11; March 11, 14, 1898; *Tacoma Daily News*, Jan. 8, 1898; *Northwest*, 15 (Sept. 1897, 33, rep. from Davenport *Times*; (Nov.

1897), 33; 16 (March 1898), 35, rep. from *West Coast Trade*, *South Bend Journal*, Sept. 17, 1897.
67. F. Talbot to Walker, Aug. 4, 1897, Puget Mill Co. Records; *Tacoma Daily Ledger*, April 13, 1898; Spokane *Spokesman-Review*, Dec. 21, 1897; *Seattle Times*, March 28, 1898; James J. Hill to Thomas Burke, April 4, 1898, Thomas Burke Papers, University of Washington Library.

Port Blakely lumber mill, October 13, 1897. *University of Washington Libraries (26804z)*

Chapter Eight

The Earnest of Coming Greatness

On the threshold of the twentieth century the Pacific begins to see the earnest of its coming greatness—a greatness commensurate with the vastness of its wandering wastes, the teeming millions of its one shore and the limitless resources of the other. On these broad waters are to ply the fleets of the twentieth century, and on this shore are to be the market places and treasure houses of the trade between the old world and the new.—Portland Oregonian.[1]

FOR MOST OF ITS LONG HISTORY, Washington Territory depended on the international Pacific Rim trade. Ships laden with green timber had sailed to the Hawaiian Islands, the Chinese mainland, the Australian gold diggings and coastal Peru and Chile. Douglas fir from Puget Sound, aptly described by an industry journal as "the one great cosmopolitan lumber in the world," was used in the construction of bridges, trestles, warehouses, buildings and the framework of deep mining shafts.[2] The transcontinental Northern Pacific, arriving late in the territorial era, for the first time truly linked the Pacific Northwest economy to America east of the Rockies. Conceived, according to a Tacoma editor, as "part of a commercial highway connecting Europe with Asia," the rail lines also stimulated further overseas expansion. The NP and the Great Northern implemented Jefferson's vision of a Pacific economic empire that decades before had sent Lewis and Clark to the faraway Columbia River.

Puget Sound, a Seattle newspaper proclaimed on the eve of Washington's admission to the Union, was "destined...in the not distant future to be the chief seat of all commerce with the Asia coast." The opening of Japan and China to outside influence and trade had made the Pacific an "ocean of promise." Tacoma, Seattle and other ports were ideally suited, by reason of geography, ocean currents and prevailing winds, to exploit the new opportunities of shipping eastern manufactures overseas in exchange for exotic luxuries and raw materials. In addition, the Asian market would encourage the further growth of local industrial enterprise, turning more of Washington's natural resources into exports to the benefit of investors, merchants and laborers. "The time is coming," claimed one Tacoman, "when a mighty commerce will sweep through this gateway, bringing the wealth of the Orient to these forest-clad shores."[3]

Interest in the lucrative Asian trade and the beckoning role for Washington was all but universal. "Gentleman, it cannot be exaggerated," Populist Governor John Rogers declared to an audience of mercantile leaders. "The commerce of the Pacific will one day…surpass the commerce of the Atlantic." In the first years of statehood, attention focused on Hawaii, as the islands attained a new strategic importance as "the key to the Pacific." In 1893, the monarchical domain had been locally converted into a self styled planter-missionary republic. Future acquisition by the United States "will compel us," expansion advocates contended, "to adopt a more vigorous foreign policy, and go on increasing our navy." The Hawaiian issue, a Spokane editor claimed, was yet another instance of America's Manifest Destiny in action:

> The situation as respects these islands is not dissimilar from that presented in the Oregon question 60 years ago. There were public men then who ridiculed the idea of territorial extension to these remote and lonely shores. They clamored for an everlasting halt at the summit of the Rocky mountains, just as public men now urge that the American flag shall pause at the shore line of the Pacific…But the judgment of history has stamped as weak and false the contention that the territorial limits of the United States must necessarily end with a range of mountains or a line of breakers.[4]

In regard to other matters of commerce, the Panic of 1893 had caused many Washingtonians to believe that "the American people would be better off if they had never borrowed one dollar of foreign money." The realities of modern finance and communications, however, made such isolation untenable. Washington's role in international financial arrangements would continue to grow. Business interests in the Pacific Northwest also called for the construction of a Nicaraguan canal across the Isthmus of Panama, which at the time was the favored plan. Such a project would substantially reduce the time and cost of commercial voyages between the Pacific Northwest and the Atlantic coast and Europe. Cuba, a Spanish ravaged colony and potential U.S. market, also drew regular attention. The necessity existed, a Yakima Valley editor argued in December 1897, "to settle the Cuban question for all time." By this date, the United States stood on the verge of becoming a recognized world power, and most Washington residents were ready to march in the vanguard of imperialism.[5]

∽≈∽

War with Spain over Cuba seemed inevitable by the early weeks of 1898. Despite their interest in overseas commercial expansion, shipping interests momentarily took pause in conducting trade. The "scare," Cyrus Walker wrote from Seattle, had disrupted travel to Alaska and precluded the seaborne export of lumber to Asia and South America. George Emerson worried about "Guerilla warfare on the Sea" directed against U.S. shipping by "Privateers" in the service of Madrid.

The potential negative impact upon wheat and flour shipments likewise caused concern east of the Cascades. Spain's Navy was "superior," warned the *Spokesman-Review*, and devoted to "the offensive, a policy quite to the liking of the impulsive Spanish people." Paradoxically, the Spokane paper also advised that America "would add nothing to the national glory or prestige" by vanquishing a decrepit foreign foe.[6]

Most public opinion, meanwhile, opposed any "toady efforts at conciliation" that might be undertaken by the McKinley administration. Spanish Cuba was "our Turkey," Washington jingoists asserted, "and we have the same responsibility for mitigating the sufferings inflicted on its people...which Europe recognizes for the unhappy peoples under the decaying Ottoman rule." The alarming destruction of the battleship USS *Maine* in Havana harbor on February 15, 1898, produced a widespread demand for vengeance in the name of civilization. Abruptly changing editorial course, the *Spokesman-Review* declared that America must enforce its will "at the cannon's mouth" upon "a nation which has been the historic foe of the Anglo-Saxon." Tacoma's *Ledger* and the *Seattle P-I*, dailies previously inclined to hand wringing, adopted a new hostile tone, dismissing as "utter nonsense" the likelihood of a Spanish assault upon west coast ports or shipping. Assuming that Spain's outmoded fleet based in the Philippines could somehow manage to cross the Pacific, U.S. war vessels and shore batteries would easily dispose of the threat.[7]

After weeks of negotiation with Spain, which to a large extent tried to be accommodating, the talks came to an impasse and war was declared on April 25, 1898. At Hoquiam, as in other communities, townspeople turned out "with banners and hurrahs to cheer" departing national guard troops "on their way" to an overseas campaign. However, the destination of the state's homegrown soldiers, sworn into federal service as the 1st Washington Volunteer Infantry, was uncertain. The detailed military analyses published in the newspapers failed to even hint at prospective Pacific theater operations.

Even after Admiral Dewey's stunning defeat of the Spanish fleet at Manila Bay and McKinley's decision to occupy the Philippines, the 1st Washington, along with numerous other state militias, initially got no further than San Francisco during the late spring and summer. "Petty personal spite" supposedly accounted for the affront to an outraged populace; some felt that the Republican administration appeared intent upon refusing the state its martial honors as punishment for the 1896 Bryan vote. Governor Rogers, moreover, had appointed Lieutenant John H. Wholley, a West Point graduate and professor of military science at the University of Washington, as colonel of the Washington regiment. Regular Army officers, Evergreen State patriots contended, were unwilling to treat a jumped-up junior as an equal and therefore declined to dispatch the Washington contingent across the Pacific. "The boys have been denied the poor satisfaction of even going to Honolulu," a Seattle editor grumped in disbelief.[8]

Merchants' fears that the conflict would be "a bad thing for the Klondike craze" were initially well founded. Instead of going north at the opening of spring, many seagoing vessels were diverted to the war effort. Persistent rumors of Spanish privateers lurking off the Queen Charlotte Islands, expecting to pick off treasure ships, also diverted interest in going to Alaska. Otherwise, however, the fight with Spain quickly turned out to be a blessing for business. Large defense expenditures pressed money into circulation, stimulating the economy. Hawaii became an important staging base in the aftermath of Dewey's triumph, requiring a major increase in lumber exports to the islands. Further operations in Asian waters were sure to benefit the Pacific Northwest.[9]

Destruction of the Spanish empire also involved, to general agreement, important non-commercial considerations, including national honor and security, and "justice to an oppressed" colonial people. Despite sympathy devoted to the Cubans' plight in recent years, however, some newspapers now began claiming that the islanders appeared to be an "illiterate, lazy, revengeful" people "not fitted for self-government." In the chauvinistic language of the *P-I*, the war was the latest battle "in the great struggle going on throughout the world in which the supremacy of the Anglo-Saxon race is the goal." Cultural and economic imperialism thus fused into a potent political force in Washington and elsewhere in America. Despite pledges previously made by the McKinley administration calling for Cuban independence, the United States must now, out of concern for trade, property and decency, exercise "for a long time to come" a self interested "moral oversight" of affairs in the former Spanish colonies.[10]

Existing trends, plus Dewey's demolition of the Spanish Asian fleet, focused the state's attention on the Pacific, rather than the Caribbean. The great ocean, Governor Rogers declared, had become "an American lake." The annexation of Hawaii, now quickly completed in the interest of national defense, drew wide support. Rogers wrote in a letter to William Randolph Hearst that the acquisition was fully "in the line of manifest destiny and military necessity." Although some concerns were expressed regarding the presence of many Chinese and Japanese laborers in the islands, the potential for trade outweighed such matters, at least in the port cities of Puget Sound. "The Hawaiians need very much that which could be shipped from here," a Seattle editor noted of the likely local benefit, "and in return we can import sugar, coffee, tropical fruits and rice."[11]

Similar arguments applied to the Philippines. Though many expansionists and critics alike conceded that the islands, if formally incorporated into a new American empire, would be "very expensive in time of peace and…a source of weakness…in time of war." Nevertheless, Spain's ancient colony could hardly be restored to Madrid's rule, nor could it be left exposed to the designs of other European powers. The Filipino population—"they have," claimed the *Seattle Times*, "that inherent Malay trait of being revengeful, even to treachery"—were, like the Cubans, supposedly unfit at the moment for self-rule. Humanitarian and strategic concerns alike made acquisition a necessity, and a responsibility that also entailed commercial benefit. Rejection of the Philippines, the *P-I* asserted, would be "a direct blow to the Pacific coast" in general and "a severe check to the prosperity…of the Pacific Northwest" in particular. Under a beneficent imperial administration in Manila, in contrast, exporters of flour, lumber and manufactured items might, without guilty conscience, exploit vast market opportunities.[12]

One prime reason for insisting on transferring the Philippines to the United States, Puget Sound newspapers had maintained, was that Americans must not betray "the insurgents who looked to us for aid" in their rebellion against Spain. Many Filipinos, however, had expected their country to become an independent republic. Upon learning that the American-Spanish peace agreement transferred the Philippines to U.S. ownership, many Filipinos led by Emilio Aguinaldo were enraged and tensions mounted, causing Washington's regiment to finally take to the field. Over 1,100 in number, the troops sailed for Manila late in 1898. When insurgent warfare finally broke out in early 1899, the 1st Washington, along with other regular Army and state volunteer units, spent six grueling months pushing the revolutionaries from the outskirts of the city and into the countryside. "While the Californians crawled to a new position on their stomachs," a Seattle daily reported in celebrating the peculiar form of regional bravery displayed in one engagement, "the Washington boys marched…upright and in skirmishing order."

By the time that the 1st Washington was ordered back to the states for mustering out, 129 men had been killed or wounded, 14 had succumbed to disease or accident, while another 239 stayed overseas in civilian capacities or enlisted in the Army's U.S. Volunteers to remain on active duty in the Philippines. The nearly 600 men arriving at Elliott Bay in the fall of 1899 were accorded the state's official "royal welcome." Wild celebrating for returning local troops also occurred in Spokane and other communities.[13]

❦

Washington's "future" was "opening…like an ocean," a Spokane editor had reflected in 1889, "and we are timid mariners who have scarcely begun the exploration of its broad bosom." The navigational metaphor was well chosen, capturing the importance of trans-Pacific commercial relationships to the residents of the new state. Regular steamship service from Tacoma to China and Japan had begun in 1892. Vessels controlled by the Great Northern first sailed from Seattle to Asian ports in 1893. "He knows," one editor observed of James J. Hill's fundamental transportation strategy, "that the time will surely come when the large and growing commerce of the Orient will pass across the state of Washington, and seek the world's great markets."[14]

Flour shipments to China had held steady through the depression years, while those to Japan mounted at an impressive rate. Four Seattle mills ran 24 hours a day, producing exclusively for the Asian market. "We have seen this trade expand so rapidly," one newspaper reported at mid-decade, "that all the steamers plying between…Puget sound…and Oriental ports are unable to handle the freight offering, and have their whole tonnage engaged for months ahead." Steel rails and rolling stock purchased in the East by transportation contractors in China and Japan were exported through the Sound. Local business interests, meanwhile, complained for the first time about competition from cheap imports. "Carpets, umbrellas, tooth brushes, [and] many articles of dry goods of Japanese manufacture," a Seattle resident noted, "are now sold…at much less price than articles of home product can be purchased for." Labor, too, faced a new threat. A Spokane editor pointed out that the low paid "Asiatic at home" had become "a more troublesome competitor than the Asiatic upon the Pacific coast of America."[15]

Times may have been "at their darkest" in the aftermath of the panic of 1893, but the people of Washington were "saved from complete stagnation," according to contemporary analysts, by the providential trade with China and Japan. Furthermore, the "rotundity of the earth," combined with "the principle of great circle sailing," put Tacoma and Seattle a thousand miles closer to Manila than rival San Francisco. Future competition between Puget Sound's major rival ports inevitably would center on dominance in the new markets. All of Washington stood to benefit from substantially increased settlement and investment, from mounting production of grain and lumber and, in general, from the nation's ongoing shifts toward an Asian orientation. "Manufactures of all kinds will spring up in the Coast towns and cities," E.V. Smalley predicted in a series of articles and editorial commentaries, "and there will come to all those communities a new epoch of activity and prosperity that will realize the old dream of the coming importance of the Pacific Slope of the continent."[16]

In August 1898, when Spain and the United States agreed to an armistice, 150 commercial vessels sailed from Elliott Bay, six times the figure for the same month in 1891. Dispatched in large part through Puget Sound ports, American exports to Asia "increased nearly seven-fold" in the same span of years according to one report. Seattle and Tacoma shipped $9 million worth of grain and flour during the 1898 season. Hawaii, an outlet historically served by lumber company schooners and barks, now took on new importance as a U.S. territory. Military and naval construction created a demand for workers and building materials, as well as profit making opportunities for merchants. The first Seattle-Honolulu steamship line commenced regular service in August 1898.[17]

James J. Hill, still celebrated in the regional press as "a calculating machine" who "never permits an invested nickel to be diverted from its duty of making more nickels," took the lead in promoting business with Asia. "The nation that has controlled the trade of the orient," he reiterated in speeches and interviews, "has held the purse strings of the world." New elevators along the Great Northern line and heavy promotion reduced costs and stimulated demand for American grain. Enormous steamships, built to specifications and directly owned by the GN, went into service at the end of the war with Spain. Contributing fully to a rational development of Seattle's harbor facilities, Hill constructed a massive dock and warehouse complex on the northern extremity of the downtown waterfront area at Smith Cove. From hilltop vantage points, townspeople gloried in a thoroughly modern view that was "rich in scenic beauty and commercial suggestiveness." The snow clad Olympics soared above sparkling salt waters, and in the foreground where "thread-like" spur tracks connected mammoth structures, "an army of men" moved among the facilities "like so many pigmies, each bent upon his separate task."[18]

Thanks to Hill, local business leaders claimed "the finger of destiny pointed unerringly" in Seattle's direction. There was no shortage, however, of competitors attempting to exploit markets beyond the home shores. The old sawmilling firms, with decades of experience in the Pacific trade, were especially energetic in reaching out for business. The Port Blakely Mill Company sold heavily to merchants in Japan and Indochina. The St. Paul & Tacoma Lumber Company sent an agent to Asia in the winter of 1897. Henry Hewitt Jr., one of the firm's senior partners, followed up with a 10-month mission to Japan, China "and even to Russia." Returning to Puget Sound, he carried orders from Chinese buyers and a fair prospect of selling the mill's "yard and common" stock to Japanese mercantile houses.[19]

Pope & Talbot, owning the historically famous mill operations at Port Gamble and Port Ludlow, was notably aggressive in Asia. Despite high freights and low priced competition, the company sold considerable Washington lumber. Special representative James Claiborne toured Japan, China and Siberia in 1899 and 1900, planning to fully develop ongoing trade connections. The Chinese, unfortunately, were preoccupied by the Boxer Rebellion—Claiborne reported in dismay that he was compelled to drink water from a "river…full of dead bodies." War loomed, meanwhile, between the Japanese and Russians. Further difficulties arose when Yokohama merchants demonstrated their willingness to "go back on a deal" whenever convenient. "Heartily disgusted, disappointed and ashamed," the Pope & Talbot agent acquired a truly informed sense of the obstacles in genuinely opening up turn-of-the-century Asian markets.[20] In addition to a desirable product and efficient transportation, U.S. companies—those operating in the state of Washington included—needed good fortune and detailed intelligence regarding foreign economic, political and cultural conditions.

⌘

Gold coming from the Klondike and other mining outposts of the frozen north could only be regarded as "mere incidents," the *Seattle Times* insisted, when compared to the wealth generated by "the new Pacific trade." Even prior to the commencement of hostilities with Spain, one observer had noted "there is already talk of pulling steamers off the Alaska run." The U.S. Army's campaign in the Philippines, first against Spanish garrisons and then the insurgents, had a compound impact on shipping—"We do not see how they are going to get the transports," a prominent businessman reported in June, "without taking nearly every available steamer on the Coast." Shipping shortages, along with the loss of would-be miners to military service, most commentators agreed, could only lead to disappointing Alaskan returns.[21]

Seeking metallic wealth, however, continued to outweigh patriotism for many Americans. "The war has to a large degree overshadowed the Klondike," a Puget Sound editor advised, "but men never forget their desire to get gold." Prospectors who went north in 1897 looked forward to springtime and the opening of the passes in 1898. The winter at Dawson had featured squabbling over supplies and mounting anger over Canadian impositions. In broadening its attack against Canada's policies regarding American miners and merchants in the Yukon, the *P-I* complained about "duty on food, license money, recording fees, a tax on fuel, tolls at every turn, and enforced gratuities to officials who have had to be paid." On the coast, Skagway merchants attempted a "purification" of the tidewater boomtown, adopting vigilante methods to curb "cut-throats, robbers, gamblers, thieves, 'sure-thing' men" and other undesirable elements from the states. Nothing was done, however, to reform the chaotic port facilities, a failure reflected in the slow unloading of cargo and substantially increased freight costs.[22]

Though delayed by wartime dislocations, a second rush to Alaska commenced in earnest in the late spring of 1898. Two dozen steamers, grossly overloaded with wealth seekers and cargo, sailed from Seattle in the first half of June. Many of the vessels were bound for St. Michael, towing river craft built in Elliott Bay yards for the 2,000 mile journey up the Yukon River. "And yet," a local newspaper scoffed, "there be those who say 'interest is lagging in the Klondike!'" The attraction of gold was, by no means, limited to the young and anonymous. Former governor John McGraw was a particularly prominent, and somewhat notorious, northbound passenger in 1898. Ezra Meeker, a well known settler since the time of Isaac Stevens and, until the depression, the largest hop rancher on Puget Sound, departed in search of a new beginning in the northern wilderness.[23]

Puget Sound residents impatiently waited for the mid-July return of the season's first treasure ships. Eventually, dust and nuggets worth $5 million were received at the Seattle assay office. San Francisco officials tallied a $3 million return for the Bay Area. John McGraw came back with a $100,000 profit, while denying rumors that he would resume a career in politics or, in an even greater affront to humanity, abandon Washington for southern California. Although total earnings for the year represented a four-fold increase over 1897, extravagant pre-war expectations caused much of the public to consider Alaska to be something of a disappointment. "Nothing but whining, kicking, snarling and general terms of execration," one of the Elliott Bay dailies exclaimed, "are heard on every hand because the amount…is not 'greater'!"[24]

Towns poorly sited to benefit from the Alaskan trade encouraged such sentiments as a means of bolstering their own local developments. "The Klondike bubble has been pricked," Spokane leaders claimed in the summer of 1898. Eastern Washington newspapers again featured stories about short supplies, dangerous trails and the inevitability of failure. "Klondike luck," a farm country weekly quipped in an attempt to dissuade harvest hands from making the trip, "seems to consist largely in the pilgrim's ability to reach the United States alive." The few prospectors actually finding gold, moreover, were the most unfortunate of all—"The Klondike millionaire does one of three things," the *Spokesman-Review* warned. "He hoards his suddenly acquired wealth with a miserly thriftiness; he branches out into the wildest speculation; or, he 'blows' his fortune in any and all forms of dissipation."[25] Intelligent persons did better by staying at home, working the mines and fields and doing business with Inland Empire merchants and bankers.

Puget Sounders dismissed this advice from east of the mountains as self-interested nonsense. Though hardly unimpressive, the official returns, for one thing, understated the true wealth of Alaska—"It is to the interests of every miner to belittle the output of his claim," a Seattle observer pointed out, for reticence acted as "a check upon the cupidity of those around him." For similar reasons, returning prospectors supposedly tended to "hide their gold" upon reaching the Sound. And, failed miners, in explaining their impoverishment, tended to exaggerate the obstacles to success. "If you don't want to go, but would like to give some excuse for staying at home," another Elliott Bay resident advised, "just consult the fellow who has...come out empty handed, and commit to memory the 'cuss words' which he will formulate against the Klondike."[26]

Investors spending heavily on constructing steamers for the run up the Yukon River to the Klondike suffered undeniable losses in 1898. Only a few of the 50 vessels first utilized that year remained in service 12 months later. The others were tied up to "rot at the bank," crushed in winter ice or sold to gullible buyers at "one-tenth their cost." The opening of the White Pass railroad from Skagway toward Whitehorse accounted, in large part, for this development. "A long...voyage of three or four weeks" up the Yukon River, one observer reported of the immediate impact on travel to the diggings, "has been abandoned for a 10-day trip which can now be made with some degree of comfort" across the Alaska panhandle. Consequently, the amount of gold shipped down the Yukon declined by 90 percent. Attention also shifted from Dawson, a transformation dramatized by the destruction of the camp in a May 1899 fire. Although the town quickly rebuilt, prospectors were "as eager to leave it as they once were feverish to behold its unlovely shacks." Lots selling for "thousands of dollars in the days of the 'boom'" found few takers at any price.[27]

Wealth seekers investigating broad Norton Sound, north of the mouth of the Yukon River, discovered enough gold in the winter of 1899 to draw miners from the Klondike. "Cape Nome has sprung into fame within a few months," a Seattle newspaper proclaimed in June, "and…the first returns are as promising as those which gave a world-wide notoriety to…the Yukon." Miners reported earning $100 and more a day from pits excavated in the sand and scrub. Nome could be reached, moreover, by an all-sea passage from Puget Sound. "Steamers go right up to the shore," one passenger noted. Bering Sea ice delayed sailings to the far north, but claim takers managed to stake "forty miles of 'pay dirt'" along the beach by late summer.[28]

Commercial interests from the state of Washington eagerly established themselves at Nome, where a sack of flour could sell for an extremely profitable $10 and lumber brought over $200 per thousand feet. Aware of the complete lack of building materials along the bleak Bering Sea, Puget Sound sawmills arranged to ship large quantities of timber to the new mines. Vessel owners again secured "very high rates" from charters for Alaska bound passengers and freight. Mercantile firms and miners alike, nonetheless, found that success was somewhat akin to purchasing "a ticket in a lottery." Goods left on the Nome beach, due to the absence of a wharf and storage facilities, suffered costly damage from storms and high tides. Gold claims staked in tidal lands were of dubious legality and therefore subject to trespass and eventual federal confiscation. The climate was harsher and the working season shorter than in southeast Alaska and the Yukon.[29]

Spokane boosters cited Nome's notoriety when arguing that gold hunters ought to avoid "hunger, cold, scurvy and the isolation of arctic life" by going instead to the mines of the interior Pacific Northwest. Ignoring such contrarian advice, thousands of prospectors sailed from Puget Sound in 1899. The first substantial returns from the new diggings swelled Alaska's mineral production for the season to $16 million. The extended gold rush also established regular economic linkages between Washington and the northern camps. Reflecting the steady aspect of things, the typical southbound steamer conveyed more gold to Seattle or Tacoma than that carried aboard the fabled *Portland* in 1897, without inducing "an extra pulsation in the veins of any inhabitant." Vessels proceeding to Skagway and Nome hauled more than enough supplies to obviate any real possibilities of starvation. Writing that he "would rather live here than in Yakima," one miner detailed the rich and varied imported cuisine: "Apples, oranges, and lemons are in the market now, as well as eastern oysters, eggs, condensed cream, prepared canned meats of all kinds, vegetables, fresh beef, fresh potatoes, pumpkin and mince pies, cranberry sauce and turkey for Thanksgiving."[30]

Fully exploiting an already dominant position in the southeast Alaskan trade, Seattle took advantage of the Nome rush to firmly establish predominance in northwest coastal waters. Elliott Bay dispatched 100,000 tons of goods to the camps in the first half of 1899, more than the combined shipments of all competing ports. Newly energized by golden profit, Seattle ended the 19th century as a colonial power of sorts, a city state drawing to it all manner of things. Back from the mines in the fall of 1899, a party of prominent citizens erected an Alaska totem pole in Pioneer Square. The only protest directed at the theft came from those Christians offended by the display of "savage idolatry" in a public place.[31]

∽∼∾

A brief designation as the newest incarnation of Chicago failed to gratify Seattle's ambitions. The "Queen City" nickname devised by the chamber of commerce also fell short of the aspirations inspired by the Asian and northern gold markets. "The vast domain tributary to Seattle and from which she derives her wealth and power," the *P-I* maintained in a celebratory screed, "is not a mere queendom, comprehending within its limits the area and people of one country, but it is an empire, reaching out to many peoples and embracing many lands." Undeniably grandiose in self promotion, the "Empire City" on Elliott Bay was hardly the sole beneficiary of America's economic resurgence. "It almost seems," an east-of-the-mountains paper declared, "as if the wild and fanciful pipe-dreams of the real-estate boomers of 1890 are coming true." Prosperity, another editor agreed, "has struck this state with a big 'P.'"[32]

Drawn to the northwest coast by commercial opportunity, the Alaska excitement and trans-Pacific expansion, immigration attained numbers "unprecedented since the boom days of 1889." Some newcomers, such as the Kansas farmers driving eight "prairie schooners" into Yakima in the late summer of 1899, arrived by venerable means of transport. Most, however, preferred the speed and comfort of the transcontinental lines, traveling aboard special trains pressed into service to accommodate the demand. The railroads encouraged relocation by reducing passenger fares and, in the case of the Northern Pacific, land prices. NP sales in the state of Washington exceeded 900,000 acres in 1898 and 600,000 acres in 1899.[33]

Recording a 50 percent upswing in their Washington transportation business in each of those years, the railroads themselves participated fully in the new prosperity. The Northern Pacific earned $60,000 in net profit for every mile of track within the state's boundaries in 1898 and could no longer, according to longtime critics, "plead poverty against proposed reductions in grain rates." Transferred in the latest Wall Street development to the sole control of the Union Pacific, the Oregon Railway & Navigation Company also returned to profitability. The railroads restored pre-1893 wage scales and planned for the first significant regional construction work since the panic.[34]

Trains also carried an ever increasing output to customers beyond the Rockies. In 1898, Washington's fields and mills produced $45 million worth of goods, half of that amount being wheat and lumber. An increasing volume of grain was shipped to foreign markets from Seattle and Tacoma. Puget Sound flour exports, meanwhile, soared by a 90 percent rate in 1899. Overall, the Sound's overseas commerce was up by a factor of seven from pre-panic levels. The local customs office ranked second in business on the Pacific coast, trailing only San Francisco.[35]

Positive returns were reported in all areas of the state's economy. Coal production was up by a third and for the first time in years Puget Sound bested British Columbia in supplying the Bay Area. The most productive mine, Roslyn on the east side of Snoqualmie Pass, installed new towers, bunkers and "every modern convenience" for the efficient handling of coal. Three times as many salmon were packed on the Sound in 1899 as on the Columbia River. The Semiahmoo cannery, just below the 49th parallel, claimed to be the largest in the world, turning out 100,000 cases (each holding 48 one pound cans) per season. Hop ranching, a long depressed endeavor in the Puyallup Valley and the Yakima vicinity, regained a measure of profitability with prices doubling between 1895 and 1899.[36]

Lumber output, all accounts agreed, was "furious" and "phenomenal," as the state moved rapidly toward becoming the nation's leading timber producer. "Times…are the liveliest we have seen for many years," one Grays Harbor manufacturer advised. "Every saw-mill…is running full blast," a region-wide survey concluded, "and most of them running night and day to keep up with the orders that have been piling in." Among the old ocean oriented operations, Port Blakely shipped 16 cargoes in October 1898, with 10 consigned to foreign ports. Pope & Talbot at ports Gamble and Ludlow exported 41 million feet in the first half of 1900, a third going to the Hawaiian Islands. Growth was most pronounced, though, in the recently opened eastern markets. Rail shipments passed the 10,000 carload mark in 1898, more than double the mid-decade rate. By trade publication estimate, a single train 400 miles in length would be needed to haul all Washington lumber and shingles sold beyond the Rockies.[37]

Major changes were reflected in the statistical returns. Because of "unhealthy competition" and the demand on seagoing tonnage by other commercial ventures, the mainstay California market had become all but obsolete. "San Francisco stands in the same position to the lumber business that a fire-pit stands in the old time mill," George Emerson claimed. "The question is into which of the two furnaces will you throw your refuse." Sending a third of the state's output east and shipping lumber to overseas outlets more than compensated for the decline of this historical relationship. "It has reached a question," Emerson noted of a complex reorientation now well underway, "of foreign credits, foreign policies, competing timber resources, export and import duties and proper foreign and eastern connections."[38]

Good times in the exploitation of all markets, plus the nation's increasing reliance on Pacific Northwest lumber, entailed predictable and potentially troublesome consequences. Washington had 300 operating sawmills by the end of 1899 and dozens more were under construction. Two million board feet of productive capacity in a single year would, in the event of an economic downturn, "become a curse to the business," Cyrus Walker warned. Encouragement of increased output would, sooner or later, lead to downward pressure on prices and negative conditions for the lumber trade.[39]

Agricultural prospects, meanwhile, grew "brighter under the hand of providence," as interior Northwest residents regularly noted of their good fortune. "There is safer and surer competency in tilling the soil of the State of Washington," a Big Bend commentator suggested, "than there is in washing the auriferous earth of the Territory of Alaska." Despite shortages of harvest machinery, warehouse space and rolling stock, excellent weather and increased planting allowed wheat farmers to deliver the "greatest crop" in regional history in 1898. The substantial upswing in production was readily absorbed by the world market, in part because of another failed harvest in Russia. Although per-bushel prices declined, the larger output resulted in profitable returns for the second year in a row. "Most of the mortgages" were, as a result, "put in pretty good condition" according to a report on the overall economic impact, while "old store debts" were for the most part "wiped out."[40]

In 1899, however, enormous production in all of the world's grain producing countries generated lower prices. Higher costs for shipping to the United Kingdom—due to the diversion of vessels for the Boer War in South Africa—added to marketing prices. Even so, earnings were sufficient in combination with the profits of 1897 and 1898 for farmers and small town merchants alike to maintain faith in the future. "The matter of tiding over until a more propitious season," one editor pointed out, "is not so deplorably urgent as it was some years ago." The continuing upward trend in Palouse, Big Bend and Walla Walla Valley land prices affirmed the retention of confidence.[41]

Ongoing reports about Alaskan gold tended, local boosters complained, to obscure the fact that Washington had "mines of its own." Like wheat, in-state prospecting opportunities deserved attention as an "at home" Klondike. For the moment, unfortunately, entrepreneurs often preferred the risk of tapping potentially greater riches in the north, than investing in more dependable closer-to-home returns. Critics also said that many miners were supposedly "compelled" to go to the Yukon and Nome because they could get grubstakes "for the new fields" from Puget Sound outfitters. The same wealth hunters, however, "could not get a cent for the equally rich and more lasting gold fields of this state." Interest was sufficient enough, however, to still draw people to the Coeur d'Alenes, the Okanogan and other sectors tributary to Spokane.[42]

Prospectors of the stay-at-home variety headed in particular to the Colville Indian Reservation, fully opened to mineral exploitation in 1898. The century's last hell-bent western mining camp opened that year at Republic on the Sanpoil River. Several thousand miners flocked to the remote location, taking up residence in makeshift cabins constructed of pine slabs and mill refuse. A "Paradise Row" of gambling dens, dance halls and saloons ran, one visitor reported, "with an open throttle." Destroyed by fire in June 1899, the town was back in business in a matter of weeks with a substantially increased number of rude structures. Hundreds of teamsters and packers, the latter leading "disconsolate...horses tied nose to tail, and half-hidden under their huge packs," were fully employed hauling supplies from Spokane. Serious planning began for at least three railroad lines. The principal Republic mine, owned by Inland Empire investors, paid a quarter million dollars in dividends in its first year, a performance explaining and justifying the attraction of the place.[43]

New energy, in fact, was on display in all activities and in all communities. "There is not a district in Washington that is not manifesting in some degree a forward movement," one newspaper noted in reporting on the end-of-the-century infusions of capital. "While a year ago you could rent almost any residence at a nominal figure," an Ellensburg resident wrote in January 1900, "today it is impossible to secure any kind of house at any figure." Yakima's population passed 3,000, answering the expectations of the "most enthusiastic of the early boomers." Stamp sales at the local post office exceeded the threshold required for introduction of free home delivery service. In Pasco, where the NP mainline crossed the Columbia, dwellings that real estate dealers claimed could not be sold for $2 during the panic now went, at minimum, for 10 times that amount.[44]

Communities west of the Cascades recorded similar advances. "Not since the boom days," a Bellingham Bay editor asserted, "has there been a healthier tone to business than today exists in New Whatcom." A half million dollars in improvements were made during 1899, as "new people" appeared "on every hand." Chehalis, on the railroad south of Olympia, had no residential or commercial vacancies, "a condition that never existed before." More property changed hands in nearby Winlock during 1899 than in the four previous years combined. On Grays Harbor, Aberdeen's population doubled, with townspeople claiming to have been "more directly changed by the return of prosperity" than any other place "on the coast."[45]

Washington's largest municipalities also prospered. In Tacoma, the resumption of investment sparked a boom in property transactions and construction. "Every house has a tenant," one of the Commencement Bay dailies reported in early 1900, "and the sound of hammer and saw attests to the truth of the building inspector's statistics showing 50 percent more building is being done than there was at this time last year." Spokane residents boasted of recovering "from the financial depression sooner than the other cities of the northwest." Sales of lots and structures in 1898 neared $4 million in valuation. Banking clearings for September that year were four times the rate of the same month in 1893. Persons renting scarce business and residential space faced regular increases in their monthly payments. "Any one who is nursing the idea that rents will soon be lower," a local paper confided, "might as well get rid of that nonsensical notion." Capitalists within and without the Inland Empire responded with funding for new housing and mercantile blocks. Spending increases for education to accommodate the growing number of school age children became an accustomed feature of Spokane life.[46]

Urban progress was most evident on the shores of Elliott Bay. Seattle "is in a condition that very closely resembles Boom," visiting lumberman George Emerson wrote in the winter of 1900. "Every man seems to be in motion as though he had something to do," another touring witness recorded, "the people were well dressed and everybody has money." The *P-I* affirmed the outlook "was never better." Despite impressive increases in the rate of construction, houses were "impossible to rent," stores were "snapped up as soon as vacant" and landlords, sitting pretty in a short market, increased rates to protest inducing figures. Banking transactions regularly exceeded the combined total for Portland, Tacoma and Spokane. "A few other little towns," one booster suggested, "might also be thrown in for good measure." Even the University of Washington prospered, achieving academic respectability for the first time and anticipating an enrollment reaching 1,000 students at the turn of the century.[47]

Tallied on a county-by-county basis for purposes of tax assessment, the state's official property valuations lagged behind the overall economic improvement by deliberate action. Property owners and their political representatives feared exposure to a demand for increased public revenue. "With the advent of better times comes danger of returning extravagance in state, county and city," a Spokane editor warned. "That would mean another long period of increasing taxation, the partial confiscation of property...and the curtailment of investment by outside capital." Prosperity compelled officials to "be careful," another journalist noted, "for that is the time when credit is good and the foundation for disaster laid." The problem was that an expanding population and economy produced pressures for spending on schools, roads, utilities and other necessities of modern life.[48]

Places coming close to, or in actual violation of, constitutional restrictions on debt practiced unavoidable fiscal restraint. Continuing a depression induced approach to spending, the city of Seattle reduced taxes in 1899. "There is a reasonable limit beyond which [the] prudent...will not go," the *Times* declared in approving a decision to postpone urban improvements. For the sake of better city management, Tacoma residents faced, in one analysis, a prospective 27 mill levy should local officials decide to repay existing municipal obligations. Traditionally frugal communities, on the other hand, emerged from the panic with finances well in hand. Wahkiakum County on the lower Columbia carried no public indebtedness. The outgoing Anacortes town council left a cash balance on the books in 1899. East of the Cascades, Kittitas County and Dayton retired outstanding bond issues from current revenues.[49]

Newly available capital, however, allowed once parsimonious governmental entities to engage in debt accumulation. Everett borrowed $60,000 for a sewer system, and bonding paid for bridge construction in Hoquiam. By overwhelming margins in a series of elections, Walla Walla voters approved installation of water and sewage works and the building of modern schools. For some communities, however, the laudable and time honored desire to inflict the cost of projects on the taxpayers of tomorrow clashed with depression reinforced traditional wisdom. After paying off a portion of its indebtedness, Yakima County decided to refinance its remaining obligations, while aggrieved residents mounted a successful legal challenge to the issuance of bonds. The alternative means of redemption, an increase in current taxation, drew a grim face-the-music endorsement from a local paper: "We have had our dance; now let us step up and pay the fiddler without groaning."[50]

Debate over taxes and spending provided but one of several un-felicitous sidelights to prosperity's otherwise welcomed return. A booming economy and the influx of population, composed in part of those bound for Alaska and those determined to fatten on the Alaska-bound, created ever increasing criminal opportunities. "The crooks, the thugs, the sneak thieves and bunco men," a Spokane citizen complained, "have rushed from all quarters of the country to the coast." Influenced by these unsavory newcomers, some home-bred youth defied authority and convention as never before. Social problems preoccupied the residents of large cities and small towns alike. The respectable elders of Wilbur in the Big Bend wheat belt bemoaned the presence of "men who are either too lazy to work or too depraved to live by honest effort." At Pasco on the Columbia, an editor wrote of a community unsettled by "hold-ups and knock-downs," which were near daily offenses perpetrated by "the scum of the earth." A survey of the regional moral order suggested that gamblers, prostitutes and confidence artists flocked to the state's urban areas just "as flies swarm around a molasses keg in mid-summer."[51]

Seattle was, appropriately, the focal point of this new era of increased lawlessness. The self-styled Empress City had become, or so a local preacher contended, the capital of the "un-godly." A new daily, the *Star*, agreed on the basic observation under the headline, "The Carnival of Crime in Seattle." Despite the chamber of commerce's claim that the metropolis was crime free, arrests increased from 4,000 in 1897 to 7,000 in 1898. Considering the shortage of police, especially of the honest variety, many other criminals surely evaded capture. Street offenses from picking pockets to brazen daylight armed robberies mounted in frequency, and saloons, gambling dens and palaces of fornication flourished. "This town can never be 'closed up,'" one Spirit-infused Seattleite noted in assessing the futile attempts by the "pure of thought" to curb the underworld.[52]

Lawbreaking in the Inland Empire provoked similar concerns. "Not one promise has been fulfilled," a Spokane editor observed of the city's officials, and "not one step has been taken to suppress or to exercise even a limited control over the many evils that exist." New pastimes of chance, such as craps and slot machines, appealed to the gullible and diverted cash from conventional channels of commerce. The operators of "cribs" and "immoral houses" robbed upstanding townsmen "of their morality" and the "women of the last shred of self-respect." Burglary was rampant and vagrancy a continuing affront to self-reliant decency.[53]

Various anti-crime expedients were unavailing for the most par. Business interests encouraged the police to be on "constant lookout and surveillance," thereby keeping would be offenders "on the move," but had to pay gratuities for this above-and-beyond the call of duty service. Attempts in many communities to apply curfews against youthful wrongdoers failed from a lack of consistent enforcement, not to mention citizen cooperation. The jailing of criminals compelled taxpayers to pay for the incarcerations. Addressing the latter outrage, several cities, Seattle included, established chain gangs, thereby putting inmates to work on projects of supposed public benefit. In another expedient, local authorities made life "too hot" for undesirables, driving away miscreants to way stations down the tracks.[54]

Economic recovery again made labor questions—dormant since the dramatic and exhausting disturbances of 1894—a prime public concern. "There is not a ghost of an excuse for [there being] an idle man in the state of Washington," one resident observed of the drastically altered post-depression situation. Due to the lure of Alaska and the boom conditions in manufacturing, agriculture and the forests, sufficient numbers of workers were, in stark contrast to previous times, decidedly scarce. Puget Sound and Grays Harbor sawmills poached laborers from one another and recruited in Oregon and California. Lumbering and logging concerns relocating from the Great Lakes attempted to secure crews from their home states. Consequently, frustration often ensued for management. "It is a fact well known to all our men," George Emerson lamented, "that any of them can leave us and get better wages without any loss of time." Moreover, so long as the supply of jobs exceeded the number of hands needed, unions would have ample opportunity to press demands.[55]

Wage scales reverted to, and then soared above, pre-panic figures. Confidential correspondence books kept by business leaders became filled with near daily complaints about increasing labor costs, reduced efficiency and the inevitable return of "the disturbing element" to the mills and woods. "In former times, men would…do what they are told," the eternal pessimist Cyrus Walker noted of prosperity's dark underside, "but now, we have but little to say how the business shall run, and for the time being, I see no other way, but to do the best we can, until we can do better." Bitterly conceding the need to "handle" his employees "with kid gloves," the elderly businessman realized that only a new economic downturn would allow for a restoration of the traditional order.[56]

Most residents of the state, as opposed to corporate executives, generally were slow to grasp the implications of the region-wide employee shortage. In expressing a widely held opinion, a Spokane editor proclaimed that strikes were "as out of date as the old style of blunderbuss would be in modern war." Supposedly, such disturbances, as amply confirmed by the 1894 events, were costly to all sectors of society, bound to fail in the end and were highly unlikely to boost the real income of workers. "Probably no less than ninety per cent of the people of the northwest...sympathize with labor," a Big Bend periodical contended. Nevertheless, the difficulty for the populace—in a continuation of past public ambivalence—arose when unions attempted to prevent non-members from accepting employment under low wage schedules offered by management. Organizing was one thing, but restraint on private freedom and property was quite another.[57]

Most of the middle class was thoroughly offended and to a considerable extent frightened by the resurgence of the Western Federation of Miners. Unrest returned, in particular, to the Coeur d'Alenes in 1898, provoked by a dispute over union recognition rather than wages, which had increased to match old time highs. Acts of violence targeted mine managers and workers attempting to defy the WFM leadership. Alarmed observers across the state line in Washington denounced such acts as a "display of folly," which was sure to drive investment from the Pacific Northwest and cause a loss of public support for labor.[58]

With all restraint abandoned, in April 1899 union members blew up the famous Bunker Hill and Sullivan mines. Dispatched to the scene at the request of the state of Idaho, federal troops imprisoned hundreds of suspected miners in a "bull pen." Given the close proximity and economic importance of the Idaho mines, many Washington residents were duly concerned and outraged. Aside from destroying a major industrial enterprise, the *Spokesman-Review* mourned, the destruction represented an "intimidation" and possible loss of capital running "into the millions." The individuals responsible "should be hung," a Walla Walla Valley editor declared. Military imprisonment, though an extraordinary development in domestic American history, was entirely justified, claimed the *P-I*, for the unionists were "too criminal to be dealt with by any other means." In the aftermath, panhandle mine owners countered organized labor by efficiently maintaining a blacklist. Meanwhile, a growing number of respectable people felt that union leaders were not only law breakers, but "enemies of society."[59]

Legislators also continued to be generally held in low regard by the public. One turn-of-the-century pundit suggested that Washington lawmakers be required to wear distinctive uniforms, fully emblazoned with lobbyist-awarded medals, when serving in Olympia. Although low anti-politician humor remained a staple of citizen discourse, the end of the depression transformed partisan affairs in the state. Still committed to "building up what ought to be...the dominant political party of the future," Governor John Rogers privately admitted that the fusionist cause was "in a chaotic condition." Patronage disputes had long since driven the victors of the free silver crusade into hostile camps. Silver Republicans, conceding the demise of their cause, had returned to old allegiances. Despite notable reductions in government spending, the general failings of the 1897 legislative session further undermined the prospects of reform.[60]

Voted into office because of the depression, the Populists and their erst-while allies could not stand against the return of prosperity. "Capital is no longer made timid by fear of a monetary revolution," one of the Seattle dailies noted in explaining the political potency of the McKinley administration. The state's fusionist congressional delegation, indeed, exercised no real influence in Repub-lican dominated Washington, D.C. Senator George Turner and Representative James Hamilton Lewis were prominent opponents of imperial expansion, stand-ing on principle contrary to the interests and views of a substantial number of their constituents. The result at the polls in November 1898 was a stunning reversal of the 1896 Bryanite verdict. The two at-large Republican U.S. house candidates, Wesley L. Jones—known as "Yakima" Jones to avoid confusion with Spokane incumbent W.C. Jones—and Francis Cushman, won by carrying 25 of the 34 counties. In state government, fusionists that had been elected to four year executive branch and senatorial positions in 1896 retained Olympia employment by default rather than by popular preference. Washington again stood in the posi-tion occupied at statehood, proudly in the ranks of the GOP.[61]

Meeting in January 1899, the regular state legislative session pitted discred-ited fusionists against the Republicans, who now were on the march toward a definitive triumph. The convoluted membership dealt first, as always, with the messy business of selecting a U.S. senator. Senator John Wilson of Spokane, a genuine partisan power and busy master of patronage, faced an overwhelming geographical obstacle as the first of eastern Washington's two incumbent senators to face reelection. Opponents included Addison Foster, a diffident and deserv-edly obscure partner in the St. Paul & Tacoma Lumber Company, Seattle Mayor Thomas Humes and Walla Walla perennial Levi Ankeny. Supporters of Spokane's other sitting U.S. senator, silver Republican George Turner, backed Foster, the Tacoman, in order to defeat their old Spokane adversary, Senator Wilson. Mean-while, incumbent Wilson had made inroads in King County by the artful dispen-sation of federal jobs.

Ballot after ballot ensued, with each round of voting increasing the likeli-hood of no candidate being elected. Finally concluding that he was better off in the long run working "a bit of a Warwick act," Senator Wilson conceded, sup-plying his votes and unexpected victory to Tacoma's Addison Foster. Defeated, but by no means vanquished, Wilson soon moved to Puget Sound, buying the *P-I* as a major facet of the campaign to remake himself as a western Washington politician.[62]

Barely four weeks remained in the 60 days mandated for legislative business. Preordained for deadlock, the Republican controlled house faced a leftover dead duck fusionist senate majority precluding the possibility of any responsible results from the session. Wheat growing regions again demanded legislation regulating the railroads, but corporate lobbyists, now nicely fortified by the results of the 1898 election, easily fought off the threat. The membership was reduced to touting passage of measures requiring barbers to be licensed and blacksmiths to pass state examinations before being allowed to shoe horses. Aware that they would not be seeing Olympia again, departing Populists absconded with "waste baskets, books, [and] ink stands," petty acts of theft providing apt metaphor for the often sorry general conduct of public affairs during Washington's first decade.[63]

⨳

People in all walks of life knew, from daily experience in the case of those living west of the Cascades, that Washington was "the state of big trees." Passengers on Puget Sound steamers and west side trains viewed "magnificent timber-lands…at every turn." Investors from the forest-depleted Great Lakes saw the practical, as opposed to the scenic, side of things. Local fir and cedar acreage was still relatively cheap compared to east-of-the-Rockies timber standards, but bound to "advance rapidly from now on" as the nation became dependent on Pacific Northwest lumber. "Millions of dollars," George Emerson wrote of the growing outsider interest in the region's natural resources, "were in the air ready to light on any tracts of timber than can be had for reasonable prices."[64]

Great Lakes lumbermen and speculators, with the future airplane enthusiast William E. Boeing among their ranks, arrived on practically every transcontinental train, eager to purchase stumpage. Michigan investors acquired 2,000 acres on northern Puget Sound in May 1899. In the same month, an eastern syndicate bought 10,000 acres along the lower Columbia River. "All the choice timber lands are being taken up," Cyrus Walker informed his partners in San Francisco. Longtime owners, able to secure substantial profit from forest stands held since pioneer days, took advantage of the opportunity to sell at wealth securing prices. "His first words almost," one newcomer noted of an encounter with a prominent Grays Harbor industrialist, "were to ask if we were in the market for timber."[65]

Convinced beyond doubt that recovery finally had taken place, Frederick Weyerhaeuser joined in the rush of capitalists to the Pacific Northwest. America's wealthiest lumberman participated with a number of regular associates in several timber related investments west of the Cascades in 1898 and 1899. Old time operators, including Pope & Talbot and Asa Simpson, the owner of George Emerson's Hoquiam mill, proffered their plants and land holdings to "the Warehouser [sic] crowd." The most persistent suitor, though, was the Northern Pacific. The NP was intent upon selling a substantial portion of its forest acreage, encompassing a quarter of the railroad's federal land grant in the state of Washington, to generate cash flow for the urgent retirement of debt. Encouraged by the GN's

James J. Hill and provided with a special NP train, Weyerhaeuser devoted the fall of 1899 to a thorough inspection of the region's timber.[66]

News that a deal was about to be made between the NP and Weyerhaeuser drew enormous interest in all corners of the Pacific Northwest. Under terms officially implemented in January 1900, the Northern Pacific sold 900,000 acres of timber scattered across 10 Washington counties, for cash and securities worth $5.4 million. Although the buyers agreed to a 15-year exclusive transportation clause, a prime concern of traffic fixated NP management, the Weyerhaeuser syndicate privately agreed to avoid manufacturing for the time being. To manage an enormous long-term investment, the partners organized the Weyerhaeuser Timber Company with headquarters in Tacoma.[67]

One overwhelmed observer claimed that the "land deal" had "taken us all off our feet and we have hardly gained our equilibrium yet." With strokes from several millionaire's pens, the new company became the nation's second largest private timber owner, and "one of the greatest, if not the greatest, lumber concerns in the world." Dwarfing the regional competition, Weyerhaeuser was the institutional culmination of a decade long trend—the exploitation of Washington's abundant natural resources by outside capital. Generating an immediate upswing in timber values—"the price of stumpage," a Puget Sound newspaper reported, "has practically doubled within thirty days"—the firm provided a foretaste of developments to come in the new century, especially regarding the increasing concentration of forest ownership. Rather than following historical practice by assigning one of their number to on-the-scene supervision, Frederick Weyerhaeuser and his partners sent a professional manager, the able George S. Long, to the west coast. Fully aware of the danger posed by fire and other destructive forces to an investment worth millions of dollars, Long became a leading advocate of conservation measures. Modernity, spreading across the Pacific Northwest since the opening of the first transcontinental railroad, had taken firm root among the forests of western Washington.[68]

⧼≈≈⧽

Duly noting the unending movement of timber from forest to mill and grain from field to dockside, one editor concluded that Washingtonians "live at a gallop." Ten years of Washington statehood had been equal to "twenty years on the other side of the Missouri river." The 1900 federal census, all residents agreed, would certainly confirm that vitality was on the march. "From every section," the *P-I* declared in anticipation, "the same story comes that lands are being occupied, a large number of employees are engaged and that houses are going up fast in every village." Washington would surely record, an onlooker from east of the Cascades contended, "a greater percentage of increase in population...than for any other state in the union." Only the departure of so many men and women for the Alaskan gold fields could possibly forestall such a deserved rating.[69]

Recorded by a legion of pencil chewing federal clerks, the actual 1900 figures were below the inflated expectations, but still undeniably impressive. Washington's official population of 517,672 represented a 48 percent increase over 1890. "Not only has this state grown in a ratio more than double that of the entire country," a Tacoma business journal asserted, "but no state of equal...development ten years ago has approached its record." The census statistics also confirmed, as a Spokane editor pointed out, that "the commercial centers of the Pacific northwest are established." Seattle solidified its in-state position, nearly doubling in size to 81,000 inhabitants. Overly dependent upon the struggling Northern Pacific and unable to secure more than a small portion of the Alaska trade, Tacoma lagged badly, adding barely 1,000 residents and tallying but half the population of its Puget Sound rival. Reflecting persistent prosperity, Spokane with 37,000 citizens had nearly caught up to Commencement Bay.[70]

A number of writers suggested that former delegates to the state constitutional convention ought to reconvene in July 1899 to deliberate on Washington's first decade and devise necessary alterations in the official framework of governance. The gathering was never held, but the approaching end of the century did encourage a general reassessment of the statehood experience. Seattleites preferred to honor the tenth anniversary of their great defining fire. Everywhere else, the celebratory focus was more comprehensive. "Twenty years ago the region...was a wild land with a sparse and scattered population," a Spokane resident noted of the Inland Empire. The countryside "was as destitute of orchard growth as the Klondike," and the beckoning Palouse and Big Bend "were lonely cattle ranges" with "hardly a schoolhouse or church...to be found." Beginning in the late territorial period and reaching fruition in post-admission times, desolation had given way to an inhabited and fully exploited paradise. "We have wrought more here," a delighted pioneer of the interior maintained, "than was wrought on the Atlantic coast in 200 years after the first colony was planted."[71]

Substantially more, however, might have been accomplished except for the prolonged depression. "Enterprises were abandoned," wrote journalist Albert Johnson, a future member of congress based for the moment in Tacoma, and "energy was stayed, prosperity halted, [and] the pinching fingers of poverty were laid...upon the people." No remedy worked prior to McKinley's election, the discovery of northern gold, and the war with Spain. The recovery, said Johnson, was "as slow as that of a man worn and wasted by the most dread disease." Economic crisis nonetheless imparted an invaluable and presumably enduring lesson—the conviction that self-sufficiency must forever displace the "riot of extravagance" that had marked and doomed "the old boom days" following upon statehood.[72]

Cynics doubted that Washington residents could long resist the allure of borrowing and debt. There was, however, no question in 1899 that the state stood on the threshold of a modern and promising era. "Opportunities are now spread before the present population," one editor exclaimed, "which excel those presented to the pioneers." America's orientation was shifting more and more, and quickly so, to include Asia. Settlers and investors, and builders of industry and cities, were on their way to the Pacific Northwest, the place best suited for the generation of profit in the dawning age. "Rivet your attention upon the Pacific ocean," the *P-I* cried. "About the shores of this new Mediterranean will cluster all the wealth, the activity, the thought, the dominance that made the old Mediterranean the market and the pleasure pavilion and the treasury of the earth." Occupying the vital spot upon the sea of the future, Washington's people were the destined beneficiaries of a "prominence and a prosperity of which the most sanguine now would scarcely dare to dream."[73]

Notes

1. Rep. in Spokane *Spokesman-Review*, Dec. 28, 1897.
2. The trading pattern prevailed into statehood. In 1889, Puget Sound dispatched well over 100 timber cargoes to foreign ports, including 32 to Melbourne, 19 to Valparaiso, 15 to Honolulu and 14 to Sydney. *Seattle Post-Intelligencer*, Nov. 16, 1898, rep. from *West Coast Lumberman*; *Tacoma Daily Ledger*, Jan. 1; July 21, 1890.
3. "The future of the Pacific coast of America," another Elliott Bay observer wrote, "is largely bound up with that of the Pacific coast of Asia." *Seattle Morning Journal*, Oct. 21, 1889; *Spokane Review*, July 23, 1893; *Tacoma Daily Ledger*, March 12, 15, 18, 1890; *Seattle Telegraph*, May 4, 1894.
4. "The annexation of Hawaii will mark a new era in the history of our country," the *Seattle Times* declared in late 1895. "We will have entered upon a road the end of which no man can see; but it is a road which the genius of the race, which is dominant in this land, will compel us to take sooner or later." The only notable opposition to annexation expressed by some Washingtonians was based on ignorance and prejudice: "As an offset to the slight possibility of the need of military protection from enemies to the west of us," a tidewater resident declared, "is the certainty of the necessity of protection from the 2,000 infectious lepers which would then be government charges." Other bigots found the prospect of equality for Polynesians, Chinese and Japanese to be more unsettling than leprosy. "The thought of an American president hobnobbing with a coffee-colored piece of debauched royalty," an eastern Washington weekly complained of the meeting between Grover Cleveland and the deposed Hawaiian monarch, "is enough to make a colonial patriot turn in his grave." Address to Tacoma Chamber of Commerce, Jan. 26, 1898, John R. Rogers Papers, Washington State University Library; *Spokane Daily Chronicle*, Jan. 6; March 28, 1898; Eugene Semple to Daughter, June 21, 1897, Eugene Semple Papers, University of Washington Library; *Seattle Telegraph*, Feb. 13, 1893; Spokane *Spokesman-Review*, May 13, 1897; Feb. 24, 1898; *Seattle Times*, Nov. 14, 1895; *South Bend Journal*, Dec. 24, 1897; *Spokane Review*, Dec. 12, 1893, rep. from Rosalia *Rustler*.
5. According to one calculation, "the difference between the route to Liverpool by the canal and that via the Horn…[would be] 61 days." The Panama Canal project, which eventually supplanted the Nicaragua scheme, would not be completed until 1914. *Tacoma Daily News*, April 18, 1890; Jan. 17, 1898; *Seattle Press-Times*, June 9, 1891; April 4, 1893; *Seattle Post-Intelligencer*, Nov. 30, 1891; *Seattle Telegraph*, Jan. 20, 1892; *Spokane Daily Chronicle*, Sept. 5, 1898; *Yakima Herald*, Dec. 9, 1897.

6. *Tacoma Daily News*, Nov. 3, 1897; Cyrus Walker to W.H. Talbot, April 13; May 2, 1898, Puget Mill Co. Records, Ames Coll., University of Washington Library; Chauncey Griggs to Anna B. Griggs, April 12, 1898, St. Paul & Tacoma Lumber Co. Records, University of Washington Library; George H. Emerson to E.J. Holt, April 20, 1898, George H. Emerson Letterbooks, University of Washington Library; Spokane *Spokesman-Review*, Feb. 25, 1896; Feb. 26, 1898.

7. The actual cause of the blowing up of the *Maine*, either due to an accident or sabotage, remains unresolved to this day. "Ocean travel on the Pacific…under the American flag," the *P-I* claimed, "is as safe as traveling on Lake Superior." *Spokane Daily Chronicle*, March 1, 24, 29, 1898; *Tacoma Daily Ledger*, April 21, 1897; April 9, 15, 23, 1898; Spokane *Spokesman-Review*, March 3, 4, 1898; *Seattle Post-Intelligencer*, May 6, 1898.

8. Washington business leaders complained that the national guard initially ought to have been stationed in Tacoma or Seattle, so that paychecks would go into the Puget Sound economy. The state's young men supposedly endured "inactivity, fretting and humiliation" in the Bay Area. The contrarian *Argus* noted, though, that the regiment was "housed in the barracks erected for the regular soldiers," providing the volunteers with better living conditions than most enjoyed at home. Emerson to Ralph D. Emerson, April 29, 1898, Emerson Letterbooks; *Tacoma Daily Ledger*, April 11; May 19, 1898; Portland *Oregonian*, May 7, 1898; Spokane *Spokesman-Review*, May 10; Aug. 8, 1898; *Tacoma Daily News*, June 13, 1898; *Seattle Times*, July 13, 1898; *Spokane Daily Chronicle*, Sept. 3, 1898; James B. Dahlquist, "Our 'Splendid Little War,'" *Columbia: The Magazine of Northwest History* [hereafter cited as *Columbia*], 14 (Spring 2000), 16–17; *Seattle Post-Intelligencer*, July 13, 1898; Seattle *Argus*, Aug. 6, 1898.

9. "If it had not been for the war," Seattle residents claimed, "the amount of gold coming down from the Klondike would have been the sensation of the year." *Spokane Daily Chronicle*, April 8, 1898; *Northwest*, 16 (May 1898), 31; Spokane *Spokesman-Review*, July 11; Aug. 8, 1898; *Seattle Times*, June 1; Sept. 11; Nov. 19, 1898; Talbot to Walker, Aug. 6; Dec. 9, 1898, Puget Mill Co. Records. For a dubious argument that the war, due to its cost, demoralized the economy, see *Tacoma Daily Ledger*, June 13, 28, 1898.

10. The *Spokesman-Review* insisted that, because of the experience gained by Army regulars in clashes with Indians, the West "has performed much the greater part of the fighting." *Tacoma Daily Ledger*, May 7, 1898; *Seattle Post-Intelligencer*, July 3, 10, 1898; Spokane *Spokesman-Review*, July 12, 13; Oct. 31, 1898.

11. "We shall have considerable difficulty in adjusting Hawaii to American principles," a Tacoma daily predicted, primarily because Asian plantation workers were "practically peons." So many Japanese had migrated to the islands, the *Seattle Times* quipped, that the likely outcome would entail "annexing Japan to Hawaii." Address at Whatcom, March 28, 1899, Rogers Papers, Washington State University Library; *Tacoma Daily Ledger*, April 12, 1898; *Tacoma Daily News*, July 8, 22, 1898; *Seattle Times*, July 9, 1898; Sept. 20, 1899; *Seattle Post-Intelligencer*, July 16; Nov. 15, 1898; John R. Rogers to W.R. Hearst, June 20, 1898, John R. Rogers Papers, Washington State Archives.

12. To some, the Philippines question represented a denial of American exceptionalism. "The unwillingness to let go anything we can get our hands on," a Tacoma editor observed, "is evidently as strong among our people as among any other." *Seattle Post-Intelligencer*, May 12; June 28; Nov. 7, 15; Dec. 25, 1898; March 25, 1899; *Seattle Times*, May 4, 1899; Spokane *Spokesman-Review*, May 9; Sept. 20, 1898; *Tacoma Daily News*, Aug. 20, 1898.

13. Military glory was still to be attained, regardless of the opponent—"It is to be where fighting, if there shall be fighting any where, will occur," a Spokane paper declared upon

receipt of details regarding action in the Philippines. "The war seems to be over," the *P-I* said regarding Spain, "but there are a lot of turbulent natives in the Philippines who may give our troops a chance to see what war is like." When returning home, the volunteers suffered an indignity during a three day celebration when Seattle moralists procured a ban on alcohol. The Filipino rebellion continued until 1902. *Seattle Post-Intelligencer*, Oct. 18; Nov. 25, 1898; March 21; Aug. 24, 1899; *Spokane Daily Chronicle*, Oct. 11, 1898; Spokane *Spokesman-Review*, Sept. 20, 1898; March 13, 1899; Dahlquist, "Our 'Splendid Little War,'" 17–22; William Woodward, "Prelude to a Pacific Century," *Columbia*, 13 (Winter 1999–2000), 6–12; *Seattle Times*, Sept. 5, 7; Oct. 11, 1899.

14. *Spokane Falls Review*, Nov. 5, 1889; Dec. 13, 1890; *Tacoma Daily Ledger*, March 2, 3, 12, 15; May 25, 1890; *Tacoma Daily News*, Feb. 19, 1890; July 6, 1893; *Seattle Telegraph*, March 14, 1891; *Northwest*, 10 (April 1892), 30; *Spokane Review*, Nov. 16, 1892; *Seattle Press-Times*, July 13, 1892; *Seattle Post-Intelligencer*, July 20; Oct. 16, 1893.

15. Puget Sound flour exports increased in value from $503,000 in 1892 to $726,000 in 1894. The Japanese Army was a major buyer of eastern Washington horses. A Spokane newspaper recorded the westbound transit of 65 Great Northern cars carrying goods for Asia on a single day in the spring of 1897. *Seattle Post-Intelligencer*, Jan. 1, 1895; *Northwest*, 15 (Aug. 1897), 35; *Seattle Press-Times*, March 14, 1895; *Seattle Times*, Oct. 6, 1896; Spokane *Spokesman-Review*, Nov. 3, 1895; Feb. 3; March 25; April 8, 1897; Seattle *Argus*, Feb. 1; March 21, 1896.

16. "The wealth of the Orient and the fertile lands of the Pacific are now within reach," the *P-I* enthused upon the defeat of Spain. Spokane *Spokesman-Review*, April 27, 1899; *Seattle Post-Intelligencer*, July 12, 1898; March 14, 31, 1899; *Tacoma Daily News*, Jan. 31; Nov. 24, 1898; *Northwest*, 15 (Jan. 1897), 28; 16 (Aug. 1898), 32; (Sept. 1898), 30; E.V. Smalley, "Four Weeks in a Car," *Northwest*, 15 (June 1897), 8.

17. With Puget Sound cargoes divided between Seattle and Tacoma, Portland retained its traditional lead in grain exports. *Seattle Post-Intelligencer*, July 12, 16; Aug. 4, 25; Sept. 5, 1898; Aug. 15, 1899; *Seattle Times*, Aug. 25, 1898; Seattle *Argus*, Aug. 27, 1898; Portland *Oregonian*, May 4, 1898.

18. "To take our surplus," Hill asserted, "the Chinese would only be required to eat a wheat loaf occasionally." The Great Northern officially declared Seattle its Pacific coast terminus in 1898. *Seattle Post-Intelligencer*, Aug. 27; Dec. 22, 1897; Nov. 12, 1898; March 3; April 23, 1899; *Seattle Times*, Dec. 31, 1896; June 4; Aug. 12; Sept. 16, 1898; Feb. 28, 1899; Spokane *Spokesman-Review*, April 30, 1897; Michael P. Malone, *James J. Hill: Empire Builder of the Northwest* (Norman: University of Oklahoma Press, 1996), 166–68; Albro Martin, *James J. Hill and the Opening of the Northwest* (New York: Oxford University Press, 1976), 472–74; *Northwest*, 16 (May 1898), 31–32. For details on Hill's conceptions regarding Seattle's harbor, see James J. Hill to Thomas Burke, Jan. 19, 1900, Thomas Burke Papers, University of Washington Library.

19. *Seattle Times*, July 27, 1898; Renton, Holmes & Co. to Port Blakely Mill Co., July 10, 1899, Port Blakely Mill Co. Records, University of Washington Library; Talbot to Walker, June 30, 1897, Puget Mill Co. Records; *Tacoma Daily News*, Oct. 7, 8, 1896; Griggs to Charles Foster, Feb. 23, 1897; to S.L. Levey, Aug. 3, 1897; to L.B. Royce, Aug. 12, 1897, St. Paul & Tacoma Lumber Co. Records.

20. Talbot to Walker, June 30, 1897; Jan. 18; Feb. 7, 1899; June 14; July 20, 1900; J.H. Claiborne, Jr. to Pope & Talbot, May 10; June 16; Aug. 19, 1900, all Puget Mill Co. Records; Robert E. Ficken, *The Forested Land: A History of Lumbering in Western Washington* (Seattle: University of Washington Press, 1987), 89.

21. *Seattle Times*, Jan. 12, 1900; *Spokane Daily Chronicle*, April 8, 1898; Talbot to Walker, June 1, 1898, Puget Mill Co. Records; *Seattle Post-Intelligencer*, Aug. 13, 1898.

22. *Tacoma Daily News*, June 30, 1898; *Seattle Post-Intelligencer*, Feb. 2, 7; Aug. 22; Nov. 19, 1898; March 24, 1899; Seattle *Argus*, Jan. 14, 1899; *Seattle Times*, July 20, 1898; L. Jensen to Renton, Holmes & Co., March 29, 1898, Port Blakely Mill Co. Records.

23. *Seattle Times*, June 12, 23, 25, 28, 1898; *Seattle Post-Intelligencer*, July 21, 1898; Howard Clifford, "Ezra Meeker's Quest for Klondike Gold," *Columbia*, 12 (Summer 1998), 24–29.

24. *Seattle Times*, June 23; July 4, 20, 21, 25; Aug. 27, 1898; *Seattle Post-Intelligencer*, July 20; Oct. 23, 1898; *Tacoma Daily News*, July 21, 1898; *Yakima Republic*, May 19, 1899; Seattle *Argus*, July 22, 1899; Spokane *Spokesman-Review*, July 31, 1899; Stephen Haycox, *Alaska: An American Colony* (Seattle: University of Washington Press, 2002), 205.

25. "The…Alaska gold boom" was, according to a Walla Walla editor, "one of the greatest false games of the year." Spokane *Spokesman-Review*, Aug. 7, 29; Oct. 15, 1898; Aug. 5, rep. from Harrington *Citizen*, 13, 1899; *Spokane Daily Chronicle*, April 11, 1898; *Seattle Post-Intelligencer*, Aug. 18, 1898, rep. from Walla Walla *Union*.

26. *Seattle Post-Intelligencer*, July 17, 20, 22; Aug. 18; Nov. 9, 1898; *Seattle Times*, Aug. 11, 1898.

27. Spokane *Spokesman-Review*, Sept. 12, 1899; Feb. 13, 1900; *Seattle Times*, May 7, 1899; Seattle *Argus*, July 22, 1899; *Northwest*, 17 (April 1899), 31; Kathryn Morse, *The Nature of Gold: An Environmental History of the Klondike Gold Rush* (Seattle: University of Washington Press, 2003), 61–63; *Seattle Post-Intelligencer*, May 22, 1899.

28. Haycox, *Alaska*, 206–7; *Seattle Post-Intelligencer*, June 11, 28; July 15; Sept. 3, 1899; *Tacoma Evening News*, Jan. 18, 24, 1900; *Seattle Times*, Sept. 26, 1899.

29. "Disgusted with the country" after a stay of eight days, John McGraw sailed from Nome on the first available steamer. Olympia *Washington Standard*, Nov. 10, 1899; Renton, Holmes & Co. to Port Blakely Mill Co., Dec. 2, 1899, Port Blakely Mill Co. Records; Talbot to Walker, Dec. 1, 1899; Walker to Talbot, March 24; July 12, 1900, all Puget Mill Co. Records; *Tacoma Evening News*, Jan. 24, 1900; Spokane *Spokesman-Review*, Aug. 1, 1899; Feb. 6, 1900; *Seattle Times*, July 17, 1899; *Seattle Post-Intelligencer*, Sept. 3, 1899.

30. Spokane *Spokesman-Review*, June 8; July 19; Sept. 5; Nov. 17, 1899; Jan. 31; Feb. 6, 1900; *Seattle Post-Intelligencer*, June 4, 25; July 3, 1899; Haycox, *Alaska*, 205; *Seattle Times*, July 1, 12; Sept. 2, 13, 1899; *Yakima Republic*, Jan. 20, 1899.

31. Portland conceded that Seattle was "the main point of arrival and departure for miners and tourists." Seattleites insisted that the totem pole had been secured in the "twilight hours" only through innocent coincidence. "The sole reason why the consent of no Indian…was asked," moreover, "was that there was nobody from whom to purchase." Besides, the visitors from Puget Sound left "some fifty or sixty other poles" undisturbed and refrained from desecration of the native "graveyard." *Seattle Post-Intelligencer*, Nov. 19; Dec. 20, 1898; July 3, 4, rep. from *Oregonian*; Oct. 16; Nov. 16, 29, 1899; *Seattle Times*, Dec. 16, 1898; Oct. 26; Nov. 10, 11, 1899; *Spokane Daily Chronicle*, April 26, 1898; *Yakima Republic*, Nov. 10, 1899; *Northwest*, 17 (Nov. 1899), 46–47.

32. Apparently conceding the sloganeering advantage to Seattle, Spokane claimed merely to be the leader of "the new west." *Seattle Post-Intelligencer*, Sept. 16, 1898; April 24; Nov. 1, rep. from Everett *Times*, 8, 1899; *Northwest*, 17 (Dec. 1899), 46, rep. from Yakima *Republic*; Spokane *Spokesman-Review*, March 16, 1899.

33. *Tacoma Daily Ledger*, April 13, 1898; Spokane *Spokesman-Review*, Dec. 21, 1897; July 13, 1898; March 10, 12, 25, 1899; Olympia *Washington Standard*, May 26; Sept. 1, 1899;

Seattle Times, March 28, 29, 1898; *Seattle Post-Intelligencer,* Oct. 2, 1898; *Yakima Herald,* Jan. 12, 1899; *Yakima Republic,* July 7, 1899.

34. *Seattle Post-Intelligencer,* Nov. 24, 1898; Feb. 27, 1899; Jan. 8, 1900; Spokane *Spokesman-Review,* Jan. 20; May 28; Sept. 18, 1898; March 28, 1899; Jan. 8, 1900; *Northwest,* 17 (Sept. 1899), 37; *Seattle Times,* July 14; Dec. 7, 1898.

35. Four vessels sailed from Tacoma in April 1898 alone with over 300,000 bushels of wheat. *Northwest,* 16 (Dec. 1898), 38; 17 (March 1899), 7; (June 1899), 16; 19 (Feb. 1901), 34; *Seattle Post-Intelligencer,* July 12; Oct. 21, 1898; March 13, 1899; Portland *Oregonian,* May 4, 1898.

36. *Seattle Post-Intelligencer,* Sept. 5; Nov. 4, 1898; Aug. 13, 1899; *Northwest,* 17 (Feb. 1899), 41; Marie S. Roberts, "Finny Folk of Puget Sound," *Northwest,* 16 (Dec. 1898), 10; *Seattle Times,* Jan. 5, 9, 1900; *Ellensburg Capital,* Oct. 28, 1899, rep. from Roslyn *Miner.*

37. Emerson to A.M. Simpson, Dec. 26, 1899, Emerson Letterbooks; C.F. White to A.W. Jackson, Aug. 5, 1899; A.W. Jackson Memorandum, Sept. 19, 1900, both Puget Mill Co. Records; Ficken, *Forested Land,* 105; Montesano *Weekly Vidette,* Aug. 5, 1898; *Northwest,* 16 (Dec. 1898), 37; 17 (Jan. 1899), 39; (Feb. 1899), 41; 18 (Aug.–Sept. 1900), 50; *Seattle Post-Intelligencer,* Nov. 16, 1898; Spokane *Spokesman-Review,* Feb. 23, 1899, citing *Pacific Lumber Trade Journal.*

38. The diversion of shipping to Asia and Alaska and to wheat carrying, one observer noted, "has practically cleared the [coastwise] market of every vessel except a few lumber schooners and a few old 'tubs.'" Increased freight rates led to ill fated experiments in the towing of timber rafts to the Bay Area. "Too many small concerns that can't shut down," a South Bend lumberman reported, "are sending lumber down the coast...for what they can get for it." South Bend *Willapa Harbor Pilot,* May 27, 1898; Spokane *Spokesman-Review,* Jan. 20, 1898, rep. from Victoria *Times; Seattle Post-Intelligencer,* Dec. 19, 1899; Ficken, *Forested Land,* 87, 105; Emerson to Simpson, Feb. 20, 1899, Emerson Letterbooks; Edw. H. Johnston to O.H. Ingram, June 29, 1898, O.H. Ingram Papers, State Historical Society of Wisconsin.

39. *Northwest,* 18 (Feb. 1900), 41; Ficken, *Forested Land,* 105; Walker to Talbot, July 24, 1900; to F.C. Talbot, July 23, 1900, Puget Mill Co. Records.

40. "Our Klondike at home," another onlooker agreed, "is less risky and almost as lucrative as the gold fields of the north." Spokane *Spokesman-Review,* May 9; July 20; Nov. 2, 1898; *Northwest,* 16 (Aug. 1898), 37; (Sept. 1898), 13, rep. from Davenport *Times; Tacoma Daily Ledger,* April 24, 1898; Portland *Oregonian,* May 5, 11; Sept. 13, 1898; *Seattle Post-Intelligencer,* June 29; Dec. 21, 1898; *Colfax Gazette,* Aug. 5, 1898; *Spokane Daily Chronicle,* April 11; May 14; Sept. 1, 1898; *Tacoma Daily News,* July 19, 1898; *Walla Walla Statesman,* Aug. 27; Nov. 19, 1898.

41. *Seattle Star,* Oct. 28, 1899; *Walla Walla Statesman,* Nov. 18, 1899; Spokane *Spokesman-Review,* Dec. 20, 1897; June 7, 1899; Jan. 14, 1900; *Seattle Post-Intelligencer,* Jan. 3, 1900; *Tacoma Daily Ledger,* April 12, 1898.

42. Profits from the Kootenay country north of the 49th parallel declined as the result of prolonged labor strife. *Seattle Post-Intelligencer,* May 13, 1898; Oct. 12, 1899; *Spokane Daily Chronicle,* Jan. 28, 1898; Spokane *Spokesman-Review,* Dec. 31, 1899.

43. Federal law prohibited the cutting of reservation timber except for direct use in mining. *Tacoma Daily Ledger,* April 11, 1898; *Wilbur Register,* June 10, Dec. 23, 1898; Spokane *Spokesman-Review,* May 11; July 15, 1898; Feb. 17, 25, 28; June 5, 1899; May 7, 1900; *Seattle Post-Intelligencer,* May 11; Dec. 26, 1898; April 6, 1899; *Northwest,* 17 (March

1899), 42; (Aug. 1899), 41; E.H. Holly, "A New El Dorado," *Northwest*, 17 (Jan. 1899), 3–4; Olympia *Washington Standard*, April 21, 1899.

44. *Seattle Post-Intelligencer*, April 24, 1899; Spokane *Spokesman-Review*, March 15; Oct. 17, rep. from Yakima *Republic*, 1899; March 8, 1900, citing Pasco *News-Recorder*; Ellensburg *Localizer*, Jan. 6, 1900; *Northwest*, 19 (Feb. 1901), 41; *Yakima Republic*, Feb. 10, 1899.

45. *Seattle Post-Intelligencer*, Oct. 13, 1899, rep. from Whatcom *Reveille*, *Northwest*, 16 (Nov. 1898), 40; 17 (July 1899), 47; (Oct. 1899), 39, rep. from Whatcom *Blade*, (Nov. 1899), 56; Olympia *Washington Standard*, June 23, 1899; Emerson to Chas. B. Emerson, June 8, 1900, Emerson Letterbooks.

46. "The growth of the city is...so rapid," one account from Spokane asserted, "that the daily papers have given up trying to publish the list of buildings being erected." *Tacoma Daily News*, Nov. 22, 1898; *Northwest*, 17 (Feb. 1899), 41; (Oct. 1899), 39; 18 (May 1900), 52, rep. from Tacoma *Ledger*; Spokane *Spokesman-Review*, Dec. 9, 1897; Oct. 1, 3, 24, 1898; Nov. 17, 1899; *Spokane Daily Chronicle*, Jan. 6, 8; Feb. 11; March 11, 14, 1898.

47. Emerson to Chas. W. Miller, Feb. 24, 1900, Emerson Letterbooks; Shelton *Mason County Journal*, Nov. 10, 1899; *Seattle Post-Intelligencer*, Aug. 21; Nov. 3, 22, 1898; April 16; July 30, 1899; Jan. 17, 21, 1900; *Northwest*, 17 (Aug. 1899), 41; Seattle *Argus*, Oct. 23, 1897; Aug. 12; Nov. 18, 1899; *Seattle Times*, Dec. 24, 1897; July 28; Sept. 11, 13, 1898; July 30; Oct. 4, 1899; Jan. 27, 29; Feb. 7, 1900; Spokane *Spokesman-Review*, Jan. 5, 1900.

48. *Seattle Post-Intelligencer*, Sept. 25, 1898; Nov. 10, 1899, rep. from Farmington *Times*; Spokane *Spokesman-Review*, Dec. 14, 1898; *Yakima Republic*, Feb. 17, 1899; *Seattle Times*, Sept. 23, 1899.

49. The Seattle tax levy declined from $489,000 in 1893 to $332,000 in 1897. Seattle's school district, on the other hand, increased its assessment in response to mounting enrollment. Kittitas County cut taxes in addition to reducing debt. *Seattle Post-Intelligencer*, Feb. 9, 1898; June 27; Nov. 18; Dec. 8, 1899; *Seattle Times*, Sept. 23, 1899; Portland *Oregonian*, Sept. 29, 1899; *Tacoma Daily Ledger*, April 4, 1898l Spokane *Spokesman-Review*, Jan. 7; Feb. 3, 1900; Olympia *Washington Standard*, March 17, 1899; *Ellensburg Localizer*, Oct. 15, 1898.

50. Spokane *Spokesman-Review*, Jan. 3, 1900; *Walla Walla Statesman*, June 24, 1899; *Northwest*, 16 (Aug. 1898), 37; 17 (Nov. 1899), 56; *Yakima Herald*, Aug. 11, 1898; *Yakima Republic*, Aug. 18; Oct. 6, 1899.

51. *Spokane Daily Chronicle*, Jan. 7; April 20, 1898; *Tacoma Daily News*, Sept. 16, 1898; *Wilbur Register*, Nov. 5, 1897; Pasco *News-Recorder*, Feb. 25, 1899; Spokane *Spokesman-Review*, April 15, 1899.

52. Olympia *Washington Standard*, Nov. 26, 1897; *Seattle Star*, Nov. 7, 1899; *Seattle Post-Intelligencer*, Aug. 30, 31, 1897; Feb. 8; May 5, 16, 1898; Jan. 20, 1899; Spokane *Spokesman-Review*, Jan. 22, 1899; *Seattle Times*, Nov. 17, 1898; Seattle *Argus*, July 29, 1899.

53. *Spokane Daily Chronicle*, Jan. 14, 20; March 30, 31; April 1, 5, 16, 20, 1898; Spokane *Spokesman-Review*, March 16; Dec. 22, 1897; July 25, 1898; March 13, 1899.

54. New Whatcom *Daily Reveille*, Dec. 14, 19, 21, 1897; *Spokane Daily Chronicle*, Jan. 7; April 20, 1898; Seattle *Argus*, Nov. 27, 1897.

55. "It seems impossible," a timber trade journal exclaimed, "to get men...to do the work." The prominent lumberman Sol Simpson returned to his native province in eastern Canada to find laborers. "Strikes occur most frequently in prosperous times," a country editor reminded readers, "not because work is scarce, but because labor is so scarce that it is master of the situation." *Seattle Post-Intelligencer*, Aug. 18, 26, rep. from Shelton *Mason County Journal*, *Wilbur Register*, Sept. 3, 1897; Emerson to Simpson Logging Co., July

12, 1898; to Simpson, July 19; Sept. 2, 1898, Emerson Letterbooks; Spokane *Spokes-man-Review*, Jan. 21, 1900; Walker to Jackson, Dec. 18, 1897, Puget Mill Co. Records; *Northwest*, 18 (Oct. 1900), rep. from *West Coast Lumber Trade Journal*.

56. Emerson to L. Harlow, Nov. 3, 1899; to Simpson, July 19; Sept. 2, 1898, Emerson Let-terbooks; Walker to Talbot, Sept. 18, 1899; March 8; May 28, 1900; to Jackson, July 9, 1900; to F. Talbot, Sept. 21, 1899, Puget Mill Co. Records; March 12, 1900, Cyrus Walker Letterbooks, Ames Coll., University of Washington Library.

57. Much of the public still believed that those who preferred to complain while in idleness, rather than continuing to work, were victims of the "laziness bacilli." Business interests and home owners also agreed that "the lawless spirit drives capital from the country." *Spo-kane Daily Chronicle*, Jan. 19; April 5, 1898; *Wilbur Register*, July 21, 1899; *Seattle Post-Intelligencer*, May 1, 1899; Spokane *Spokesman-Review*, May 15, 1897; Oct. 26, 1898.

58. Spokane *Spokesman-Review*, May 16, 1897; Jan. 2; Oct. 26; Nov. 7, 1898; April 28, 29, 1899; *Seattle Post-Intelligencer*, April 27; May 1, 1899.

59. Spokane *Spokesman-Review*, April 30; May 3, 6, rep. from *Washington Independent*, 11; Nov. 24, 1899; Mark Wyman, *Hard Rock Epic: Western Miners and the Industrial Rev-olution, 1860–1910* (Berkeley: University of California Press, 1979), 170; Carlos A. Schwantes, *In Mountain Shadows: A History of Idaho* (Lincoln: University of Nebraska Press, 1991), 157–59; *Seattle Post-Intelligencer*, May 10; July 20, 1899.

60. *Northwest*, 17 (Feb. 1899), 36; Rogers to W.W. Langhorne, Feb. 26, 1898; to George Turner, May 4, 1898, Rogers Papers, Washington State Archives; *Seattle Post-Intelligencer*, July 8; Aug. 20; Oct. 24, 29, 30, 1898; *Seattle Times*, Sept. 22; Oct. 26; Nov. 15, 1898.

61. "The American people must have some prevailing topic for discussion," a Tacoma editor observed in 1898. "Two years ago it was the silver question. Now it takes but a little to change a conversation on almost any topic into an argument about annexation." The 1898 outcome was "as great a surprise to the victors as to the losers," one observer exclaimed. The substantial reduction in turnout compared to 1896 suggested that the return of good times had reduced public interest in politics. Seattle's J.H. Lewis finished first in King County, which otherwise voted Republican. Upon completion of his single congressional term, Lewis moved to Chicago, becoming a member of that city's Democratic organiza-tion and, many years later, returning to the nation's capital as U.S. senator from Illinois. *Seattle Post-Intelligencer*, June 28; July 17; Aug. 29; Oct. 30; Nov. 10, 12, 15, 16, 1898; Jan. 24, 1900; *Spokane Daily Chronicle*, Aug. 30; Oct. 6, 1898; Spokane *Spokesman-Review*, Dec. 22, 1897; *Yakima Republic*, Jan. 27; Feb. 3, 1899; *Seattle Times*, Nov. 9–11, 18, 1898; Jan. 25, 1900; *Tacoma Daily News*, Dec. 24, 1898; Thomas W. Riddle, "Popu-lism in the Palouse: Old Ideals and New Realities," *Pacific Northwest Quarterly* [hereafter cited as *PNQ*], 65 (Jan. 1974), 97.

62. Complaining that "practically all the appropriations" had gone to the tidewater counties in spite of both senators being Inland Empire residents, Spokane vainly claimed that "the West side has been the gainer, and the East side has lost, by the existing arrangement." According to brief rumor, the unlamented Watson Squire intended to return to the Pacific Northwest and contend for the senate seat. Colleagues in the timber industry disparaged Addison Foster as a "lazy man...only willing to work hard when his own interests are at stake." Spokane *Spokesman-Review*, Nov. 29, 1898; Jan. 7; Feb. 1, 4, 1899; *Seattle Times*, June 18; Aug. 22, 25; Sept. 17, 1898; Jan. 5, 14; Feb. 2, 1899; Olympia *Washington Standard*, Feb. 3, 1899; *Yakima Republic*, Feb. 3, 24, 1899; *Walla Walla Statesman*, Feb. 4, 1899; Talbot to Walker, Feb. 2, 1899, Puget Mill Co. Records.

63. *Seattle Post-Intelligencer*, Jan. 14; Feb. 3, 16; March 3, 13, rep. from Olympia *Olympian*, 1899; Spokane *Spokesman-Review*, Nov. 25, 1898; Jan. 15; Feb. 28; March 4, 5, 1899; *Yakima Republic*, Feb. 3, 24; March 10, 1899.

64. "Little timber is left in the [east-of-the-Rockies] states...that formerly were thought to hold supplies that would last forever," a regional newspaper pointed out. "In a few years it will all be gone, and then the saw mills will close down, and the many men who have gained a livelihood in the timber...business will have to look elsewhere for their bread and butter." *Seattle Times*, Sept. 1, 1899; Marion Patton, "A Voyage Down Puget Sound," *Northwest*, 17 (April 1899), 24; Renton, Holmes & Co. to Port Blakely Mill Co., Sept. 15, 1899, Port Blakely Mill Co. Records; Griggs to Henry F. Dimmock, Oct. 22, 1898, St. Paul & Tacoma Lumber Co. Records; Walker to Talbot, Nov. 1, 1899, Walker Letterbooks; Emerson to C.A. Congdon, Oct. 26, 1899, Emerson Letterbooks; Spokane *Spokesman-Review*, Nov. 16, 1899, rep. from Portland *Telegram*.

65. "It is apparent from the way...timber lands are being gobbled up," a coast based editor advised, "that the capitalists have at last discovered the value of timber in this section." Ficken, *Forested Land*, 100; Olympia *Washington Standard*, May 5; June 23, 1899; *Seattle Times*, May 3, 1899; Walker to Talbot, Oct. 26, 1899, Walker Letterbooks; A.G. Foster to Ingram, Nov. 3, 1899, Ingram Papers; R.D. Merrill to T.D. Merrill, Aug. 20, 1898, Merrill & Ring Lumber Co. Records, University of Washington Library; *Seattle Post-Intelligencer*, Sept. 15, 1899, rep. from South Bend *Journal*.

66. Charles Weyerhaeuser to J.P. Weyerhaeuser, May 3, 1899, Weyerhaeuser Family Papers, Minnesota Historical Society; Robert E. Ficken, "Weyerhaeuser and the Pacific Northwest Timber Industry, 1899–1903," *PNQ*, 70 (Oct. 1979), 147–48; Annual Statement, Dec. 10, 1900, Sound Timber Co. Records, Minnesota Historical Society; W.I. Ewart to Ingram, July 21, 1899; Johnston to Ingram, Nov. 19, 1899, both Ingram Papers; Walker to Talbot, Oct. 26, 1899, Walker Letterbooks; *Seattle Times*, Nov. 21, 1899; C.S. Mellon to J.M. Hannaford, Sept. 27, 1899, Northern Pacific Railroad Records, Minnesota Historical Society; Shelton *Mason County Journal*, Nov. 17, 1899. The proper spelling of Weyerhaeuser was invariably a challenge. "If Frederick Weyerhaeuser...should patronize a press clipping bureau," one trade publication suggested, "and read all the items printed concerning his business he would probably be more amused over the variegated spelling given to his name than impressed by the recognized magnitude of his operations." *Pacific Lumber Trade Journal*, 6 (Sept. 1900), 9. For a reference to pending "Warehouse" transactions, see Portland *Oregonian*, Nov. 13, 1899.

67. Northern Pacific executives believed that Weyerhaeuser intended to "commence cutting and manufacturing immediately." The purchasers apparently engaged in deliberate deception on this point. "The shipping clause," one syndicate insider remarked in a private letter, "does not make any more difference to the company...than though we had received a clear deed, and made no contract whatever." Frederick Weyerhaeuser owned 30 percent of the shares and Laird, Norton & Company 20 percent. The remaining stock went to a number of individuals, including O.H. Ingram, Robert L. McCormick and Sumner T. McKnight. Portland *Oregonian*, Nov. 13, 1899; Shelton *Mason County Journal*, Nov. 10, 17, 1899; Jan. 19, 1900; Frederick Weyerhaeuser to Ingram, Dec. 11, 27, 1899; A.E. Macartney to Ingram, Jan. 3, 1900, all Ingram Papers; Mellon to C.H. Coster, Dec. 27, 1899; Jan. 2, 5, 1900; to Edward D. Adams, Jan. 2, 5, 1900; to Wm. H. Phipps, Dec. 4, 1899, Northern Pacific Railroad Records; Ficken, "Weyerhaeuser," 149, 151; and *Forested Land*, 95; Olympia *Washington Standard*, Nov. 10, 1899; Ralph W. Hidy, Frank Ernest

Hill and Allan Nevins, *Timber and Men: The Weyerhaeuser Story* (New York: Macmillan, 1963), 212–13.

68. W.H. Boner to Ingram, Feb. 18, 1900; Hugh Bellas to Ingram, March 9, 1900, both Ingram Papers; Robert E. Ficken, "Gifford Pinchot Men: Pacific Northwest Lumbermen and the Conservation Movement, 1902–1910," *Western Historical Quarterly*, 13 (April 1982), 165–78; and "Weyerhaeuser," 146; Spokane *Spokesman-Review*, Jan. 14, 1900, rep. from Tacoma *Ledger*; Charles E. Twining, *George S. Long: Timber Statesman* (Seattle: University of Washington Press, 1994), 19–22.

69. Looking far into the future, a leading newspaper predicted that Washington would have a population of at least 10 million by the year 2000. *Spokane Daily Chronicle*, April 14, 1898; *Seattle Post-Intelligencer*, Aug. 11, 1899; Jan. 30, 1900; *Yakima Republic*, Oct. 13, 1899; Spokane *Spokesman-Review*, Jan. 20, 1899.

70. Oregon tallied a one-third increase, but now trailed Washington by 100,000 people. Starting from a relatively small base in 1890, Idaho and Montana grew, respectively, by 92 and 84 percent. Portland retained the lead among the region's cities with a population of 90,000 in 1900. Walla Walla, at 10,000, remained Washington's fourth largest community. Two in five Washingtonians lived in urban areas in 1900, compared to one in three Oregonians and one in sixteen Idaho residents. *Northwest*, 18 (Nov. 1900), 43; (Dec. 1900), 18, rep. from *West Coast Trade*, 35, 44; Spokane *Spokesman-Review*, Feb. 8, 1900; Carlos A. Schwantes, *The Pacific Northwest: An Interpretive History* (Lincoln: University of Nebraska Press, 1989), 192.

71. "The material advance of the State of Washington…is nothing short of marvelous," a Yakima paper remarked at the end of 1899, "even to those of us who, during the last eight years, have prophesied and have never lost faith." *Seattle Post-Intelligencer*, Jan. 29; June 6, 1899; Spokane *Spokesman-Review*, Oct. 6, 1897; *Northwest*, 17 (Dec. 1899), 46, rep. from Yakima *Republic*.

72. *Tacoma Daily News*, Nov. 17, 1898.

73. Spokane *Spokesman-Review*, Sept. 25, 1898; *Tacoma Daily News*, Jan. 31; Nov. 19, 1898; *Seattle Post-Intelligencer*, Sept. 8, 1898; June 26; Dec. 17, 1899.

❧

Bibliography

Archival Collections

Federal Records Center, Seattle—
  Portland District Records, U.S. Army Corps of Engineers, RG 77
  Seattle District Records, U.S. Army Corps of Engineers, RG 77

Library of Congress—
  Gifford Pinchot Papers

Minnesota Historical Society—
  Northern Pacific Railroad Records
  Sound Timber Company Records
  Weyerhaeuser Family Papers

National Archives—
  Records of the Office of Chief of Engineers, 1894–1923, RG 77

State Historical Society of Wisconsin—
  O.H. Ingram Papers

University of Washington Library—
  Thomas Burke Papers
  George H. Emerson Letterbooks
  Elisha P. Ferry Papers
  Daniel H. Gilman Papers
  Harry C. Heermans Papers
  Merrill & Ring Lumber Company Records
  Oregon Improvement Company Records
  Port Blakely Mill Company Records
  Puget Mill Company Records, Ames Collection
  Eugene Semple Papers
  Watson C. Squire Papers
  St. Paul & Tacoma Lumber Company Records
  Stimson Mill Company Records
  Cyrus Walker Letterbooks, Ames Collection

Washington State Archives—
  John R. Rogers Papers

Washington State University Library—
  John R. Rogers Papers
  Washington Water Power Company Records

Articles and Essays

Andrews, Clarence L., ed. "Some Notes on the Yukon by Stewart Menzies," *Pacific Northwest Quarterly*, 32 (April 1941).

Avery, Bailey. "Spokane Falls," *Northwest*, 8 (April 1890).

Beardsley, Arthur S. "The Codes and Code Makers of Washington, 1889–1937," *Pacific Northwest Quarterly*, 30 (Jan. 1939).

_____. "Later Attempts to Relocate the Capital of Washington," *Pacific Northwest Quarterly*, 32 (Oct. 1941).

Berner, Richard C. "The Port Blakely Mill Company, 1876–89," *Pacific Northwest Quarterly*, 57 (Oct. 1966).

Bicha, Karel D. "Peculiar Populist: An Assessment of John R. Rogers," *Pacific Northwest Quarterly*, 65 (July 1974).

Blankenship, Russell. "The Political Thought of John R. Rogers," *Pacific Northwest Quarterly*, 37 (Jan. 1946).

Boening, Rose M. "History of Irrigation in the State of Washington," *Washington Historical Quarterly*, 10 (Jan. 1919).

Brainerd, Erastus. "Seattle," *Harper's Weekly*, 41 (Nov. 13, 1897).

Brown, Richard Maxwell. "Rainfall and History: Perspectives on the Pacific Northwest," in G. Thomas Edwards and Carlos A. Schwantes, eds., *Experiences in a Promised Land: Essays in Pacific Northwest History.* Seattle: University of Washington Press, 1986.

Burnet, Ruth A. "Mark Twain in the Northwest, 1895," *Pacific Northwest Quarterly*, 42 (July 1951).

C.A.H. "Washington's Five Contrasting Climates," *Northwest*, 10 (May 1892).

Campbell, Robert A. "Blacks and the Coal Mines of Western Washington, 1888–1896," *Pacific Northwest Quarterly*, 73 (Oct. 1982).

Catton, Theodore. "The Campaign to Establish Mount Rainier National Park, 1893–1899," *Pacific Northwest Quarterly*, 88 (Spring 1997).

Chittenden, H.M. "Ports of the Pacific," American Society of Civil Engineers, *Transactions*, 76.

Clifford, Howard. "Ezra Meeker's Quest for Klondike Gold," *Columbia: The Magazine of Northwest History*, 12 (Summer 1998).

Cole, Terrence. "One Man's Adventure in the Klondike," *Columbia: The Magazine of Northwest History*, 11 (Winter 1997–1998).

Coulter, Calvin B. "The Victory of National Irrigation in the Yakima Valley, 1902–1906," *Pacific Northwest Quarterly*, 42 (April 1951).

Dahlquist, James B. "Our 'Splendid Little War,'" *Columbia: The Magazine of Northwest History*, 14 (Spring 2000).

Daniels, Joseph L. "History of Pig Iron Manufacture on the Pacific Coast," *Washington Historical Quarterly*, 17 (July 1926).

Davies, Kent R. "Sea of Fire," *Columbia: The Magazine of Northwest History*, 15 (Summer 2001).

Ducker, James H. "Gold Rushers North: A Census Study of the Yukon and Alaskan Gold Rushes, 1896–1900," *Pacific Northwest Quarterly*, 85 (July 1994).

Dumke, Glenn S. "The Real Estate Boom of 1887 in Southern California," *Pacific Historical Review*, 11 (Dec. 1942).

"Establishing the Navy Yard, Puget Sound," *Washington Historical Quarterly*, 2 (July 1908).

Fahey, John. "The Million-Dollar Corner: The Development of Downtown Spokane, 1890–1920," *Pacific Northwest Quarterly*, 62 (April 1971).

_____. "When the Dutch Owned Spokane," *Pacific Northwest Quarterly*, 72 (Jan. 1981).

Ficken, Robert E. "Columbia, Washington or Tacoma? The Naming and Attempted Renaming of Washington Territory," *Columbia: The Magazine of Northwest History*, 17 (Spring 2003).

_____. "Gifford Pinchot Men: Pacific Northwest Lumbermen and the Conservation Movement, 1902–1910," *Western Historical Quarterly*, 13 (April 1982).

_____. "Rufus Woods, Wenatchee, and the Columbia Basin Reclamation Vision," *Pacific Northwest Quarterly*, 87 (Spring 1996).

_____. "Seattle's 'Ditch': The Corps of Engineers and the Lake Washington Ship Canal," *Pacific Northwest Quarterly*, 77 (Jan. 1986).

_____. "Weyerhaeuser and the Pacific Northwest Timber Industry, 1899–1903," *Pacific Northwest Quarterly*, 70 (Oct. 1979).

Finger, John R. "The Seattle Spirit, 1851–1893," *Journal of the West*, 13 (July 1974).

Gates, Charles M. "Daniel Bagley and the University of Washington Land Grant, 1861–1868," *Pacific Northwest Quarterly*, 52 (April 1961).

Griffiths, David B. "Far-western Populist Thought: A Comparative Study of John Rogers and Davis H. Waite," *Pacific Northwest Quarterly*, 60 (Oct. 1969).

Hanford, C.H. "The Orphan Road and the Rams Horn Right of Way," *Washington Historical Quarterly*, 14 (April 1923).

Hanscom, John. "Company Coal Town: Franklin and the Oregon Improvement Company," *Columbia: The Magazine of Northwest History*, 8 (Spring 1994).

Holly, E.H. "A New El Dorado," *Northwest*, 17 (Jan. 1899).

Howard, William Willard. "The City of Tacoma," *Harper's Weekly*, 35 (June 20, 1891).

_____. "Spokane Falls and Its Exposition," *Harper's Weekly*, 34 (Aug. 30, 1890).

Hunt, William R. "Goldfield Gateway," *Columbia: The Magazine of Northwest History*, 4 (Winter 1990–1991).

Hynding, Alan A. "Eugene Semple's Seattle Canal Scheme," *Pacific Northwest Quarterly*, 59 (1968).

Johnson, Claudius O. "George Turner: The Background of a Statesman," *Pacific Northwest Quarterly*, 34 (July 1943).

Johnston, Norman J. "A Capitol in Search of an Architect," *Pacific Northwest Quarterly*, 73 (Jan. 1982).

_____. "The Washington State Capitol Campus and Its Peripatetic Planning," *Columbia: The Magazine of Northwest History*, 13 (Spring 1999).

Jonasson, Jonas A. "Portland and the Alaska Trade," *Pacific Northwest Quarterly*, 30 (April 1939).

Kingston, C.S. "Franz Ferdinand in Spokane, 1893," *Washington Historical Quarterly*, 16 (Jan. 1925).

Kraig, Beth. "The Bellingham Bay Improvement Company: Boomers or Boosters?" *Pacific Northwest Quarterly*, 80 (Oct. 1989).

Larson, T.A. "The Woman Suffrage Movement in Washington," *Pacific Northwest Quarterly*, 67 (April 1976).

Leonard, Frank. "'Wise, Swift and Sure'? The Great Northern Entry into Seattle, 1889–1894," *Pacific Northwest Quarterly*, 92 (Spring 2001).

LeWarne, Charles Pierce. "Equality Colony: The Plan to Socialize Washington," *Pacific Northwest Quarterly*, 59 (July 1968).

Lindeman, Glen. "Golden Harvest: Wheat Farming on the Columbia Plateau," *Columbia: The Magazine of Northwest History*, 6 (Summer 1992).

MacDonald, Norbert. "The Business Leaders of Seattle, 1880–1910," *Pacific Northwest Quarterly*, 50 (Jan. 1959).

_____. "Seattle, Vancouver and the Klondike," *Canadian Historical Review*, 49 (Sept. 1986).

Magnusson, C. Edward. "Hydro-Electric Power in Washington," *Washington Historical Quarterly*, 19 (April 1928).

McDonald, Robert T. "Photographs of Washington Governors," *Pacific Northwest Quarterly*, 34 (Oct. 1943).

Meany, Edmond S. "The Pioneer Association of the State of Washington," *Washington Historical Quarterly*, 8 (Jan. 1917).

Miyamoto, S. Frank. "The Japanese Minority in the Pacific Northwest," *Pacific Northwest Quarterly*, 54 (Oct. 1963).

Mohler, Samuel R. "Boom Days in Ellensburg, 1888–1891," *Pacific Northwest Quarterly*, 36 (Oct. 1945).

Morris, T.S. "Aberdeen, Washington," *Northwest*, 8 (Jan. 1890).

Munroe, Kirk. "The Cities of the Sound," *Harper's Weekly*, 38 (Jan. 13, 1894).

———. "Eastern Washington and the Water Miracle of Yakima," *Harper's Weekly*, 38 (May 19, 1894).

Murray, Keith. "Issues and Personalities of Pacific Northwest Politics, 1889–1950," *Pacific Northwest Quarterly*, 41 (July 1950).

Nesbit, Robert C., and Charles M. Gates, "Agriculture in Eastern Washington, 1890–1910," *Pacific Northwest Quarterly*, 37 (Oct. 1946).

Nichols, Jeannette Paddock. "Advertising and the Klondike," *Washington Historical Quarterly*, 13 (Jan. 1922).

Northwest, Vols. 8–11 (1890–1893), and Vols. 15–19 (1897–1901).

Ochsner, Jeffrey Karl. "A.B. Chamberlain: The Illustration of Seattle Architecture, 1890–1896," *Pacific Northwest Quarterly*, 81 (Oct. 1990).

———. "The University That Never Was: The 1891 Boone and Wilcox Plan for the University of Washington," *Pacific Northwest Quarterly*, 90 (Spring 1999).

———. "Willis A. Ritchie: Public Architecture in Washington, 1889–1905," *Pacific Northwest Quarterly*, 87 (Fall 1996).

O'Neil, J.P. "The Last Home of the Elk," *Northwest*, 10 (July 1892).

Patton, Marion "A Voyage Down Puget Sound," *Northwest*, 17 (April 1899).

Pendergrass, Lee F. "The Formation of a Municipal Reform Movement: The Municipal League of Seattle," *Pacific Northwest Quarterly*, 66 (Jan. 1975).

Pfeifer, Michael J. "'Midnight Justice': Lynching and Law in the Pacific Northwest," *Pacific Northwest Quarterly*, 94 (Spring 2003).

Phelps, William F. "In the Cascade Mountains: A Tramp in Search of Silver Mines," *Northwest*, 10 (Dec. 1892).

Pierce, J. Kingston. "The Panic of 1893," *Columbia: The Magazine of Northwest History*, 7 (Winter 1993–1994).

———. "River of Gold," *Columbia: The Magazine of Northwest History*, 11 (Summer 1997).

———. "Words of Gold," *Columbia: The Magazine of Northwest History*, 12 (Spring 1998).

Purvis, Neil H. "History of the Lake Washington Canal," *Washington Historical Quarterly*, 25 (April 1934).

Renk, Nancy F. "Off to the Lakes: Vacationing in North Idaho during the Railroad Era, 1885–1917," *Idaho Yesterdays*, 34 (Summer 1990).

Riddle, Thomas W. "Populism in the Palouse: Old Ideals and New Realities," *Pacific Northwest Quarterly*, 65 (July 1974).

Roberts, Marie S. "Finny Folk of Puget Sound," *Northwest*, 16 (Dec. 1898).

Rothman Hal K. "Tourists in Wonderland: Early Railroad Tourism in the Pacific Northwest," *Columbia: The Magazine of Northwest History*, 7 (Winter 1993–1994).

Roush, J.F. "Legislative Reapportionment in Washington State," *Pacific Northwest Quarterly*, 28 (July 1937).

Russell, Israel C. "The Wheat-Lands of Washington," *Harper's Weekly*, 41 (July 24, 1897).

Schafer, Louise. "Report from Aberdeen," *Pacific Northwest Quarterly*, 47 (Jan. 1956).

Schwantes, Carlos A. "The Concept of the Wageworkers' Frontier: A Framework for Future Research," *Western Historical Quarterly*, 18 (Jan. 1987).

———. "Tourists in Wonderland: Early Railroad Tourism in the Pacific Northwest," *Columbia: The Magazine of Northwest History*, 7 (Winter 1993–1994).

Sherrard, William R. "The Kirkland Steel Mill: Adventure in Western Enterprise," *Pacific Northwest Quarterly*, 53 (Oct. 1962).

Smalley, E.V. "Anacortes: New Seaport at the Lower End of Puget Sound," *Northwest*, 9 (April 1891).
_____. "Everett, Washington: The New Manufacturing and Commercial Town on Puget Sound," *Northwest*, 10 (April 1892).
_____. "Four Weeks in a Car," *Northwest*, 15 (June 1897).
_____. "The Gray's Harbor Basin," *Northwest*, 8 (March 1890).
_____. "In the Big Bend Country," *Northwest*, 8 (May 1890).
_____. "In the Palouse Country," *Northwest*, 10 (Sept. 1892).
_____. "The Rebuilding and Remarkable New Growth of the Chief City of Washington," *Northwest*, 9 (Feb. 1891).
_____. "Seattle in 1898," *Northwest*, 16 (July 1898).
_____. "South Bend: A New Commercial City on the Pacific Coast of Washington," *Northwest*, 9 (May 1891).
_____. "Tacoma: Remarkable Progress of the New Commercial City on Puget Sound," *Northwest*, 9 (July 1891).
_____. "Westward in Winter: A February Journey from St. Paul to Puget Sound," *Northwest*, 10 (April 1892).
Smart, Douglas. "Spokane's Battle for Freight Rates," *Pacific Northwest Quarterly*, 45 (Jan. 1954).
Snowden, C.A. "Another Account," *Harper's Weekly*, 41 (Aug. 7, 1897).
Stevens, John F. "Great Northern Railway," *Washington Historical Quarterly*, 20 (April 1929).
Thorson, Winston B. "Washington State Nominating Conventions," *Pacific Northwest Quarterly*, 35 (April 1944).
Tollefson, Kenneth. "The Snoqualmie Indians as Hop Pickers," *Columbia: The Magazine of Northwest History*, 8 (Winter 1994–1995).
Warnock, James. "Entrepreneurs and Progressives: Baseball in the Northwest, 1900–1901," *Pacific Northwest Quarterly*, 82 (July 1991).
West Shore, Vols. 15–17 (1889–1891).
White, W. Thomas. "Railroad Labor Protests, 1894–1917: From Community to Class in the Pacific Northwest," *Pacific Northwest Quarterly*, 75 (Jan. 1984).
Whitney, Caspar. "The Stampede to Alaska for Gold," *Harper's Weekly*, 40 (April 4, 1896).
Willis, Park Weed. "A Journey to Seattle, 1883," *Pacific Northwest Quarterly*, 34 (Jan. 1943).
Wing, Robert C. "Washington Lights Up," *Columbia: The Magazine of Northwest History*, 2 (Fall 1988).
Wood, Robert L. "The O'Neil Expeditions," *Columbia: The Magazine of Northwest History*, 4 (Summer 1990).
Woodward, William. "Prelude to a Pacific Century," *Columbia: The Magazine of Northwest History*, 13 (Winter 1999–2000).
Woody, Carroll H. "Populism in Washington: A Study of the Legislature of 1897," *Washington Historical Quarterly*, 21 (April 1930).
Zeisler-Vralsted, Dorothy. "Reclaiming the Arid West: The Role of the Northern Pacific Railway in Irrigating Kennewick, Washington," *Pacific Northwest Quarterly*, 84 (Oct. 1993).

Books and Reports

Annual Report of the Chief of Engineers (Washington, D.C.); *1891, 1893, 1895, 1896, 1898.*
Armbruster, Kurt E. *Orphan Road: The Railroad Comes to Seattle, 1853–1911.* Pullman: Washington State University Press, 1999.
Berner, Richard C. *Seattle 1900–1920: From Boomtown, Urban Turbulence to Restoration.* Seattle: Charles Press, 1991.
Berton, Pierre. *Klondike: The Last Great Gold Rush, 1896–1899.* Toronto: McClelland and Stewart, 1958, 1987 rev. ed.

Boswell, Sharon A., and Lorraine McConaghy. *Raise Hell and Sell Newspapers: Alden J. Blethen and the Seattle Times.* Pullman: Washington State University Press, 1996.

Boxberger, Daniel L. *To Fish in Common: The Ethnohistory of Lummi Indian Salmon Fishing.* Seattle: University of Washington Press, 1989, 1999 ed.

Britton, Diane F. *The Iron and Steel Industry in the Far West: Irondale, Washington.* Niwot: University Press of Colorado, 1991.

Bryan, Enoch A. *Historical Sketch of the State College of Washington, 1890–1925.* Pullman: Alumni Association, 1928.

Bryce, James. *The American Commonwealth.* New York: Macmillan, 2 vols., 3d ed., 1895.

Bunting, Robert. *The Pacific Raincoast: Environment and Culture in an American Eden, 1778–1900.* Lawrence: University Press of Kansas, 1997.

Clark, Norman H. *The Dry Years: Prohibition and Social Change in Washington.* Seattle: University of Washington Press, rev. ed., 1988.

_____. *Mill Town.* Seattle: University of Washington Press, 1970.

_____. *Washington: A Bicentennial History.* New York: W.W. Norton, 1976.

Cronon, William. *Nature's Metropolis: Chicago and the Great West.* New York: W.W. Norton, 1991.

Daniels, Roger. *Asian America: Chinese and Japanese in the United States since 1850.* Seattle: University of Washington Press, 1988.

Edwards, G. Thomas. *Sowing Good Seeds: The Northwest Suffrage Campaigns of Susan B. Anthony.* Portland: Oregon Historical Society Press, 1990.

Fahey, John. *Inland Empire: D.C. Corbin and Spokane.* Seattle: University of Washington Press, 1965.

_____. *The Inland Empire: Unfolding Years, 1879–1929.* Seattle: University of Washington Press, 1986.

Ferguson, Niall. *Empire.* New York: Basic Books, 2003.

Ficken, Robert E. *The Forested Land: A History of Lumbering in Western Washington.* Seattle: University of Washington Press, 1987.

_____. *Rufus Woods, the Columbia River, and the Building of Modern Washington.* Pullman: Washington State University Press, 1995.

_____. *Unsettled Boundaries: Fraser Gold and the British-American Northwest.* Pullman: Washington State University Press, 2003.

_____. *Washington Territory.* Pullman: Washington State University Press, 2002.

Ficken, Robert E., and Charles P. LeWarne, *Washington: A Centennial History.* Seattle: University of Washington Press, 1988.

Frykman, George A. *Creating the People's University.* Pullman: Washington State University Press, 1990.

_____. *Seattle's Historian and Promoter: The Life of Edmond S. Meany.* Pullman: Washington State University Press, 1998.

Gough, Barry M. *The Royal Navy and the Northwest Coast of North America, 1810–1914: A Study of British Maritime Ascendancy.* Vancouver: University of British Columbia Press, 1971.

Hak, Gordon. *Turning Trees into Dollars: The British Columbia Coastal Lumber Industry, 1858–1913.* Toronto: University of Toronto Press, 2000.

Hawthorne, Julian, ed., *History of Washington: The Evergreen State.* New York: American Historical Publishing, 2 vols., 1893.

Haycox, Stephen. *Alaska: An American Colony.* Seattle: University of Washington Press, 2002.

Hidy, Ralph W., Frank Ernest Hill, and Allan Nevins, *Timber and Men: The Weyerhaeuser Story.* New York: Macmillan, 1963.

Hines, Neal O. *Denny's Knoll: A History of the Metropolitan Tract of the University of Washington.* Seattle: University of Washington Press, 1980.

Hundley, Norris, Jr., *The Great Thirst: Californians and Water, 1770s–1990s.* Berkeley: University of California Press, 1992.

Hunt, Herbert, and Floyd C. Kaylor. *Washington, West of the Cascades.* Chicago: S.J. Clarke, 3 vols., 1917.

Hynding, Alan A. *The Public Life of Eugene Semple: Promoter and Politician of the Pacific Northwest.* Seattle: University of Washington Press, 1973.

Johnston, Norman J. *Washington's Audacious State Capitol and Its Builders.* Seattle: University of Washington Press, 1988.

Lang, William L. *Confederacy of Ambition: William Winlock Miller and the Making of Washington Territory.* Seattle: University of Washington Press, 1996.

Laskin, David. *Rains all the Time: A Connoisseur's History of Weather in the Pacific Northwest.* Seattle: Sasquatch, 1997.

LeWarne, Charles Pierce. *Utopias on Puget Sound, 1885–1915.* Seattle: University of Washington Press, 1975.

Lewty, Peter J. *Across the Columbia Plain: Railroad Expansion in the Interior Northwest, 1885–1893.* Pullman: Washington State University Press.

Lukas, J. Anthony. *Big Trouble.* New York: Simon and Schuster, 1997.

MacDonald, Norbert. *Distant Neighbors: A Comparative History of Seattle and Vancouver.* Lincoln: University of Nebraska Press, 1987.

Malone, Michael P. *James J. Hill: Empire Builder of the Northwest.* Norman: University of Oklahoma Press, 1996.

Marks, Paula Mitchell. *Precious Dust, The American Gold Rush Era: 1848–1900.* New York: William Morrow, 1994.

Martin, Albro. *James J. Hill and the Opening of the Northwest.* New York: Oxford University Press, 1976.

McCune, Don. *Trail to the Klondike.* Pullman: Washington State University Press, 1997.

McGregor, Alexander Campbell. *Counting Sheep: From Open Range to Agribusiness on the Columbia Plateau.* Seattle: University of Washington Press, 1982.

Meinig, D.W. *The Great Columbia Plain: A Historical Geography, 1805–1910.* Seattle: University of Washington Press, 1968.

Meyerson, Harvey. *Nature's Army: When Soldiers Fought for Yosemite.* Lawrence: University Press of Kansas, 2001.

Mills, Randall V. *Stern-Wheelers Up Columbia: A Century of Steamboating in the Oregon Country.* Palo Alto: Pacific Books, 1947.

Montgomery, David R. *King of Fish: The Thousand-Year Run of Salmon.* Boulder: Westview Press, 2003.

Morgan, Murray. *The Mill on the Boot: The Story of the St. Paul and Tacoma Lumber Company.* Seattle: University of Washington Press, 1982.

_____. *Puget's Sound: A Narrative of Early Tacoma and the Southern Sound.* Seattle: University of Washington Press, 1979.

_____. *Skid Road: An Informal Portrait of Seattle.* Seattle: University of Washington Press, 1951, 1982 ed.

Morrissey, Katherine G. *Mental Territories: Mapping the Inland Empire.* Ithaca: Cornell University Press, 1997.

Morse, Kathryn. *The Nature of Gold: An Environmental History of the Klondike Gold Rush.* Seattle: University of Washington Press, 2003.

Moynihan, Ruth Barnes. *Rebel for Rights: Abigail Scott Duniway.* New Haven: Yale University Press, 1983.

Nesbit, Robert C. *"He Built Seattle": A Biography of Judge Thomas Burke.* Seattle: University of Washington Press, 1961.

Oliphant, J. Orin. *On the Cattle Ranges of the Oregon Country.* Seattle: University of Washington Press, 1968.

Pisani, Donald J. *From the Family Farm to Agribusiness: The Irrigation Crusade in California and the West, 1850–1931.* Berkeley: University of California Press, 1984.

_____. *To Reclaim a Divided West: Water, Law, and Public Policy, 1848–1902.* Albuquerque: University of New Mexico Press, 1992.

Pomeroy, Earl. *In Search of the Golden West: The Tourist in Western America.* Lincoln: University of Nebraska Press, 1957, 1990 ed.

Pyne, Steven J. *Fire in America: A Cultural History of Wildland and Rural Fire.* Princeton: Princeton University Press, 1982.

Reynolds, Maryan E., with Joel Davis. *The Dynamics of Change: A History of the Washington State Library.* Pullman: Washington State University Press, 2001.

Riddle, Thomas W. *The Old Radicalism: John R. Rogers and the Populist Movement in Washington, 1891–1900.* New York: Garland, 1991.

Robbins, William G. *Colony and Empire: The Capitalist Transformation of the American West.* Lawrence: University Press of Kansas, 1994.

———. *Landscapes of Promise: The Oregon Story, 1800–1940.* Seattle: University of Washington Press, 1997.

Rothman Hal K. *Devil's Bargains: Tourism in the Twentieth-Century American West.* Lawrence: University Press of Kansas, 1998.

Sale, Roger. *Seattle: Past to Present.* Seattle: University of Washington Press, 1976.

Schwantes, Carlos A. *Coxey's Army: An American Odyssey.* Lincoln: University of Nebraska Press, 1985.

———. *In Mountain Shadows: A History of Idaho.* Lincoln: University of Nebraska Press, 1991.

———. *Long Day's Journey: The Steamboat and Stagecoach Era in the Northern West.* Seattle: University of Washington Press, 1999.

———. *The Pacific Northwest: An Interpretative History.* Lincoln: University of Nebraska Press, 1989, 1996.

———. *Radical Heritage: Labor, Socialism, and Reform in Washington and British Columbia, 1885–1917.* Seattle: University of Washington Press, 1979.

———. *Railroad Signatures across the Pacific Northwest.* Seattle: University of Washington Press, 1993.

Steen, Harold K. *The U.S. Forest Service: A History.* Seattle: University of Washington Press, 1976, 2004 ed.

Stimson, William L. *Going to Washington State.* Pullman: Washington State University Press, 1989.

Strom, Claire. *Profiting from the Plains: The Great Northern Railway and Corporate Development of the American West.* Seattle: University of Washington Press, 2003.

Taylor, Joseph E., III, *Making Salmon: An Environmental History of the Northwest Fisheries Crisis.* Seattle: University of Washington Press, 1999.

Taylor, Quintard. *In Search of the Racial Frontier: African Americans in the American West, 1528–1990.* New York: W.W. Norton, 1998.

Twining, Charles E. *George S. Long: Timber Statesman.* Seattle: University of Washington Press, 1994.

White, Richard. *Land Use, Environment, and Social Change: The Shaping of Island County, Washington.* Seattle: University of Washington Press, 1980.

———. *The Organic Machine.* New York: Hill and Wang, 1995.

Wyman, Mark. *Hard Rock Epic: Western Miners and the Industrial Revolution, 1860–1910.* Berkeley: University of California Press, 1979.

Youngs, J. William T. *The Fair and the Falls: Spokane's Expo '74; Transforming an American Environment.* Cheney: Eastern Washington University Press, 1996.

Regional Newspapers

Aberdeen *Bulletin*
Aberdeen *Herald*
Anacortes American
Anacortes *Progress*
Astoria *Columbian*
Bellingham Bay *Express*

Big Bend Empire
Blaine *Journal*
Chehalis Bee
Chehalis *Nugget*
Chelan Falls *Leader*
Chelan *Leader*

Cheney *Sentinel*
Colfax *Gazette*
Colfax *Palouse Gazette*
Conconully *Okanogan Outlook*
Corvallis *Gazette*

Cosmopolis *Enterprise*
Coulee City *News*
Coulee City *Times*
Coupeville *News*
Cowlitz *Advocate*
Davenport *Lincoln County Times*
Davenport *Times*
Dayton *Columbia Chronicle*
Ellensburg(h) *Capital*
Ellensburg(h) *Localizer*
Ellensburgh *Register*
Everett Herald
Everett News
Everett *Times*
Fairhaven *Herald*
Farmington *Journal*
Farmington *Register*
Farmington *Times*
Garfield *Enterprise*
Grays Harbor *Times*
Harrington *Citizen*
Hoquiam *Tribune*
Hoquiam Washingtonian
Ilwaco *Journal*
Index Miner
Island County *Times*
Juneau *Mining Record*
Kettle Falls *Pioneer*
Lincoln County *Populist*
Montesano *Vidette*
Montesano *Weekly Vidette*
Mount Vernon *Post*
Nanaimo *Free Press*
New Whatcom *Daily Reveille*
Oakesdale *Advocate*
Oakesdale *Sun*
Okanogan *Outlook*
Olympia *Capital*
Olympia *Morning Olympian*
Olympia *Olympian*
Olympia *Tribune*
Olympia *Washington Standard*

Orting *Oracle*
Palouse City *News*
Palouse *News*
Pasco *News*
Pasco *News-Recorder*
Pendleton *East Oregonian*
Pomeroy *Independent*
Pomeroy *Washington Independent*
Pomeroy *Washingtonian*
Port Angeles *Democrat-Leader*
Port Angeles *Times*
Port Angeles *Tribune*
Port Angeles *Tribune-Times*
Port Townsend *Democrat*
Port Townsend *Leader*
Port Townsend *Morning Leader*
Port Townsend *Weekly Leader*
Portland *Oregonian*
Portland *Telegram*
Post Falls *Post*
Pullman Tribune
Rosalia *Rustler*
Roslyn *Miner*
San Francisco *Chronicle*
San Juan *Graphic*
Seattle *Argus*
Seattle Morning Journal
Seattle Post-Intelligencer
Seattle Press
Seattle *Press-Times*
Seattle *Puget Sound Dispatch*
Seattle *Star*
Seattle *Telegraph*
Seattle *Times*
Seattle *Weekly Intelligencer*
Shelton *Mason County Journal*
Snohomish *Eye*
Snohomish *Sun*
South Bend Enterprise
South Bend Journal
South Bend *Willapa Harbor Pilot*

Spangle *Record*
Spokane *Chronicle*
Spokane Daily Chronicle
Spokane Falls Review
Spokane Falls *Spokesman*
Spokane *Outburst*
Spokane Review
Spokane *Spokesman*
Spokane *Spokesman-Review*
Sprague *Advertiser*
Sprague *Herald*
Sprague *Mail*
Stevens County *Miner*
Sumner *Hellas*
Tacoma Daily Ledger
Tacoma Daily News
Tacoma Evening News
Tacoma *Ledger*
Tacoma Morning Globe
Tacoma *Sun*
Tekoa *Globe*
Tekoa *Times*
The Dalles Times-Mountaineer
Union City *Tribune*
Vancouver *Independent*
Victoria *Times*
Waitsburg *Times*
Walla Walla Statesman
Walla Walla Union
Walla Walla Union-Journal
Waterville *Big Bend Empire*
Waterville *Democrat*
Waterville *Immigrant*
Wenatchee Advance
Wenatchee *Graphic*
Westport *World*
Whatcom *Blade*
Whatcom *Bulletin*
Whatcom *Reveille*
Wilbur *Register*
Yakima *Herald*
Yakima *Republic*

Index